The Bradshaw Family Cookbook

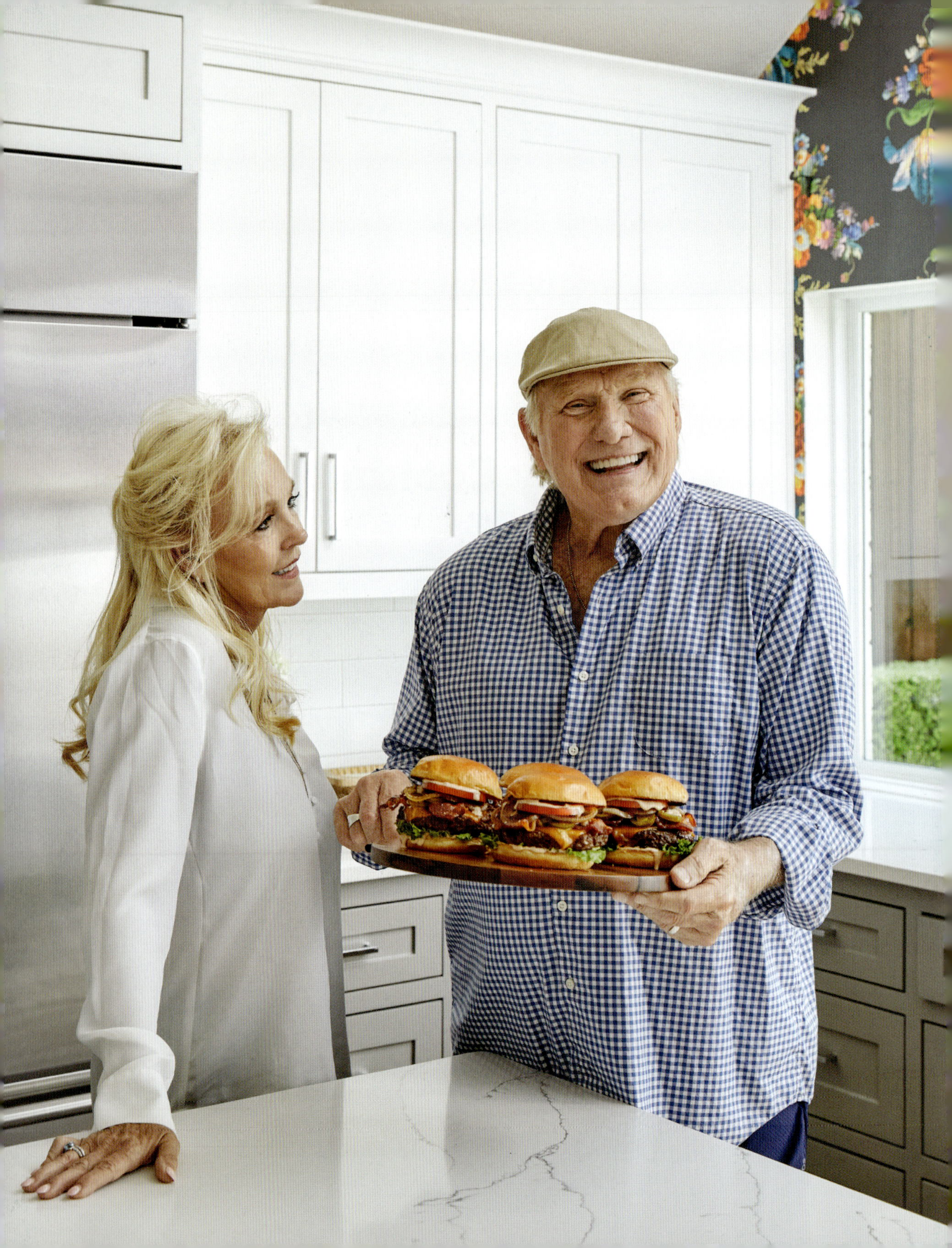

The Bradshaw Family Cookbook

OUR FAVORITE RECIPES FOR
GAME DAYS, WEEKDAYS, AND ANY DAY

Terry and Tammy Bradshaw

Rachel Bradshaw
Noah and Lacey Hester
and
James O. Fraioli

FLATIRON BOOKS
NEW YORK

THE BRADSHAW FAMILY COOKBOOK.
Copyright © 2025 by Terry Bradshaw and the Bradshaw family.
Photographs copyright © 2025 by Charity Burggraaf.
All rights reserved. Printed in China.
For information, address Flatiron Books, 120 Broadway,
New York, NY 10271.

www.flatironbooks.com

Designed by Lynne Yeamans

Library of Congress Cataloging-in-Publication Data

Names: Bradshaw, Terry, author. | Bradshaw, Tammy, 1961- author.
Title: The Bradshaw family cookbook : winning recipes
from our kitchen to yours / Terry and Tammy Bradshaw,
Rachel Bradshaw, Noah and Lacey Hester, and James O. Fraioli.
Description: First edition. | New York, NY : Flatiron Books, 2025.
| Includes index.
Identifiers: LCCN 2024052346 | ISBN 9781250344939 (paper over board) |
ISBN 9781250422538 (signed edition) | ISBN 9781250344922 (ebook)
Subjects: LCSH: Cooking. | Bradshaw family. | LCGFT: Cookbooks.
Classification: LCC TX714 .B675 2025 | DDC 641.5—dc23/eng/20241205
LC record available at https://lccn.loc.gov/2024052346

Our books may be purchased in bulk for promotional,
educational, or business use. Please contact your local
bookseller or the Macmillan Corporate and Premium Sales Department at
1-800-221-7945, extension 5442, or by email
at MacmillanSpecialMarkets@macmillan.com.

First Edition: 2025

10 9 8 7 6 5 4 3 2 1

This book is dedicated to my remarkable grandmother, whom I affectionately named "Hoodie Baby." Thank you for inspiring me and my family to appreciate and enjoy life in the kitchen.

—TERRY BRADSHAW

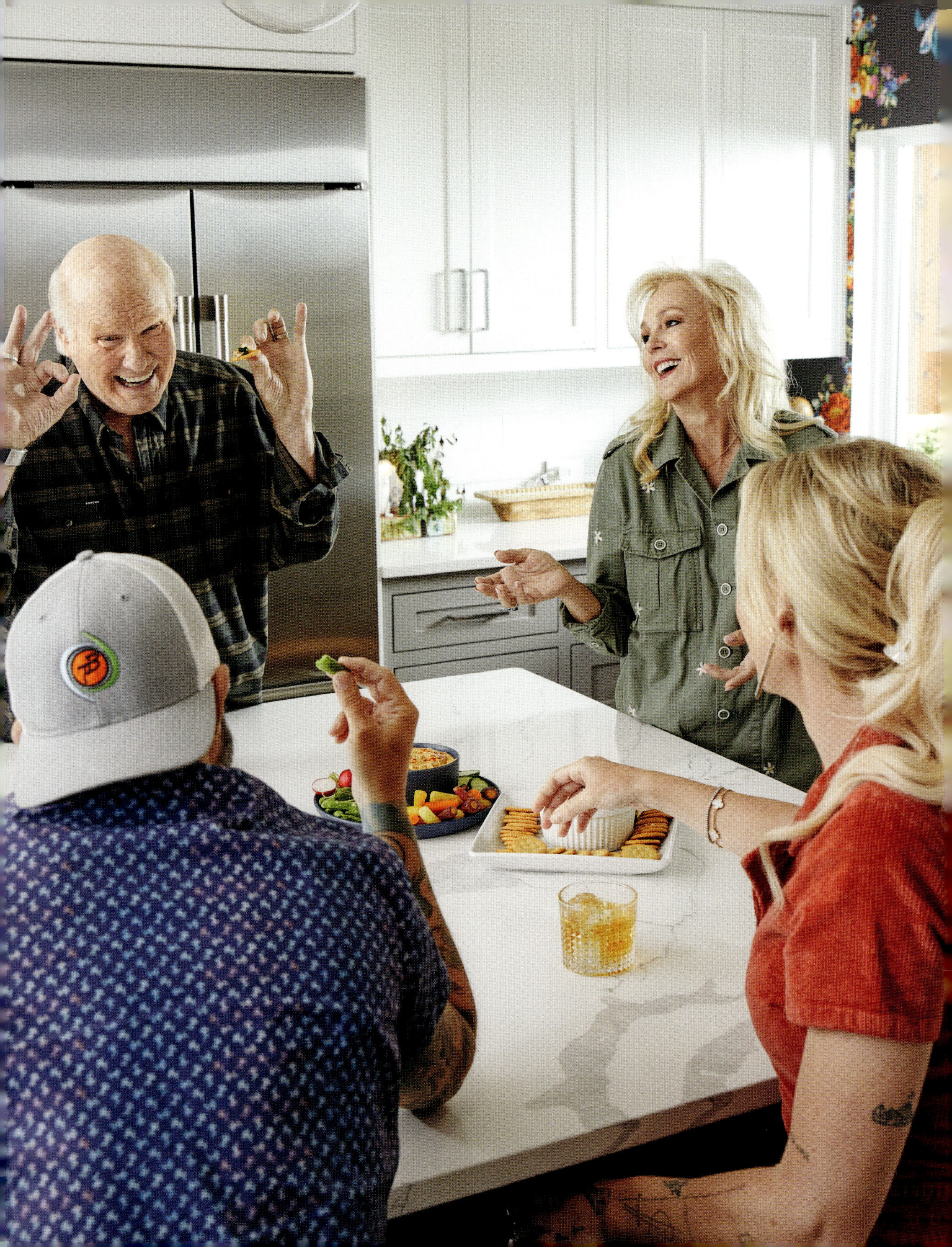

Contents

Introduction: Meet the Bradshaws! 13

A Peek Inside Our Kitchen and Pantry 21

Must-Have Tools 23

Grilling and Smoking—a Bradshaw Family Primer 27

What's Cooking in Our Kitchen 31

1 // Breakfasts and Brunches

Brunch Punch 37

Creamy Vanilla Fruit Salad 41

Baked Cinnamon Doughnuts 42

Ooey Gooey Apple Monkey Bread 45

Funfetti Chocolate Chip Banana Pancakes 46

Cinnamon Apple Waffles 49

French Toast Casserole 50

Ham and Old English Cheese Casserole 51

Overnight Stuffed Brioche French Toast Casserole ... 52

Sausage and Cheddar Cheese Biscuits 57

Nannie Bradshaw's Sausage Gravy 58

Spicy Breakfast Casserole with Onion and Bell Peppers 60

One-Skillet Breakfast Frittata 61

Bacon, Onion, and Mushroom Quiche 63

Breakfast Tacos with Chipotle Crema 64

Toad in the Hole 67

Terry's Favorite Omelet 68

2 // Starters and Snacks

Blond Bomber 74

Fourth and One Bourbon Smash 77

The Immaculate Refreshment 78

Gainesville Grande Margarita 82

Nannie's Ranch Crackers 83

Ranch-Style Pretzel Snacks 85

Homemade Focaccia with Herb Dipping Oil 86

Beet Deviled Eggs 89

Garlic Pull-Apart Pigs in a Blanket 90

Crispy Egg Rolls with Shrimp, Sprouts, and Peanut Butter 93

Chicken Fried Steak "Fries" with Zesty Dip 94

Toasted Ham and Swiss Cheese Sliders 97

Poppa Hester's Savory Herb Pimento Cheese 98

Cheesy Smoked Buffalo Chicken Dip 101

Famous Gridiron Nine-Layer Dip 102

Missouri Crab Grass Dip 105

Hawaiian Summer Tuna Fish Dip 106

Sriracha Curry Dip 109

3 // Grilling and Smoking

Finger-Lickin' Barbecue Bourbon Chicken Wings 114

Garlic Shrimp, Cheddar, and Bacon Phyllo Cups 117

Asian-Inspired Sticky-Finger Ribs 118

Juicy Braised Korean Short Ribs 123

Smoked Maple-Bourbon Pork Belly Bites 124

Spicy Pork Canoes with Cilantro Sour Cream 127

Spinach Bacon Sports Balls 128

Loaded Wagyu Hot Dogs 131

Bison Burgers with Balsamic Glazed Onions and Hot Honey Mustard 132

Brisket, Bacon, and Jalapeño Burgers 137

Smoked Brisket Sliders with Homemade Biscuits 138

Bradshaw Bourbon Barbecue Sauce 141

Grilled Tomahawk Steak with Chimichurri 143

4 // Get-Togethers and Potlucks

Aloha Bread 148

Apple Butter Bread 150

Cabbage and Potato Kettle 151

Spicy Italian Sausage, Vegetable, and Kale Soup 153

Fire-Roasted Hatch Chile Chicken Stew 154

Cannellini Chicken Chili 157

Creamy Sun-Dried Tomato Chicken with Orzo 158

Cheesy Chicken Enchiladas 161

South of the Border Lasagna 162

Roasted-Chicken Tetrazzini 164

Sunday Family Casserole 165

Baked Eggplant Parmesan with Marinara 167

Italian Sausage–Stuffed Peppers 168

Sunday Glazed Meatloaf 171

5 // Salads and Sides

Iceberg Salad with Terry's Favorite Dressing 176

Waldorf Salad with Walnut Pumpkin Seed Brittle 179

German Country Potato Salad 180

Red Potato Salad with Pimento and Sweet Pickle 183

Old-Fashioned Ambrosia Salad 184

Greek Orzo Salad with Oil, Vinegar, and Honey Dressing 187

Mexican Street Corn Salad 188

Missouri Corn Salad with Lime and Paprika 190

Green Beans with Bacon, Onion, and Garlic 191

Chicken Stock Scalloped Potatoes 193

Havarti and Gouda Mac 'n' Cheese 194

Honey Balsamic Farmers Market Carrots 197

Terry's Legendary Bradshaw Beans 198

6 // Roots and Relatives

Slow-Cooked Collard Greens with Bacon, Hot Sauce, and Balsamic ... 205

Nannie's Cornbread Dressing 206

Sweet Potato Casserole with Chopped Pecans 208

Fried Green Garden Tomatoes 209

Homemade Organic Chicken Stock 212

Buttermilk and Hot Sauce Fried Chicken 213

Herb-Roasted Chicken and Biscuit Dumplings 217

Fried Bologna Sandwich on Texas Toast 218

Maryland-Style Crab Cakes with Sweet Pickle Tartar Sauce 221

Old Bay Shrimp, Andouille, and Vegetable Boil 224

Gumbo with Chicken, Andouille, and Crawfish 227

Spam (Hawaiian) Musubi with Homemade Teriyaki Sauce 229

Terry's Ranch-Style Fish Fry 233

7 // Desserts and Sweets

Wild Blackberry Muffins with Powdered Sugar 239

Banana Pudding with Nilla Wafers 240

Keller's Granny Smith Apple Turnovers 243

Old-Fashioned Blackberry Pie 244

Buttermilk Pecan Pie 247

Louisiana Coconut Cream Pie 248

Italian Olive Oil–Lemon Cake 251

Sweet Orchard Peach Cobbler 252

Cherry Crisp with Crushed Pineapple and Pecans 255

Warm Chocolate Chip Cookies with Sea Salt 256

Pappy's Midnight Spoon 259

Acknowledgments 261

Index 263

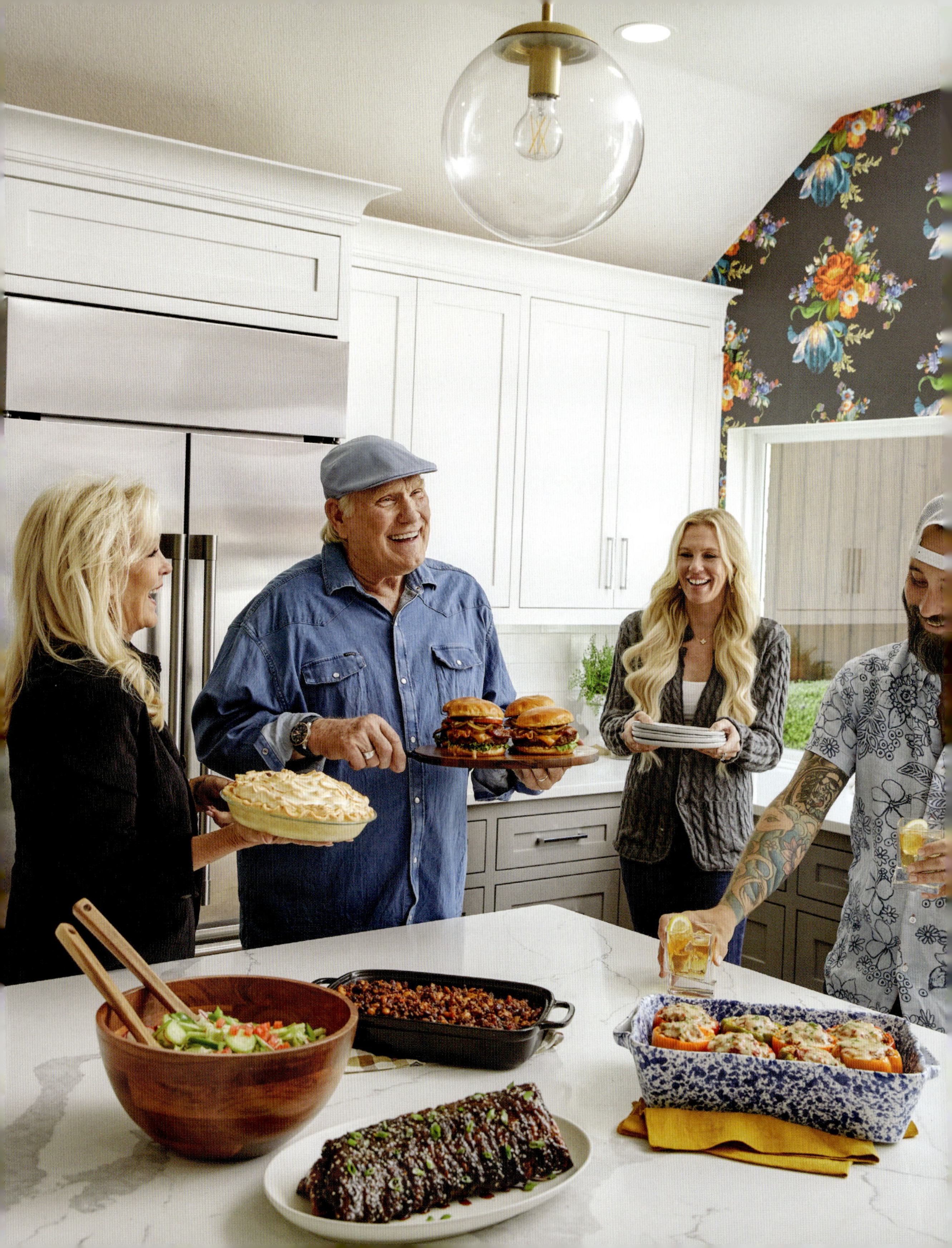

INTRODUCTION
Meet the Bradshaws!

WE CAN'T TELL YOU HOW EXCITED WE ARE TO SHARE OUR COOKBOOK with you. This book represents a whole lot of passion—about the delicious food and drinks we love to make as a family and serve to our friends.

So, who are we? If you're a football fan, you've probably heard of TB, aka Terry Bradshaw, the leader of our clan. A beefy, six-foot-three man with hands almost as big as baseball mitts, Terry led the Pittsburgh Steelers to four Super Bowl championships as team quarterback, earning two MVPs in the process. With one of the most powerful arms in NFL history, Terry played fourteen seasons for the Steelers and is now a three-time Emmy-winning broadcaster. But there's two things you likely don't know about the Hall of Famer. The first is Terry was drafted over a coin flip. True fact. The Pittsburgh Steelers and the Chicago Bears had equally bad records of 1-13. At the draft, a coin was tossed, and Pittsburgh won, giving them the number one pick. They chose Terry, and the rest is history. The second, and more relevant, piece of trivia for the purpose of this book is that Terry likes to cook. In fact, his culinary roots span generations.

Terry's grandmother lived in the small, sleepy town of Hall Summit, Louisiana. A remarkable woman of German descent whom Terry fondly called "Hoodie Baby," she was short in stature but mighty in spirit. Hoodie Baby's culinary prowess was renowned far and wide. Her kitchen was the heart of her home, a place where magic happened and happiness was served on every plate.

Hoodie Baby had an uncanny ability to transform simple ingredients into mouth-watering feasts. Every dish was made from scratch, with fresh foods she meticulously selected herself. Her philosophy was simple: Cooking was an act of love, and every meal was a gift to those she cared about.

Biscuits were one of her signature creations. Hoodie Baby had a unique way of kneading the dough, using her elbow to achieve perfect consistency. Terry recalls that watching her work was like witnessing a well-rehearsed dance, each movement precise and filled with purpose. The biscuits that emerged from her oven were golden, flaky, and melt-in-your-mouth delicious.

Her legendary classics, like Old-Fashioned Ambrosia Salad (page 184) and Sweet Orchard Peach Cobbler (page 252), were crafted to perfection and always warmed the soul. Friends and family often gathered around her table, savoring the memorable dishes and comforting ambience Hoodie Baby created effortlessly.

Despite the conveniences that crept into most homes, Hoodie Baby's kitchen remained a sanctuary of tradition. The bucket of lard that hung in a corner of her kitchen was a testament to the old-world techniques she brought with her from Germany, as much a symbol of a time-honored craft, passed down through generations, as her unique methods and insistence on quality ingredients. Today her legacy lives on in the hearts of those who had the privilege of sitting at her table, tasting the fruits of her labor and experiencing the magic of her cooking.

Today, Hoodie Baby has inspired Terry and the rest of the family to appreciate and enjoy life in the kitchen. And that's what this book is all about—how family recipes and the memories behind them bind us all together. And that begins at home with Terry and Tammy.

If you ever saw our reality show, *The Bradshaw Bunch*, you know Terry and Tammy have a lot in common, particularly ranch life in Texas and good ol'-fashioned cooking. Thumb through the pages ahead and you'll discover some of Terry's favorites, including his Legendary Bradshaw Beans (page 198) and celebrated Texas Ranch-Style Fish Fry (page 233). Being a bourbon man, the football legend is also going to show you how to make some of his lip-smacking cocktails.

Tammy and Terry were a couple for thirteen years before finally tying the knot in Hawaii in 2014. Tammy is the mother of Lacey and Cody and the stepmom to Terry's daughters, Erin and Rachel. Lacey owns and operates Hamm's Meat + Market butcher shop in McKinney, Texas, along with her husband, Austin native Noah Hester. Noah, who spent more than twenty years in Hawaii as a chef, blends his love of Southern hospitality with a hankering for Pacific Rim flavors. In this book, Noah and Lacey come together to share some of their mouthwatering dishes, particularly from the Aloha State. Trust us, one bite and you'll be dreaming of swaying coconut palms and strums of the ukulele. Noah and Lacey have two children, Zurie and Jebediah, who inspired a handful of recipes in this book as well.

Terry's older daughter, Rachel, meanwhile, is an award-winning singer and songwriter. In this book you'll find many of the signature recipes she and her husband, Chase, an executive in the gas and oil industries, love to cook and share. Getting together with the family is always at the top of Rachel, Chase, and their son Cason's list of favorite things to do, and they have a knack for creating fun dishes that can be shared.

And then there's Erin, the younger daughter, who's a world champion equestrian. She has a daughter named Jessie with her husband, Scott Weiss. Scott's a successful horse trainer, and they often head over to Terry and Tammy's house on the weekends to hang out, join in on the fun and excitement, and cook alongside the family.

And that's the Bradshaws in a culinary nutshell.

Whether it's in the kitchen or grilling out in the backyard, we love preparing and enjoying easy, delicious, family-driven recipes inspired by our roots and relatives, and our passion for cooking amid the rolling pastures of the Texas landscape that we're proud to call home.

As you'll discover throughout the pages of this book, we each bring our own specialties to the family table, from Terry's Southern-inspired dishes and Tammy's Missouri-based recipes to Rachel's quick and delicious meals and Noah and Lacey's Hawaiian culinary surprises. We also bring with us a laid-back, unpretentious lifestyle and a deep commitment to one another. Terry believes good food needs good atmosphere, and setting the proper ambience is very important to him, especially when family and friends come over. Terry always has a wood fire crackling in the kitchen and

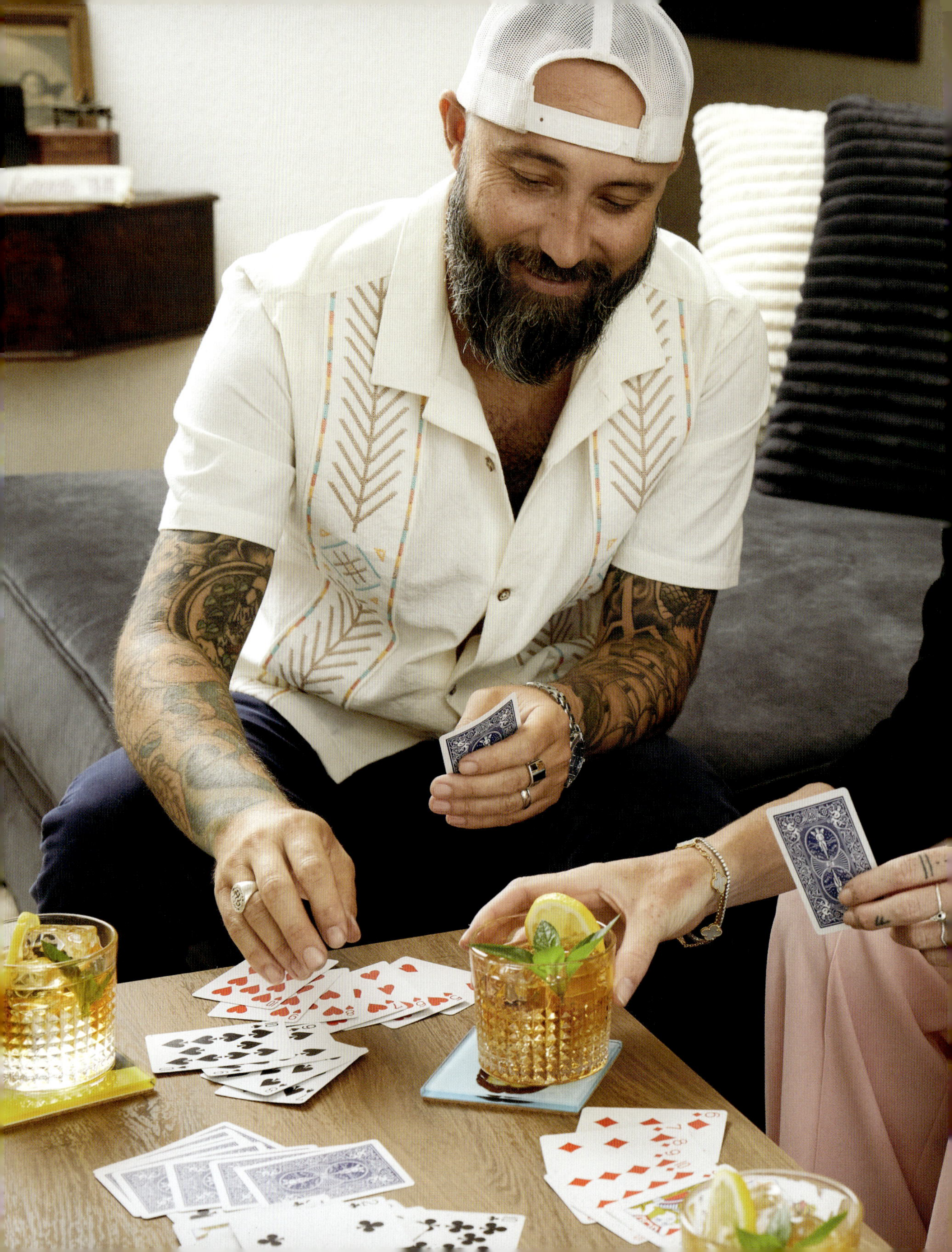

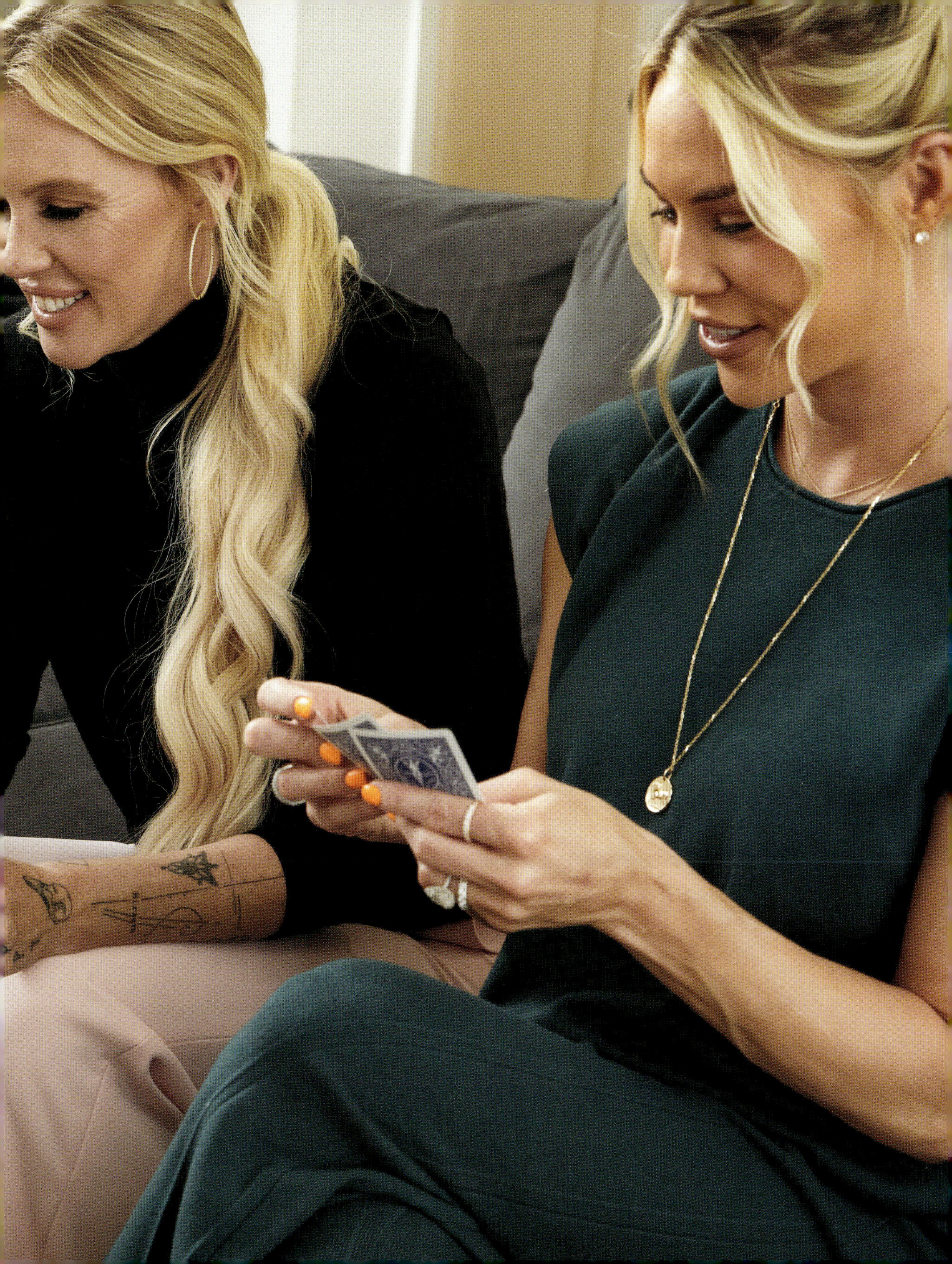

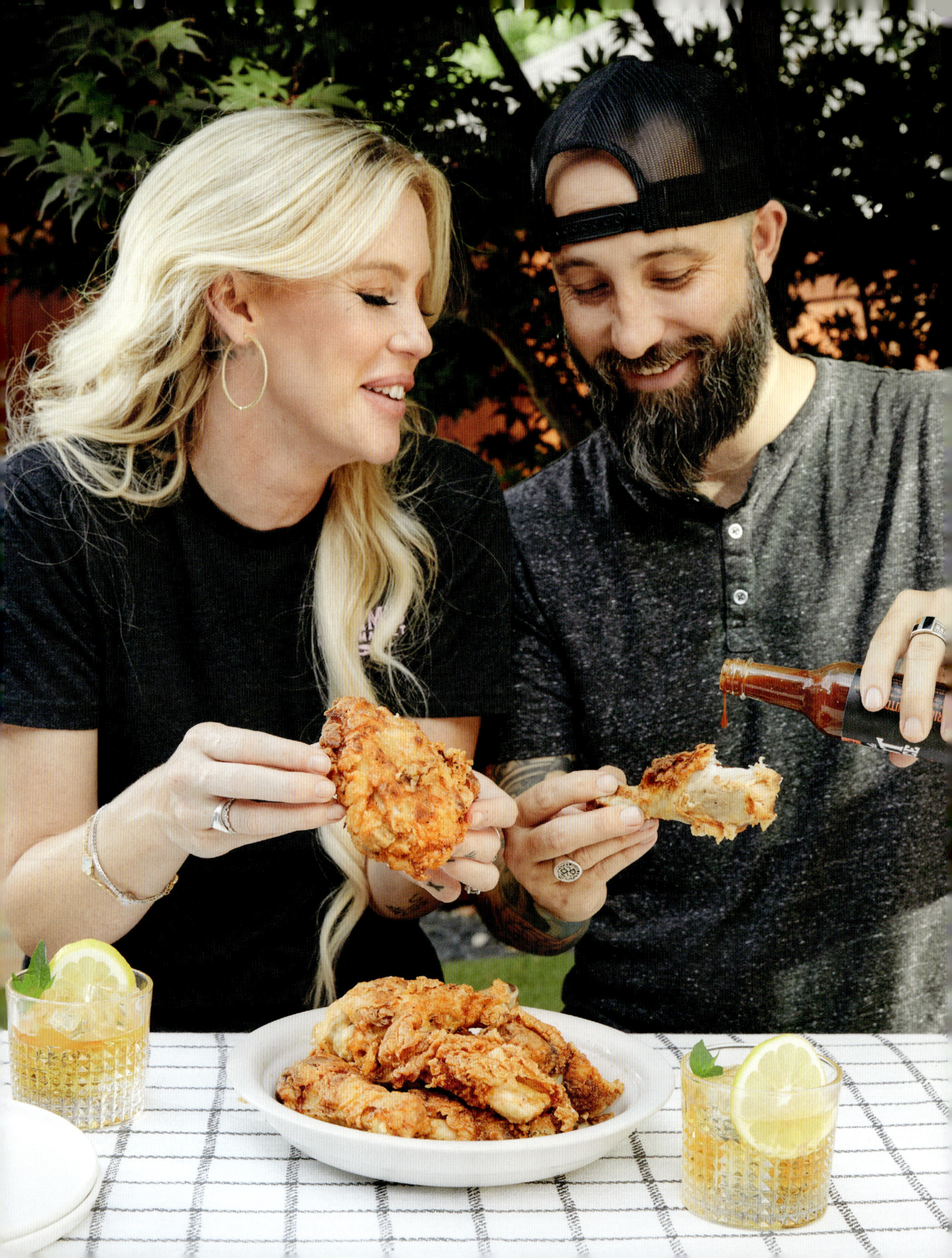

living room, regardless of the weather outside, and the Eagles' "Take It to the Limit" can be heard thrumming through the speakers. As usual, Terry will have the big screen on as well, with the sound on mute so as not to disturb his favorite band, but football, golf, or a classic movie like John Wayne's *True Grit* will be playing.

Once Terry fetches the wood and gets the fires going, he'll slip cautiously past the pool (we've pushed him in countless times) to refresh everyone on the finer points of horseshoes. Terry loves playing horseshoes (actually, any game for that matter; he's competitive). Investing time and energy in family activities is important to him. And that means plenty of humor and laugh-out-loud moments. Like the time one of the girls hid a remote-control rubber snake under Pappy's chair at the kitchen table. When he sat down to enjoy his French Toast Casserole (page 50), he felt something slithering across his feet. Looking down and seeing the snake, he jumped from the chair and screamed like we'd never heard before! We all thought he was going to have a heart attack!

Speaking of family laughter, this cookbook is filled with all the celebratory foods that put smiles on our faces and that we've grown to know and love. We've arranged our recipes to reflect the way we like to gather, whether for a leisurely weekend breakfast or brunch, for one of our legendary cookouts or tailgates, or for a casual potluck with the whole rambunctious bunch of us. You'll also find plenty of inspiration for snacks to fuel your game day, salads and sides, desserts and sweets, plus an extraspecial section of cherished family recipes that have graced our family's tables for generations, including a couple from Hoodie Baby herself. We've also included some great Bradshaw spins and surprises here and there. We hope they will become a regular part of your household traditions, as they have with ours.

Now, let's get cooking!

CHEF NOAH Hester
Hawaiian
CHILI WATER
FRANK'S
RedHot
ORIGINAL

A Peek Inside Our Kitchen and Pantry

The contents of cooks' refrigerators and kitchen pantries offer a culinary window into their family's cooking habits and preferences, and ours are no exception. Below, you'll find some of the ingredients we like to keep on hand and that are used in this book, with some helpful notes on what they taste like, where to find them, and their role in our kitchen.

Bisquick Original Pancake and Baking Mix
We all depend on this versatile baking mix, which dates back to 1930 and remains a staple in our kitchens. The mix is convenient and sure simplifies the preparation of pancakes (page 46) and biscuits (page 57), as well as the Herb-Roasted Chicken and Biscuit Dumplings (page 217).

Bradshaw Bourbon Barbecue Sauce
Whether we're making it from scratch (page 141) or using it from the bottle, our signature barbecue sauce is a sweet and savory condiment crafted with straight bourbon whiskey, tomato paste, vinegar, and spices. It infuses foods with rich, smoky flavor and hints of caramel and oak from the bourbon. When we're wanting to add such depth to our backyard dishes, like our Spicy Pork Canoes with Cilantro Sour Cream (page 127) or Terry's Legendary Bradshaw Beans (page 198), this sauce is the ticket.

Chef Noah's Hawaiian Chili Water
Because Noah makes and sells this spicy concoction at his and Lacey's butcher shop in McKinney, we always have a good supply on hand. A traditional Hawaiian condiment, the seasoned water is infused with fiery Hawaiian chili peppers, vinegar, and salt. It packs a punch of heat and flavor, which is why we reach for it when we're wanting to add depth and heat to dishes such as our Finger-Lickin' Barbecue Bourbon Chicken Wings (page 114).

Frank's RedHot Sauce
Another beloved condiment, Frank's RedHot has a fiery kick and tangy taste that elevates

our meals with its signature heat. Made from cayenne peppers, vinegar, garlic, and spices, this versatile and iconic sauce adds a bold zing to many of our dishes, particularly Finger-Lickin' Barbecue Bourbon Chicken Wings (page 114) and Cheesy Smoked Buffalo Chicken Dip (page 101).

Lit'l Smokies

Made from seasoned meat, typically pork or beef, these bite-sized sausages are bursting with flavor and always a hit at our parties and gatherings, especially when used in our Garlic Pull-Apart Pigs in a Blanket (page 90).

Old English Cheese Spread

This versatile and nostalgic spread is a tangy blend of aged cheddar, mustard, and spices. We always keep a jar on hand, as the creamy texture and robust taste never fail to satisfy. Try it in our comforting Ham and Old English Cheese Casserole (page 51).

Pimentos

When we need a pop of color and subtle sweetness in our recipes, like Poppa Hester's Savory Herb Pimento Cheese (page 98) or Hawaiian Summer Tuna Fish Dip (page 106), we'll reach for pimentos to enhance the taste and visual appeal of our dishes. These small, red, heart-shaped peppers, known for their mild, sweet flavor, are ideal for our various culinary creations.

Premade Piecrusts and Shells

Another convenient shortcut for baking homemade pies, like our Old-Fashioned Blackberry Pie (page 244), refrigerated crusts save time and frustration for those challenged by pie dough. They come in various sizes and types, including traditional, gluten-free, and vegan options. You can also buy pie shells, which you simply prebake and then fill, making pie-making accessible to all levels of bakers and dietary preferences.

Refrigerated Biscuit Dough

Premade doughs, like Pillsbury's Grands! Original Flaky Layers used in our Ooey Gooey Apple Monkey Bread (page 45) and Pillsbury's dough sheets used in our Garlic Pull-Apart Pigs in a Blanket (page 90), simplify baking with their ready-to-use convenience. They are extremely versatile, easy to handle, and have a consistent texture, making them perfect for quick and easy dishes.

Slap Ya Mama Original Blend Cajun Seasoning

We enjoy this great mixture of spices, which we'll add to Southern dishes like our Gumbo with Chicken, Andouille, and Crawfish (page 227). Not too spicy and full of flavor, you'll love how this Cajun seasoning enhances your food. For those of you, like Terry, who want extra heat, Slap Ya Mama offers a Hot Blend that's sure to set your mouth on fire.

Wagyu Hot Dogs

We like to keep a package or two of these hot dogs on hand for a luxurious twist on the classic that elevates the humble dog to gourmet status. Made with high-grade Wagyu beef, the hot dogs are known for their marbling and tenderness as well as their rich, buttery flavor and juicy bite. They're perfect for our Loaded Wagyu Hot Dogs (page 131).

Must-Have Tools

As important as having the necessary ingredients on hand, having the right kitchen tools is an essential part of cooking efficiently and successfully. From basic barware and blenders to the right pans and electric appliances, these tools play a vital role in our cooking process. Investing in quality utensils also ensures smoother preparation and better-tasting dishes. Here's a short list of the kitchen tools we keep at the ready:

Aluminum Pans
These convenient and hassle-free pans are ideal for baking, roasting, and grilling. Lightweight and inexpensive, aluminum pans eliminate the need for cleanup, making them perfect for parties, cookouts, and tailgates. Make sure you have these pans on hand for dishes like Terry's Legendary Bradshaw Beans (page 198).

Baking Dishes and Pans
You don't need a huge variety of baking pans to make the recipes in this book, but for a few specific baked goods, like our Baked Cinnamon Doughnuts (page 42), having the right pan is nonnegotiable. To make *all* the yummy sweets in this book, you'll need these items:

- Two 6-hole doughnut pans
- Two 12-cup standard-sized muffin pans
- One 2-quart round glass or ceramic baking dish
- Two 5 × 9-inch loaf pans
- Two 13 × 18-inch rimmed baking sheets
- One 9-inch pie dish (preferably glass)
- One 9-inch round cake pan (preferably uncoated light-colored aluminum)
- One 9 × 9-inch baking dish (preferably glass)

These pans deliver consistent results and enhance the presentation of the baked items.

Basic Bar Tools
Essential bar tools like a shaker, muddler, jigger, and strainer are crucial for crafting our signature cocktails (pages 74 to 82) with precision and style. A shaker mixes the ingredients thoroughly while the

muddler crushes herbs and fruit to release their essential oils and juices. A jigger delivers accurate measurements, and a strainer removes unwanted ice and pulp, resulting in perfectly balanced and visually appealing drinks.

Blenders

It seems every kitchen these days has an electric appliance that can mix, puree, or emulsify food and beverages. Blenders, whether countertop or immersion (stick) types, are an extremely versatile and efficient way to blend soups, sauces, and more—from our refreshing Brunch Punch (page 37) to blending beans for our cozy Cannellini Chicken Chili (page 157).

Dutch Oven

Usually made of cast iron, often with a heavy enamel coating, the Dutch oven is a durable and versatile cooking pot with a tight-fitting lid. It's ideal for slow-cooking, braising, roasting, and baking due to its excellent heat retention and even distribution. We like to use the Dutch oven for our Juicy Braised Korean Short Ribs (page 123), Cannellini Chicken Chili (page 157), and Gumbo with Chicken, Andouille, and Crawfish (page 227), among others.

Mandoline

If you like to cut your fruits and vegetables consistently every time, invest in a mandoline. This handy tool features a flat, adjustable blade that creates thin, even slices or julienne strips. Not only does the mandoline ensure precision and consistency but it makes food preparation quicker and more efficient. Use a mandoline when thinly slicing the vegetables for Iceberg Salad with Terry's Favorite Dressing (page 176) or the potatoes for our Chicken Stock Scalloped Potatoes (page 193).

Musubi Mold

This fun tool is used to shape rice into compact, rectangular blocks, essential for making our Spam (Hawaiian) Musubi with Homemade Teriyaki Sauce (page 229), a popular Hawaiian snack. Typically made of plastic, the mold ensures uniformity and makes it easy to press the rice and fillings together.

Outdoor Grill and Smoker

When it comes to backyard barbecues and tailgates, we think you need to have both a grill and a smoker. The grill is perfect for giving the meats, hot dogs, and hamburgers in our Cookouts and Tailgates chapter a smoky char over high or indirect heat. The outdoor smoker, meanwhile, is meant to slow-cook at low temperatures, infusing foods with a rich, smoky taste from the wood being used.

Pressure Cooker or Multicooker

Whether you prefer a dedicated pressure cooker (Tammy swears by her electric pressure cooker) or an appliance like an Insta-Pot that can sauté, slow-cook, or cook under pressure, these appliances are great time-savers. Check out our Green Beans with Bacon, Onion, and Garlic (page 191).

Waffle Maker

It's not breakfast in the Bradshaw household without waffles, especially our Cinnamon Apple Waffles (page 49). Waffle makers are available in various styles, from traditional to Belgian, with some having adjustable temperature controls for perfect browning.

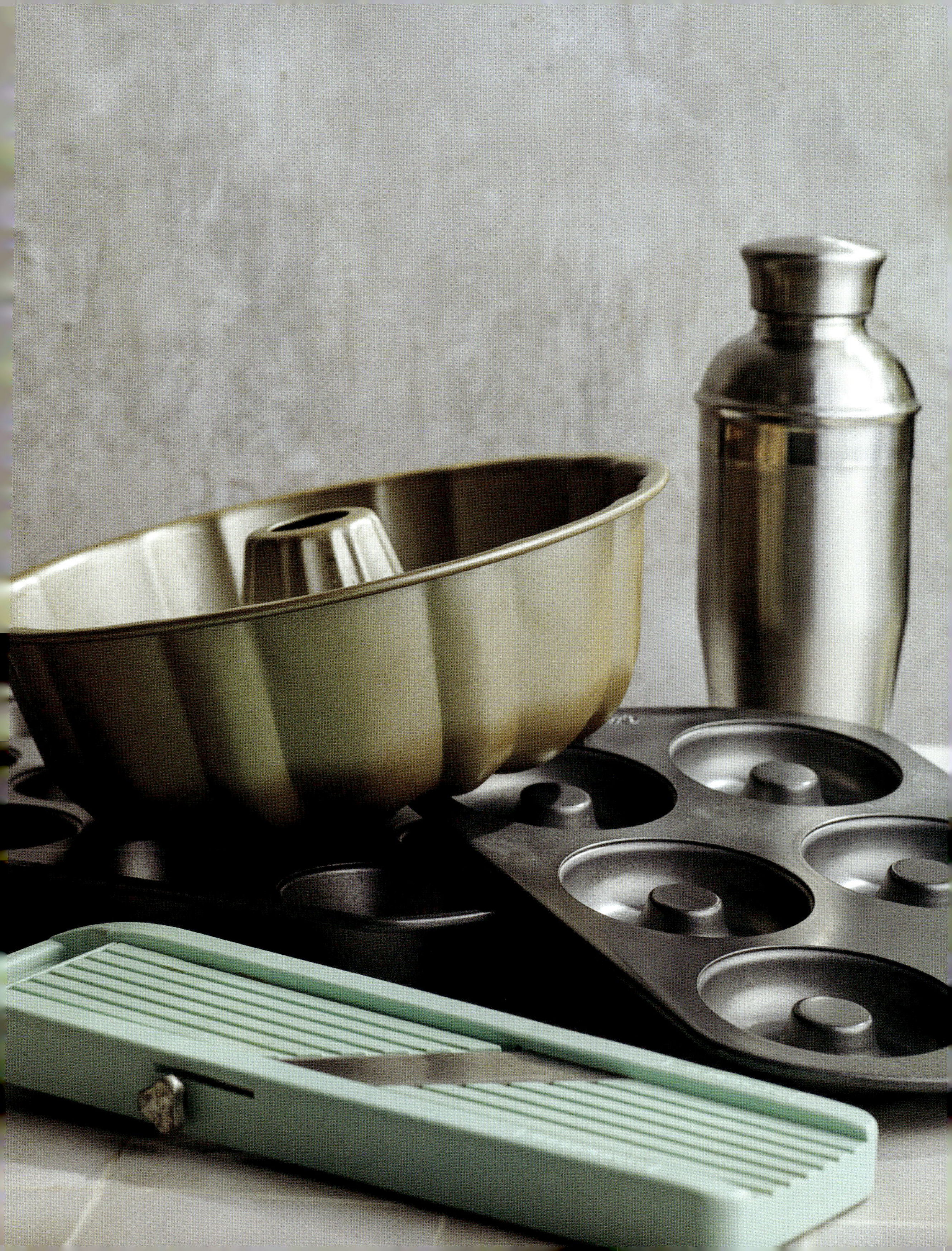

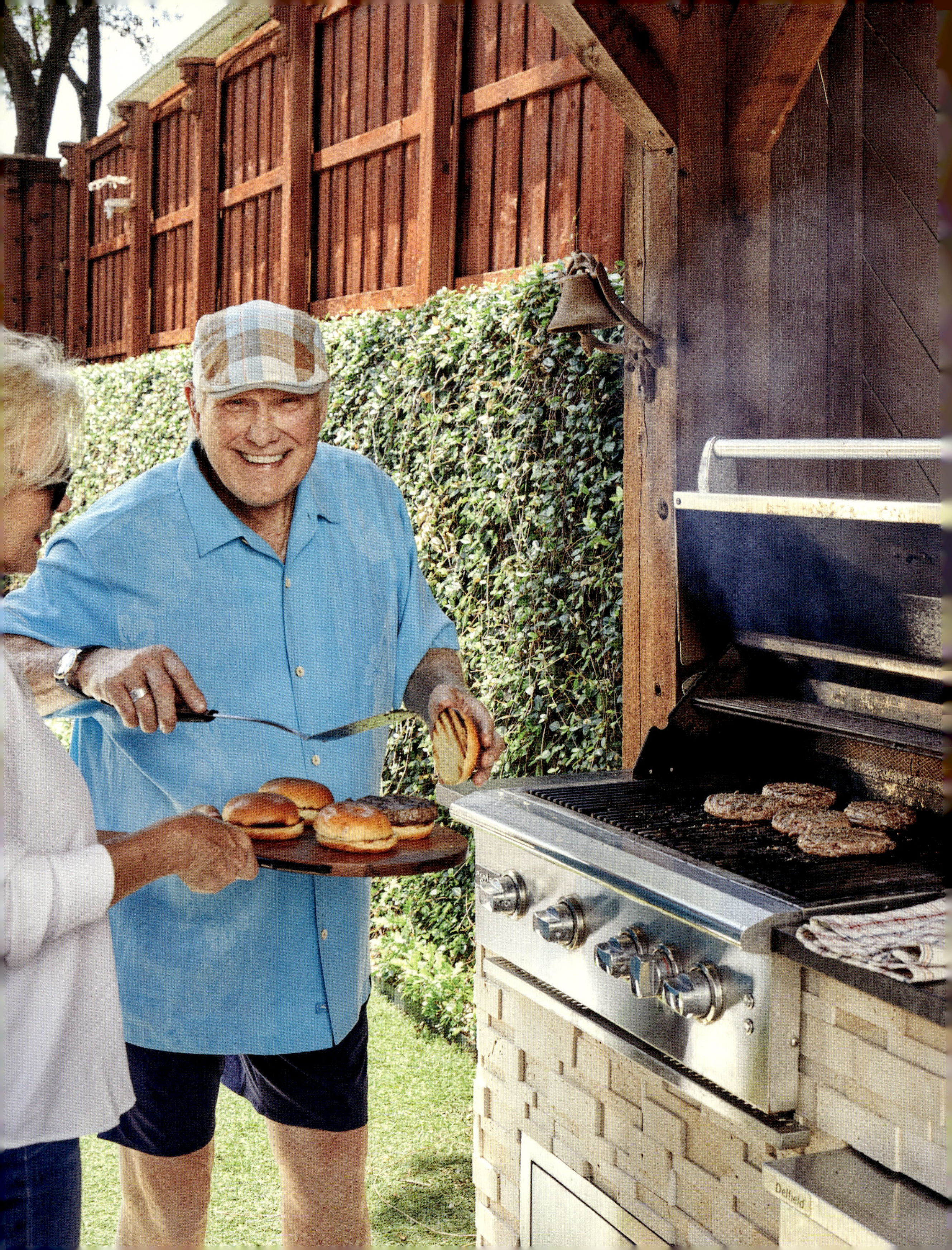
Delfield

Grilling and Smoking— a Bradshaw Family Primer

Grilling

If you are ever invited to one of our cookouts, you'll definitely find us working over an outdoor grill—or two! We consider them essential for cooking delicious meals, whether in our backyard, at a tailgate, or at the ranch. Whether you opt for gas, charcoal, electric, or pellet is a matter of personal choice, and each has its own unique characteristics.

We all use gas grills at home because they're convenient and easy, running on propane or natural gas. They offer precise temperature control, making them ideal for both beginners and experienced grillers.

Terry and Noah both also have charcoal grills, which they like to use when cooking steaks or other cuts of beef. Noah, who cooks a lot with charcoal, prefers the Kamado Joe Big Joe, a versatile ceramic grill known for its superior heat retention and temperature control. It's ideal for smoking and grilling, making it a premium choice for outdoor cooking enthusiasts.

Cleaning

Before firing up the grill, it's always important to prepare it properly. We recommend cleaning the cooking grates as the first step. This removes any leftover food particles to prevent flare-ups and ensure even cooking. Start by brushing the grates to remove the food residue. If we've been using our gas grills quite a lot, we'll scrub the burners, too. And if your grill has a drip pan to catch the grease, make sure you clean that as well to prevent grease buildup. Sometimes we'll wash the cooking grates and burners with warm, soapy water and a sponge, depending on how dirty they got, making sure to rinse them thoroughly. Otherwise, a clean rag soaked in some oil is effective for cleaning and oiling the grates after scrubbing to ensure the grates are clean and that the food won't stick. For charcoal grill maintenance, it's a good practice to dispose of any leftover ash from the previous cooking session before preparing and lighting up for more grilling.

Preheating

Once the grill and grates are clean and well-oiled, you need to allow the grill to reach optimal temperature before putting your food over the heat. When we're in a hurry, sometimes we skip this step, but we shouldn't. Preheating is important to making delicious grilled foods because it prevents food from sticking to the grates while ensuring consistent heat distribution. Preheating also brings food to the proper temperature more quickly, reducing cook times.

We like to preheat our gas grills for about 15 minutes. For charcoal grills, we'll pile a pyramid of coals on the bottom grate, light them using a natural lighter fluid, and wait for about 15 minutes for the coals to ash over before spreading them out. Other times we may mound the coals into a chimney starter. It takes about 15 minutes for the flames to flicker at the top of the chimney and for the coals to turn gray and ashy, which means they're ready. We'll carefully pour the charcoal onto the bottom grate and spread it out. The clean, oiled grate goes on top, and we're ready for business.

Cooking

When it comes to grilling, timing and temperature control are key. Different foods require different cooking times and heat levels, so it's essential to monitor the grill closely and adjust as needed. For gas grills, it's relatively easy to adjust the temperature by turning the knobs. For charcoal grills it's not that easy. What we'll do is push the prepared charcoal to one side of the grill, leaving the other side exposed. This allows us to control the cooking. We can cook on the side with the coals for high heat, on the side with no coals for low heat, or in the middle for medium heat. Because we never want to overcook or burn our food, we like to use a digital meat thermometer. This ensures our meats are cooked to our liking.

Lastly, please don't forget about safety. Keep a fire extinguisher nearby, and never leave the grill unattended while it's lit. Also, make sure the grill is away from any flammable materials and on a stable, flat surface.

There you have it. Now you have the basics to mastering the art of outdoor grilling.

Smoking

If you've ever had good ol'-fashioned Texas barbecue, you know the outdoor smoker is an essential piece of equipment. Prized by professional pitmasters and barbecue enthusiasts alike, the smoker is paramount when it comes to infusing food with rich, smoky flavors. Like barbecue grills, smokers come in various types, including offset smokers, vertical water smokers, and electric smokers. Here are the basics:

Offset smokers feature a separate firebox adjacent to the cooking chamber, allowing for indirect heat and smoke circulation. They're favored for their traditional smoking methods and large cooking capacities, perfect for smoking large pieces of meat like brisket or ribs. Vertical water smokers, also known as bullet smokers, consist of stacked chambers with a water pan at the bottom to regulate temperature and humidity. They're affordable, compact, and easy to use, making them a good entry-level smoker for beginners.. Electric smokers are convenient and easy to use, requiring minimal effort to maintain consistent temperatures. They're ideal for urban environments or areas where open flames are restricted. Some electric smokers even come with digital controls and smartphone connectivity for precise temperature monitoring and adjustment.

Regardless of the kind of smoker you opt for, mastering the art of smoking requires attention to detail and patience. We like to start by choosing the right wood—from hickory and mesquite to apple and cherry—to complement the flavor of our food. For example, when smoking pork, we like to use a fruit wood like apple or peach for a subtle, sweet, and fragrant smoke. When smoking brisket or ribs, hickory and mesquite work well because the smoke given off from these woods penetrates deep into the meat. Next, we'll prepare our smoker by cleaning the grates and adding water to the pan if necessary to create excess moisture (this protects the meat from drying out). Then we'll preheat the smoker to the desired temperature, ensuring it's stable before adding the food. We've included a few smoking recipes in this book to get you acquainted with the smoking process, such as our Spicy Pork Canoes (page 127), Pork Belly Bites (page 124), and Smoked Brisket Sliders (page 138).

GRILLING AND SMOKING—A BRADSHAW FAMILY PRIMER

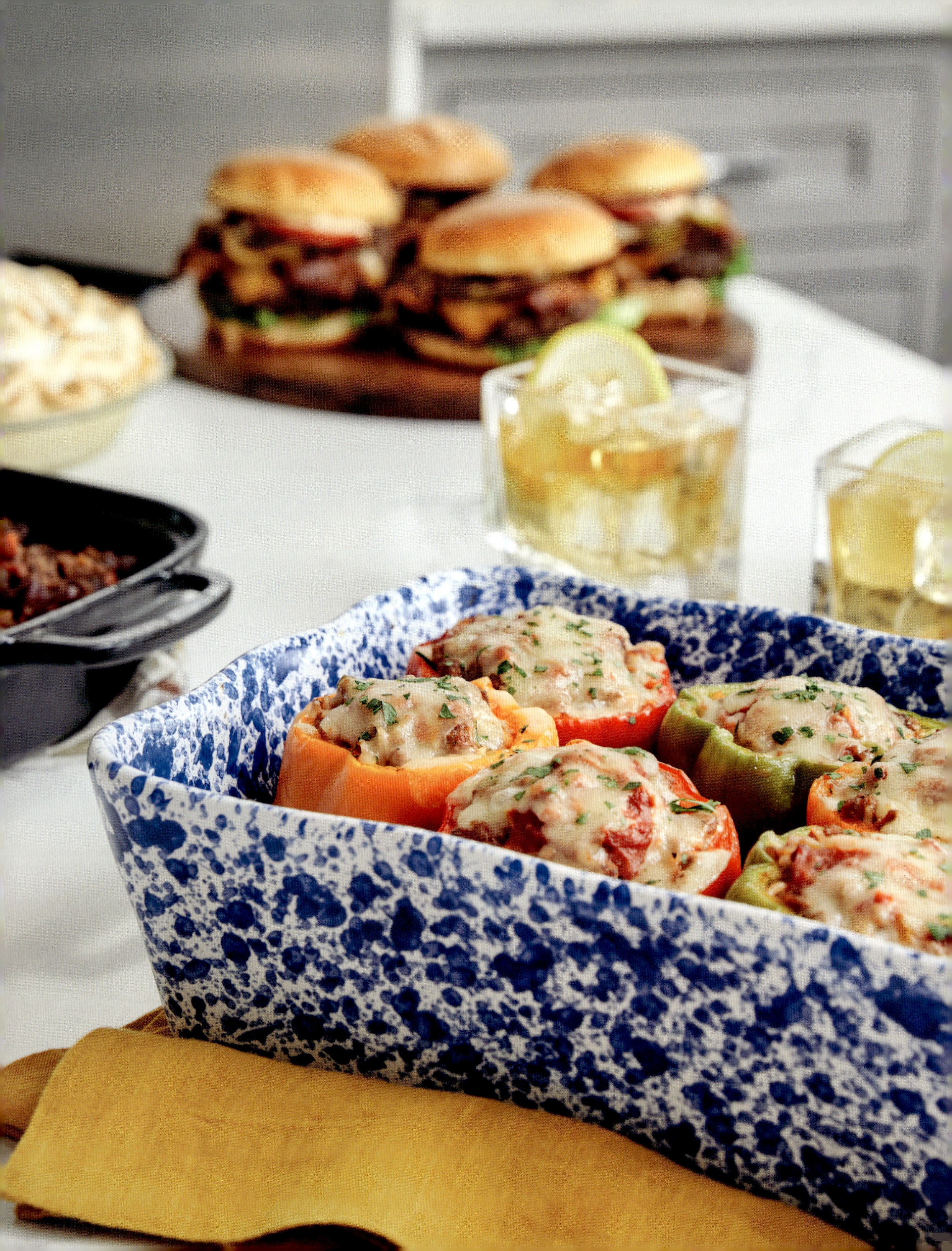

What's Cooking in Our Kitchen

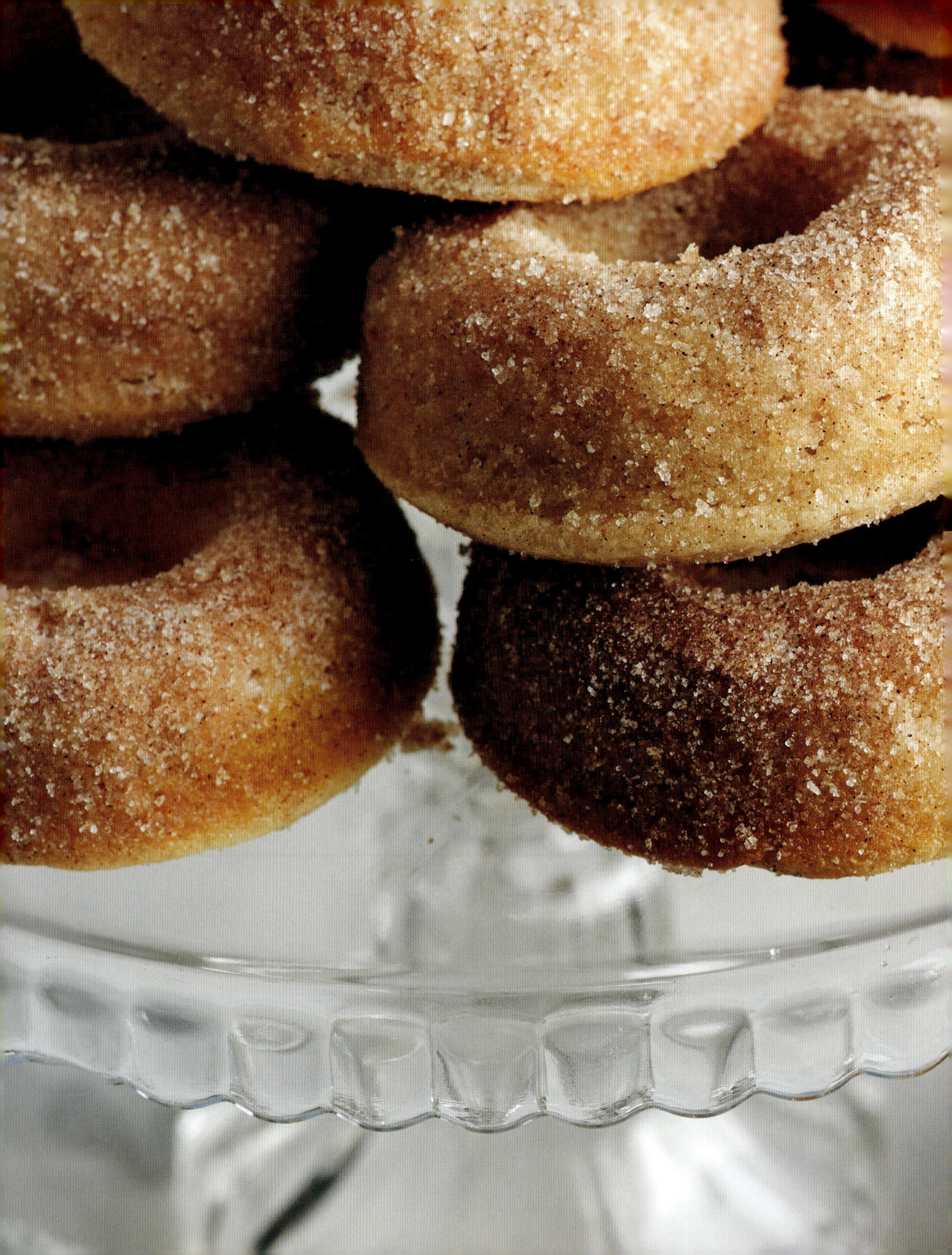

1 // Breakfasts and Brunches

Brunch Punch

Creamy Vanilla Fruit Salad

Baked Cinnamon Doughnuts

Ooey Gooey Apple Monkey Bread

Funfetti Chocolate Chip Banana Pancakes

Cinnamon Apple Waffles

French Toast Casserole

Ham and Old English Cheese Casserole

Overnight Stuffed Brioche French Toast Casserole

Sausage and Cheddar Cheese Biscuits

Nannie Bradshaw's Sausage Gravy

Spicy Breakfast Casserole with Onion and Bell Peppers

One-Skillet Breakfast Frittata

Bacon, Onion, and Mushroom Quiche

Breakfast Tacos with Chipotle Crema

Toad in the Hole

Terry's Favorite Omelet

MORNINGS AT THE BRADSHAW HOME ARE A TRUE FAMILY AFFAIR where love is served with every plate. Picture this: daylight streaming through the windows as Terry's got the food of the gods—bacon—sizzling on the stove, Tammy's pouring fresh-brewed coffee, and the whole clan—dogs included—is congregating around the big wooden table that's the heart of our kitchen. That table's seen it all, from Rachel's buttery Ooey Gooey Apple Monkey Bread (page 45) to Noah and Lacey's Funfetti Chocolate Chip Banana Pancakes (page 46), which their kids can't get enough of.

Breakfast here is more than just fuel for the day—it's a time to slow down, swap stories, and savor the dishes that have become cherished Bradshaw family favorites—and occasionally a few that are new to the rotation. We adore watching the children's faces light up as they listen to Terry's tales from the football field, their eyes wide with wonder as they munch on Cinnamon Apple Waffles (page 49).

When we say brunch, we mean leisurely Sunday mornings with omelets, fresh doughnuts, and a round or two of our Brunch Punch (page 37), because what's a weekend without a little indulgence? But most of the time, the breakfast dishes we savor are the ones we've been making for years. Maybe it's Nannie Bradshaw's Sausage Gravy (page 58) over fluffy, buttery biscuits (page 57), or Terry's Bacon, Onion, and Mushroom Quiche (page 63) that gets everyone coming back for seconds. It's in these moments, over plates piled high with our favorite comfort foods, that we create bonds we'll cherish long after the dishes are done.

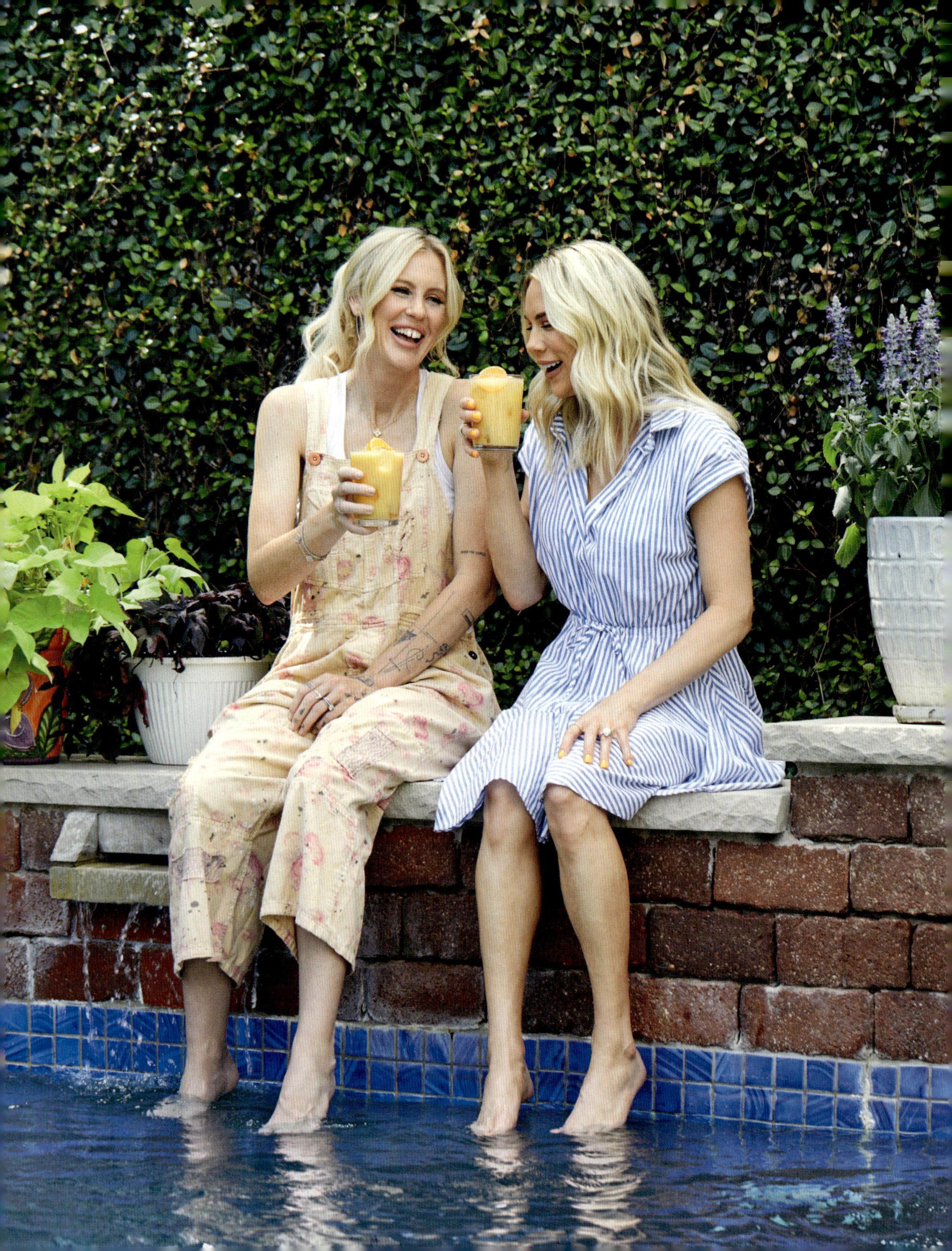

Brunch Punch

My mom, Charla, says I remind her of fruit punch, always cheerful and happy. When I was young, we'd have afternoon tea parties and sip this punch from adorable little cups. Naturally sweetened with banana and the juices of bright orange and pineapple, this wonderful brunch beverage is a cool splash of paradise. —RACHEL

Makes 2 quarts

3 large ripe bananas

¾ cup fresh orange juice

1 (23-ounce) can 100% pineapple juice

Simple Syrup (see Coach's Corner, page 77), **to taste**

Ginger ale, to taste (see Coach's Corner)

Add the bananas to a blender and puree until smooth, about 1 minute. Add the orange juice and pineapple juice, then blend to combine. Add simple syrup to taste, depending on how sweet the fruit is. Place the blender pitcher in the freezer and freeze the mixture until slushy, 1 or 2 hours. (Freezing the mixture in the blender allows you to blend it back to a slushy consistency should it freeze too solid.) Transfer the mixture to a pitcher.

To serve, pour the punch into tall, ice-filled glasses until about three-quarters full. Top with ginger ale and serve.

COACH'S CORNER

For the adults, sometimes we'll spike the punch with champagne or vodka; how much is up to you.

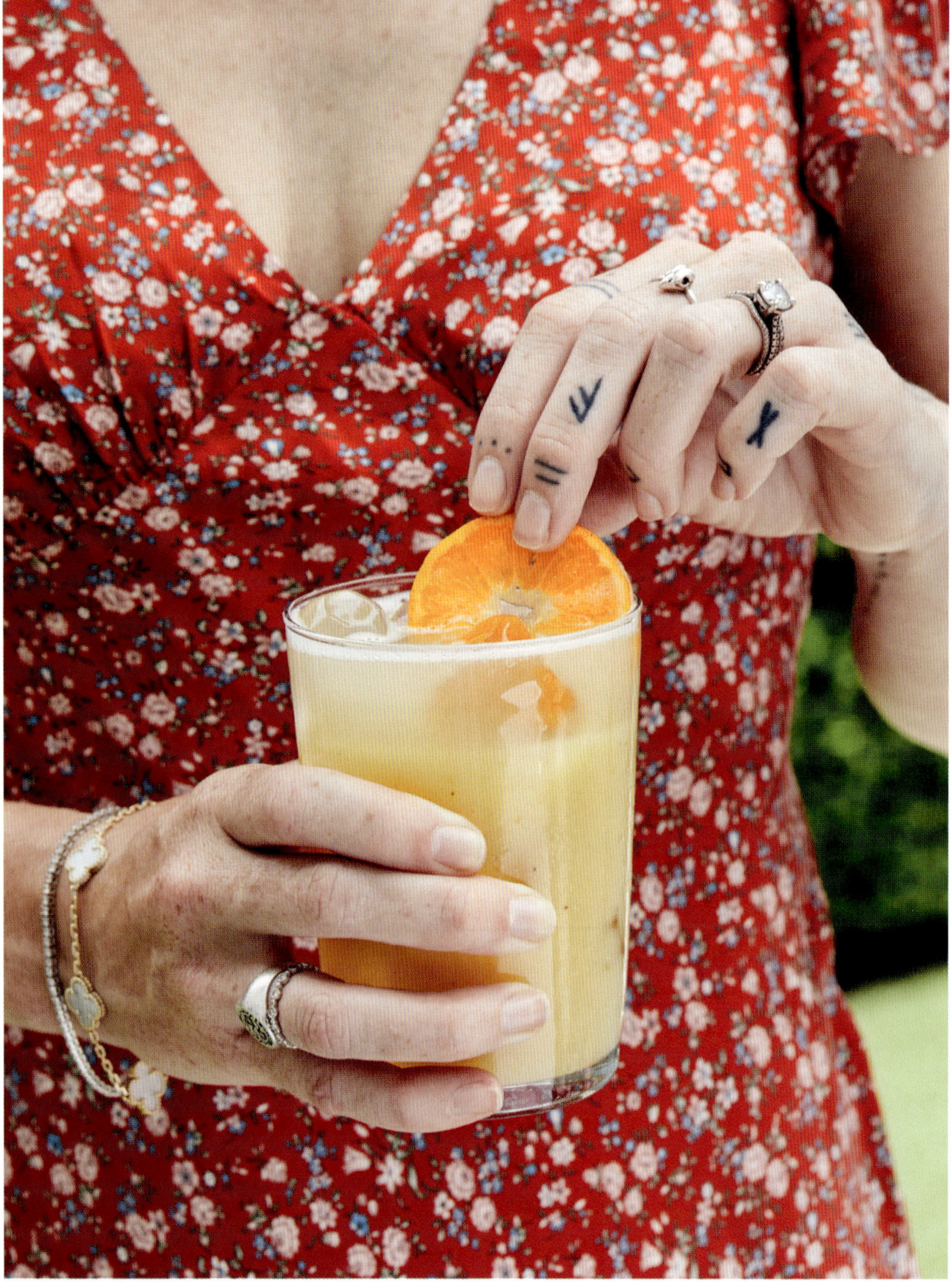

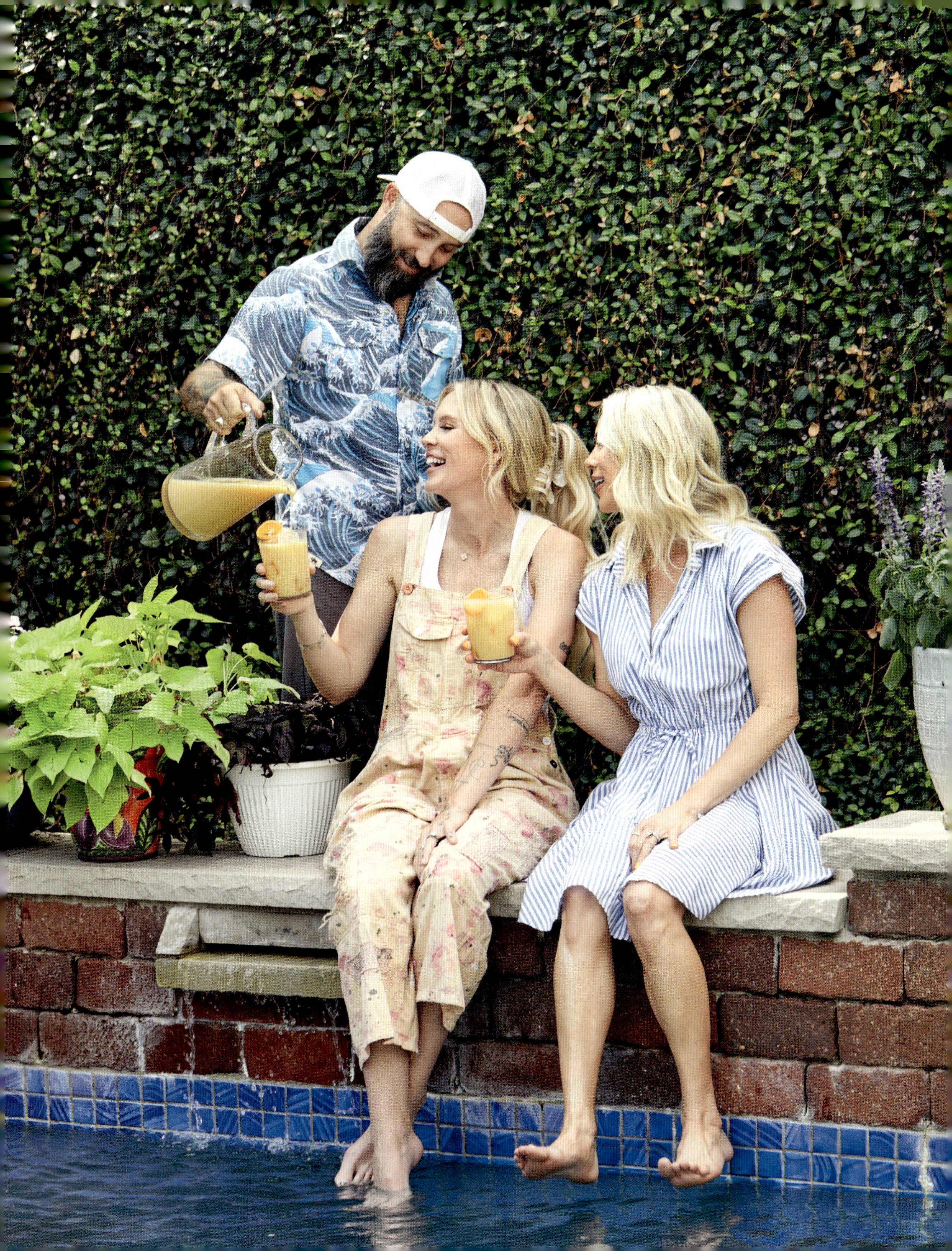

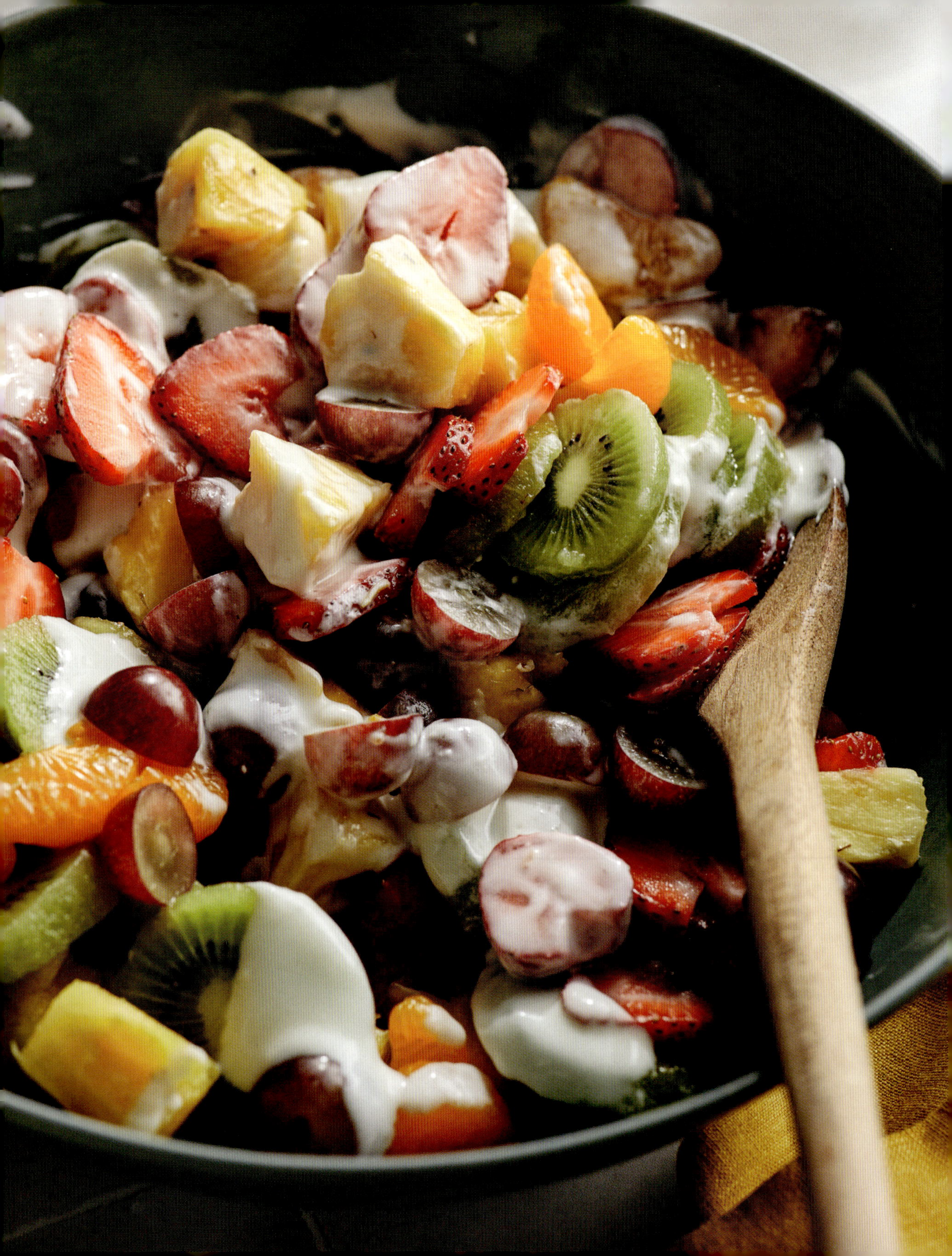

Creamy Vanilla Fruit Salad

Nothing beats a refreshing fruit salad on a hot summer day. If you grew up in the South, like us, you know a good fruit salad is a must for special occasions and holiday breakfasts. This sweet, velvety version features a medley of fresh fruit, including strawberries, oranges, grapes, kiwi, and pineapple. **—TERRY**

Serves 4 to 6

4 ounces cream cheese, at room temperature

1 teaspoon pure vanilla extract

1 cup vanilla yogurt

¼ cup granulated sugar, to taste

2 cups sliced fresh strawberries

1 cup canned mandarin orange segments

1½ cups halved seedless red grapes

4 kiwifruit, peeled and sliced

1½ cups chopped fresh pineapple

Combine the cream cheese and vanilla in a mixing bowl and beat with an electric mixer until blended and smooth. Add the yogurt and continue to mix until incorporated. Taste and add the sugar, if necessary.

Add the strawberries, oranges, grapes, kiwi, and pineapple to a serving bowl. Add the cream cheese "dressing" and toss gently to coat. Refrigerate until chilled. Gently toss before serving.

Baked Cinnamon Doughnuts

During my pregnancy, I craved all things sweet, especially anything flavored with cinnamon. To satisfy my hankering, I went out one day and bought myself a doughnut baking pan to make these "little drops of heaven." (If you've ever seen *Friends*, you'll understand this reference.) You too can satisfy your sweet tooth with these baked doughnuts. Bursting with warm, comforting flavors, these golden cakelike morsels are coated in a fragrant butter and cinnamon sugar mixture, which adds a delightful crunch and extra dose of sweetness. **—RACHEL**

Makes 12 to 16 doughnuts

Nonstick cooking spray

2 cups all-purpose flour

1½ cups granulated sugar

2 teaspoons baking powder

1 teaspoon ground cinnamon, or more to taste

½ teaspoon ground nutmeg

½ teaspoon kosher salt

1 extra-large egg, lightly beaten

1¼ cups whole milk

2 tablespoons unsalted butter, melted

2 teaspoons pure vanilla extract

TOPPING

½ cup (1 stick) unsalted butter

¾ cup granulated sugar

½ teaspoon ground cinnamon

Preheat the oven to 350°F. Spray two 6-hole doughnut pans with nonstick cooking spray.

Sift the flour, sugar, baking powder, cinnamon, nutmeg, and salt together in a large bowl.

Combine the egg, milk, melted butter, and vanilla in a small bowl and whisk to combine. Add the egg mixture to the dry ingredients and stir with a wooden spoon until just combined.

Spoon the batter into the prepared pans, filling each one a little more than three-quarters full. Bake until a toothpick inserted into the center of a doughnut comes out clean, 17 to 20 minutes. Cool the doughnuts in the pans for about 5 minutes, then turn them out onto a sheet pan.

For the topping, melt the butter in an 8-inch skillet over medium heat, then remove from the heat. Stir the sugar and cinnamon together in a small bowl. Dip each doughnut first in the butter and then in the cinnamon sugar, coating one or both sides. Serve warm or at room temperature. Store any extras in a sealed container at room temperature for a day or two.

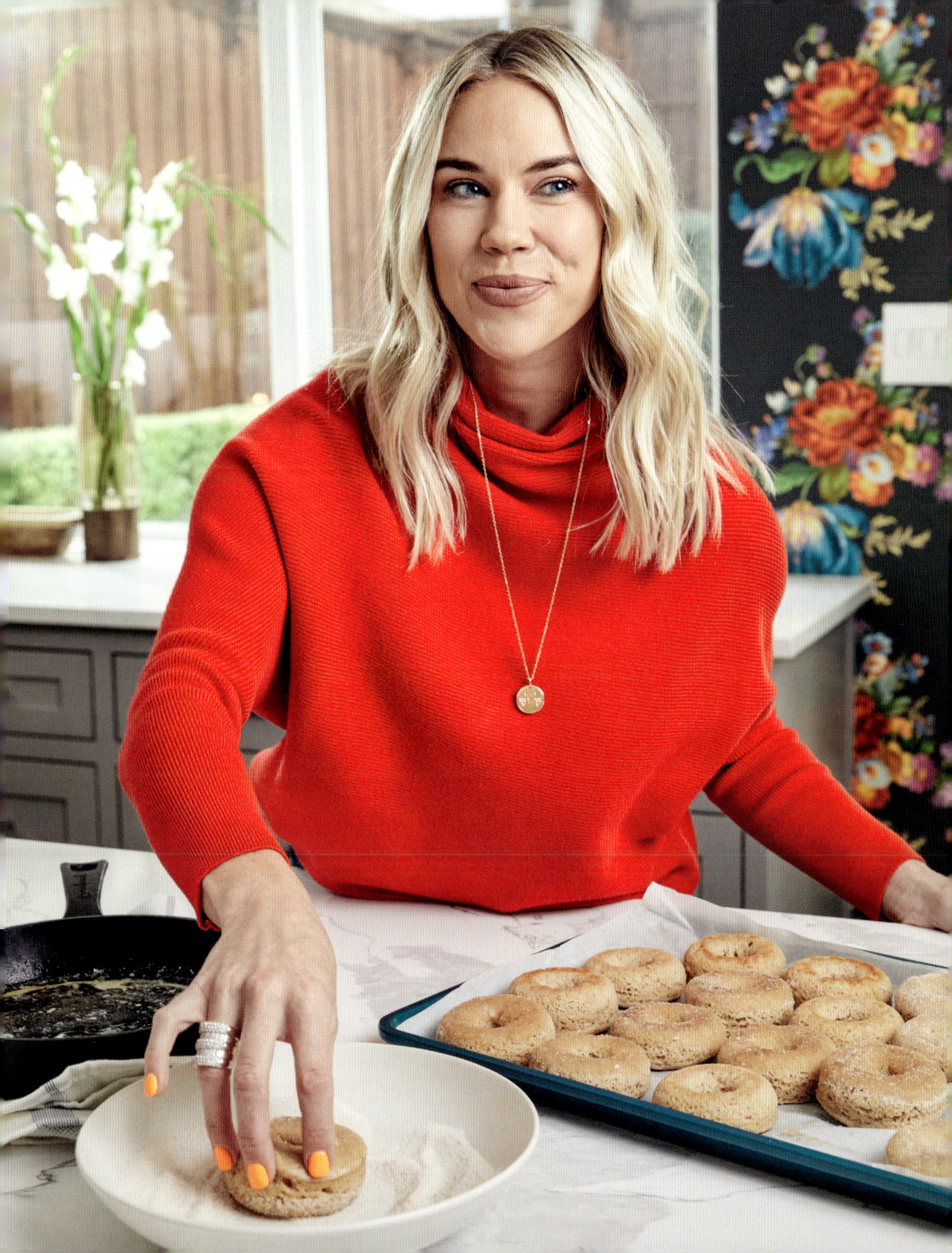

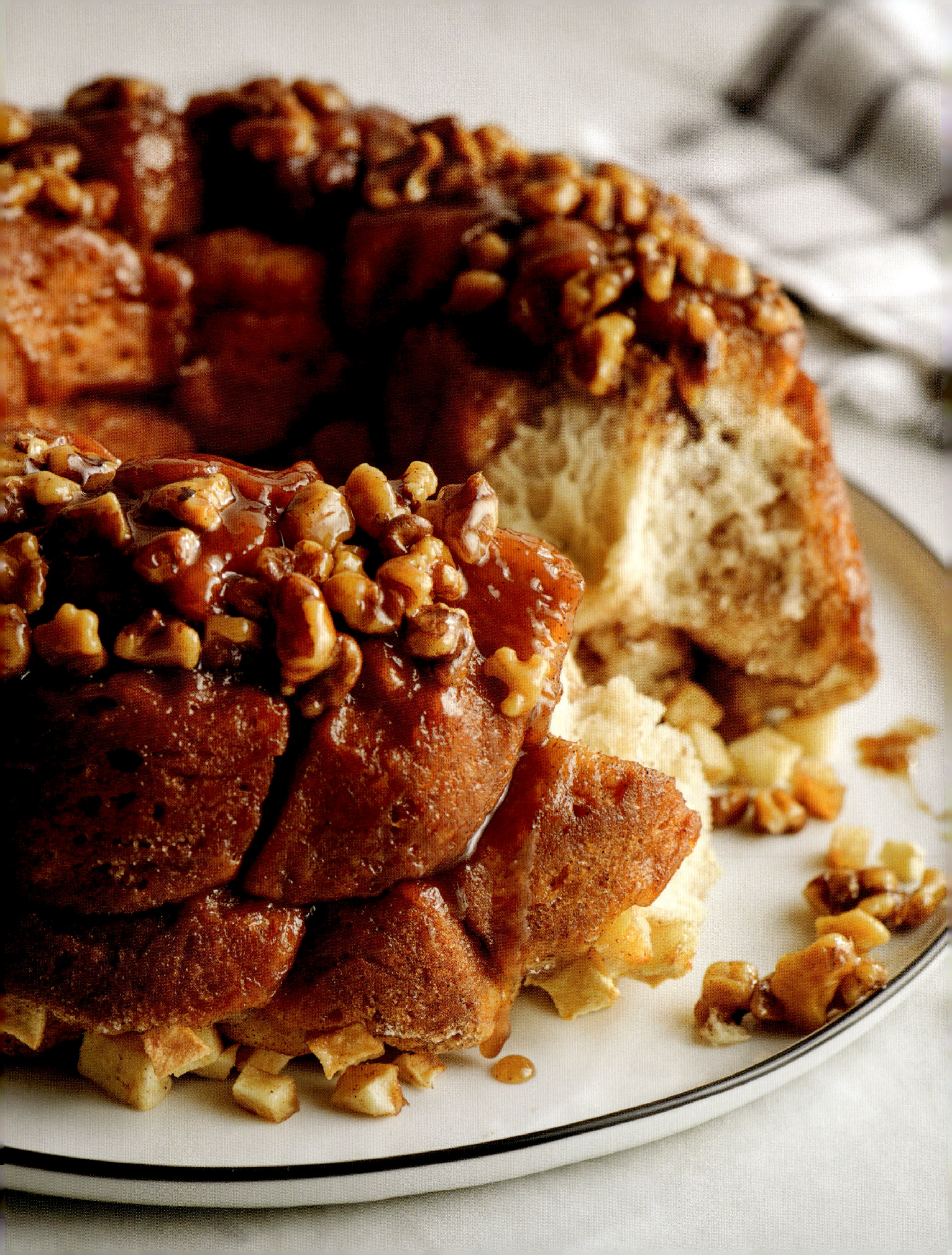

Ooey Gooey Apple Monkey Bread

Because monkey bread will retain its shape for hours, I often bring it along when attending a brunch or early game day gathering. The warm, fluffy balls of dough coated in cinnamon sugar, layered on a base of brown sugar, melted butter, and walnuts, topped with fresh apple, and baked to golden perfection are a real crowd pleaser. —RACHEL

Serves 8 to 12

Nonstick cooking spray

½ cup packed brown sugar

4 tablespoons (½ stick) butter, melted

½ cup chopped walnuts (optional)

½ cup granulated sugar

1 teaspoon ground cinnamon

2 (16.3-ounce) Pillsbury Grands! Original Flaky Layers (see Coach's Corner)

2 apples, cored, peeled, and diced (about 1½ cups)

Preheat the oven to 350°F. Coat a Bundt pan with nonstick cooking spray.

In a small bowl, stir together the brown sugar, melted butter, and walnuts (if using). Scrape the mixture into the prepared pan.

Add the granulated sugar and cinnamon to another bowl. Mix to combine.

Remove the biscuit dough from the packaging and cut each piece into quarters. Dip each quarter into the sugar-and-cinnamon mixture and add to the pan, filling in the spaces with more pieces of dough. When all the pieces have been added, top with the diced apple.

Bake until golden brown, 40 to 50 minutes. Let cool slightly, invert onto a platter, and serve.

COACH'S CORNER

If, for some reason, you cannot find Pillsbury Grands, you can substitute Pillsbury's Southern Homestyle Big Biscuits. They're not as flaky and ride heavily on that buttermilk flavor, but they're still delicious and will work well for this recipe.

Funfetti Chocolate Chip Banana Pancakes

This spontaneous recipe came to be one Saturday morning when our daughter Zurie woke up early and wanted to make herself breakfast. She was so proud her parents didn't have to cook. Despite the enormous mess that followed, her pancakes turned out delicious, and we think it's important to let kids have fun in the kitchen. We now make these on the regular, and top the warm stack with sliced bananas, more chocolate chips, sprinkles, and a drizzle of maple syrup. —**NOAH AND LACEY**

Makes 10 to 12 (2-to-3-inch) pancakes

1½ cups Bisquick

1 tablespoon granulated sugar

1 large egg

½ cup mashed ripe banana (about 1 small banana), plus sliced bananas for serving

¾ cup whole milk

¼ cup chocolate chips, plus more for serving

2 tablespoons rainbow sprinkles, plus more for serving

Butter or nonstick cooking spray

Maple syrup, for serving

Preheat the oven to 200°F.

In a large mixing bowl, stir together the Bisquick and sugar. Add the egg, banana, and milk and mix until the batter is smooth. Fold in the chocolate chips and rainbow sprinkles.

Preheat a large skillet over medium heat. Add a small amount of butter to the skillet. When the skillet is hot, spoon small portions of the batter into the pan to form pancakes. Cook until bubbles form on the surface, 2 to 3 minutes, then flip the pancakes and cook the other side until golden brown, another 2 to 3 minutes. Remove the pancakes and keep warm in the oven while you cook the remaining pancakes.

To serve, stack the pancakes on a platter or plate and, if desired, top with sliced bananas, additional chocolate chips, and more sprinkles. Finish with a drizzle of maple syrup.

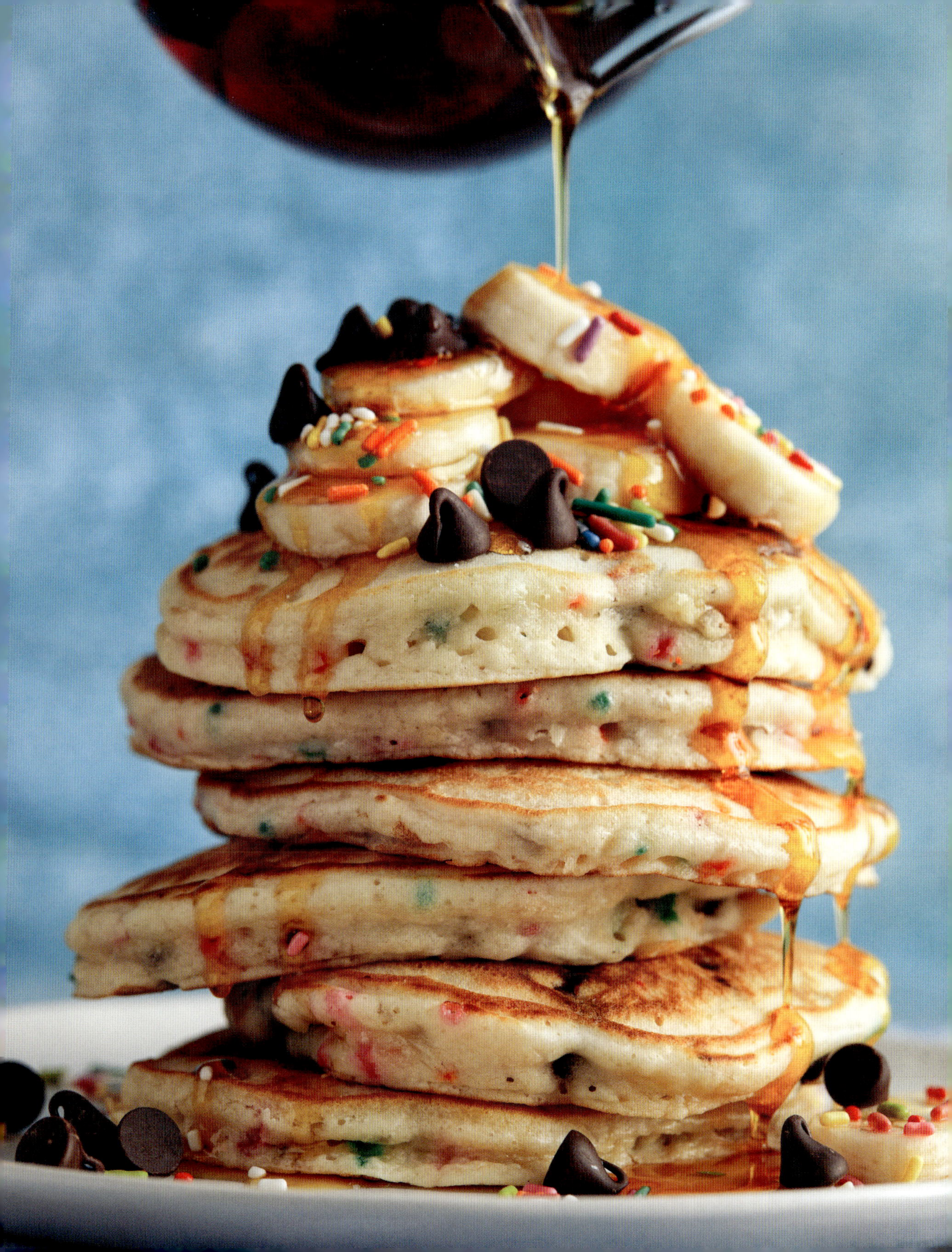

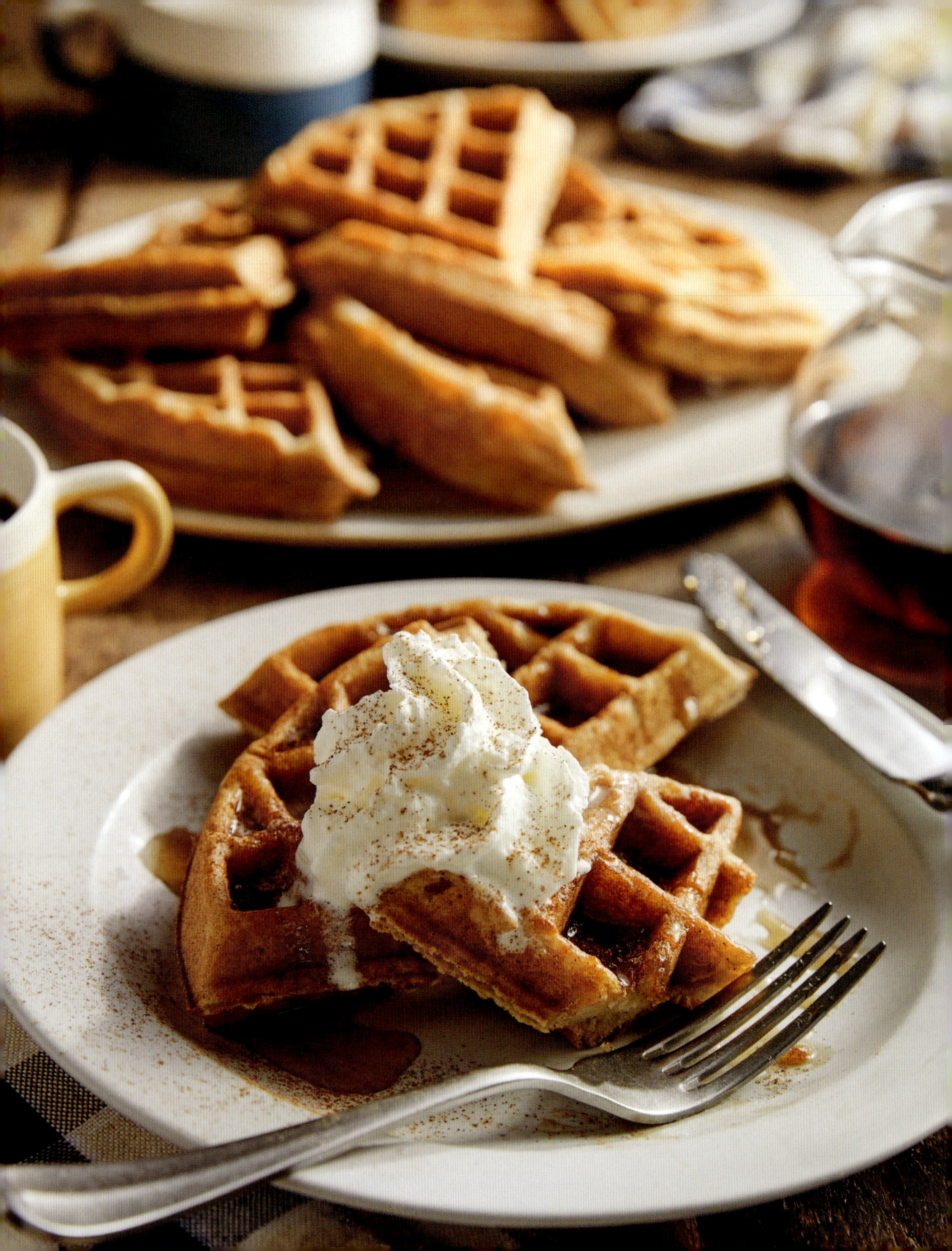

Cinnamon Apple Waffles

Not long ago, while rummaging through my parents' attic, I unearthed this recipe from an old *Southern Living* article that our grandmother Nannie Bradshaw cut out and taped in her recipe book. I've since tweaked the dish, but it's still darn delicious. Whether enjoyed with a drizzle of maple syrup or a dollop of whipped cream, these waffles are a great way to kick-start your day. —RACHEL

Makes 4 to 6 waffles

1 cup all-purpose flour

½ teaspoon kosher salt

1 teaspoon ground cinnamon, plus more for serving

2 teaspoons baking powder

2 packed tablespoons dark brown sugar

2 large eggs

1 cup whole milk

4 tablespoons (½ stick) unsalted butter, melted

1 Granny Smith apple, peeled, cored, and grated

Whipped cream and warm maple syrup, for serving

Preheat a waffle iron. Preheat the oven to 200°F.

Combine the flour, salt, cinnamon, baking powder, brown sugar, eggs, milk, and melted butter in a large bowl and whisk until smooth. Fold in the apple and continue to whisk until the batter is smooth and has the consistency of pancake batter.

Ladle the batter onto the waffle iron and cook until golden brown. The amount of time will vary with the size and type of waffle iron, so start checking once steam is no longer escaping from the sides of the iron. Transfer the cooked waffle to a baking sheet and keep warm in the oven while you cook the remaining waffles.

Serve the waffles with a sprinkle of cinnamon, a dollop of whipped cream, and some warm maple syrup, or the toppings of your choice.

French Toast Casserole

Peek into Terry and Tammy's kitchen any holiday morning when Terry isn't covering a game and you'll be greeted by this delicious dish as everyone gathers around the kitchen table. Our French Toast Casserole is baked until golden and puffed, with a soft, custardy inside and slightly crisp outside. Although this twist on the classic can be served any time of year, we enjoy serving it during the holidays. —NOAH AND LACEY

Serves 6

Nonstick cooking spray

1 cup plus 1 tablespoon packed brown sugar, divided

½ cup (1 stick) unsalted butter

1 loaf crusty French bread, cut into 1-inch pieces

2 cups whole milk

6 large eggs

2 teaspoons pure vanilla extract

¼ teaspoon ground cinnamon

Spray a 9 × 13-inch baking dish with nonstick cooking spray.

Combine 1 cup of the brown sugar and the butter in a small saucepan. Stir over medium-low heat until the butter is melted and the sugar is dissolved, 2 to 4 minutes. Remove from the heat and pour into the prepared baking dish. Scatter the bread pieces on top, creating a 1½- to 2-inch layer.

Whisk the milk, eggs, and vanilla together in a bowl until well combined. Pour the mixture over the bread pieces, pressing the bread down with a spatula to help the bread absorb the liquid. Cover the dish and refrigerate for at least 8 hours, preferably overnight.

When ready to bake, preheat the oven to 350°F.

In a small bowl, stir together the remaining 1 tablespoon brown sugar and the cinnamon. Sprinkle over the casserole. Bake, uncovered, until browned and bubbling, 50 to 60 minutes (see Coach's Corner).

Cool slightly before cutting into squares and serving.

COACH'S CORNER

When baking the casserole, you might see the top browning before the inside is cooked through. If this happens, simply cover the casserole with aluminum foil for the remainder of the baking time.

Ham and Old English Cheese Casserole

Robust Old English cheese and smoky ham—it's a winning combination (like my years with the Steelers!). When it comes to Old English cheese, Kraft makes this excellent spread that delivers a nostalgic sharp cheddar taste. Our family grew up on this dish, and it's still in frequent rotation at family breakfasts. **—TERRY**

Serves 8

3 cups whole milk

6 large eggs

½ teaspoon kosher salt

¼ teaspoon freshly cracked black pepper

16 slices white bread, crusts removed

1½ pounds thinly sliced deli ham

2 (5-ounce) jars Kraft Old English spread, at room temperature

4 tablespoons (½ stick) unsalted butter, melted, plus more for greasing

4 cups corn flakes

In a large measuring cup, whisk together the milk, eggs, salt, and pepper until combined.

Grease a 9 × 13-inch baking dish with butter. Arrange half the bread slices in the pan in a single layer. You may need to trim the bread slices so they fit perfectly. Layer the ham onto the bread, then cover with the Old English spread. If the cheese is too stiff to spread, microwave for 10 to 15 seconds. Top with the remaining bread slices. Pour the custard over all the bread so it seeps down through the cracks. Cover the pan and refrigerate overnight.

Preheat the oven to 350°F.

Stir the melted butter and corn flakes together in small bowl and mix until combined. Spread the buttered flakes over the top of the casserole. Loosely cover the pan with foil and bake until the custard is set, about 90 minutes. Let cool slightly before serving.

Overnight Stuffed Brioche French Toast Casserole

This casserole is a riff on Terry and Tammy's French Toast Casserole (page 50), and it wouldn't be Christmas morning in my home without it. I'll tuck the dish in the refrigerator overnight before helping Noah stuff the stockings and place presents around the tree. On Christmas morning, just before we wake the kids, I'll slip into the kitchen and bake the dish. —LACEY

Serves 4 to 6

Nonstick cooking spray

1 loaf brioche, cut into 1-inch cubes

8 large eggs

2 cups whole milk

½ cup heavy cream

½ cup granulated sugar

¼ cup packed brown sugar

2 teaspoons pure vanilla extract

1 teaspoon ground cinnamon

¼ teaspoon ground nutmeg

¼ teaspoon kosher salt

½ cup softened cream cheese

½ cup raspberry or apricot preserves

TOPPING

½ cup (1 stick) unsalted butter

1 cup chopped pecans

1 cup packed dark brown sugar

2 tablespoons maple syrup, plus more for serving

½ teaspoon ground cinnamon

⅛ teaspoon kosher salt

Powdered sugar and fresh seasonal berries or sliced fruit, for serving

Spray a 9 × 13-inch baking dish with nonstick cooking spray, then arrange the cubed bread evenly in the prepared dish.

Combine the eggs, milk, cream, granulated sugar, brown sugar, vanilla, cinnamon, nutmeg, and salt in a large measuring cup or mixing bowl, whisking to blend thoroughly. Pour half the mixture over the bread cubes.

Stir the cream cheese and raspberry preserves together in a small bowl until smooth. Dollop spoonfuls of the cream cheese mixture onto the bread cubes and top with the remaining egg mixture. Press down on the bread with a spatula to ensure it absorbs the custard. Cover the dish with plastic wrap and refrigerate overnight.

When ready to bake, preheat the oven to 350°F.

To make the topping: Heat the butter in a saucepan over medium heat until melted. Add the pecans, dark brown sugar, the maple syrup, cinnamon, and salt. Cook, stirring constantly, until the mixture thickens and the pecans are caramelized, about 5 minutes. Remove from the heat and spoon the praline topping evenly over the casserole.

Bake until the top is golden brown and the center is set, 45 to 50 minutes. Let cool for several minutes. To serve, dust the top with powdered sugar and serve with the berries and a drizzle of maple syrup.

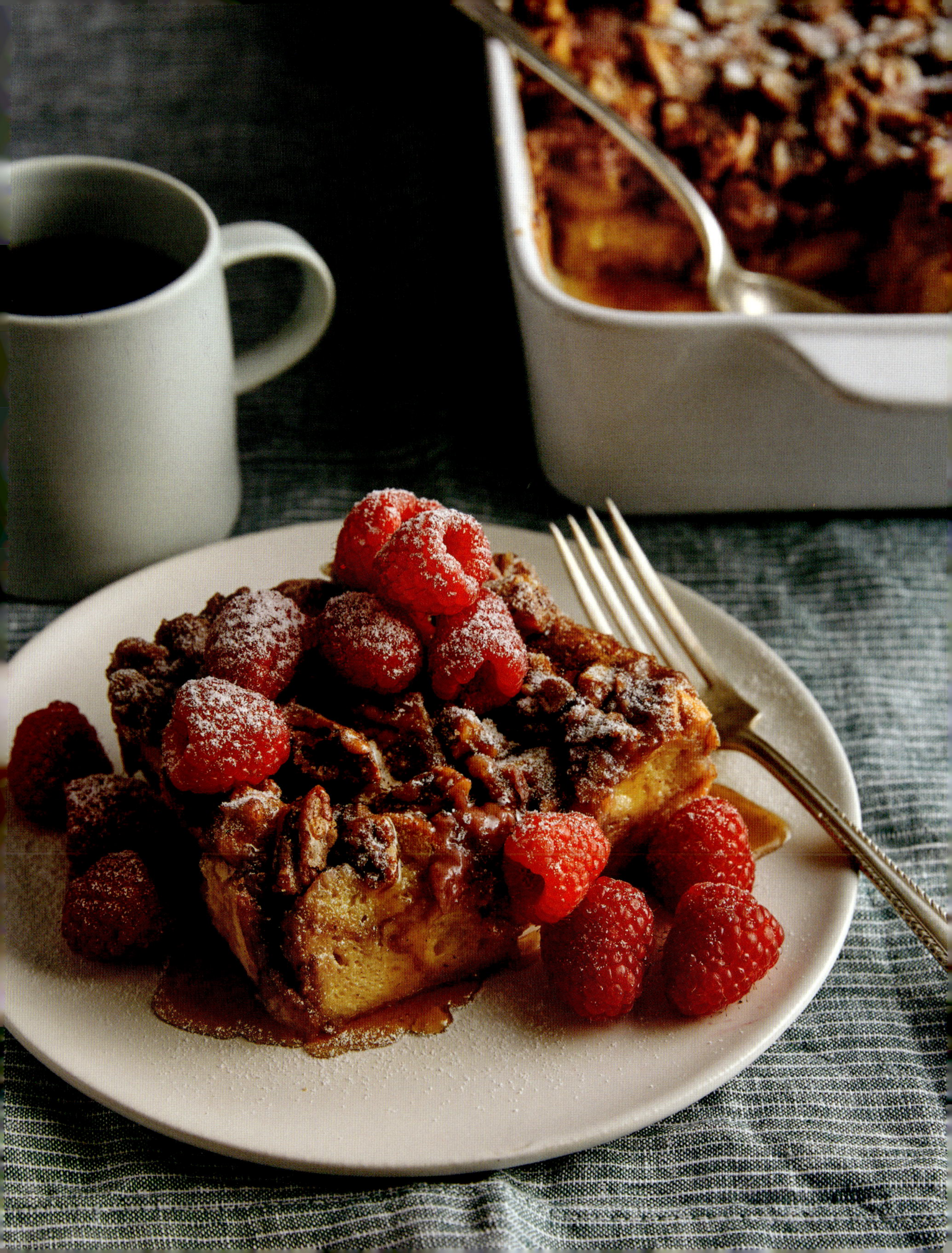

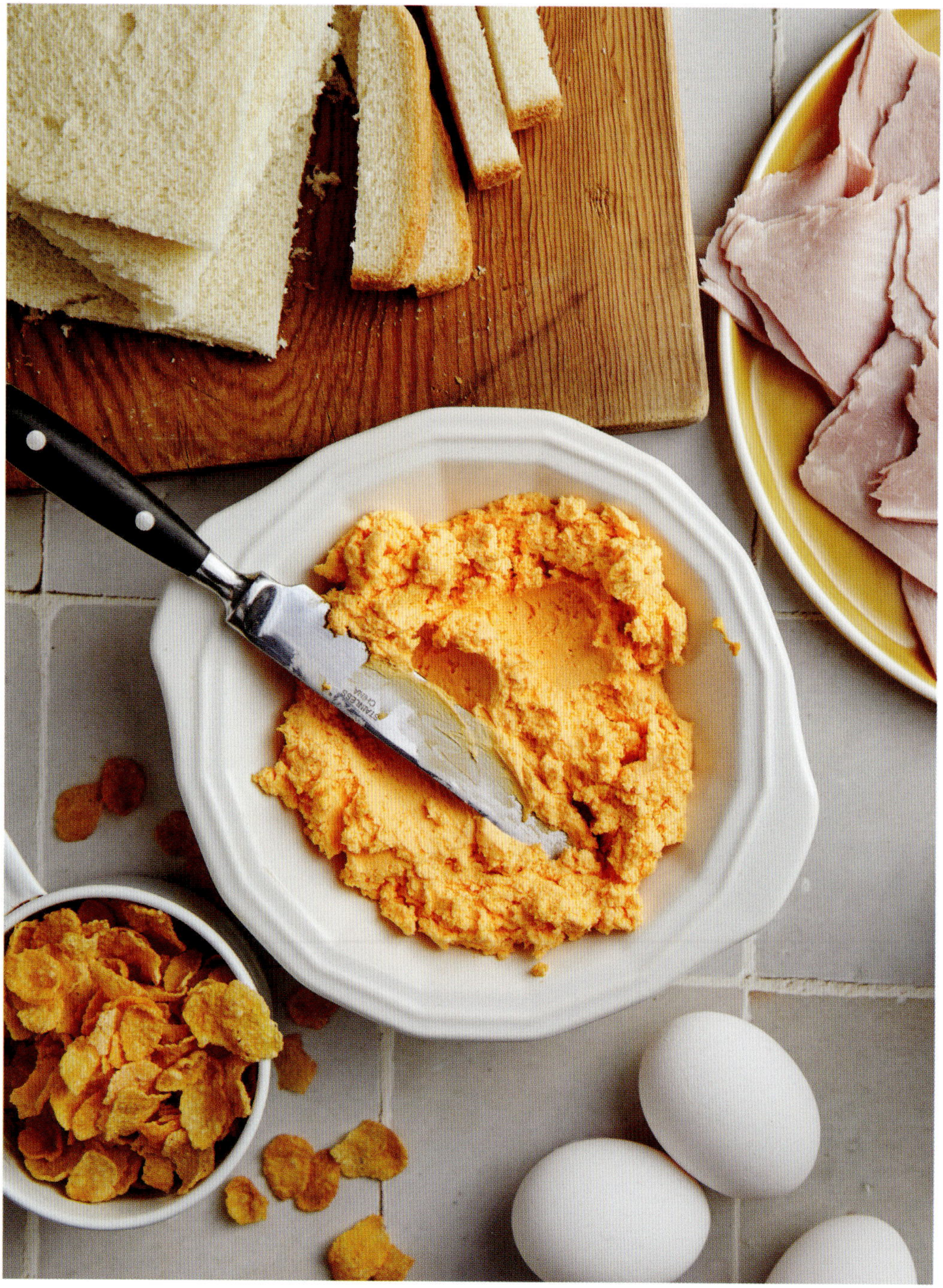

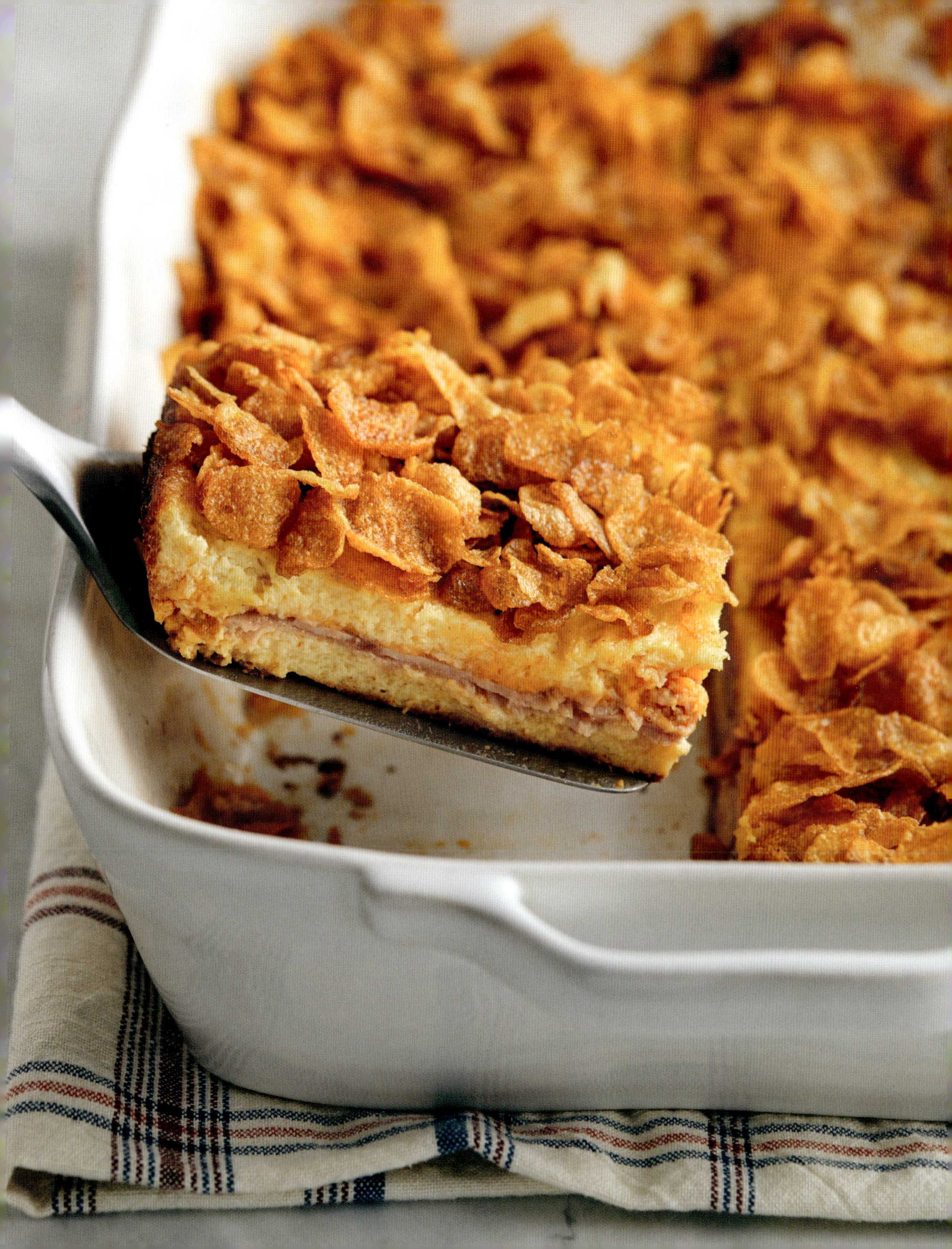

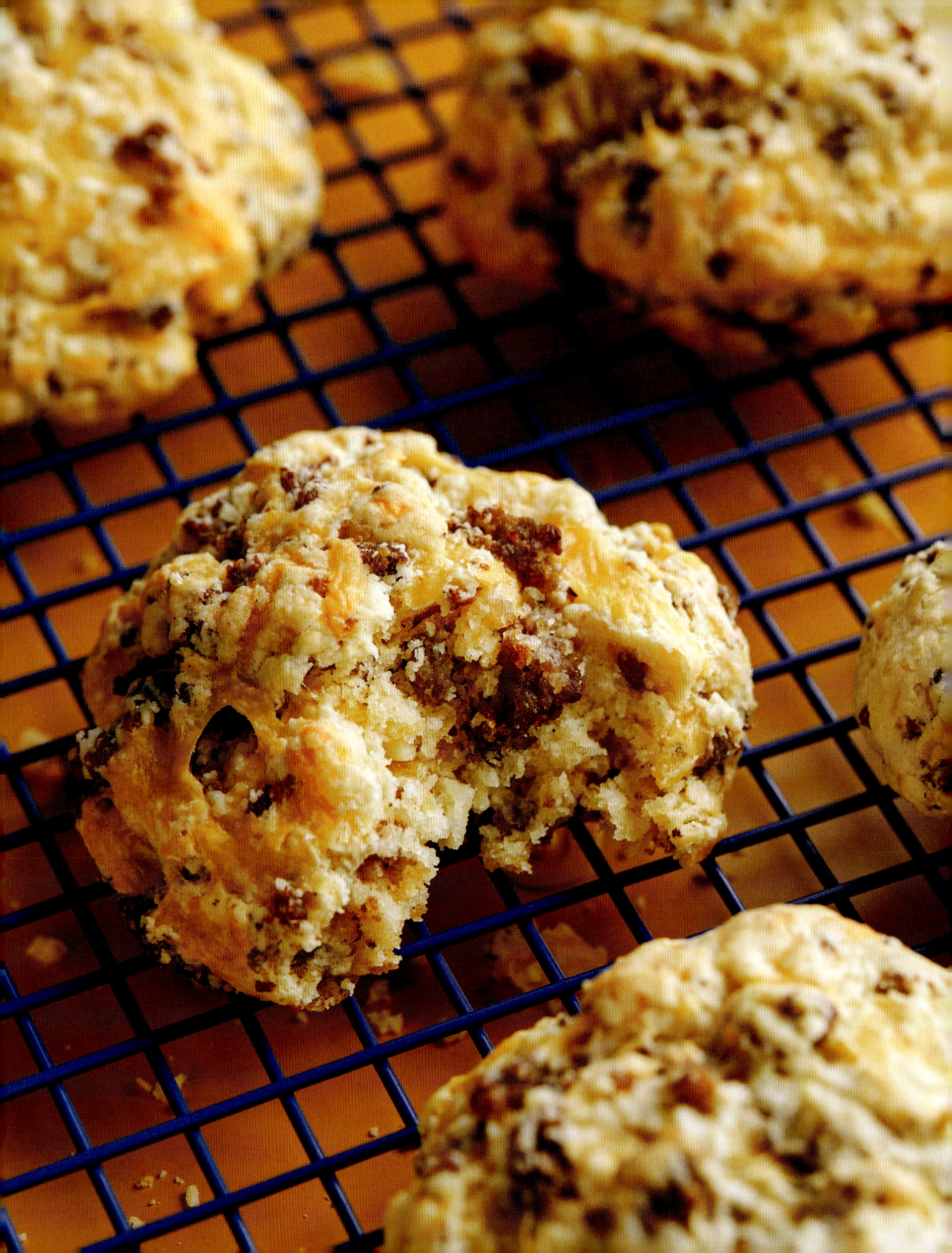

Sausage and Cheddar Cheese Biscuits

I've been known to holler, "I'm on national television in front of millions. I hate making mistakes!" We don't want you making mistakes, either, so when kneading the dough for these warm and buttery biscuits, don't overmix or you'll end up with biscuits that are tough and deflated. Filled with a savory blend of sausage and cheddar cheese, they are the perfect thing to chow down on while you wait for the pregame show to come on. —TERRY

Serves 6

Nonstick cooking spray
½ pound bulk pork sausage
2 cups Bisquick
½ pound grated cheddar cheese
2 large eggs
¼ cup heavy cream

Preheat the oven to 325°F. Spray a rimmed baking sheet with nonstick cooking spray.

Cook the sausage in a large skillet over medium heat, using a wooden spoon to break up the sausage, until the sausage is crumbled and brown, 6 to 8 minutes. Drain off the fat and transfer the sausage to a mixing bowl. Add the Bisquick, cheddar, eggs, and heavy cream to the sausage. Mix lightly until a dough forms. Gather into a ball and lightly knead six to eight times, just until it's no longer sticky. Divide the dough into six equal pieces and roll into balls to make the biscuits.

Arrange the balls on the baking sheet and bake for 30 to 40 minutes, or until golden brown. Transfer the biscuits to a cooling rack and cool slightly before serving (see Coach's Corner).

COACH'S CORNER

For hearty sausage biscuits, split the biscuits and top with Nannie Bradshaw's Sausage Gravy (page 58).

Nannie Bradshaw's Sausage Gravy

Terry's mother's soul-warming gravy is more than just a morning meal. It's a recipe for memories and a family legacy that will remain in our hearts for generations. We ladle generous portions over homemade biscuits, like our Sausage and Cheddar Cheese Biscuits (page 57). —TAMMY

Serves 4

¾ cup bulk pork sausage

Up to ¼ cup bacon grease, vegetable oil, or shortening, if needed

6 tablespoons all-purpose flour

1½ cups whole milk

¼ teaspoon kosher salt

¼ teaspoon freshly cracked black pepper

Place the sausage in a high-sided skillet and cook over medium-high heat, using a wooden spoon to break up the sausage until crumbled and brown, 6 to 8 minutes. Pour off all but ¼ cup of the rendered fat. If the sausage didn't render enough fat, add some bacon grease, vegetable oil, or shortening. Stir in the flour, whisking until incorporated. Reduce the heat to medium and whisk in the milk. Continue to whisk until incorporated and the mixture reaches a thick, gravylike consistency without any lumps, about 3 minutes. Remove from the heat, season with salt and pepper, and serve immediately.

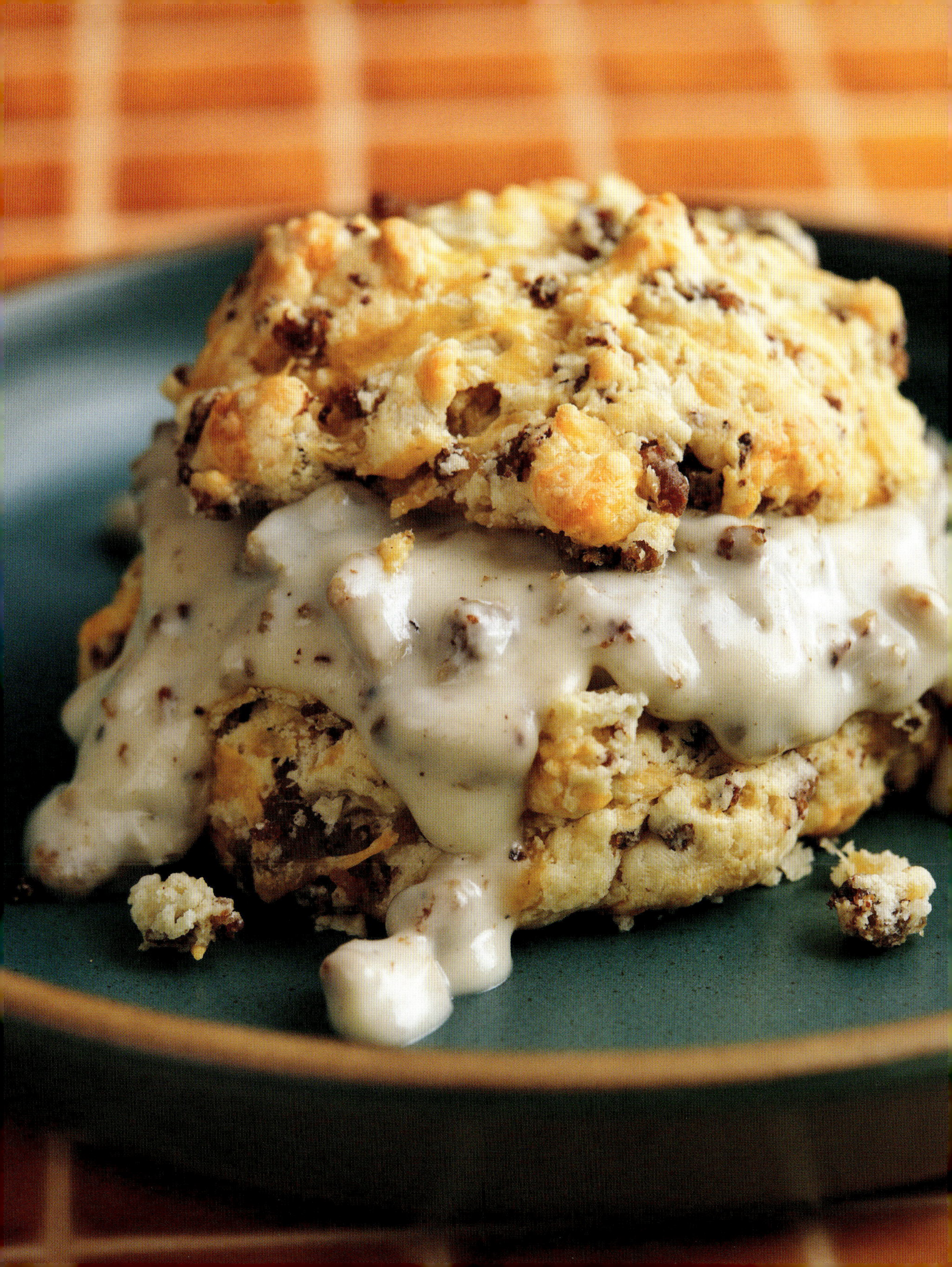

Spicy Breakfast Casserole with Onion and Bell Peppers

This happens to be one of Chase's favorite breakfasts. In fact, he loves it so much I find myself making it on a weekly basis. For the flavor-packed casserole, we prefer Jimmy Dean Hot Premium Pork Sausage because it adds the right amount of zing while complementing the sweetness of the sautéed onion and peppers. —RACHEL

Serves 6 to 8

Nonstick cooking spray

1 pound spicy breakfast sausage

1 cup diced yellow onion

¼ cup diced red bell pepper

¼ cup diced yellow bell pepper

6 large eggs, beaten

1 cup heavy cream

1 teaspoon kosher salt

½ teaspoon freshly cracked black pepper

1 cup shredded cheddar, Monterey Jack, or Swiss cheese

Preheat the oven to 350°F. Spray a 9 × 13-inch baking dish with nonstick cooking spray.

Add the sausage to a medium skillet and cook over medium heat, using a wooden spoon to crumble the meat. When the sausage is about halfway browned, add the onion and peppers. Cook until the meat is browned and the vegetables are soft, 5 to 8 minutes. Remove from the heat and drain.

Add the eggs, cream, salt, pepper, and cheddar to the sausage mixture. Mix well and pour into the prepared baking dish.

Bake for 35 to 45 minutes or until the eggs are cooked and set. Remove from the oven and allow to cool slightly before serving.

One-Skillet Breakfast Frittata

When we lived in Hawaii, we often indulged in local delicacies like loco moco—layers of rice and hamburger with gravy and a fried egg on top. I found eating breakfast in Hawaii was a sensory feast that captured the essence of the islands. Here in cattle country, our breakfast go-to is a one-skillet frittata that I find best represents a Texas ranch-style breakfast. We make it in a cast-iron skillet and without the fuss of a crust. **—NOAH**

Serves 6 to 8

1 tablespoon extra-virgin olive oil

½ pound smoked sausage, cut into ¼- to ½-inch slices

½ pound baby red potatoes, cut into ¼-inch slices

10 large eggs

⅓ cup whole milk

1 tablespoon chopped fresh Italian flat-leaf parsley

1 tablespoon chopped fresh chives

1 teaspoon kosher salt

½ teaspoon freshly cracked black pepper

4 ounces shredded Monterey Jack cheese (about 1 cup)

2 ounces goat cheese, for serving (optional)

Set a rack in the middle of the oven and preheat to 300°F.

Heat the oil in an ovenproof skillet over medium-high heat. Add the sausage and potatoes. Cook, stirring often, until the sausage browns and the potatoes are lightly browned and slightly tender, about 10 minutes. Drain the grease from the skillet.

In a medium bowl, whisk together the eggs, milk, parsley, chives, salt, and pepper until combined. Pour the mixture over the sausage and potatoes. Sprinkle with the shredded Monterey Jack.

Bake the frittata until the eggs are no longer jiggly in the center, 30 to 40 minutes. Let cool for 5 to 10 minutes. Place a large plate on top of the skillet and, using oven mitts, quickly invert the skillet and plate so the frittata comes out of the pan. Garnish with goat cheese, if using, and serve.

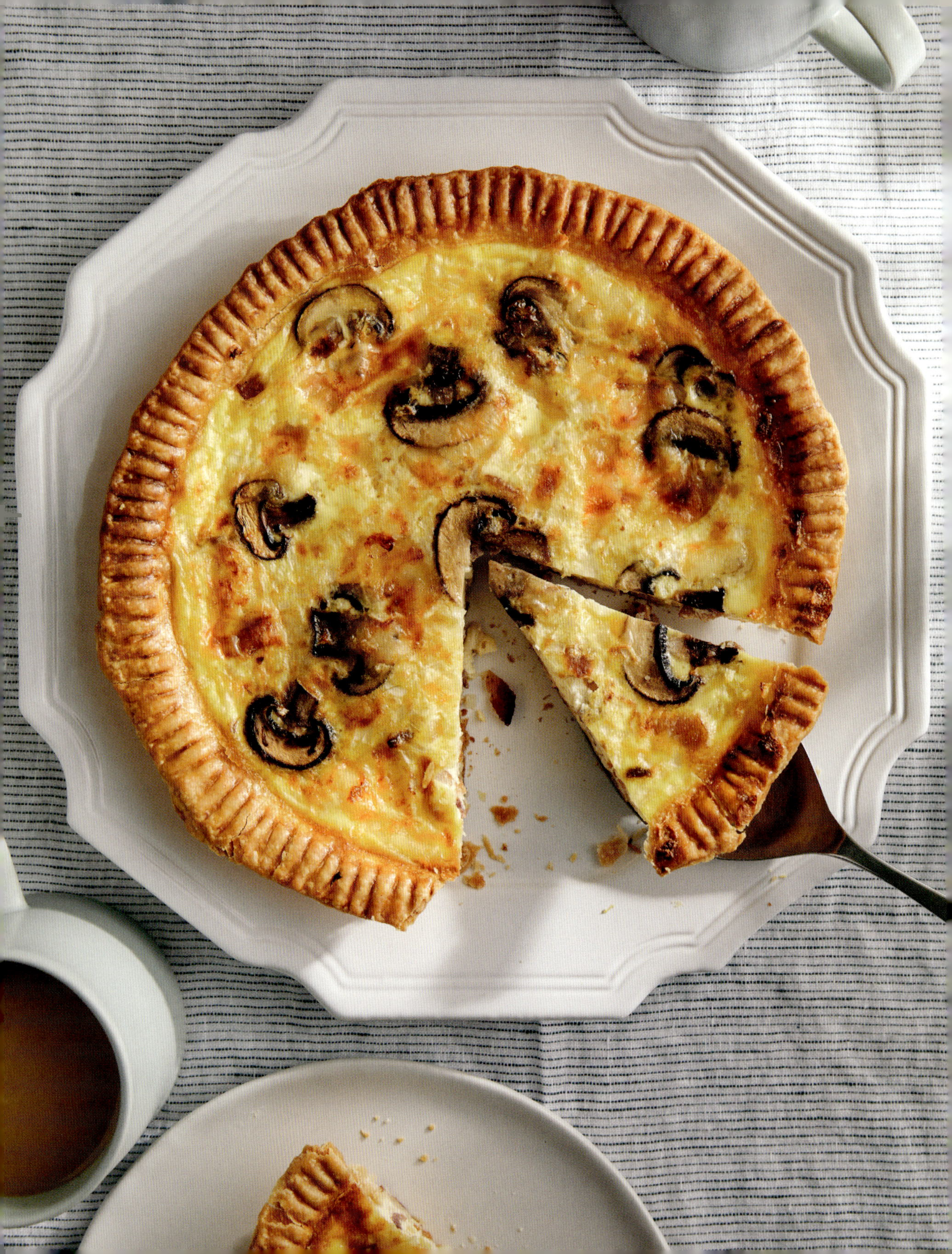

Bacon, Onion, and Mushroom Quiche

Quiche is our go-to when the kids come over unexpectedly and we need to make something fast. We also like that quiche is a dish that adapts easily to whatever we have in the refrigerator. Stop by when football season's over, and there's a good chance you'll find us in the kitchen assembling this comforting quiche. Crisp bacon from Noah and Lacey's Hamm's Meat + Market in McKinney, Texas, infuses the custardy filling with smoky depth while the onion and mushrooms add sweet and robust dimensions. **—TERRY AND TAMMY**

Serves 4 to 6

1 (9-inch) premade pie shell

¼ cup sliced button or cremini mushrooms

½ cup shredded Swiss cheese

¼ cup finely chopped yellow onion

½ cup cooked and crumbled bacon (about 8 strips)

4 large eggs

2 cups half-and-half

Place a rack in the middle of the oven and preheat to 300°F.

With a fork, poke holes in the bottom of the pie shell. Line the pie shell with parchment and fill with pie weights. Bake for 15 minutes, then remove the weights and parchment and return to the oven. Bake for another 10 minutes or until light golden brown. Remove the crust from the oven and set aside.

Add the mushrooms to a medium skillet. Sauté over medium heat for several minutes, stirring occasionally. The goal is just to draw out some of the moisture before adding the mushrooms to the filling. Remove the mushrooms from the pan and set aside.

Increase the oven temperature to 400°F. Spread the Swiss cheese evenly over the bottom of the crust. Top with the onion in an even layer, followed by the cooked bacon and the mushrooms. Place the crust on a rimmed baking sheet.

Add the eggs to a bowl and whisk until incorporated, then whisk in the half-and-half. Carefully pour the mixture over the filling.

Bake for 15 minutes. Reduce the oven temperature to 350°F and continue baking until the filling is set, about 45 minutes. Let the quiche cool slightly before serving.

Breakfast Tacos with Chipotle Crema

Hearty breakfast tacos are a terrific way to start the morning. During football season, I have a hectic schedule, especially on Fridays when I'm off to Los Angeles for the pregame show. If I don't have time to sit down for breakfast before my flight, I'll grab a taco or two, wrap them in foil, and enjoy them in the car on my way to the airport. They're fast and easy, and the aroma of sausage, onion, and cilantro draws everyone to the kitchen. —**TERRY**

Serves 4

CHIPOTLE CREMA
Makes 1 cup

¼ cup canned chipotle peppers in adobo
(see Coach's Corner)

1 cup sour cream

2 tablespoons fresh lime juice

Kosher salt, to taste

FILLING

½ pound breakfast sausage

4 large eggs

1 tablespoon whole milk

¼ teaspoon kosher salt

¼ teaspoon freshly cracked black pepper

1 tablespoon unsalted butter

4 (4- to 5-inch) flour or corn tortillas

1 cup diced fresh tomatoes

1 cup shredded cheddar cheese

½ cup diced red onion

¼ cup chopped fresh cilantro

1 avocado, pitted, peeled, and thinly sliced

Hot sauce or salsa, for serving (optional)

To make the crema: Puree the chipotle peppers and transfer to a small bowl. Stir in the sour cream, lime juice, and salt. Set aside until ready to serve.

To make the filling: Cook the breakfast sausage in a medium skillet over medium heat, using a wooden spoon to break it into small pieces, until the meat is well crumbled and cooked through, 5 to 7 minutes. Transfer the sausage to a bowl and set aside. Wipe the pan clean.

Whisk the eggs, milk, salt, and pepper in a mixing bowl until blended. Return the skillet to the stove and melt the butter over medium heat. Add the egg mixture and scramble until fully cooked, about 4 minutes. Remove the eggs from the pan and keep warm.

Wipe the pan clean and add the tortillas, one at a time, to warm, about 15 seconds on each side or until pliable. Keep warm until ready to assemble.

To assemble, divide the scrambled eggs among the tortillas and top with the sausage, tomatoes, cheddar, onion, and cilantro. Add two or three slices of avocado to each taco and drizzle with the chipotle crema. Fold the tacos in half and serve immediately with hot sauce or salsa, if using.

COACH'S CORNER

Chipotle peppers are smoked and dried jalapeños, which means they are spicy hot. If you prefer your dishes on the mild side, make the crema, adding the pepper puree in small increments until it reaches your desired heat level.

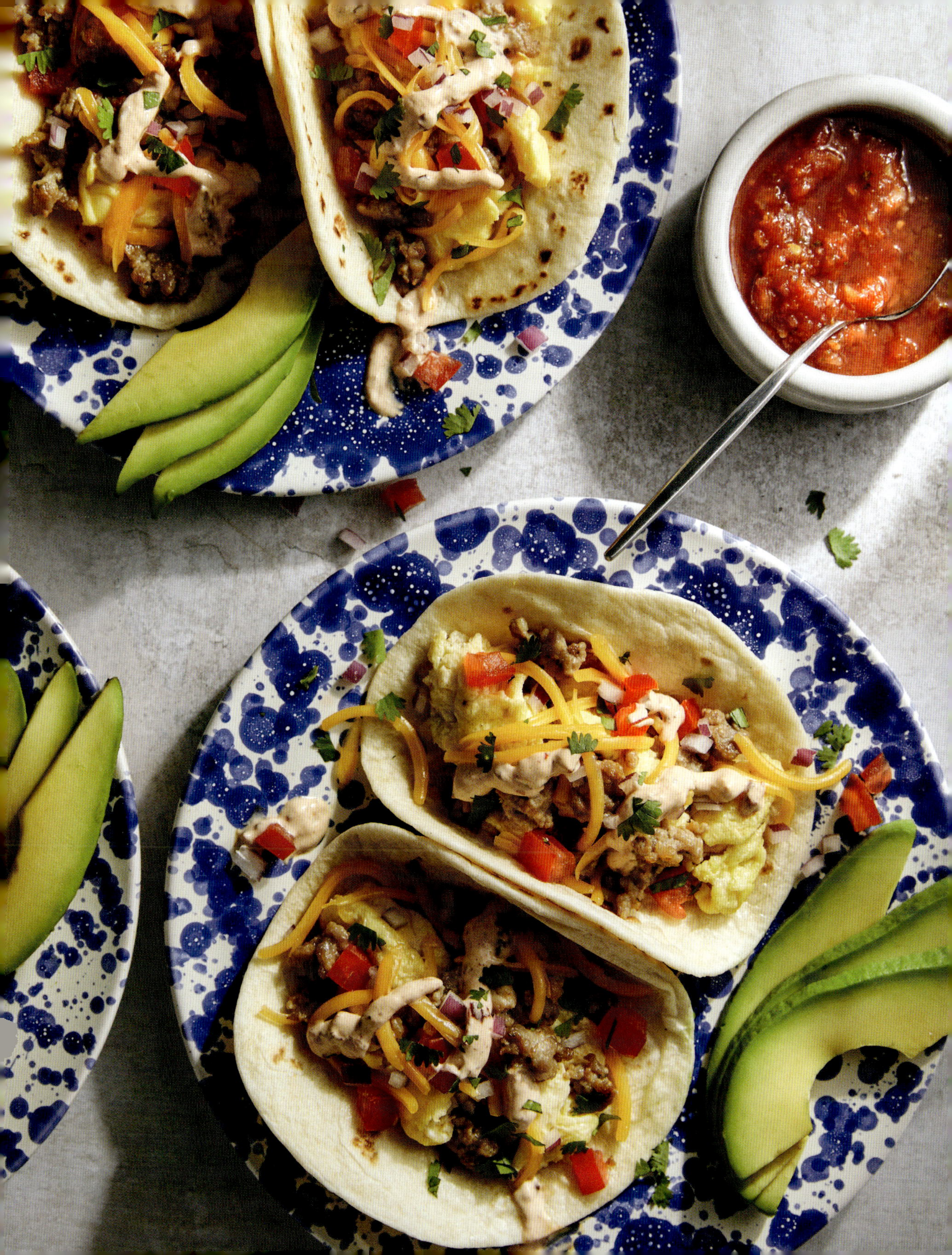

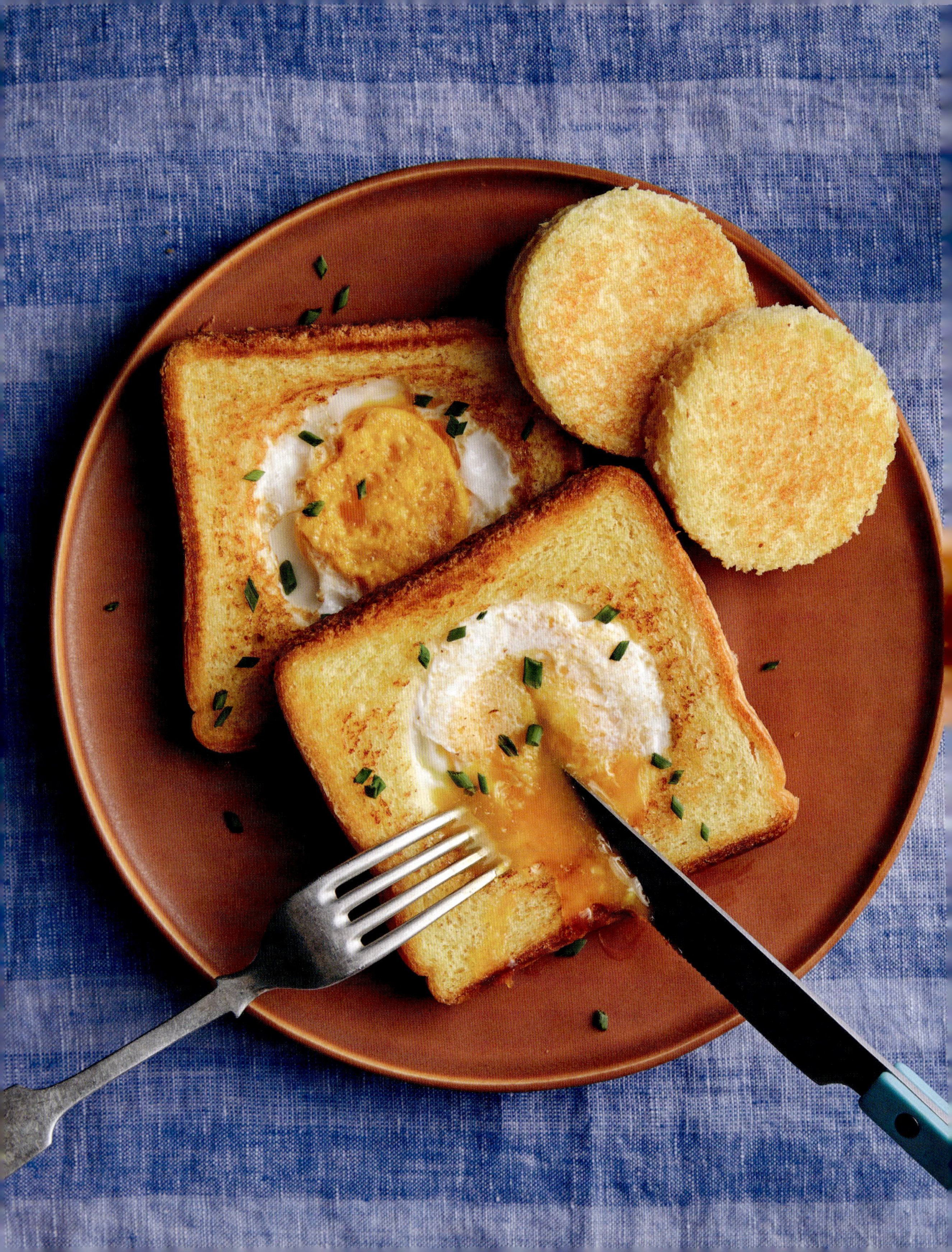

Toad in the Hole

Noah's mother used to make Toad in the Hole for him on lazy mornings. Now we make it for our kids. It's Jeb's favorite. For Noah and me, we'll garnish the toast and eggs with fresh herbs from our garden, along with a splash of hot sauce for a subtle kick. **—LACEY**

Serves 4

4 thick-cut bread slices (Texas toast style)
(see Coach's Corner)

2 tablespoons unsalted butter, divided

4 large eggs

Kosher salt and freshly cracked black pepper, to taste

Fresh chopped herbs, such as chives and Italian flat-leaf parsley, plus hot sauce, for serving (optional)

Use a round cookie cutter or the rim of a glass to punch out a hole from the center of each slice of bread, reserving the cut-out circles.

Add 1 tablespoon of the butter to a large skillet over medium heat. When the butter has melted, add two bread slices along with the cut-out circles. Crack an egg into each hole and season with salt and pepper. Allow the eggs to cook until the whites are set but the yolks are still runny, about 2 minutes. Carefully flip the bread and cut-out circles and cook for another 2 minutes. Remove from the skillet. Repeat with the remaining butter, bread slices, and cut-out circles and eggs.

Arrange on plates with the cut-out circles placed on the side for dipping into the yolks. Garnish with fresh herbs and hot sauce, if using, and serve.

COACH'S CORNER

If you can't find thick-cut Texas toast–style bread, you can always buy an unsliced loaf of the bread of your choice and cut the thick slices yourself.

Terry's Favorite Omelet

To me, there's nothing more fulfilling than a day of ranch work. When football season's over, you'll find me in the kitchen most mornings, enjoying this omelet before heading out to tend to the cattle and horses. An omelet filled with asparagus, ham, and cheddar cheese really keeps me going right through to lunchtime. **—TERRY**

Serves 1

¼ cup chopped fresh asparagus (about 4 spears)

3 large eggs

¼ cup half-and-half

Kosher salt and freshly cracked black pepper, to taste

¼ cup chopped deli ham

½ cup shredded cheddar cheese, divided

Heat a small pot of water over high heat. When boiling, add the asparagus and blanch for 30 seconds to 1 minute, depending on how tender you like your asparagus. Drain and set aside.

Heat a 10-inch nonstick skillet over medium heat.

Add the eggs and half-and-half to a small mixing bowl. Season with salt and pepper. Mix, then pour into the hot skillet, creating a thin, smooth layer. Sprinkle the asparagus, ham, and ¼ cup of the cheddar on top. Continue to cook until the eggs are set, 5 to 6 minutes. Using a spatula, fold the omelet in thirds like a letter. Remove from the heat and slide the omelet onto a plate. Top with the remaining ¼ cup cheddar and serve.

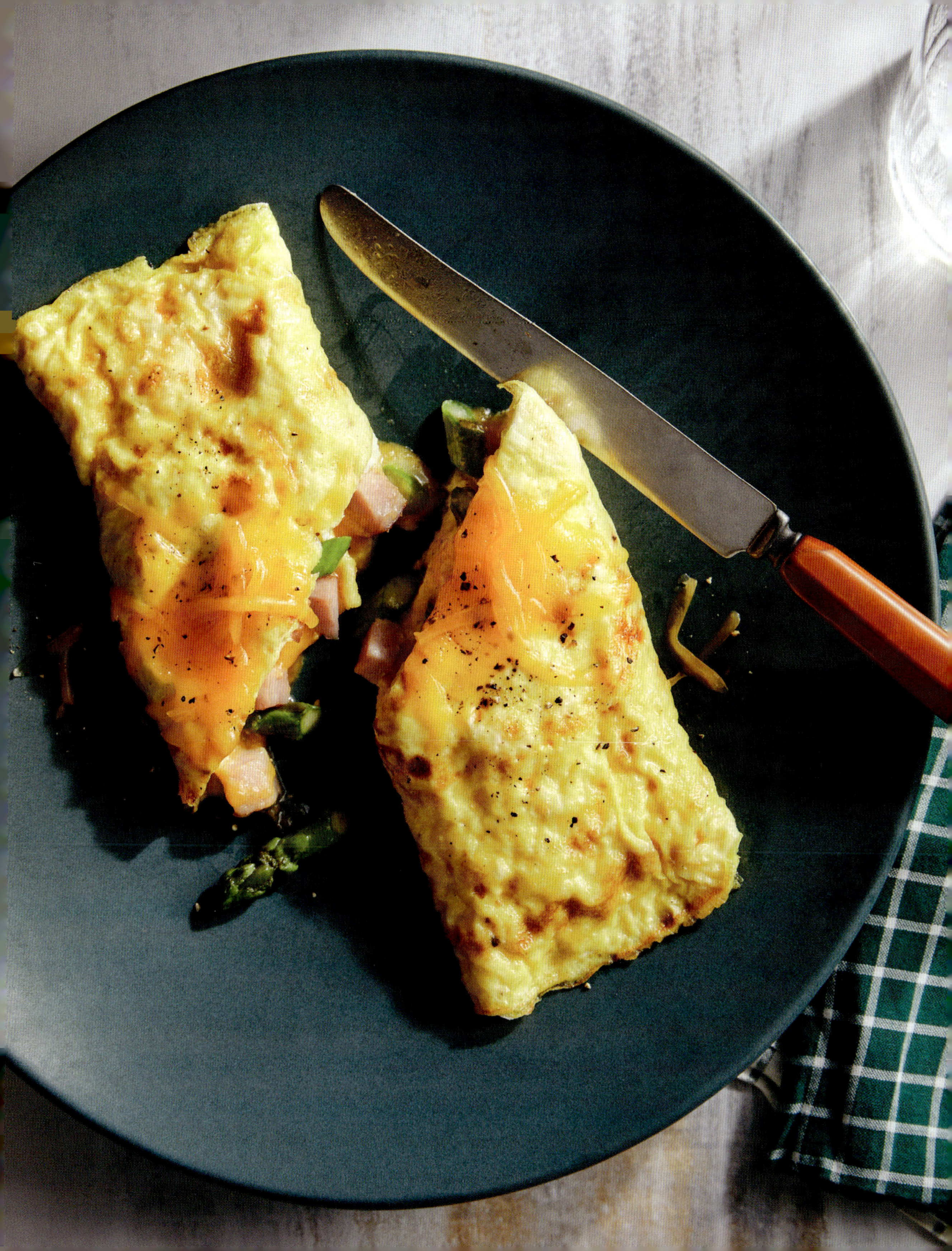

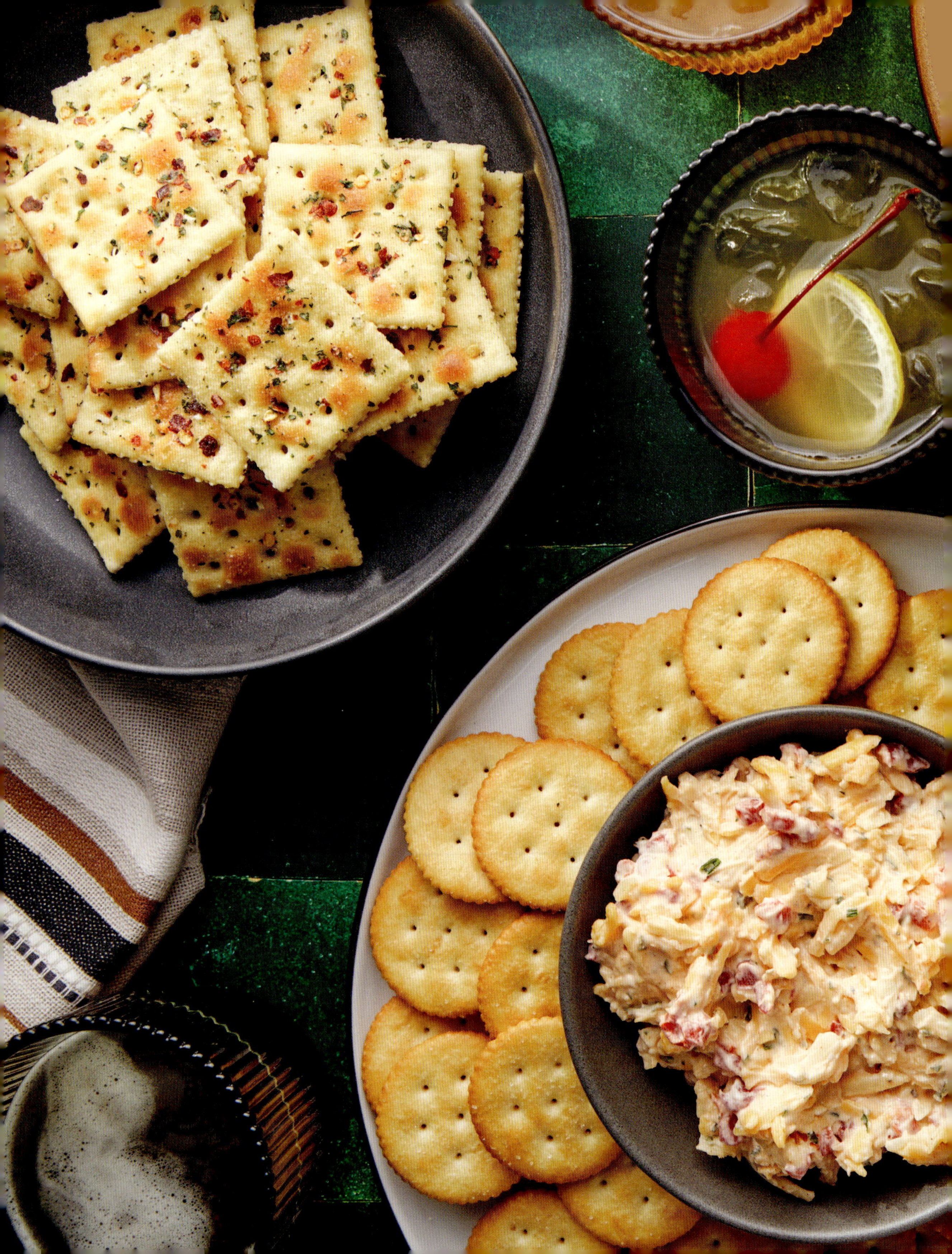

2 // Starters and Snacks

Blond Bomber

Fourth and One Bourbon Smash

The Immaculate Refreshment

Gainesville Grande Margarita

Nannie's Ranch Crackers

Ranch-Style Pretzel Snacks

Homemade Focaccia with Herb Dipping Oil

Beet Deviled Eggs

Garlic Pull-Apart Pigs in a Blanket

Crispy Egg Rolls with Shrimp, Sprouts, and Peanut Butter

Chicken Fried Steak "Fries" with Zesty Dip

Toasted Ham and Swiss Cheese Sliders

Poppa Hester's Savory Herb Pimento Cheese

Cheesy Smoked Buffalo Chicken Dip

Famous Gridiron Nine-Layer Dip

Missouri Crab Grass Dip

Hawaiian Summer Tuna Fish Dip

Sriracha Curry Dip

GAME DAY OR A LAID-BACK AFTERNOON AT OUR HOME IS ALL ABOUT the spread, where every dish is prepared with a dash of affection and a sprinkle of fun. After all, our family firmly lives by the adage that a family who cooks together, stays together. Whether it's the anticipation of the big game or just gathering with friends and family, the starters and snacks we set out are almost as important as the event itself. Imagine Terry eyeing Rachel's Famous Gridiron Nine-Layer Dip (page 102) and strategizing his next move while Tammy brings out her legendary Missouri Crab Grass Dip (page 105) and Sriracha Curry Dip (page 109), perfect for keeping the crowd happy.

Noah and Lacey's Cheesy Smoked Buffalo Chicken Dip (page 103) always steals the show, loaded with melted cheese and all the spicy flavors of hot wings. But it's the unexpected twists that really keep things interesting. One year, Lacey decided to have some fun and told Terry she made his popular Crispy Egg Rolls with Shrimp, Sprouts, and Peanut Butter (page 93) but for vegetarians. Little did he know they were filled with the shrimp that's made them a Bradshaw classic.

Of course, no spread is complete without something to wash it all down. We keep our guests refreshed with a variety of cocktails, from the tart, lip-smacking Fourth and One Bourbon Smash (page 77) to the always-popular Blond Bomber (page 74). These drinks, along with Nannie's Ranch Crackers (page 83) and Ranch-Style Pretzel Snacks (page 85) round out a lineup that has something for everyone.

So, whether you're cheering on your favorite team or just enjoying the company, you'll find a snack to keep you coming back. Just watch out for Terry, who's been known to pull a fast one by hiding the last of the Garlic Pull-Apart Pigs in a Blanket (page 90)—proof that at the Bradshaw house, anything can happen.

Blond Bomber

As football fans may know, Terry had flowing blond locks back in the day, along with a strong right arm, giving him the nickname the Blond Bomber. Our namesake drink, a twist on the whiskey sour, features caramel and vanilla flavors from the bourbon balanced with the perfect tartness of the lemon juice. When we created this drink, we wanted people to enjoy it and have fun with it, but also to make it their own. Feel free to experiment with other flavors and see how they pair with the bourbon. —NOAH

Makes 1 cocktail

2 ounces straight bourbon whiskey

¾ ounce fresh lemon juice

¾ ounce Simple Syrup
(see Coach's Corner, page 77)

Cocktail cherry and lemon wheel, for serving

Add the bourbon, lemon juice, and simple syrup to a cocktail shaker filled with ice. Shake vigorously for 10 to 20 seconds, then strain into a rocks glass filled with ice. Serve with a cherry and lemon wheel.

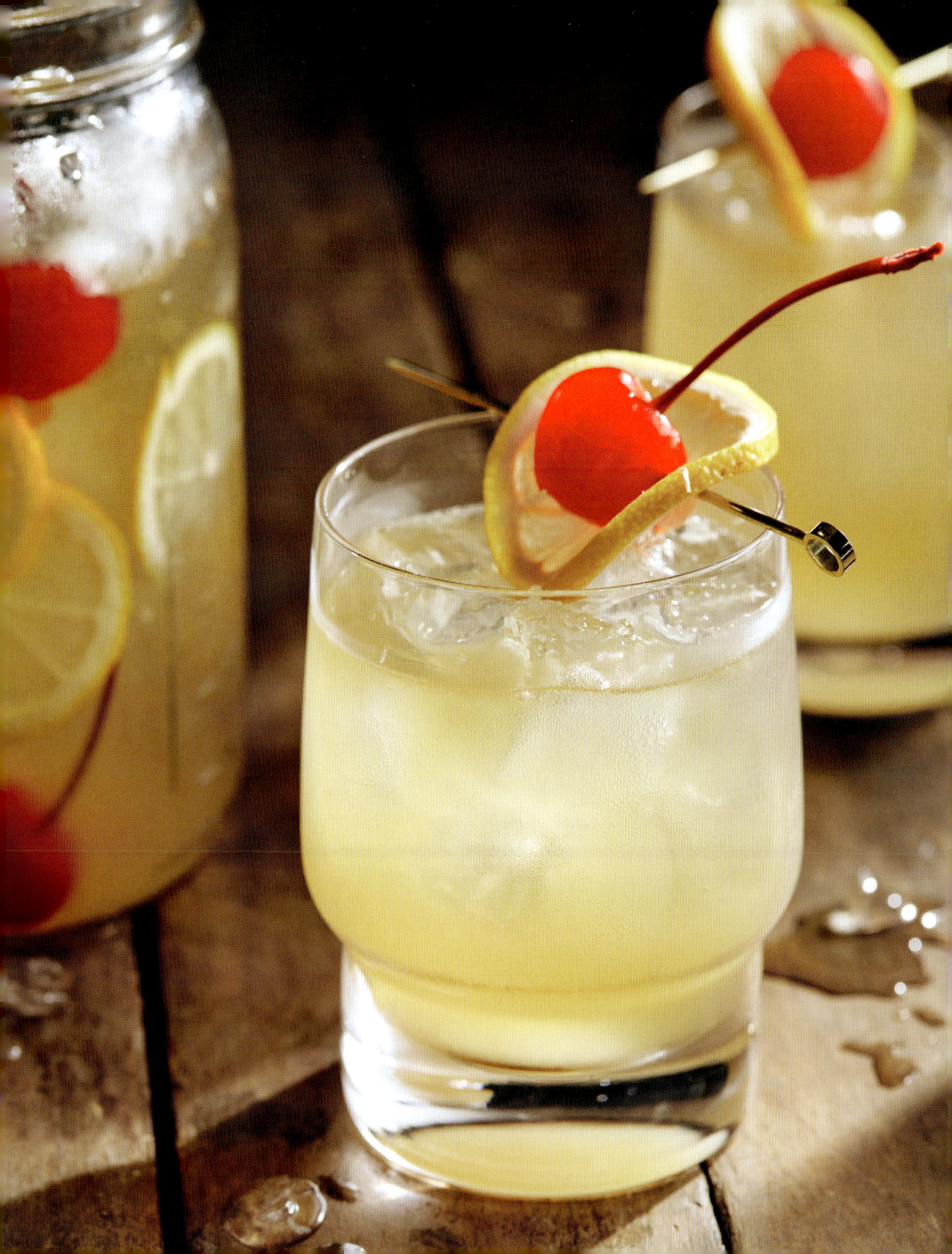

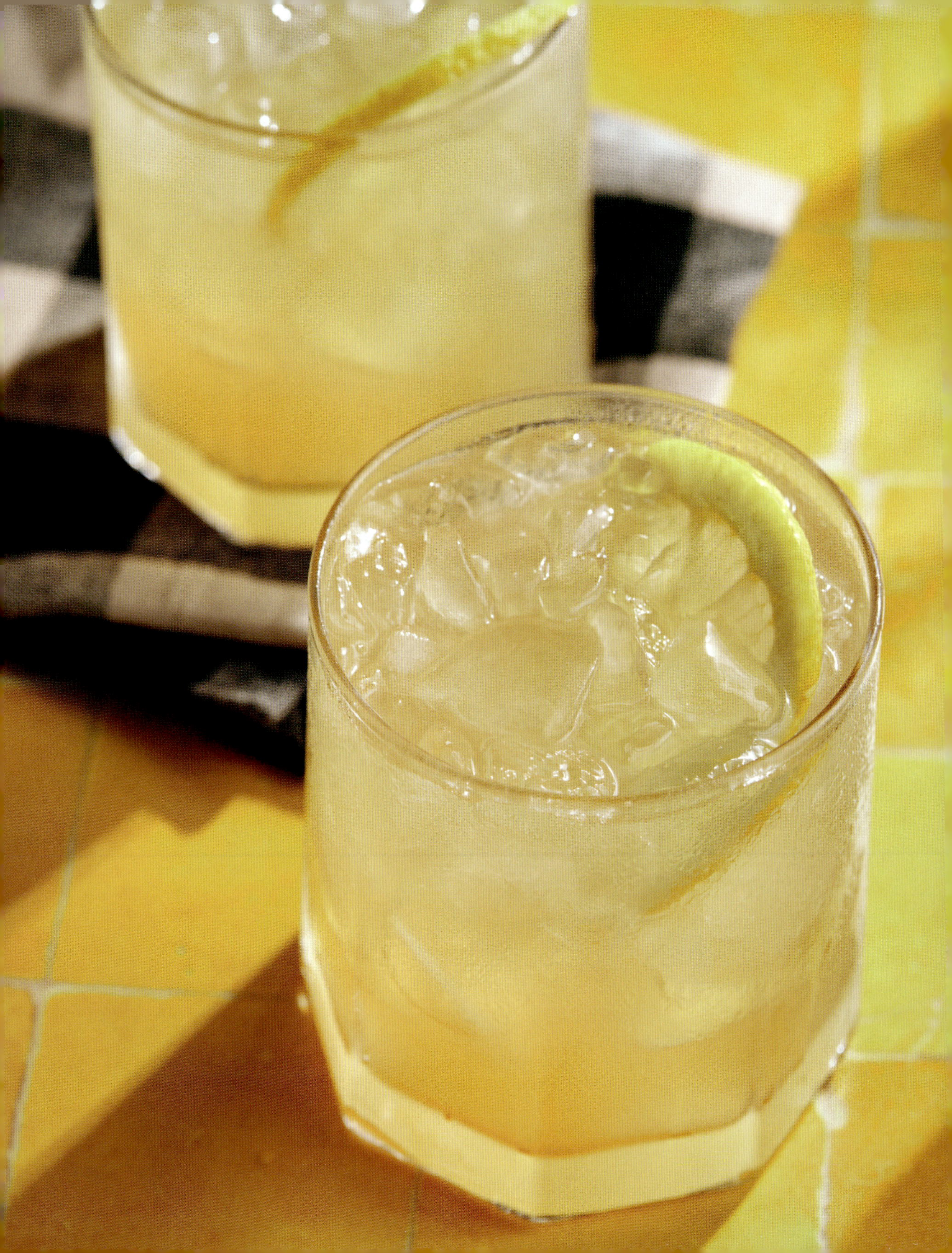

Fourth and One Bourbon Smash

The smash is a popular pregame drink of ours that requires minimal effort and just a few ingredients. The idea behind it is, by shaking the crushed lemon and mint, simple syrup, and bourbon, you coax out the flavors. Sort of like fourth and one for the offense. Sometimes shaking up the play call, to coax the defenders into thinking something different will happen, results in a touchdown. This drink is also a touchdown and worth celebrating at your next gathering. **—TERRY**

Makes 1 cocktail

1 lemon, cut into quarters

3 large fresh mint leaves (optional)

¾ ounce Simple Syrup (see Coach's Corner)

2 ounces straight bourbon whiskey

Fresh lemon wheel, for serving

Add the lemon quarters; mint leaves, if using; and simple syrup to a cocktail shaker. Using a muddler, crush the ingredients together to release the essential oils. Add a handful of ice and the bourbon. Shake vigorously for 10 to 20 seconds, strain into a rocks glass filled with ice, and serve with a lemon wheel.

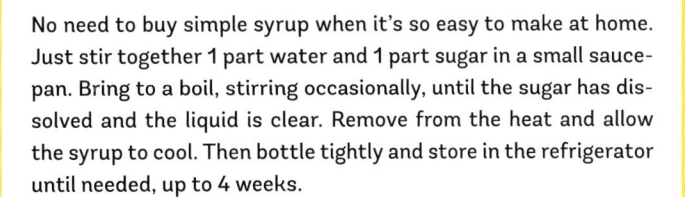

COACH'S CORNER

No need to buy simple syrup when it's so easy to make at home. Just stir together 1 part water and 1 part sugar in a small saucepan. Bring to a boil, stirring occasionally, until the sugar has dissolved and the liquid is clear. Remove from the heat and allow the syrup to cool. Then bottle tightly and store in the refrigerator until needed, up to 4 weeks.

The Immaculate Refreshment

This refreshing bourbon drink with hints of bright basil, citrus, and strawberry will be the star of any party or pregame celebration. The name stems from the famous Immaculate Reception, that legendary play in 1972 when Steelers running back and future Hall of Famer Franco Harris caught my deflected pass and scored the game-winning touchdown during our AFC Divisional Playoff game against the Oakland Raiders. Noah and I recently made this drink on live television for *Houston Life*, and it was an instant win. **—TERRY**

FOR 1 COCKTAIL

2 ounces straight bourbon whiskey

¾ ounce Simple Syrup (see Coach's Corner, page 77)

1 ounce fresh lime juice

1 large strawberry, hulled and cut into quarters

4 fresh basil leaves

1 strawberry half and 1 basil sprig, for serving

BIG BATCH FOR A TEAM
(makes about 10 cocktails)

1¼ cups straight bourbon whiskey

3½ ounces Simple Syrup (see Coach's Corner, page 77)

¾ cup lime juice

5 large strawberries, hulled and cut into quarters

12 fresh basil leaves

5 strawberries, hulled and halved, and 10 basil sprigs, for serving

For one cocktail: Add the bourbon, simple syrup, lime juice, strawberry quarters, and basil leaves to a cocktail shaker with several ice cubes. Shake vigorously for 4 to 6 seconds. Pour the contents of the shaker into a Collins glass, or a glass of your choice, without straining. Garnish with the basil sprig and strawberry half and serve.

For a big batch (see Coach's Corner): Add the bourbon, simple syrup, lime juice, strawberry quarters, and basil leaves to a pitcher with a handful of ice. Mix the ingredients and pour into glasses of your choice, without straining, and top with fresh ice. Serve with the strawberry halves and basil sprigs.

COACH'S CORNER

For convenience and easy transport, make a big batch and refrigerate overnight. The next day, transfer it to a half-gallon insulated thermos and it's ready to go for your tailgate or serving at home.

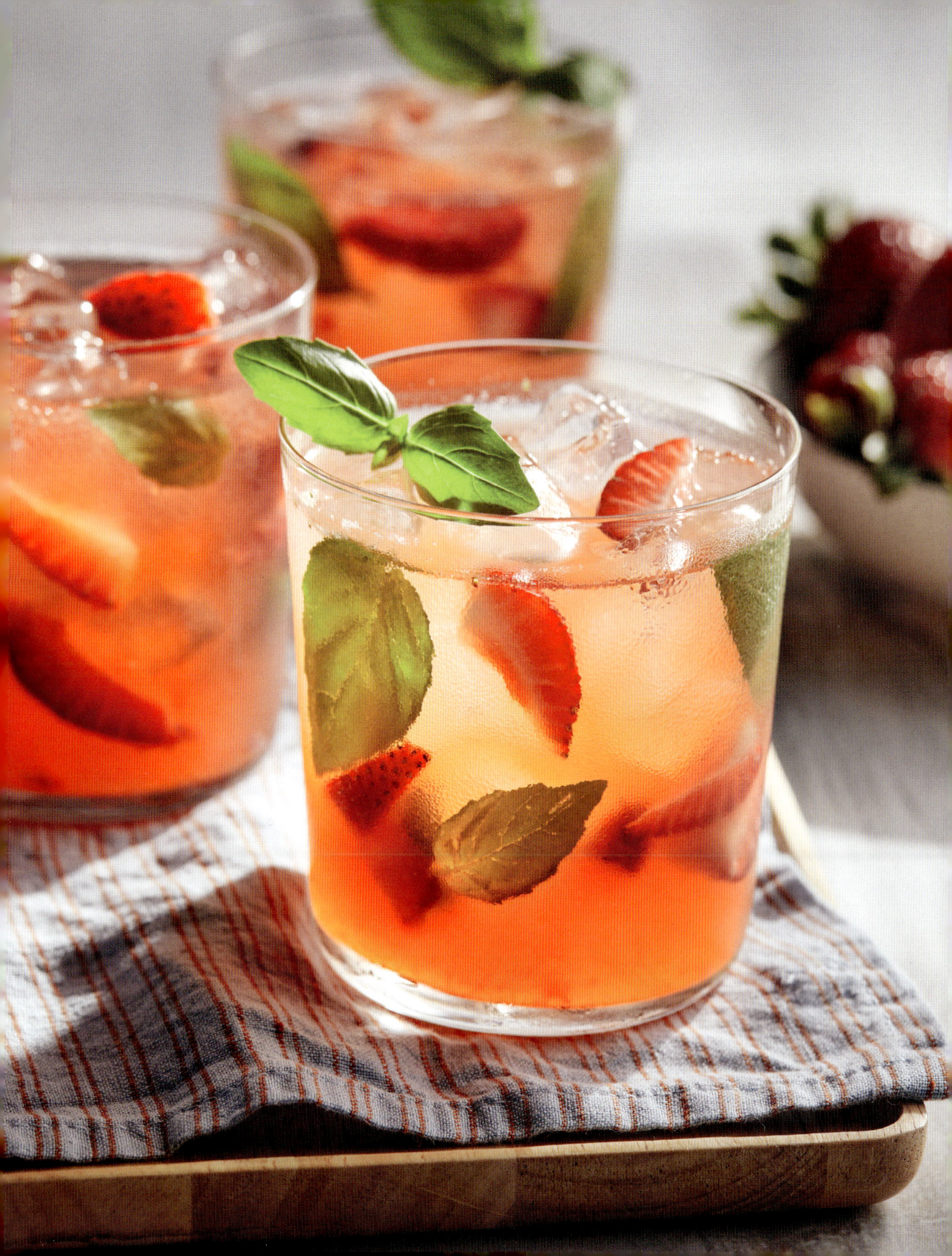

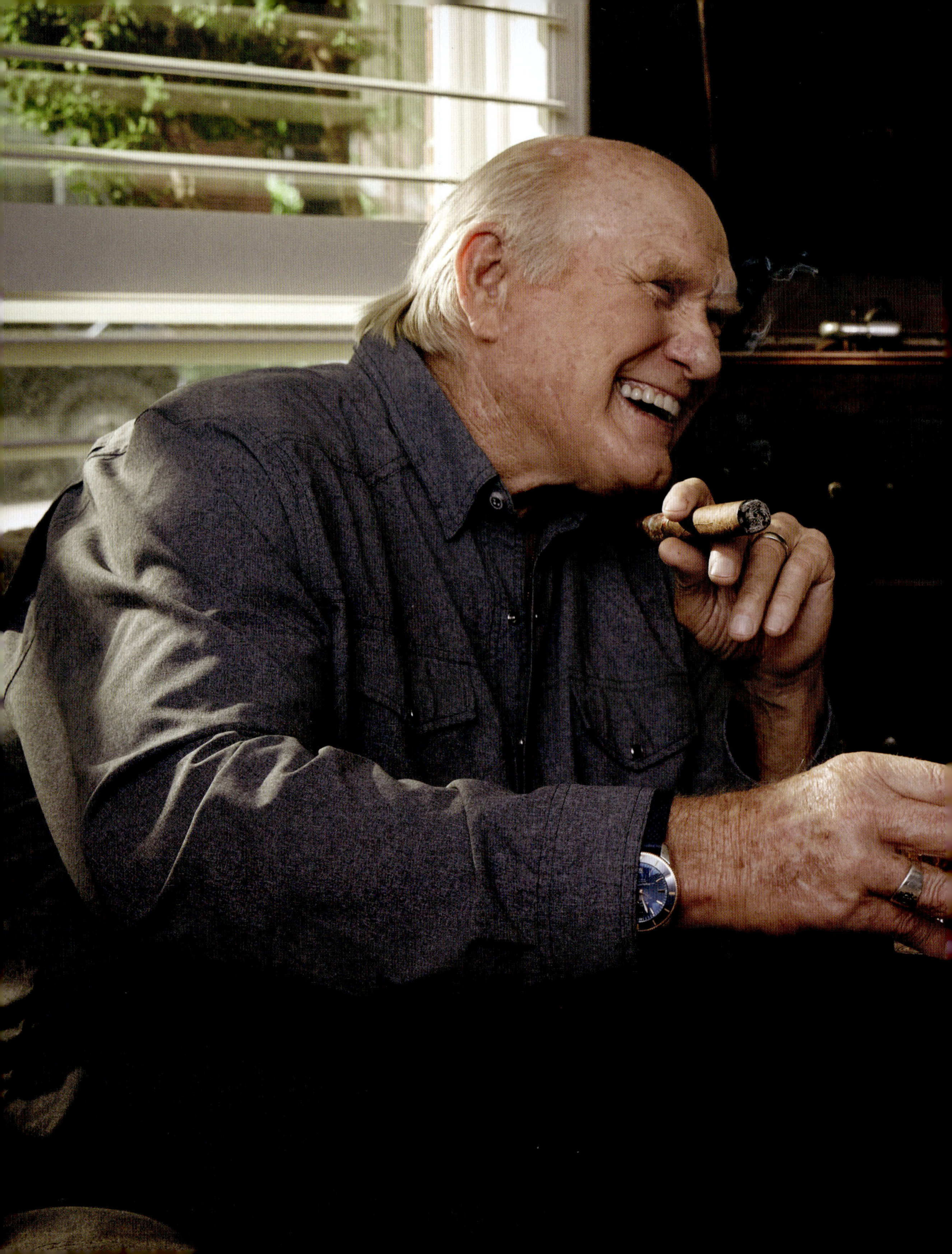

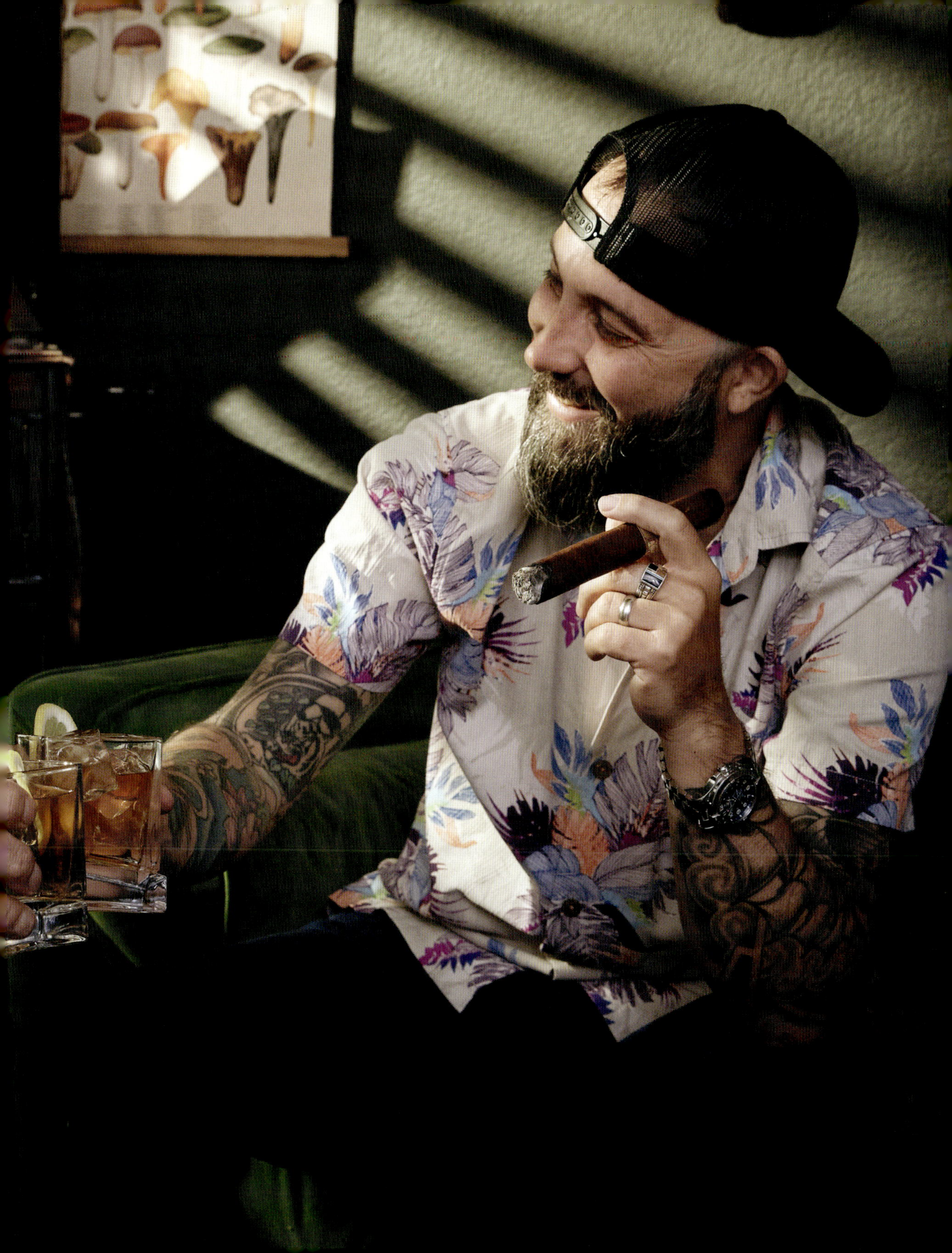

Gainesville Grande Margarita

Everyone at our ranch loves Mexican food. Once a week, Tammy and I will take our friends and helpers out for a fun dinner at Villa Grande Mexican Restaurant, a quaint little eatery in Gainesville, Texas. That's where they'll retrieve a couple icy glasses and make us this refreshing and unique margarita featuring tequila and bourbon. It's a terrific combination with the right amount of "bite." —TERRY

Makes 1 cocktail

1 lime wedge

Tajin spice mix, for the glass rim

1-ounce piece fresh pineapple

1½ ounces fresh lime juice

¾ ounce honey or agave syrup

1 ounce 100% agave tequila

¾ ounce straight bourbon whiskey

½ ounce Cointreau (or other orange liqueur)

4 to 5 drops Tabasco hot sauce

Run the lime wedge around half the rim of a chilled rocks glass. Roll the moistened rim in the Tajin and set the glass aside.

Add the pineapple, lime juice, and honey to a cocktail shaker. Using a muddler, firmly crush the ingredients together. Add the tequila, bourbon, Cointreau, hot sauce, and a handful of ice. Shake vigorously for 10 to 20 seconds, strain into the prepared glass, and serve.

Nannie's Ranch Crackers

Our grandmother Nannie Bradshaw was a fantastic cook who made extravagant dishes as well as simple bites like this one. I vividly remember these zesty crackers that she gently tossed in olive oil, red pepper flakes, and Hidden Valley Ranch seasoning. They have an herbaceous bite and remain a family favorite. —RACHEL

Serves 12 to 15

16 ounces saltine crackers (4 sleeves, or about 120 crackers)

1 cup olive oil

1 tablespoon crushed red pepper flakes, plus more for serving (optional)

1-ounce packet Hidden Valley Original Ranch Dips Mix

Add the crackers to a large bowl or pot with a lid. Add the olive oil, red pepper flakes, and ranch mix. Seal and gently tumble the crackers over and over until they are well and evenly coated. Try to avoid breaking them as you mix them with the seasonings. Arrange the crackers on a large platter and serve with extra red pepper flakes, if using.

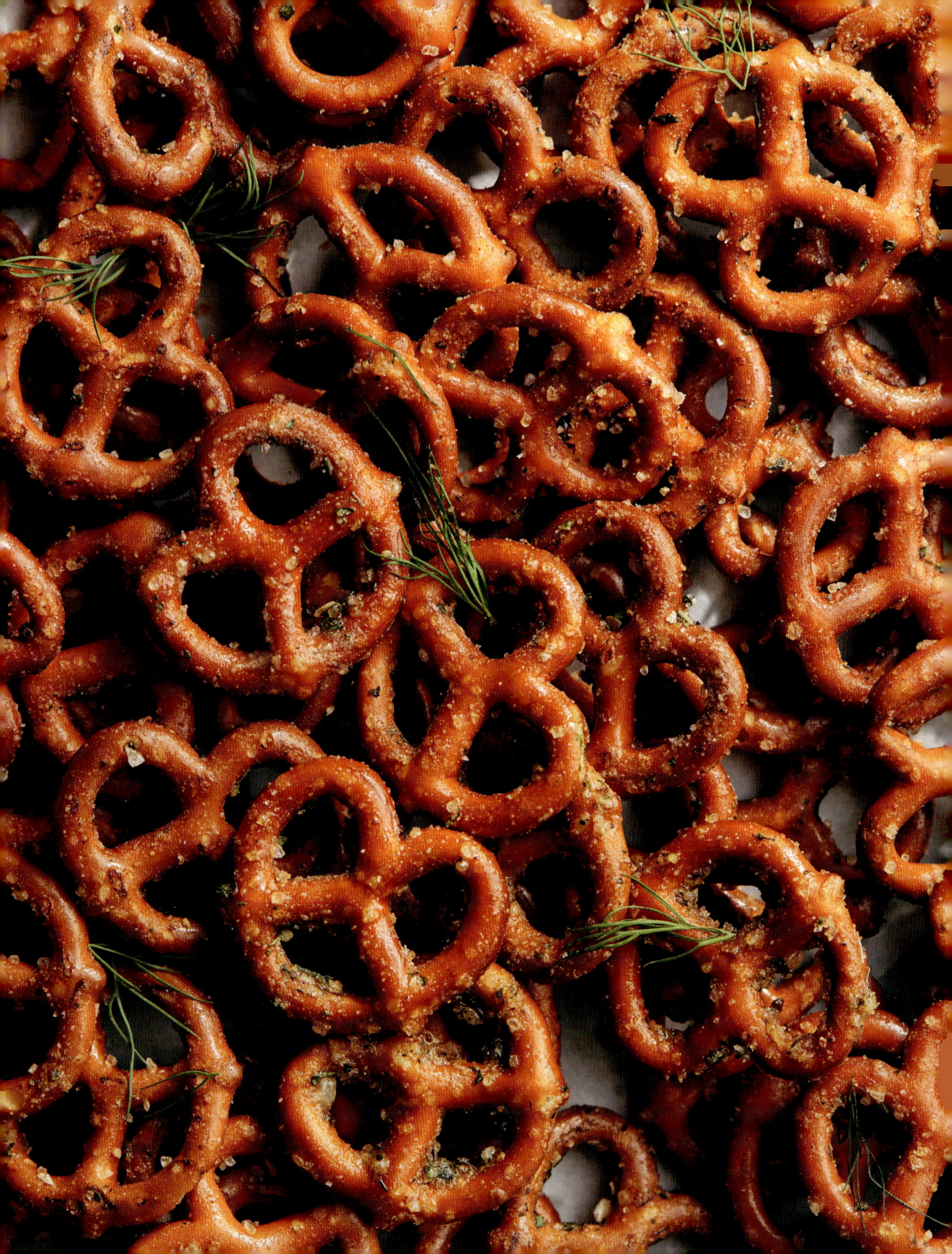

Ranch-Style Pretzel Snacks

These incredibly addicting pretzels, gently tossed with olive oil and an array of herbs and spices, are easy to make and hold up well. They're perfect for snacking throughout the day and you'll often find a bowl on our kitchen counter. They travel well, too. I like to take a bag with me when I'm heading out to watch one of Zurie's horse shows. —TAMMY

Serves 12

1-ounce packet Hidden Valley Original Ranch Seasoning, Salad Dressing, and Recipe Mix

1½ teaspoons garlic powder

½ teaspoon cayenne pepper, to taste

1 teaspoon lemon pepper

½ teaspoon chopped fresh dill, plus 4 or 5 dill fronds for serving

¾ cup vegetable oil

1 (16-ounce) package mini pretzels

Combine the seasoning mix, garlic powder, cayenne, lemon pepper, and dill in a mixing bowl, using a whisk to combine. Drizzle in the oil while continuing to mix until incorporated. Add the pretzels and toss well to coat. Cover the bowl with plastic wrap and let sit at room temperature overnight, tossing the pretzels occasionally. Serve the pretzels with some dill fronds.

Homemade Focaccia with Herb Dipping Oil

Who doesn't love warm, salty bread dipped into herb-infused olive oil? While pregnant with Cason, I was gaining confidence in the kitchen and turned to baking for fun. Soon, I started playing around with different types of breads. With its golden crust, olive oil infusion, and touch of salt and herbs, this focaccia never disappoints. Feel free to dress up your focaccia with any toppings you like, or keep it simple like we do. Either way, your friends and family will be impressed with your baking prowess. —RACHEL

Serves 4 to 6

2 cups lukewarm water

2 teaspoons granulated sugar

2 teaspoons instant or active dry yeast

1 tablespoon unsalted butter

3 or 4 tablespoons chopped fresh herbs, such as basil, thyme, or rosemary, to taste

2 garlic cloves, minced

4½ to 5 cups all-purpose flour, plus more for dusting

¼ cup olive oil, plus more for greasing, brushing, and dipping

1 tablespoon kosher salt

Nonstick cooking spray (optional)

Coarse kosher salt and freshly cracked black pepper, plus Italian seasoning, to taste

In a medium bowl, stir together the water, sugar, and yeast. Set aside for 5 minutes.

Combine the butter, herbs, and garlic in a small saucepan. Stir over medium-low heat until the butter is melted and the mixture is fragrant, 1 or 2 minutes, stirring often to prevent the garlic from burning. Set aside.

In the bowl of a standing mixer with a dough hook attachment, add the yeast mixture. With the mixer on low, add 4½ cups of the flour, the olive oil, salt, and butter-herb mixture. Mix until the dough is firm yet elastic, about 10 minutes. If the dough is too sticky, add more flour, 1 tablespoon at a time, until the dough comes away from the sides of the bowl. Remove the dough ball and knead it on a floured surface. Form the dough back into a ball and place it in a greased bowl, cover with a damp kitchen cloth or plastic wrap, and let rise until doubled in size, 2 to 3 hours.

Spray a rimmed baking sheet with olive oil or nonstick spray. Punch down the dough to release any air bubbles. With your fingers, stretch and flatten the dough to fit onto the baking sheet, being careful not to tear it (see Coach's Corner). Let sit at room temperature for about 1 hour.

Preheat the oven to 350°F.

Brush the dough generously with some olive oil and sprinkle with coarse salt and black pepper. Bake until golden brown, 25 to 35 minutes.

Serve warm with a small bowl of olive oil mixed with a little Italian seasoning for dipping.

COACH'S CORNER

If you find that your dough is shrinking back from the sides as you stretch it on the baking sheet, cover the dough and baking sheet with a kitchen towel and allow the dough to rest another 10 minutes before continuing. This will give the gluten time to relax, making the dough easier to shape.

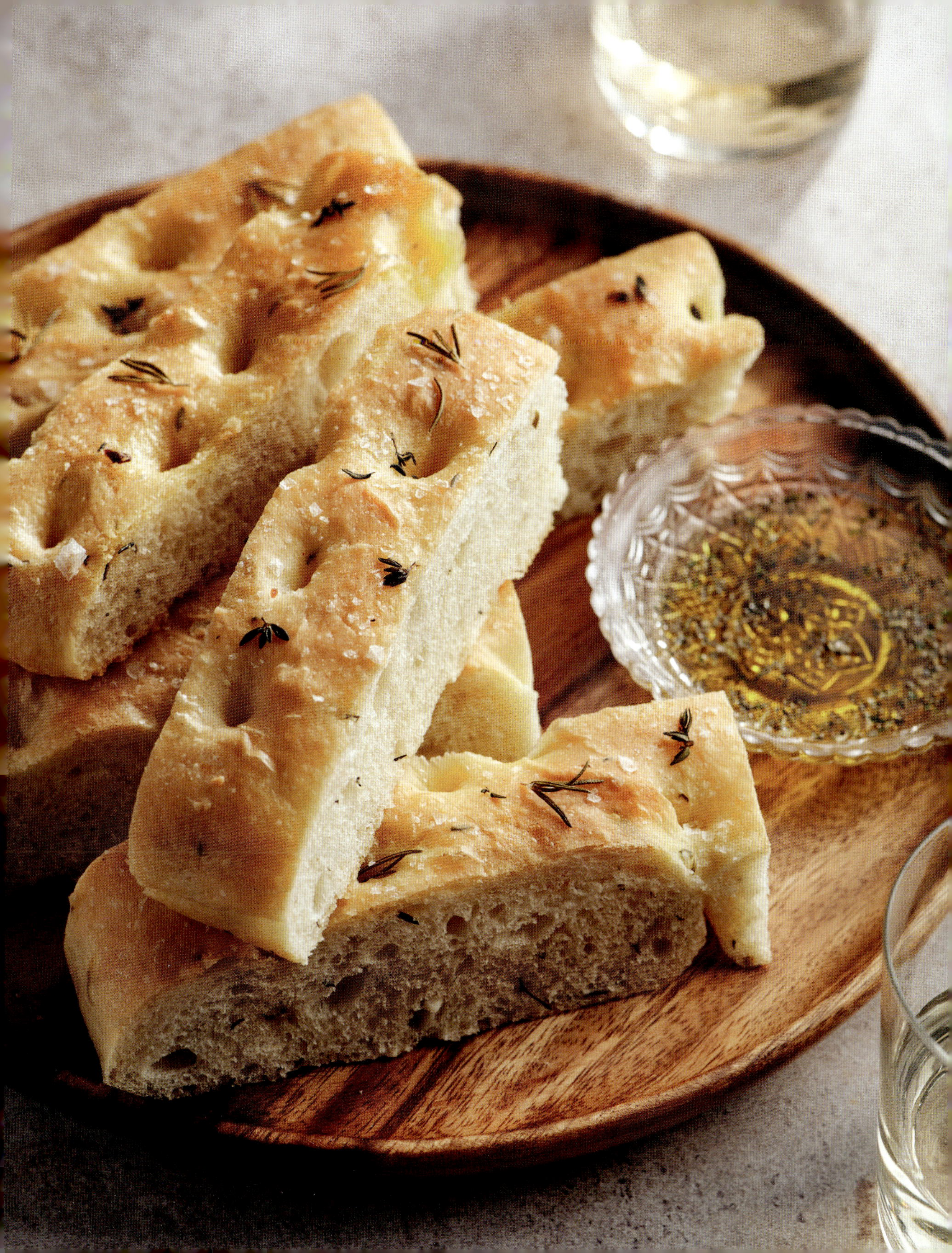

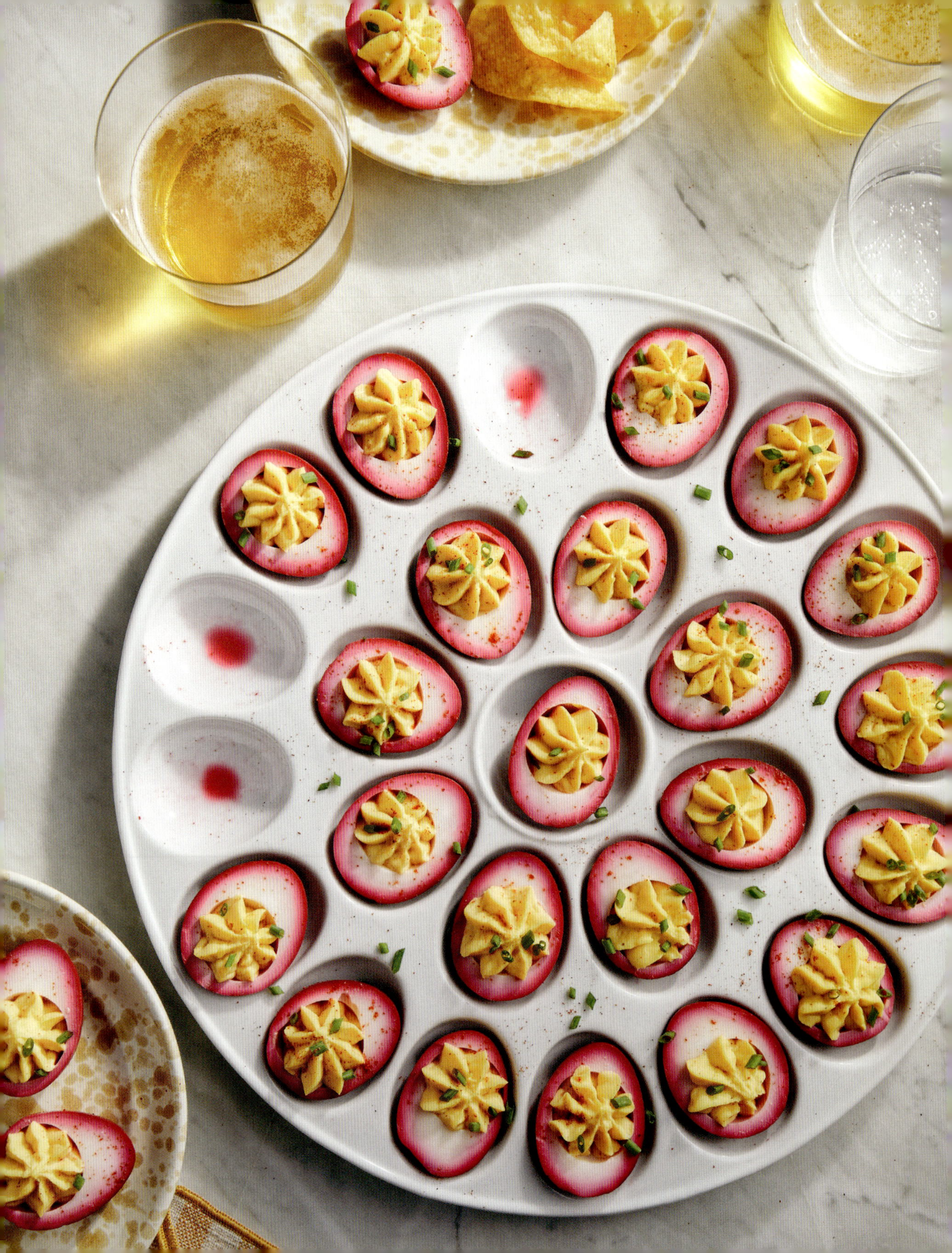

Beet Deviled Eggs

Minnesota Vikings fans, you'll appreciate these. For those who don't care for beets, we can assure you these eggs don't taste like beets at all. We simply use the natural color of beets to dye the eggs a vibrant purple. The brightly colored eggs highlight the creamy yolks flavored with tangy mustard and a sprinkle of paprika. They're sure to get as much attention as the halftime show. No matter which team you're pulling for, these deviled eggs are a winner. —**TERRY**

Makes 12 deviled eggs

PICKLED BEET EGGS

6 large eggs

2 medium red beets, peeled and shredded (see Coach's Corner)

1 cup apple cider vinegar

½ cup granulated sugar

1 teaspoon kosher salt

½ teaspoon black peppercorns

2 or 3 whole cloves

1 bay leaf

DEVILED EGG FILLING

3 tablespoons mayonnaise

2 teaspoons Dijon mustard

1 teaspoon apple cider vinegar

1 teaspoon honey

¼ teaspoon kosher salt

¼ teaspoon freshly cracked black pepper

Chopped fresh chives and paprika, for serving

To make the pickled beet eggs: Place the eggs in a medium saucepan with enough water to cover. Bring to a boil over high heat, then reduce the heat to low and simmer gently for 10 minutes. Use a slotted spoon to transfer the eggs to a bowl of ice water to cool completely.

While the eggs are cooling, prepare the pickling liquid. In a small saucepan, combine the shredded beets, vinegar, sugar, salt, peppercorns, cloves, bay leaf, and ¼ cup water. Bring to a boil over medium-high heat, then reduce the heat to low and simmer for 5 minutes. Let the pickling liquid cool to room temperature.

Strain the cooled pickling liquid into a resealable plastic bag. Peel the eggs (see Coach's Corner) and nestle them into the cooled pickling liquid, ensuring they are fully submerged. Refrigerate for at least 4 hours, or overnight, for a consistent purple color.

To make the deviled egg filling: Remove the eggs from the pickling liquid and pat dry. Cut each egg in half lengthwise, and carefully transfer the yolks to a small bowl. With a fork, mash the yolks, then add the mayonnaise, mustard, vinegar, honey, salt, and cracked pepper. Mix until smooth and creamy. Spoon or pipe the filling into the depression of the egg white halves where the yolks once were. Garnish with chives and a sprinkle of paprika.

COACH'S CORNER

Wear gloves when shredding the beets. This will ensure you don't end up with red fingertips. And here's a trick for easier egg peeling: Once the eggs have cooled, gently crack one side of the shell and return the eggs to the ice water. The water will seep into the cracks, getting underneath the shells and releasing the shells from the whites. When it's time to peel, you'll find it much easier.

Garlic Pull-Apart Pigs in a Blanket

One year, Chase and I were having friends over to watch the Super Bowl and realized we needed another finger food. I scoured my cookbooks for a pigs-in-a-blanket recipe, but none of them had the flavor I was after, so I added some garlic powder and butter to elevate the taste. It was an instant hit, and will be a must-have snack for your next celebration. —RACHEL

Makes 30 to 32 pieces

Nonstick cooking spray (optional)

6 tablespoons (¾ stick) butter, melted

2 tablespoons honey mustard, plus more for dipping

2 teaspoons paprika

½ teaspoon garlic powder

All-purpose flour, for dusting

1 (8-ounce) tube Pillsbury Crescent Dough Sheet

1 (14-ounce) package Hillshire Farm Lit'l Smokies or cocktail franks (30 to 32 pieces)

1 teaspoon poppy seeds

Preheat the oven to 400°F. Spray a rimmed baking sheet with nonstick cooking spray or line with parchment paper and set aside.

Stir together the melted butter, honey mustard, paprika, and garlic powder in a microwave-safe container. Mix and set aside. (If the mixture sits too long, the butter will harden. If this happens, just pop the mixture into the microwave for a few seconds to remelt.)

Sprinkle a little flour on a clean work surface. Place the dough sheet on the floured surface and spread it out with your hands. Brush the top of the dough with 4 tablespoons of the butter mixture. Using a pizza or pastry cutter, cut the dough lengthwise into 8 equal strips, then cut the strips in half (making 16 strips in total), then cut lengthwise in half again to make 32 thin strips (see Coach's Corner). Roll up a frank in a strip and place on the prepared baking sheet. Repeat the process with the remaining dough strips and franks. Brush the tops of the wrapped franks with the remaining butter mixture and sprinkle them with poppy seeds.

Cover the baking sheet with foil and bake for 30 minutes. Remove the foil and bake until the dough is a rich, golden brown, 3 to 5 minutes. Let cool slightly before serving with a side of honey mustard.

COACH'S CORNER

If you prefer a sweet, doughy bite with your pigs in a blanket, follow our recipe as is. If you would rather taste more meat and less dough, roll out the dough and cut the sheet into thinner strips for wrapping the meat (you will end up with leftover dough). Either way, you'll enjoy these tasty little beauties.

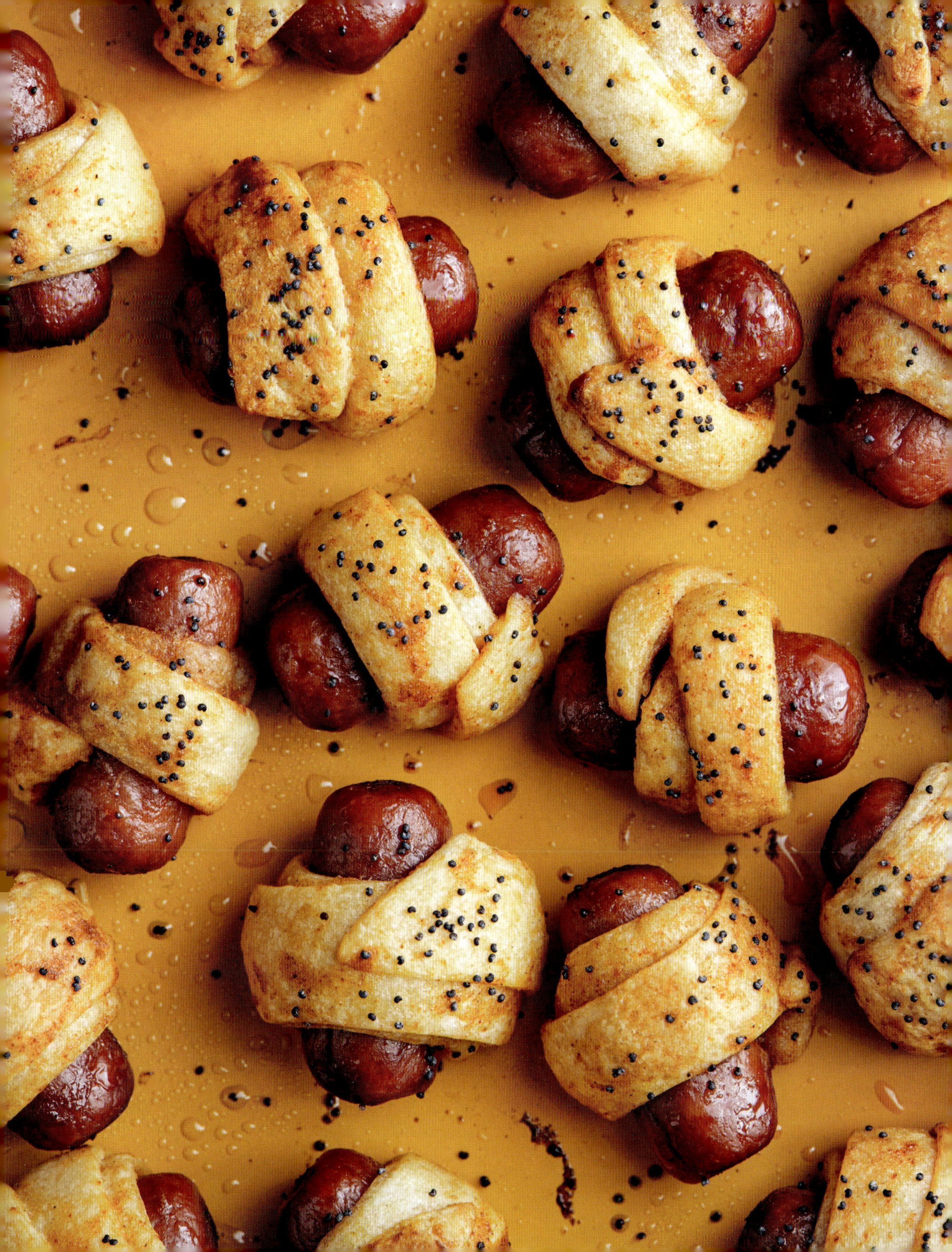

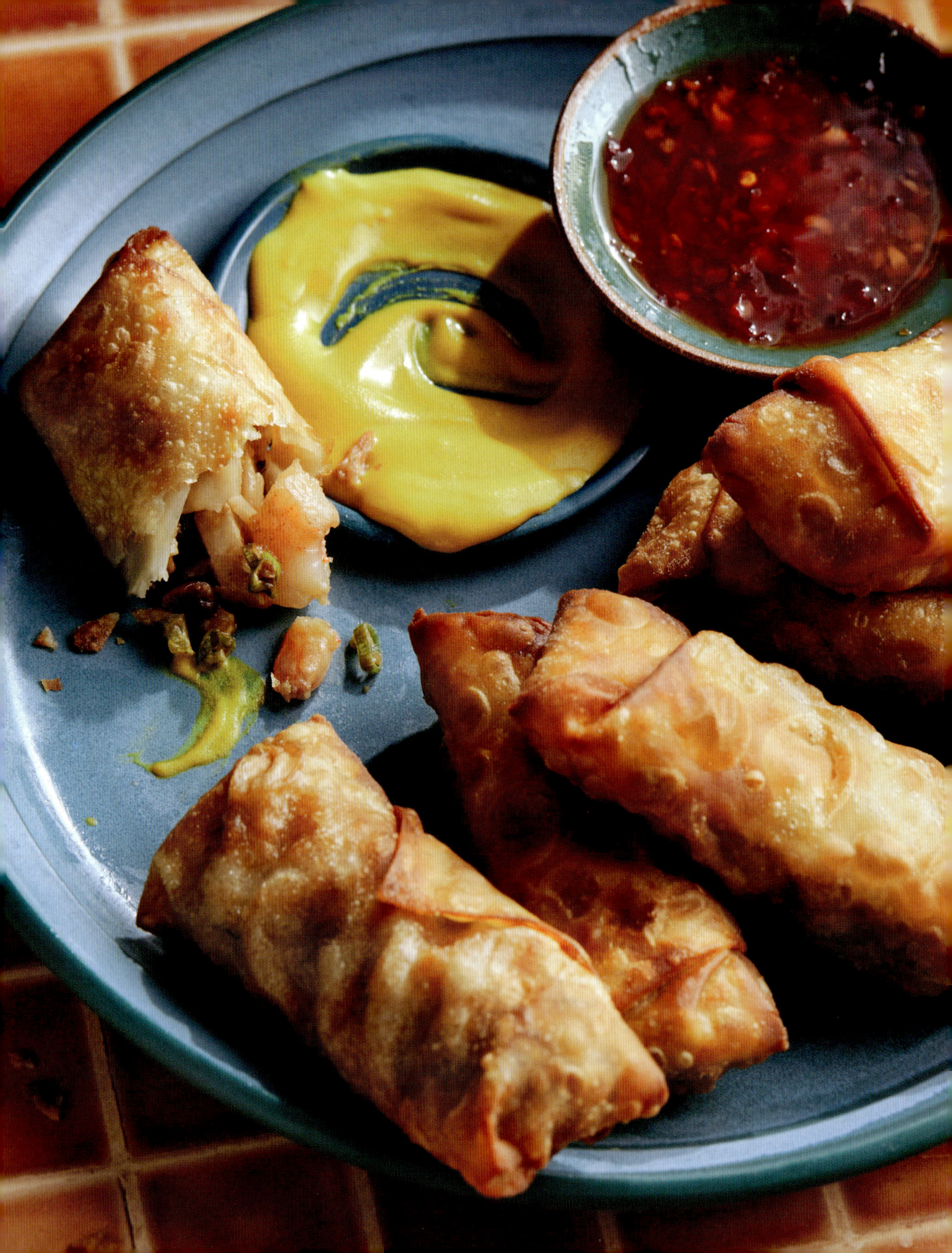

Crispy Egg Rolls with Shrimp, Sprouts, and Peanut Butter

When it comes to appetizers with a crunchy and delicious bite, these are often our go-to. Terry and I enjoy making these delectable bundles of crispy perfection because they are so much better than store-bought. The savory combination of shrimp and sprouts paired with the touch of sweetness from the peanut butter is one enormous flavor explosion. —TAMMY

Makes 10 egg rolls

1 cup chopped cooked shrimp

¼ cup chopped green bell pepper

½ cup bean sprouts

½ cup chopped water chestnuts

¼ cup chopped green onions, green and white parts

¼ cup smooth peanut butter

2 teaspoons soy sauce

1 teaspoon granulated sugar

10 egg roll wrappers

Canola or vegetable oil, for frying

Hot mustard and/or sweet chili sauce, for dipping

Add the shrimp, bell pepper, bean sprouts, chestnuts, green onions, PB, soy sauce, and sugar to a large bowl. Mix well to ensure all the flavors are evenly distributed.

Lay one egg roll wrapper on a clean work surface. Place 3 tablespoons of the filling in a strip diagonally across the center of the wrapper, from one corner to the opposite one. Fold the bottom corner of the wrapper up and over the filling, then fold the sides inward, and roll tightly until you reach the top corner. Seal the roll by brushing a bit of water on the edges. (Sealing the edges will ensure the filling doesn't spill out during frying.) Repeat to make 10 egg rolls.

Add at least 2 inches of oil to a high-sided frying pan or pot. Heat the oil to 350°F over medium to medium-high heat, using a candy or digital thermometer to check the oil temperature.

When the oil is at temperature, carefully place three or four egg rolls into the hot oil and fry, turning occasionally, until golden brown, 4 or 5 minutes. Use tongs or a slotted spoon to transfer the cooked egg rolls to a paper towel–lined plate to drain. Continue the process with the remaining egg rolls (see Coach's Corner).

Arrange the egg rolls on a platter with small bowls of hot mustard and/or sweet and sour sauce for dipping.

COACH'S CORNER

If you would like to prepare the egg rolls ahead of time, simply cook them completely, cool, then refrigerate for up to 3 days until ready to serve. To reheat, place the egg rolls on a microwave-safe plate and microwave for a couple minutes, until hot. You can also heat the egg rolls in a 350°F oven for about 10 minutes (5 minutes per side) to get them crispy again.

Chicken-Fried Steak "Fries" with Zesty Dip

There aren't many things more Texan than chicken-fried steak, that Southern comfort classic featuring tenderized beef coated in seasoned flour and fried until crispy. When we moved back to Texas from Hawaii with our kids, Jeb and Zurie, we had a lot of fun experimenting with the local cuisine. Both our kids are big fans of steak and French fries, so we thought, why not combine the two? —NOAH AND LACEY

Serves 8 to 10 (makes about 20 steak "fries")

ZESTY DIP
Makes 1 cup

½ cup mayonnaise

¼ cup sour cream

2 tablespoons Dijon mustard

2 garlic cloves, minced

Grated zest and 1 tablespoon juice from 1 lemon

1 teaspoon hot sauce, or to taste

Kosher salt and freshly cracked black pepper, to taste

STEAK "FRIES"

4 (8-ounce) top round cube steaks

Kosher salt and freshly cracked black pepper, to taste

Vegetable oil, for frying

2 cups all-purpose flour

2 cups panko breadcrumbs

4 teaspoons garlic powder

4 teaspoons onion powder

2 teaspoons paprika

4 large eggs

2 cups buttermilk

To make the zesty dip: Add the mayonnaise, sour cream, mustard, garlic, lemon zest, lemon juice, hot sauce, salt, and pepper to a small bowl and mix until thoroughly combined. Taste and adjust the seasoning and spiciness level to your preference. Set aside.

To make the steak "fries": Place each steak between two sheets of plastic wrap or parchment paper and gently pound with a meat mallet to tenderize and flatten to about ¼ inch thick. You can also have your butcher run the steaks through a meat tenderizer and thinly slice each steak for you.

Cut the pounded cutlets into strips about ½ inch wide. Season the strips with salt and pepper.

Combine the flour and panko in a shallow dish. Add the garlic powder, onion powder, and paprika and stir to distribute well. In another shallow dish, use a fork to beat the eggs and buttermilk together. Place a rimmed baking sheet next to the bowls.

Dip one strip of beef first into the flour-panko mixture, coating both sides, then into the egg mixture, then back into the flour-panko mixture, pressing the coating onto the meat. Set the coated beef strip on the baking sheet and repeat with the remaining strips.

Pour the vegetable oil into a large skillet until ½ inch deep. Heat over medium-high heat until the oil is shimmering. Preheat the oven to 200°F.

Carefully add four to six strips of the breaded beef to the hot oil. (Work in batches to avoid overcrowding the skillet, which lowers the temperature of the oil and prevents the meat from becoming crisp.) Fry the strips until golden brown and crispy, 3 to 4 minutes on each side. Transfer the fried beef strips to a paper towel–lined plate to drain. Then place in the oven to keep warm. Repeat with the remaining strips, skimming the oil of any crispy bits and allowing it to become hot again between batches. Serve with the zesty dip on the side.

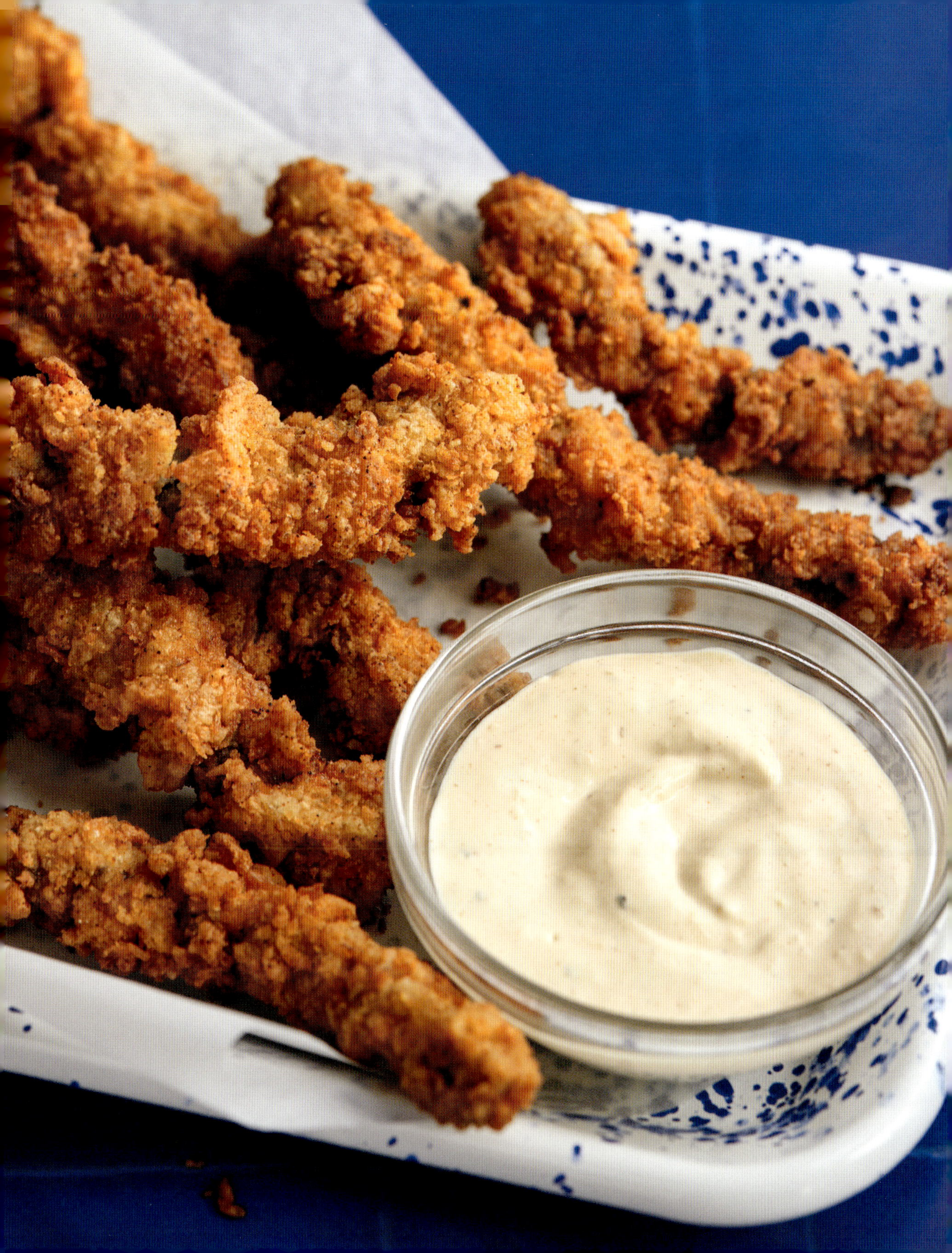

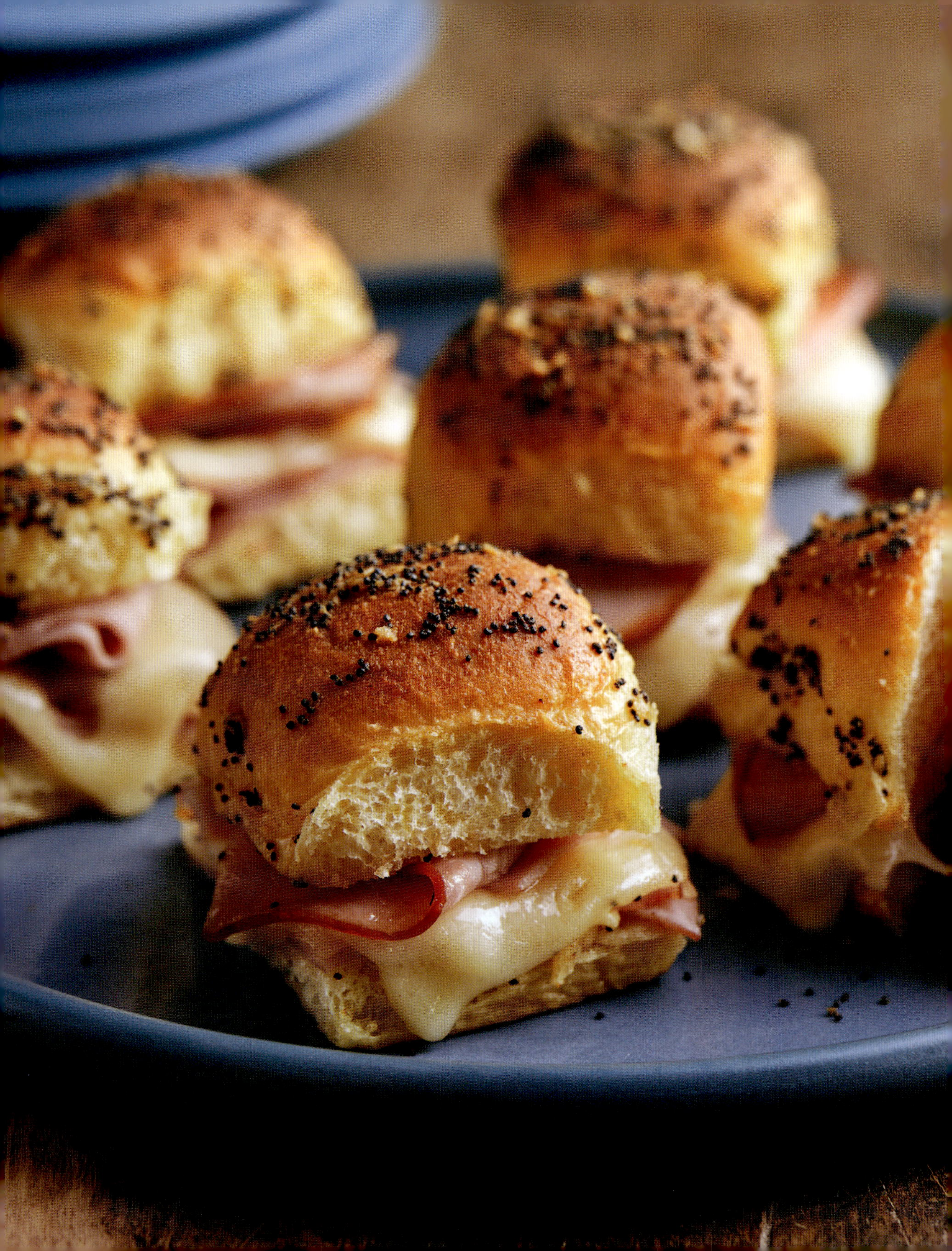

Toasted Ham and Swiss Cheese Sliders

Since I was a little girl, these little toasted sandwiches have been my favorite snack. These days, I like to serve them when I have friends over. Brush the tops with seasoned butter and bake them until golden and gooey. These sliders are a good choice for those of you who like to host rather than be stuck in the kitchen because they are quick to make and look impressive on a platter. — **RACHEL**

Makes 24 sliders

Nonstick cooking spray

24 King's Hawaiian Original Hawaiian Sweet Rolls

1 pound thinly sliced deli ham, cut to fit the slider buns

1 pound thinly sliced Swiss cheese, cut to fit the slider buns

¾ cup (1½ sticks) unsalted butter, melted

1½ tablespoons Dijon mustard

1½ teaspoons Worcestershire sauce

1½ tablespoons poppy seeds

1 tablespoon dried minced onion

Preheat the oven to 350°F. Spray a 9 × 13-inch baking dish with nonstick cooking spray.

Separate the tops of the rolls from the bottoms. Arrange the bottom halves in the prepared baking dish. Layer about half the ham slices on the bottom rolls, followed by a layer of Swiss and then the remaining ham. Set aside.

Combine the melted butter, mustard, Worcestershire sauce, poppy seeds, and dried onion in a small mixing bowl, stirring with a fork. Brush the tops of the rolls evenly with the butter mixture and place on top of the sandwiches.

Bake the sliders until nicely browned and the Swiss has melted, 10 to 12 minutes. If you find the rolls are browning too quickly, cover the pan with a sheet of aluminum foil.

Remove from the oven, arrange on a serving platter, and serve.

COACH'S CORNER

It's easy to customize your sliders to satisfy you and your guests. Sometimes we'll use pepper jack cheese and turkey or add pickles and pesto. Just be sure to brush the tops of the buns with the butter sauce. That's the secret to these fabulous bites.

Poppa Hester's Savory Herb Pimento Cheese

Here's another exciting bite that will tantalize your taste buds and impress your guests, courtesy of Noah's father. Poppa's flavorful spread is creamy and tangy, blending sharp cheddar and Monterey Jack, sweet pimentos, and a hint of spice. During our football get-togethers, we like to serve this savory cheese spread with Ritz crackers and some crusty bread, but it's also terrific on sandwiches. —**NOAH AND LACEY**

Makes 4 cups

- 2 cups shredded sharp cheddar cheese
- 1 cup shredded Monterey Jack cheese
- ½ cup mayonnaise
- ¼ cup cream cheese, at room temperature
- 1 teaspoon Dijon mustard
- ¼ cup drained and diced pimentos
- 1 teaspoon onion powder, or more to taste
- 1 teaspoon garlic powder, or more to taste
- 1 teaspoon smoked paprika, or more to taste
- 1 or 2 dashes hot sauce, to taste (optional)
- Kosher salt and freshly cracked black pepper, to taste
- 1 tablespoon finely chopped fresh chives
- 1 tablespoon finely chopped fresh Italian flat-leaf parsley
- Ritz crackers or crusty bread, for serving

Mix the Monterey Jack, cheddar, mayonnaise, cream cheese, and mustard in a large mixing bowl until combined. Fold in the pimentos, ensuring they are evenly distributed. Add the onion powder, garlic powder, smoked paprika, and hot sauce, if using. Mix thoroughly. Season with salt and pepper. Gently fold in the chives and parsley, ensuring the herbs are evenly distributed. Taste and adjust the seasonings to your preference. Cover and refrigerate for at least 1 hour to allow flavors to meld.

To serve, give the spread a final stir and transfer to a serving bowl. Serve with the crackers.

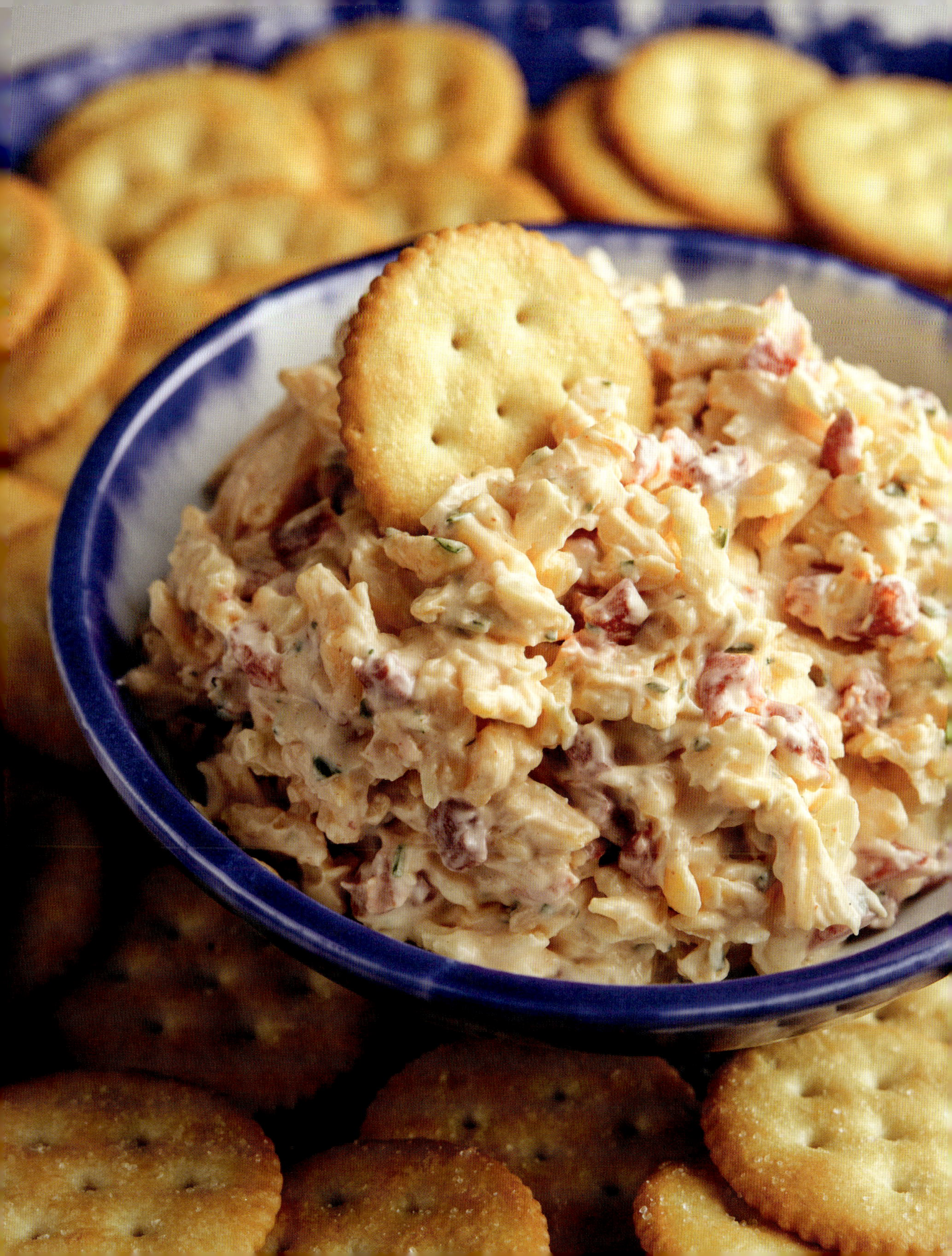

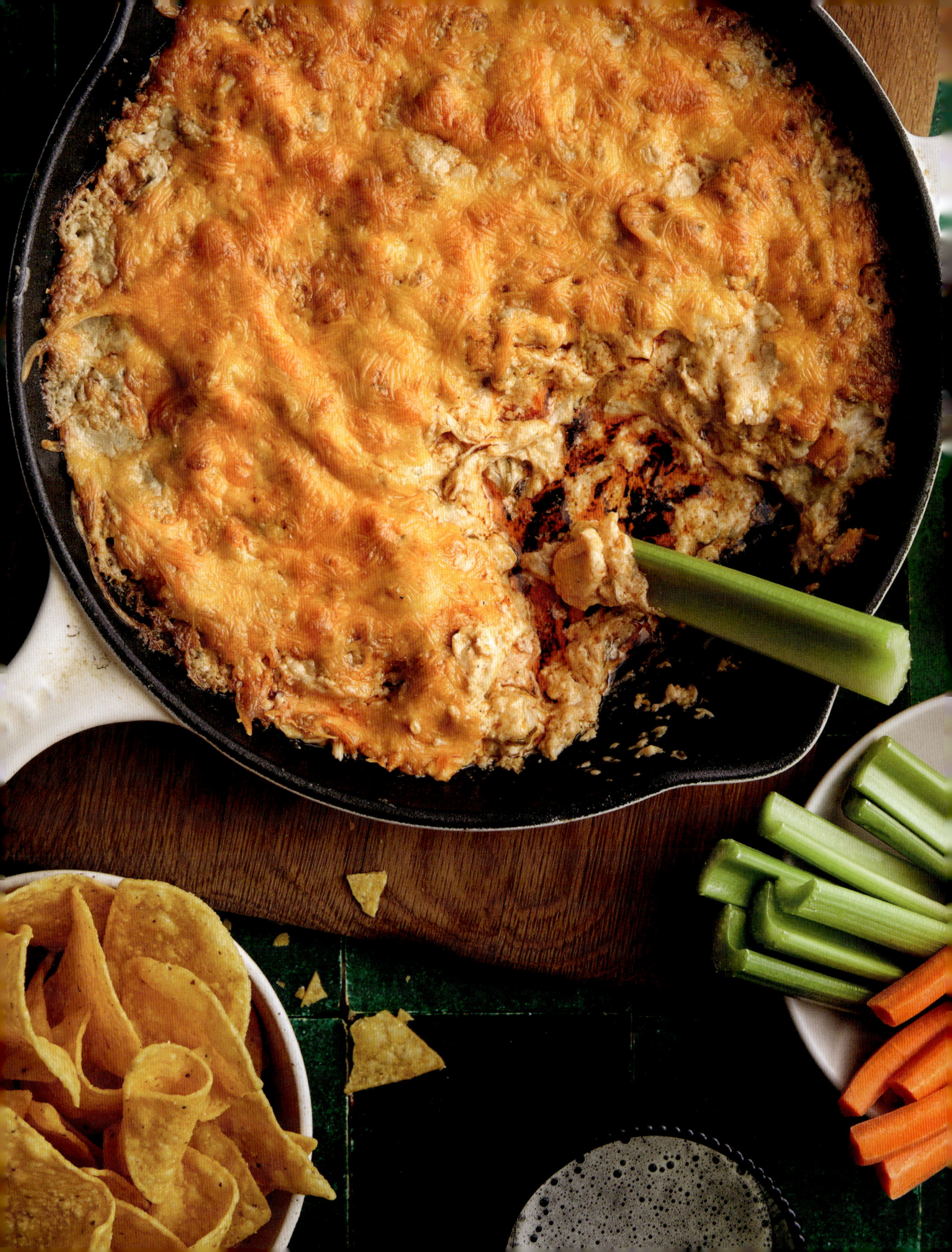

Cheesy Smoked Buffalo Chicken Dip

Do you know how many professional football teams Terry played for during his fourteen-year career? If you guessed one—the Pittsburgh Steelers—you're correct. Talk about loyalty. We are almost as loyal to this dip because it features the flavors of hot wings without the mess. It's one of those fun dishes you can enjoy in the kitchen, head over to the couch to check on the game, then return to dip again. Wait, who are we fooling? Just take the entire pan right to the coffee table and enjoy it without missing any of the action. —NOAH

Serves 8 to 10

SMOKED BUFFALO CHICKEN

1 teaspoon smoked paprika

½ teaspoon garlic powder

Kosher salt and freshly cracked black pepper, to taste

2 (8-ounce) boneless, skinless chicken breasts

1 tablespoon olive oil

CHEESY DIP
Makes about 3½ cups

1 cup (8 ounces) cream cheese, at room temperature

½ cup mayonnaise

½ cup Frank's RedHot sauce, or more to taste

1½ cups shredded cheddar cheese, divided

½ cup crumbled blue cheese

2 green onions, green and white parts, finely chopped

2 garlic cloves, minced

1 teaspoon Worcestershire sauce

1 teaspoon onion powder

½ teaspoon smoked paprika

Kosher salt and freshly cracked black pepper, to taste

Tortilla chips, celery sticks, and/or carrot sticks, for serving

To make the smoked Buffalo chicken: Preheat an outdoor smoker to 225°F. (See Grilling and Smoking—a Bradshaw Family Primer, page 27.) For the wood chips, hickory, mesquite, or oak works well.

Stir together the paprika, garlic powder, salt, and pepper in a small bowl. Lightly coat the chicken breasts on both sides with the olive oil, then rub liberally with the spice mixture.

Smoke the chicken until the internal temperature of the breasts reaches 165°F, about 90 minutes. Set aside to cool while you start the dip.

To make the cheesy dip: Preheat the oven to 350°F.

Combine the cream cheese, mayonnaise, hot sauce, 1 cup of the cheddar, the blue cheese, green onions, minced garlic, Worcestershire sauce, onion powder, smoked paprika, salt, and pepper in a large bowl. Mix well.

Using two forks or your fingers, shred the chicken finely. Add to the bowl and stir until the chicken is evenly distributed. Taste and add more hot sauce to achieve your preferred spiciness.

Transfer the dip to an oven-safe dish or cast-iron skillet. Sprinkle the remaining ½ cup cheddar evenly over the top. Bake until the dip is hot and bubbly and the cheese on top is melted and slightly browned, 20 to 25 minutes. If you like, further brown the cheese topping on the broil setting for 1 or 2 minutes.

Serve with tortilla chips, celery sticks, and/or carrot sticks.

Famous Gridiron Nine-Layer Dip

Here's a recipe that's been in our family ever since we can remember. For us, football-watching parties aren't a party without this multilayer dip. The bean-dip layer is earthy and robust, the cheese layer is forceful and flavorful, and the olives add a much-needed salty, briny tang. Add to that the "magic layers" of sour cream and taco seasoning, plus guacamole, pico de gallo, lettuce, tomato, and tender tasty bites of green onion, and you're on your way to tailgate goodness. **—RACHEL**

Serves 6 to 8

1 (16-ounce) can bean dip

1½ cups sour cream

2 tablespoons taco seasoning

3 ripe avocados, halved, pitted, and peeled

¼ teaspoon fresh lemon juice

¼ teaspoon garlic powder

¼ teaspoon kosher salt

¼ teaspoon freshly cracked black pepper

1½ to 2 cups freshly shredded cheddar cheese

Fresh pico de gallo, to taste

1 cup shredded romaine lettuce

1 (14.5-ounce) can diced tomatoes

1 small (2.25-ounce) can sliced black olives (about ⅓ cup), drained

⅓ cup sliced green onions, both green and white parts

Fritos Scoops or other sturdy dippers, for serving

Spread the bean dip in a 9 × 12-inch casserole dish.

In a small bowl, stir together the sour cream and taco seasoning until smooth. Spread evenly over the beans.

Add the avocado, lemon juice, garlic powder, salt, and pepper to another bowl. Mash until a guacamole-like consistency is reached, then spread in an even layer over the sour cream.

Sprinkle the cheddar over the guacamole, then top with the pico de gallo, lettuce, diced tomatoes, black olives, and green onions, in that order. Serve with a basket of your preferred dippers (see Coach's Corner).

COACH'S CORNER

Our dip can be served cold or at room temperature, making it the perfect snack for a barbecue, picnic, or tailgate.

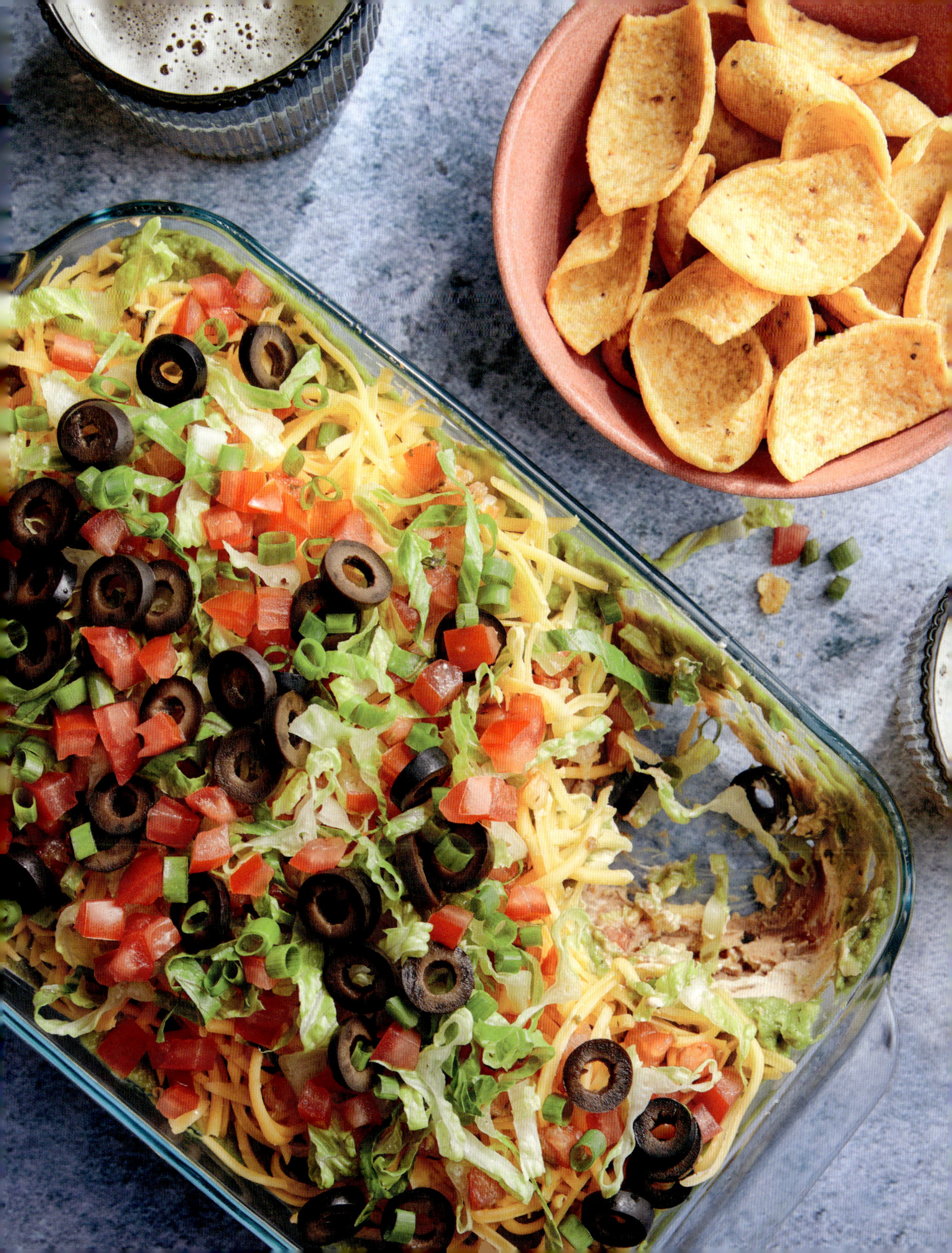

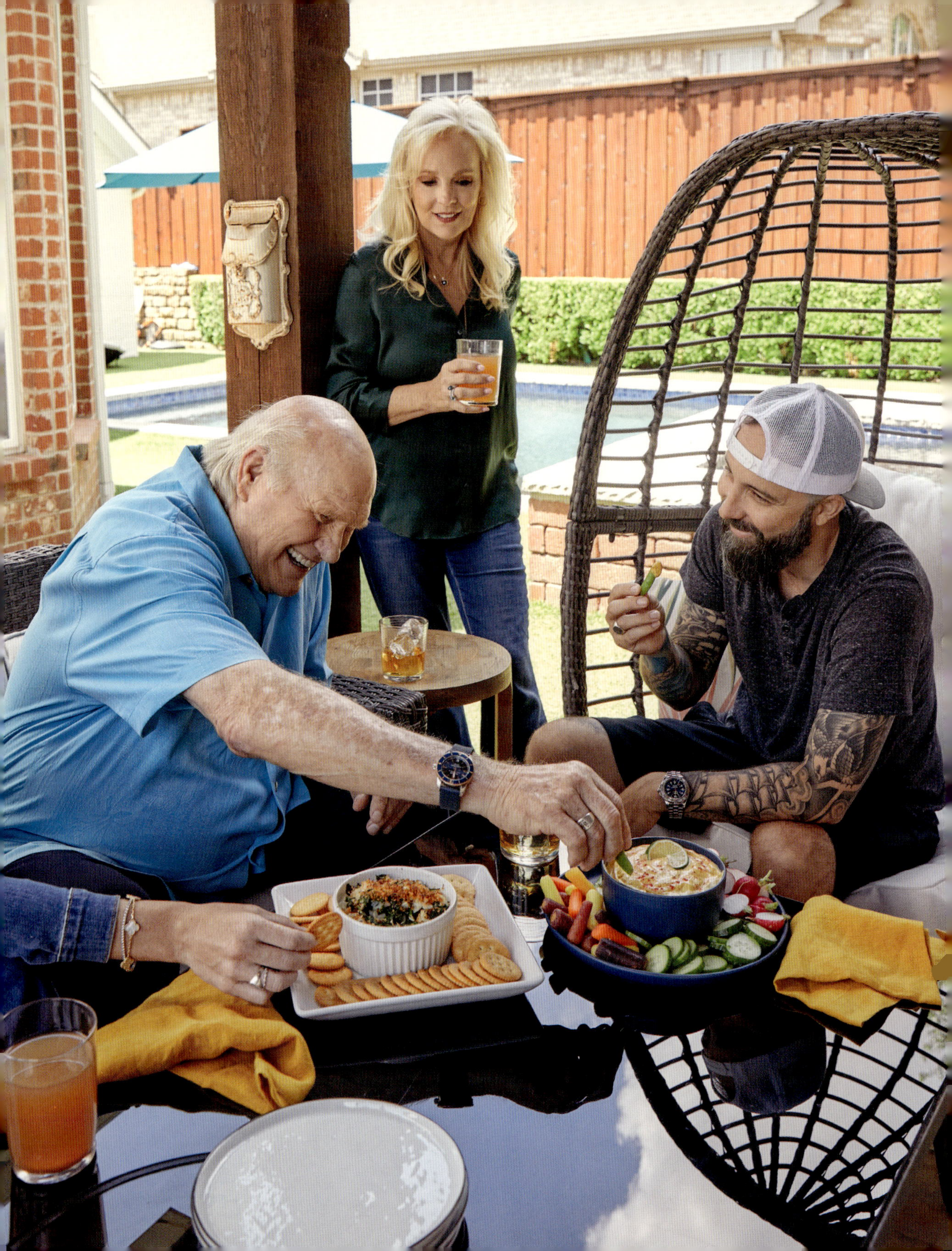

Missouri Crab Grass Dip

One thing about us: We always like to have plenty of good food for everyone. The Missouri Crab Grass Dip is Tammy's spin on a traditional crab dip, named after the crabgrass that grew outside her window growing up in Missouri. —**TERRY AND TAMMY**

Serves 10 to 12

½ cup (1 stick) unsalted butter

½ cup chopped white or yellow onion

1 teaspoon chopped fresh garlic

1 (10-ounce) package frozen chopped spinach, cooked and drained

8 ounces fresh crab meat (about 1 cup)

¾ cup freshly grated Parmesan cheese

½ cup seasoned breadcrumbs

Ritz crackers, for serving

Preheat the oven to broil. Grease a 8 × 8 × 2-inch Pyrex dish (or similar) and set aside.

Melt the butter in a medium skillet over medium-high heat. Add the onion and garlic and sauté until the onion is translucent, 2 to 3 minutes. Add the spinach, crab, and Parmesan. Stir until combined and hot, about 4 minutes. Transfer the mixture to the prepared dish and sprinkle the top evenly with the breadcrumbs. Place under the broiler until golden brown, about 4 minutes. Serve hot with crackers.

Hawaiian Summer Tuna Fish Dip

When the kids were young, Terry and I would take them to Hawaii during their summer vacations. Terry, who had the summers off before returning to football in the fall, fell in love with the tropical islands. Hawaii is still our favorite place to visit. Inspired by one of the islands' tuna fish dips, this fresh dip that Rachel likes to make is crisp and crunchy, and the touch of salt on the Ritz crackers really brings out the flavors. If this doesn't take you to Hawaii, you're not going. —TAMMY

Serves 6 to 8

5 (5-ounce) cans water-packed tuna, drained (see Coach's Corner)

½ cup mayonnaise

⅓ cup finely chopped celery (about 1 rib)

2 tablespoons minced red onion

2 tablespoons sweet pickle relish

1 tablespoon fresh lemon juice

1 clove garlic, minced

2 hard-boiled large eggs, peeled and chopped

1 (4-ounce) jar sliced pimentos, drained

1 (2.25-ounce) can sliced black olives, drained (about ⅓ cup)

Kosher salt and freshly cracked black pepper, to taste

Ritz crackers, for serving

Break the tuna into fine pieces, and add to a large mixing bowl. Add the mayonnaise, celery, onion, relish, lemon juice, garlic, eggs, pimentos, and olives. Toss until combined and season with salt and pepper. Refrigerate until chilled. Serve cold with crackers.

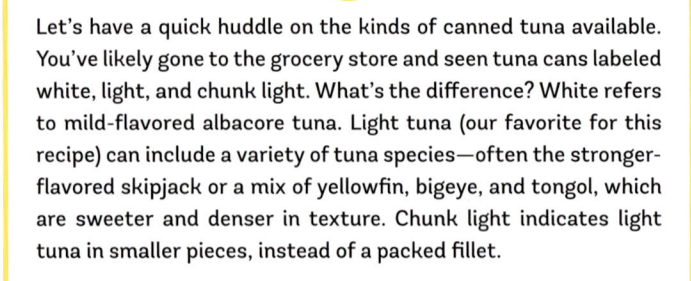

COACH'S CORNER

Let's have a quick huddle on the kinds of canned tuna available. You've likely gone to the grocery store and seen tuna cans labeled white, light, and chunk light. What's the difference? White refers to mild-flavored albacore tuna. Light tuna (our favorite for this recipe) can include a variety of tuna species—often the stronger-flavored skipjack or a mix of yellowfin, bigeye, and tongol, which are sweeter and denser in texture. Chunk light indicates light tuna in smaller pieces, instead of a packed fillet.

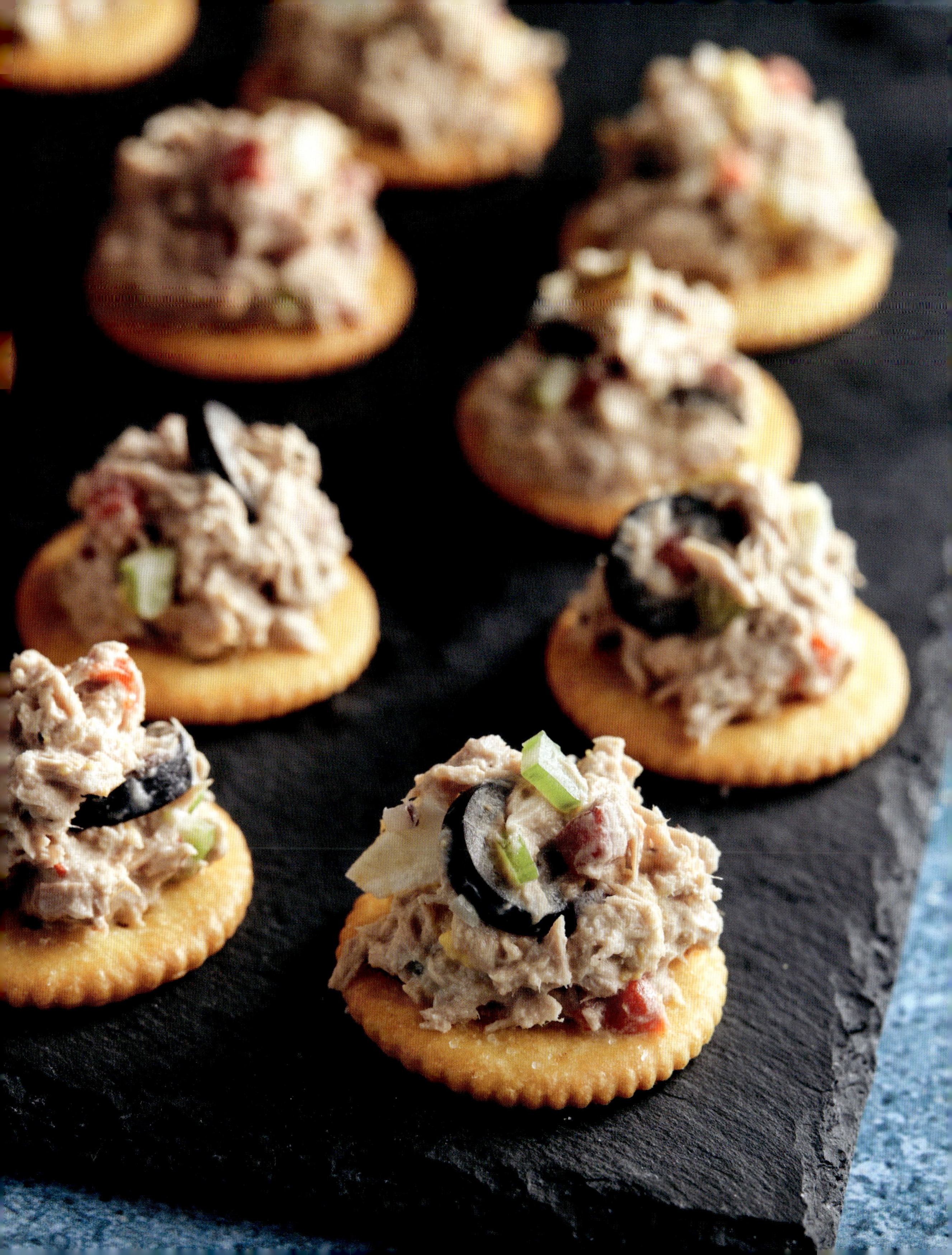

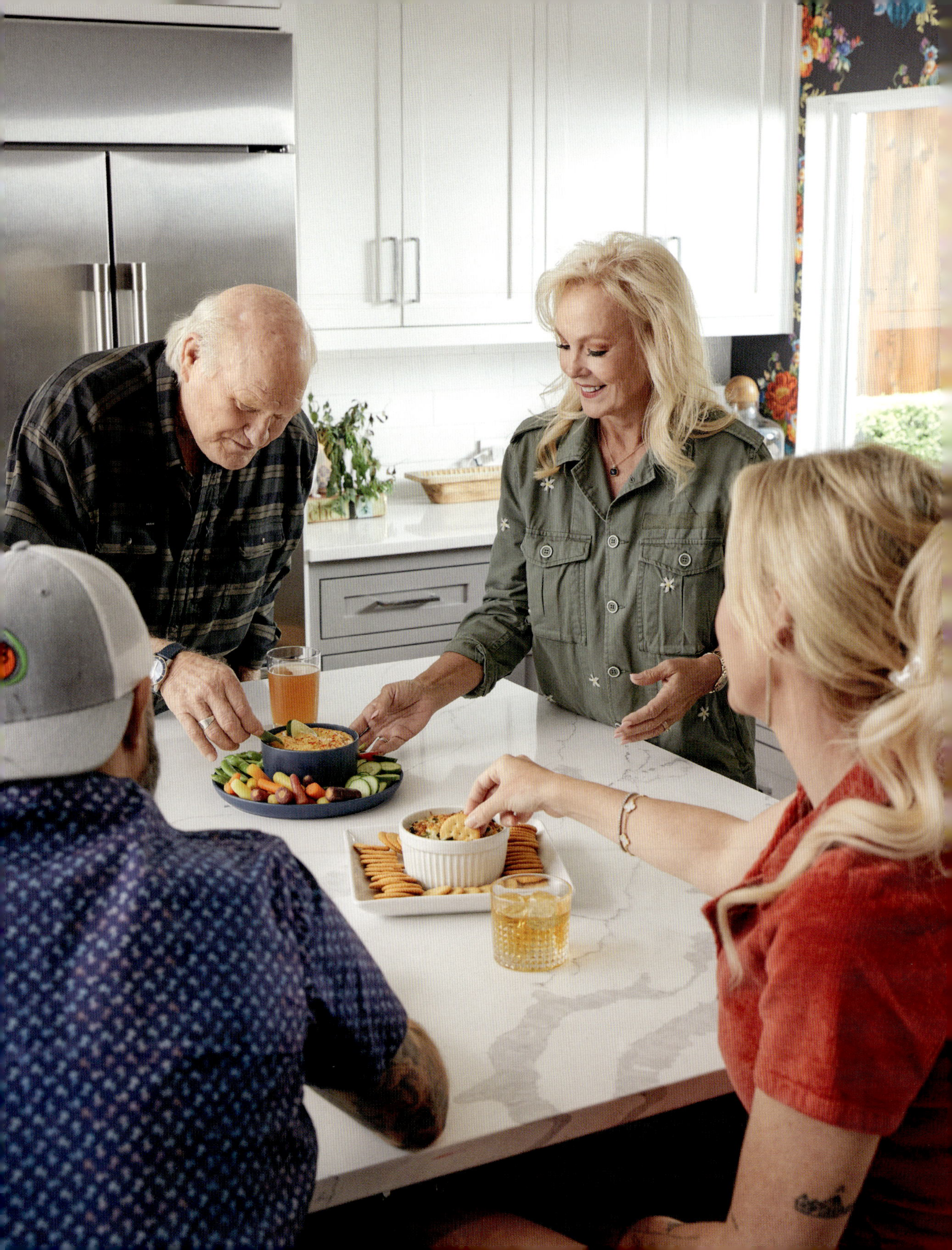

Sriracha Curry Dip

When we're hosting a gathering, we'll make this dip to kick off the fun. Thanks to a touch of spice and a dash of curry powder, this recipe is another crowd-pleaser. Serve it with the crispy fresh vegetables, or with Ritz crackers. —TERRY AND TAMMY

Serves 8 to 10

2 cups mayonnaise

¼ cup sriracha (or your favorite hot chili sauce)

2 tablespoons fresh lime juice

1 tablespoon white vinegar

1½ tablespoons curry powder

1 teaspoon paprika

1 teaspoon ground cumin

½ teaspoon kosher salt

¼ teaspoon freshly cracked black pepper

Sprinkle of paprika, for serving

Lime wheel and fresh vegetables, such as baby carrots, snap peas, and cucumber slices, for serving

In a medium bowl, stir together the mayonnaise, sriracha, lime juice, vinegar, curry powder, paprika, cumin, salt, and pepper until combined. Cover and refrigerate for at least 3 hours to allow the flavors to meld.

Transfer to a serving bowl and top the dip with a sprinkle of paprika and a lime wheel. Serve with fresh vegetables.

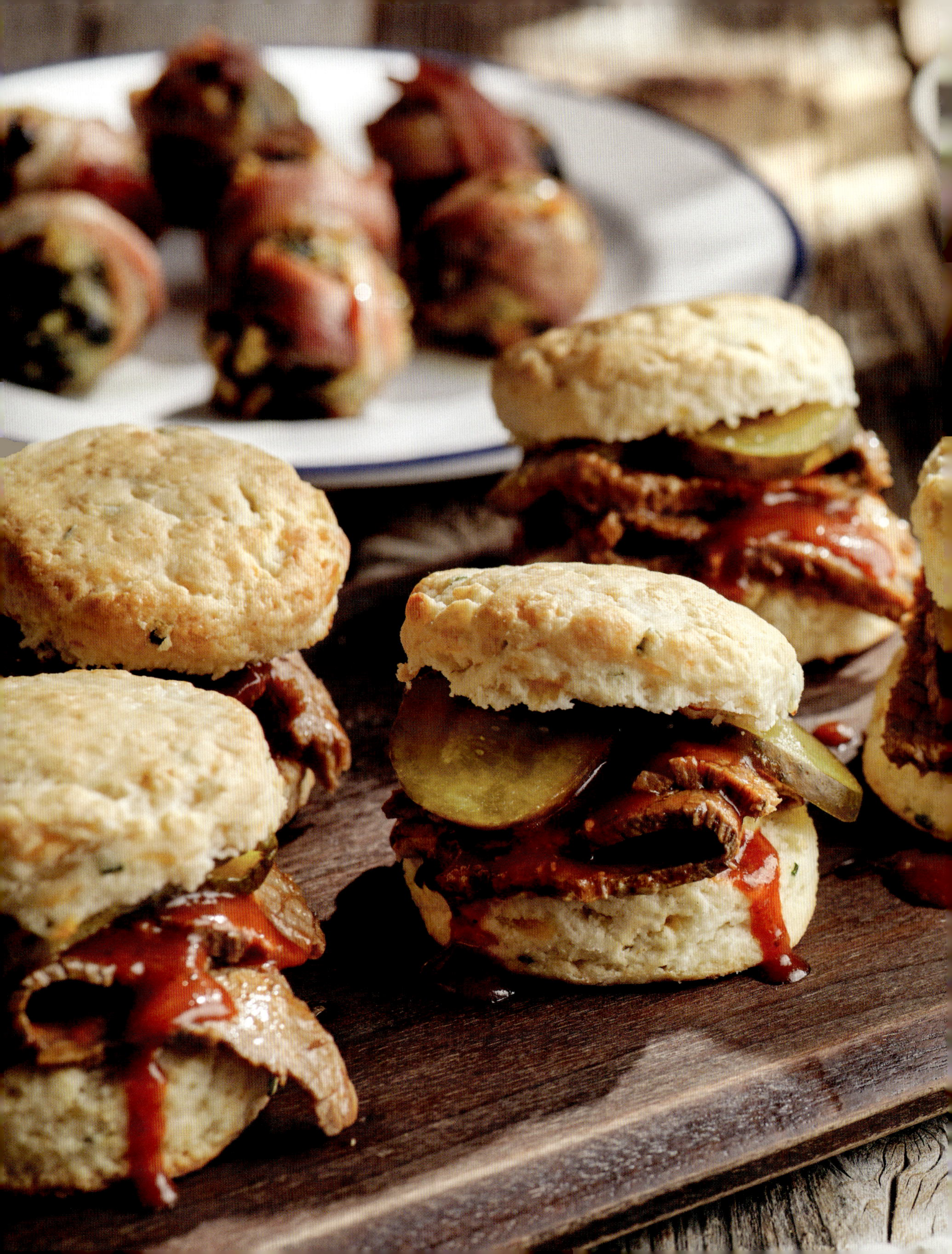

3 // Grilling and Smoking

Finger-Lickin' Barbecue
Bourbon Chicken Wings

Garlic Shrimp, Cheddar, and Bacon
Phyllo Cups

Asian-Inspired Sticky-Finger Ribs

Juicy Braised Korean Short Ribs

Smoked Maple-Bourbon Pork Belly Bites

Spicy Pork Canoes
with Cilantro Sour Cream

Spinach Bacon Sports Balls

Loaded Wagyu Hot Dogs

Bison Burgers with Balsamic Glazed
Onions and Hot Honey Mustard

Brisket, Bacon, and Jalapeño Burgers

Smoked Brisket Sliders
with Homemade Biscuits

Bradshaw Bourbon Barbecue Sauce

Grilled Tomahawk Steak
with Chimichurri

COOKOUTS ON THE BRADSHAWS' BACK DECK ARE LEGENDARY. DURING the hot Texas summers before Terry gets ready for the upcoming football season, the whole crew gathers to fire up the grill and let the good times roll. Envision a sunny day with the smell of charcoal in the air, Terry flipping Bison Burgers with Balsamic Glazed Onions and Hot Honey Mustard (page 132) while Noah's tending to his secret weapon: perfectly smoked Spicy Pork Canoes with Cilantro Sour Cream (page 127).

As the day unfolds, the table fills with more crowd-pleasers like our Finger-Lickin' Barbecue Bourbon Chicken Wings (page 114) and Spinach Bacon Sports Balls (page 128), which are perfect for snacking between rounds of horseshoes. And of course, the grill wouldn't be complete without a few slabs of our Asian-Inspired Sticky-Finger Ribs (page 118), slow-cooked until they're falling off the bone.

Just when you think the grill has done its job, out comes the massive Grilled Tomahawk Steak with Chimichurri (page 143), seared to perfection. To wash it all down, a pitcher of Gainesville Grande Margaritas (page 82) keeps everyone refreshed as the sun dips below the horizon. And be sure to round out the gathering with a few recipes from the starters and sides chapters, plus as many desserts as timing and your waistine allow!

It should go without saying that just about all of these cookout favorites would make superior tailgating fare, whether fired up in the parking lot pregame or cooked at home and reheated on-site. Whether it's the food, the laughter, or the occasional prank, our cookouts are all about enjoying good times with even better company.

Finger-Lickin' Barbecue Bourbon Chicken Wings

Honestly, who doesn't love wings when watching the big game? The balance between sweet and heat makes these a surefire hit at our parties. If you're like some of our family members and prefer a little more heat, use more hot sauce and less barbecue sauce when tossing and coating the wings. You can also serve them the way I like them, with the sauce on the side. —TERRY

Makes 14 to 16 chicken wings

Nonstick cooking spray

2 pounds fresh chicken wings (drumettes, flats, or a combination of both)

1 teaspoon smoked paprika

1 teaspoon granulated garlic

Kosher salt and freshly cracked black pepper, to taste

1 tablespoon unsalted butter, melted

½ cup Bradshaw Bourbon Barbecue Sauce (page 141)

¼ cup Chef Noah's Hawaiian Chili Water (optional) (see Coach's Corner)

Ranch dressing and celery sticks, for serving

Preheat the oven to 450°F. Lightly grease a rimmed baking sheet with nonstick cooking spray.

Add the chicken wings, paprika, and granulated garlic to a large bowl. Toss to combine and season with salt and pepper.

Transfer the seasoned wings to the prepared baking sheet and spread out in a single layer. Bake until the wings reach the desired level of crispiness, about 20 minutes. Ensure the wings reach an internal temperature of at least 165°F.

Stir to combine the melted butter, barbecue sauce, and chili water, if using, in a small bowl.

Place the baked wings in a large bowl and pour half the barbecue sauce mixture over them. Toss until the wings are well coated. Lightly grease the baking sheet with more nonstick cooking spray, transfer the wings back to the baking sheet, and bake for an additional 10 minutes, or until cooked through. Remove the wings and return them to the bowl. Toss the wings with the remaining barbecue sauce mixture until well coated. Serve with a side of ranch dressing and celery sticks.

COACH'S CORNER

Chili pepper water, which is quite popular in Hawaii, is traditionally made with red chili peppers, water, and salt. Noah likes it so much he created his own version and now sells it under the label Chef Noah's Hawaiian Chili Water, which you can order online at www.chefnoahhester.com. For this chicken wing recipe, don't fret if you can't get your hands on chili pepper water. Simply add some Frank's RedHot sauce if you like. You'll still win at your cookout or tailgate.

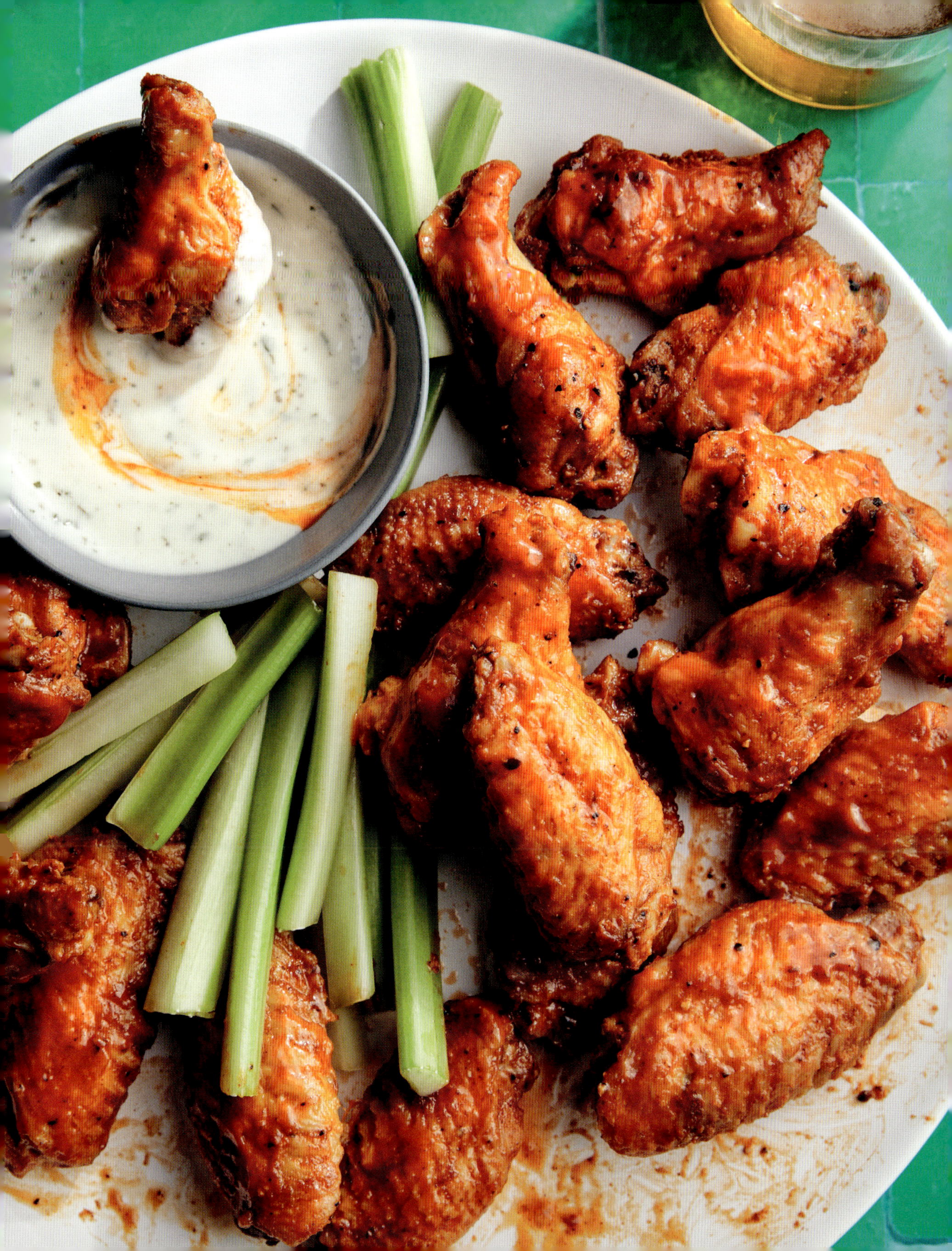

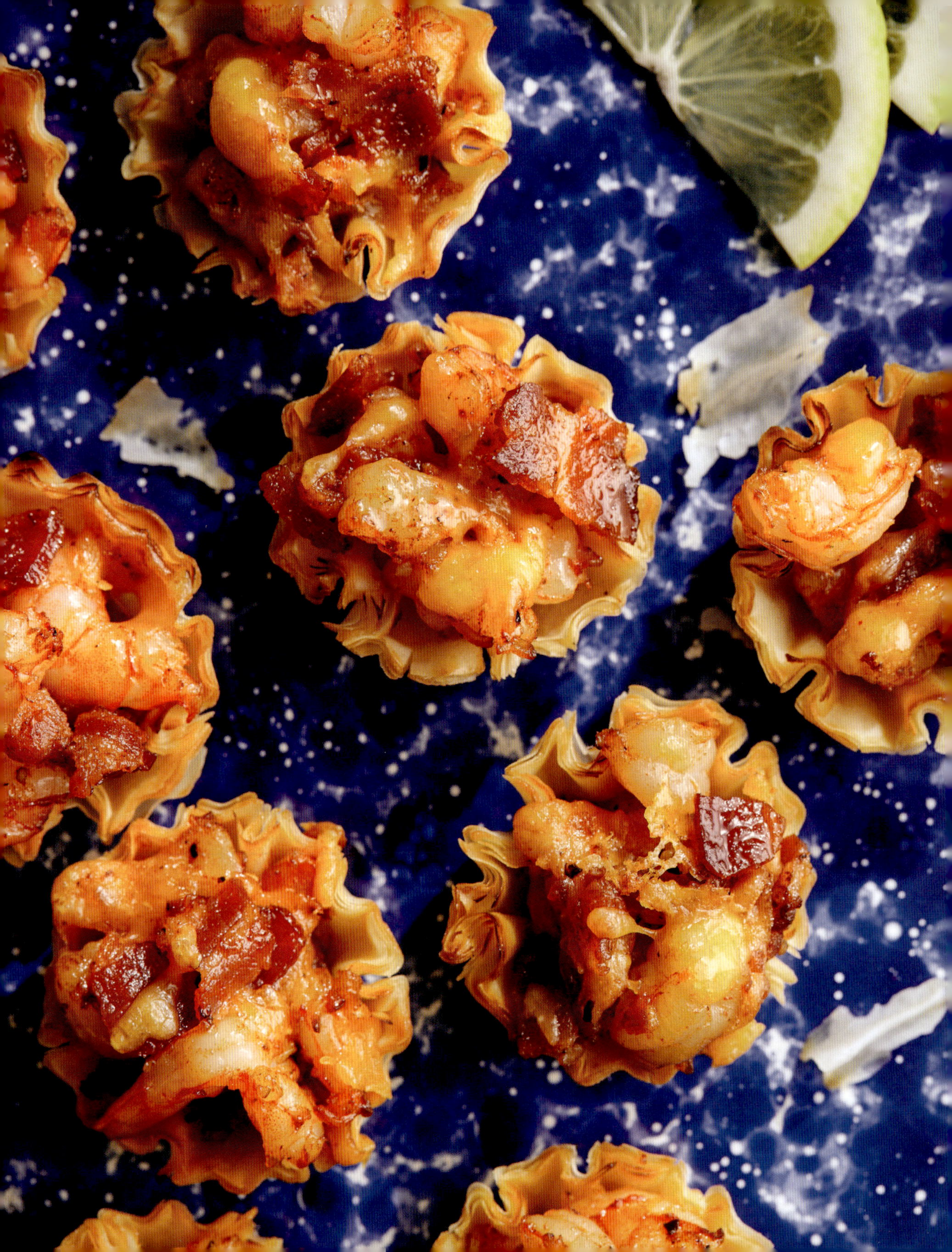

Garlic Shrimp, Cheddar, and Bacon Phyllo Cups

This delicious favorite of mine is actually a fluke. With little time to prepare for a party one night, I searched our kitchen and found some shrimp, bacon, garlic, cheddar, and a package of phyllo cups in the freezer. With a hope and a prayer, I assembled the ingredients into this recipe, popped them in the oven, and they were an enormous hit. Now I'm expected to arrive at any Bradshaw cookout with a platter of these delicious morsels. —LACEY

Makes 15 shrimp cups

1 pound raw large (31/40) shrimp, peeled and deveined, tails removed (see Coach's Corner)

1 teaspoon smoked paprika

Kosher salt and freshly cracked black pepper, to taste

8 slices bacon

3 garlic cloves, minced

1 tablespoon olive oil, if needed

1 cup shredded cheddar cheese

1 package (15-count) frozen phyllo cups, thawed

Half of 1 lemon

Preheat the oven according to the phyllo cups' package instructions (typically 350°F). Line a rimmed baking sheet with parchment paper.

Pat the shrimp dry and chop them into small pieces. Add to a bowl and season with the smoked paprika, salt, and pepper. Set aside.

Cook the bacon in a skillet over medium heat until crisp, 3 to 4 minutes. Use tongs to remove the cooked bacon, leaving the grease in the pan, and crumble the slices into a small bowl. Set aside.

Add the garlic to the skillet with the bacon grease. If there's not enough bacon grease to cook the garlic and shrimp, add the olive oil. Cook the garlic over medium heat until fragrant, about 30 seconds. Add the seasoned shrimp and sauté for 2 minutes. Add the crumbled bacon to the skillet and toss everything together to combine. Sprinkle the cheddar over the top. When the cheddar is partly melted and coats the shrimp and bacon, remove the skillet from the heat.

Arrange the phyllo cups on the lined baking sheet. Spoon some of the shrimp mixture into each cup, distributing evenly. Bake the filled phyllo cups until golden brown, 12 to 15 minutes. Let cool slightly. Squeeze a little fresh lemon juice over each cup and serve.

COACH'S CORNER

You've likely seen shrimp at your local supermarket with numbers like 51/60, 41/50, and 31/35. When you buy shrimp, remember this good rule of thumb: The smaller the numbers, the bigger the shrimp, as these numbers indicate the number of shrimp that make up one pound. If there are 51 to 60 shrimp per pound, they are considered small shrimp, 41 to 50 shrimp per pound are medium, and 31 to 35 shrimp per pound are large. There's also jumbo (16 to 20 per pound) and even bigger sizes, the largest being extra colossal (fewer than 10 per pound).

Asian-Inspired Sticky-Finger Ribs

Kick off your tailgate right by starting with these easy ribs that have the perfect balance of sweet, savory, and umami flavors along with a sticky glaze that makes them incredibly mouthwatering. Asian ingredients like these, and those in the Juicy Braised Korean Short Ribs (page 123), can bring an exciting new twist to some of your old standbys! —**NOAH AND LACEY**

Serves 10 to 14

MARINADE AND RIBS

½ cup soy sauce

¼ cup hoisin sauce

¼ cup honey
(see Coach's Corner)

2 tablespoons natural rice vinegar

2 tablespoons grated fresh ginger

2 garlic cloves, minced

½ teaspoon Chinese five-spice powder

Kosher salt and freshly cracked black pepper, to taste

2 racks baby back ribs (about 7 pounds total)

GLAZE

¼ cup hoisin sauce

2 tablespoons honey
(see Coach's Corner)

1 tablespoon soy sauce

1 teaspoon sesame oil

Sliced green onions, green and white parts, plus sesame seeds, for serving

To make the marinade and ribs: Stir together the soy sauce, hoisin, honey, rice vinegar, ginger, garlic, five-spice powder, salt, and pepper in a medium bowl.

Remove the ribs' silver skin—the thin white membrane on the bony side of the ribs—if it hasn't been previously removed. To do so, slide a kitchen knife under one edge of the silver skin to loosen it. Grip the loosened skin with a paper towel for a better hold, and slowly peel the skin away from the meat. The silver skin will often come off easily in one piece.

Place both racks of ribs in a large resealable bag or a shallow dish. Pour the marinade over the ribs, making sure they are well coated. For the best flavor, seal the bag or cover the dish and refrigerate for at least 4 hours, or overnight.

Preheat the outdoor grill to medium-high heat (375°F). (See Grilling and Smoking—a Bradshaw Family Primer, page 27).

Remove the ribs from the marinade, allowing any excess to drip off. Reserve the marinade for basting.

Place the ribs, bone-side down, on the preheated grill and cook over direct heat for 20 minutes. Baste with the reserved marinade.

To make the glaze: While the ribs cook, make the glaze by combining the hoisin sauce, honey, soy sauce, and sesame oil in a small bowl.

Turn the ribs over and baste again. Grill, meat side down, for 20 minutes. Brush the ribs with the glaze on both sides and continue to cook for another 20 minutes, turning the ribs and basting with the glaze a couple times to create a sticky, flavorful coating. When the ribs are tender and have a nice char, after another 30 to 40 minutes of cooking, remove from the grill and let them rest for several minutes. Slice the ribs between the bones and arrange on a platter. Garnish with sliced green onions and a sprinkle of sesame seeds.

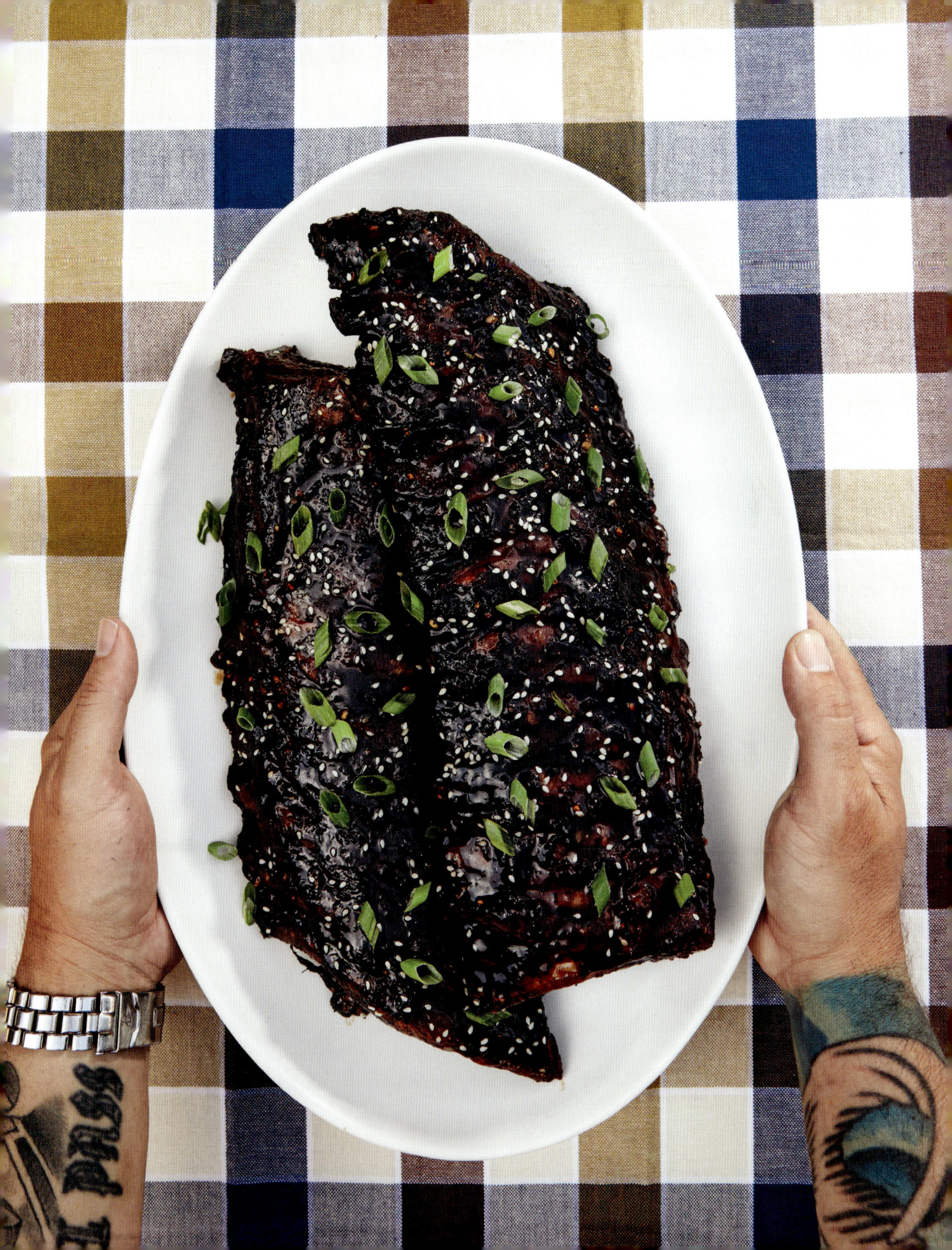

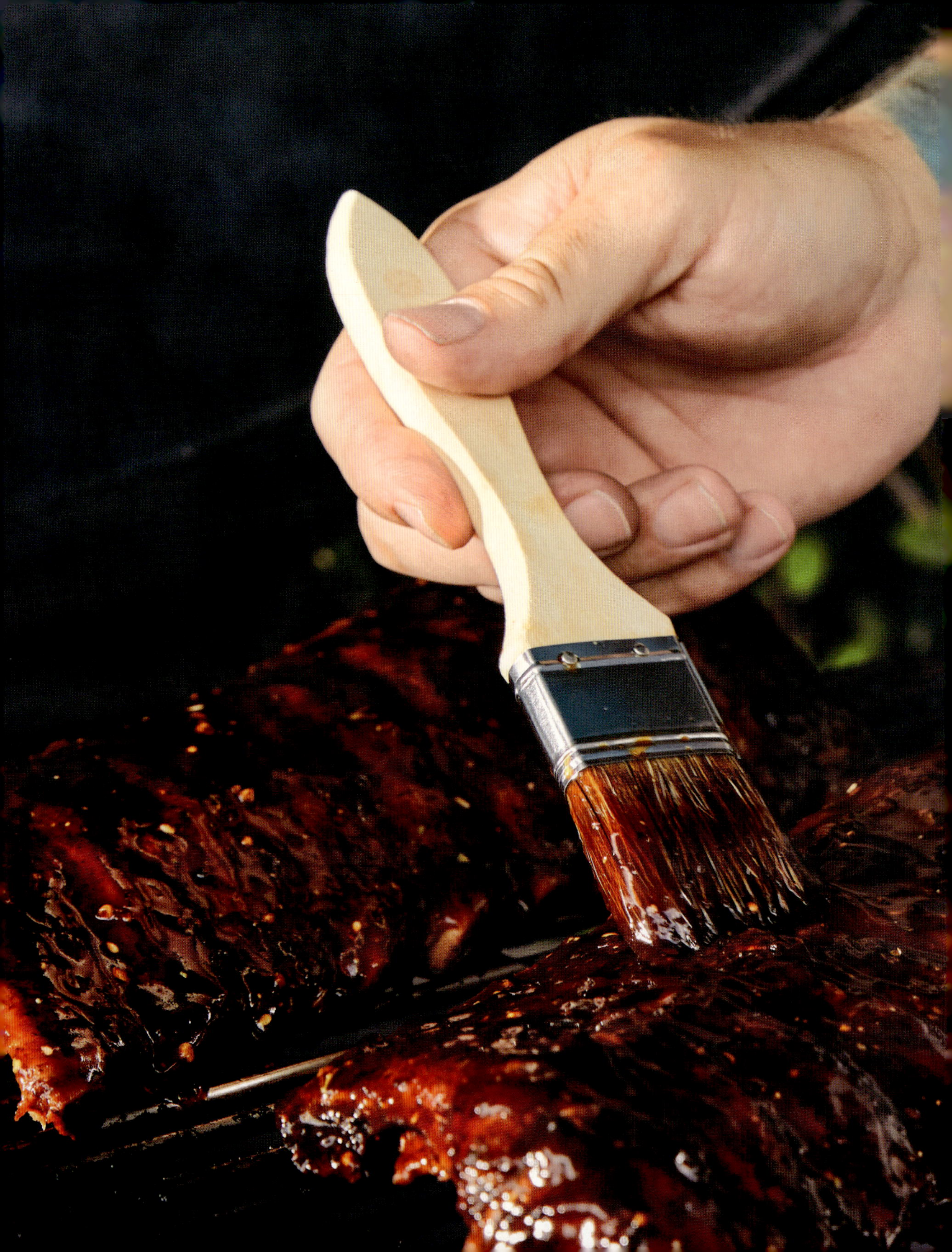

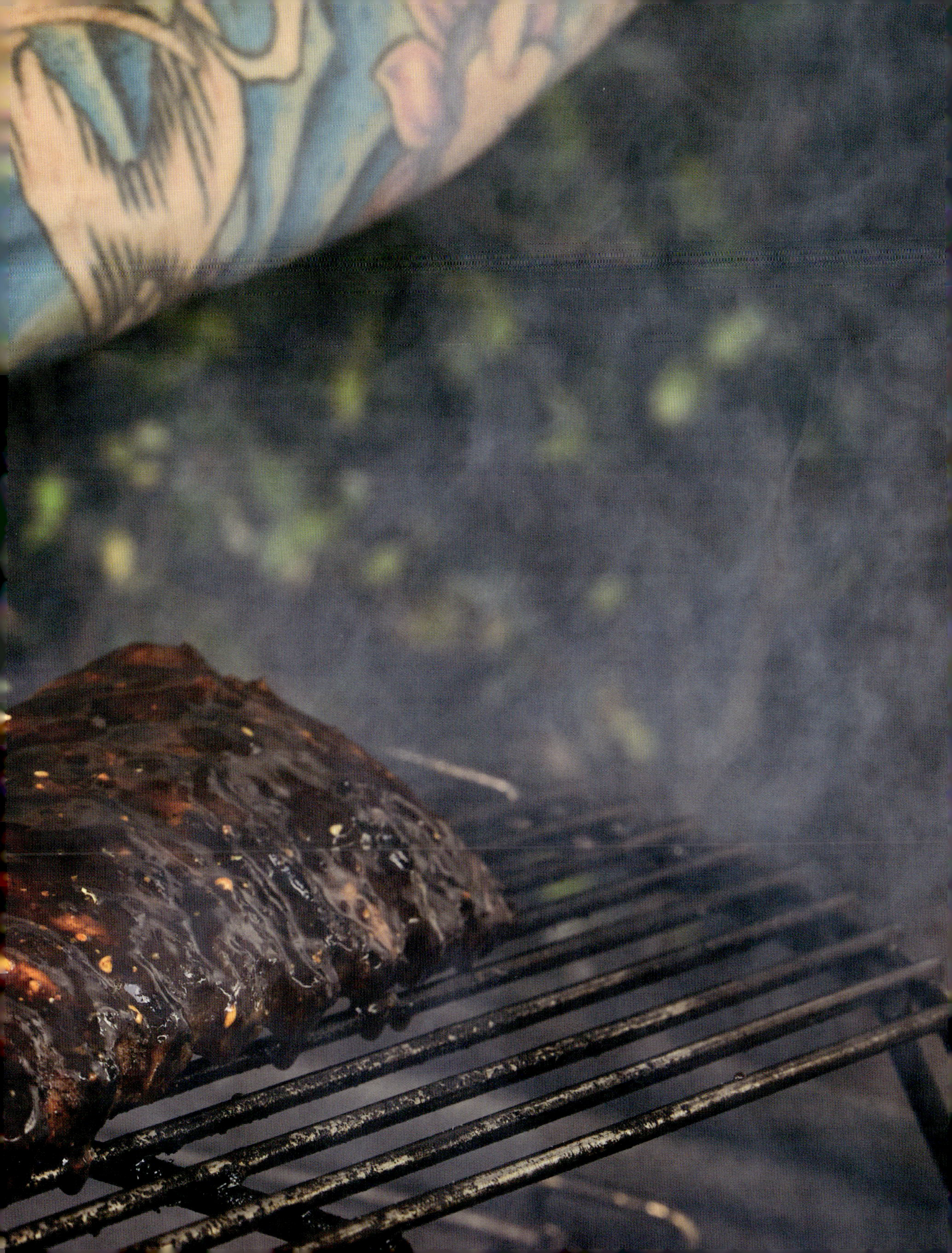

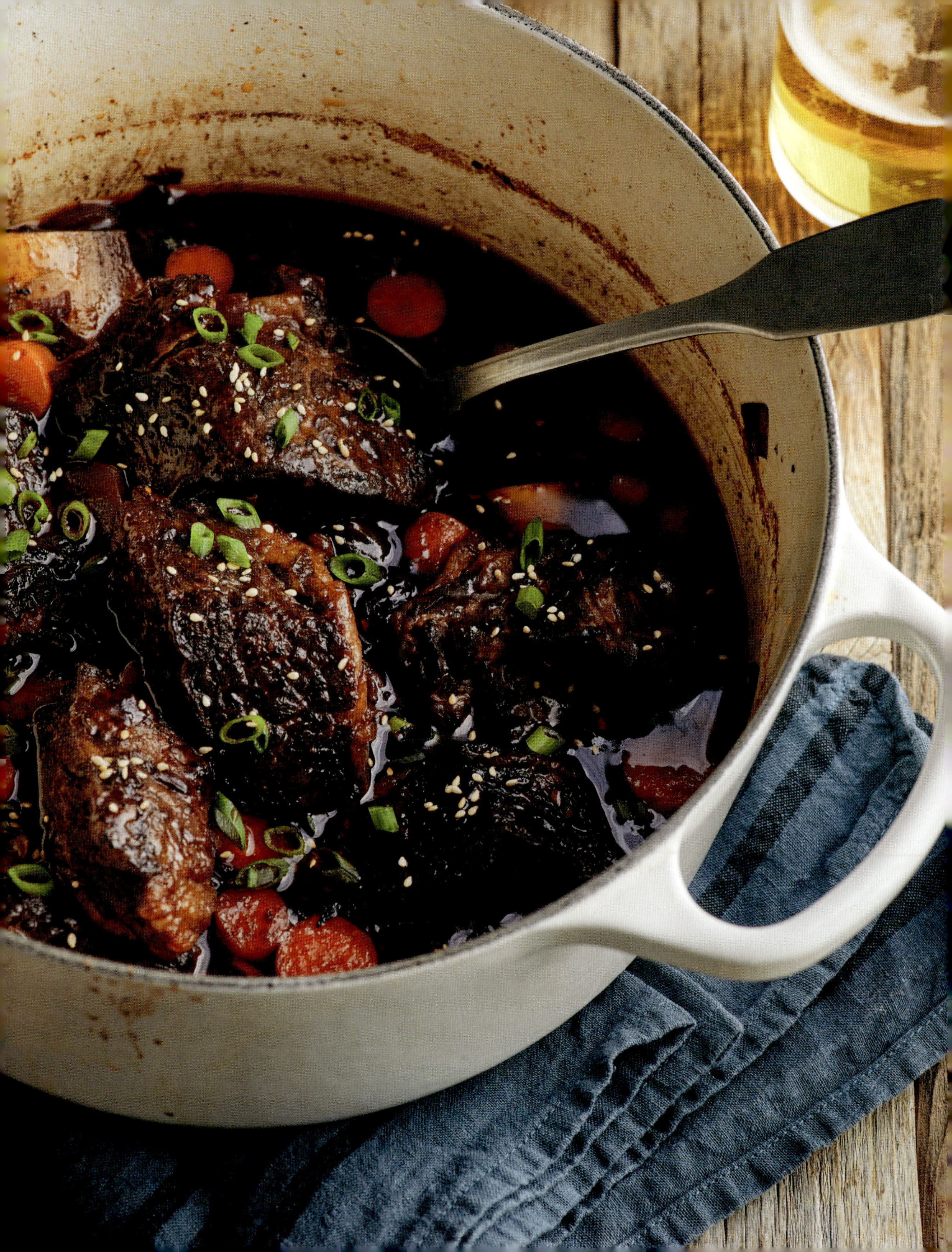

Juicy Braised Korean Short Ribs

Korean short ribs aren't only for game days. Serve them when you want someone to fall in love with you—that's what happened to me. I made this dish for Lacey early in our relationship, and she still admits it was short ribs that sealed the deal. The tender, succulent ribs are marinated with a sweet-savory flavor profile and slow-cooked to perfection. —**NOAH**

Serves 4 to 6

3 pounds beef short ribs

Freshly cracked black pepper, to taste

2 tablespoons vegetable oil

1 large yellow onion, diced

3 carrots, peeled and sliced

1 cup beef broth

1 cup soy sauce

½ cup mirin

¼ cup natural rice vinegar

2 tablespoons hoisin sauce

2 tablespoons gochujang (red chili paste) (see Coach's Corner)

2 tablespoons packed brown sugar

2 tablespoons toasted sesame oil

2 tablespoons grated fresh ginger

1 star anise pod or a pinch of Chinese five-spice powder

4 garlic cloves, minced

2 green onions, green and white parts, sliced, for serving

Sesame seeds, for serving

Cooked jasmine rice, for serving (optional)

Preheat the oven to 325°F.

Season the short ribs with pepper.

Add the vegetable oil to a large oven-safe pot or Dutch oven and heat over medium-high heat. Working in batches to avoid overcrowding the pot, add the ribs a few at a time and sear on all sides until browned, about 8 minutes per batch. Remove the seared ribs and set aside. To the same pot, add the yellow onion and carrots. Sauté until the onion is soft and translucent, about 5 minutes.

While the onion is sautéing, make the braising liquid. In a large measuring cup, stir together the beef broth, soy sauce, mirin, rice vinegar, hoisin, gochujang, brown sugar, sesame oil, ginger, and star anise until the sugar dissolves. Set aside.

When the onion starts to look translucent, add the garlic to the pot and sauté for 1 or 2 minutes. Return the seared ribs to the pot and pour the braising liquid over them. Bring the liquid to a simmer, then reduce the heat to low, cover the pot, and braise until the ribs are tender and almost falling off the bone, 2½ to 3 hours. Divide the ribs among individual plates, garnish with green onions and sesame seeds, and serve with cooked jasmine rice, if using.

COACH'S CORNER

If you like sriracha, you're going to enjoy gochujang, if you haven't tried it already. Just don't get them confused. Even though both are made from fermented red peppers, gochujang has a thicker, pastelike texture and a much more salty-umami flavor. Culturally, sriracha is used in Thai and Vietnamese cooking (Southeast Asia), and gochujang is distinctly Korean (East Asia).

Smoked Maple-Bourbon Pork Belly Bites

What's the worst thing that can happen to a quarterback? He loses his confidence. We sure don't want you losing your confidence when manning the smoker, so be sure to have your preheated smoker standing by and ready to go to make these pork belly bites before the big game kicks off. They feature a decadent glaze of bourbon and maple syrup, creating a caramelized exterior with a tender, melt-in-your-mouth interior—the result of slowly smoking the pork. **—TERRY**

Serves 12 to 14

4 tablespoons packed dark brown sugar, divided

1 tablespoon freshly cracked black pepper

1 teaspoon ground cinnamon

1 teaspoon kosher salt

5 pounds pork belly, skin removed, cut into 1-inch cubes

½ cup plus 2 ounces straight bourbon whiskey, divided

½ cup maple syrup

6 tablespoons (¾ stick) unsalted butter, cut into tablespoon-sized pieces

Preheat an outdoor smoker with hickory, mesquite, or oak to 225°F. (See Grilling and Smoking—a Bradshaw Family Primer, page 27).

Mix 2 tablespoons of the brown sugar, the pepper, cinnamon, and salt in a large bowl until combined. Add the cubed pork belly and toss to coat. Set aside.

In a small bowl, stir together ½ cup of the bourbon and the maple syrup and set aside.

When the smoker is at temperature, place the seasoned pork belly cubes on a wire rack. Smoke until the internal temperature of the pork reaches 165°F, 1½ to 2 hours (depending on your smoker). Remove the cubes from the smoker and transfer to a foil pan. Pour the bourbon-syrup mixture over the pork until well coated. Sprinkle with the remaining 2 tablespoons of brown sugar and add the pieces of butter. Cover the pan with aluminum foil.

Increase the heat of the smoker to 325°F. Return the pork in the covered pan to the smoker. Smoke for 30 minutes. If you have a smoker that doesn't reach 325°F, smoke at 225°F until tender, about 1 hour. While the pork is smoking, add the remaining 2 ounces of bourbon to a glass containing one ice cube. Sip the bourbon leisurely while the pork continues to smoke.

When the pork is tender, uncover the pan, then continue to smoke to caramelize the pork belly, about 30 minutes more, and serve.

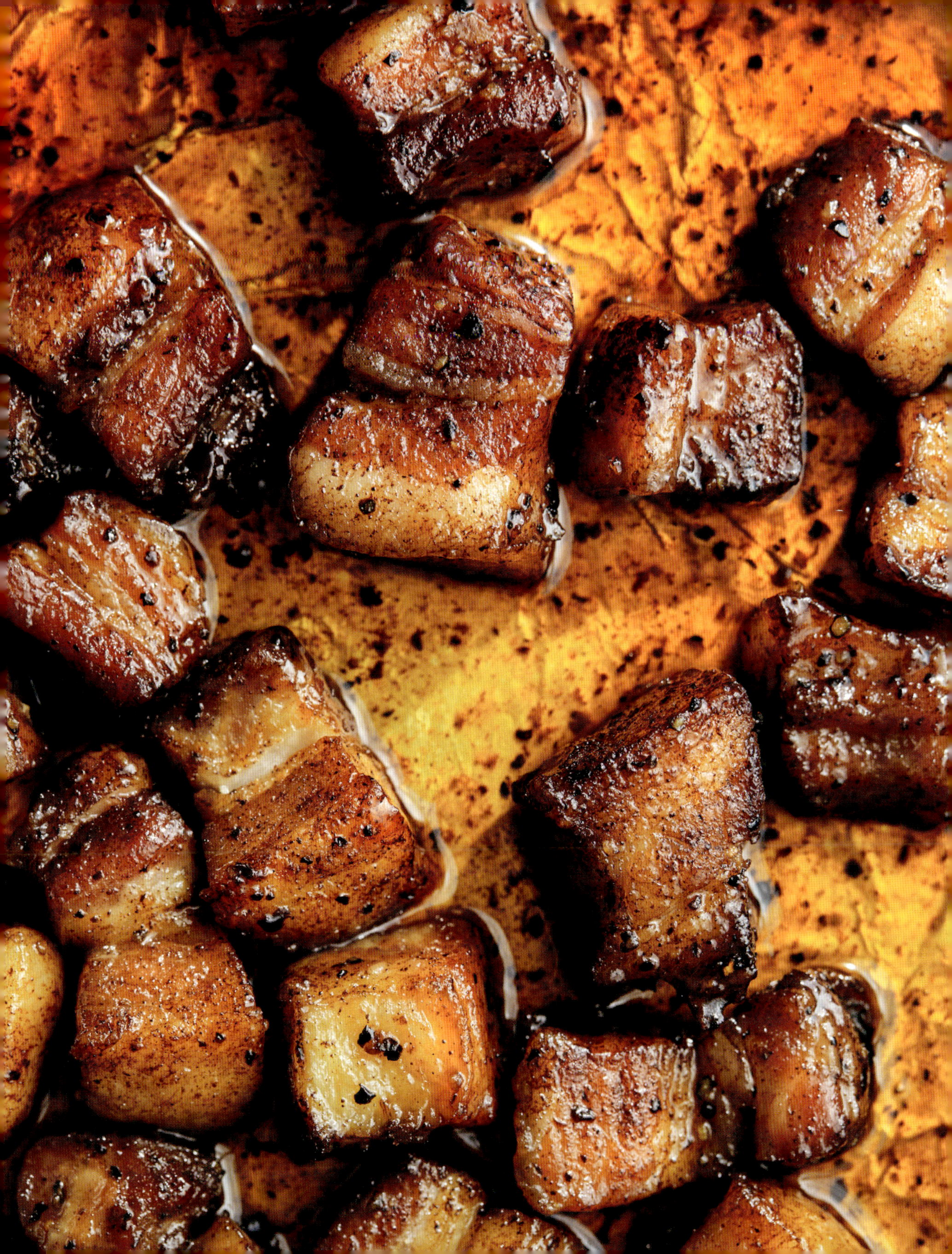

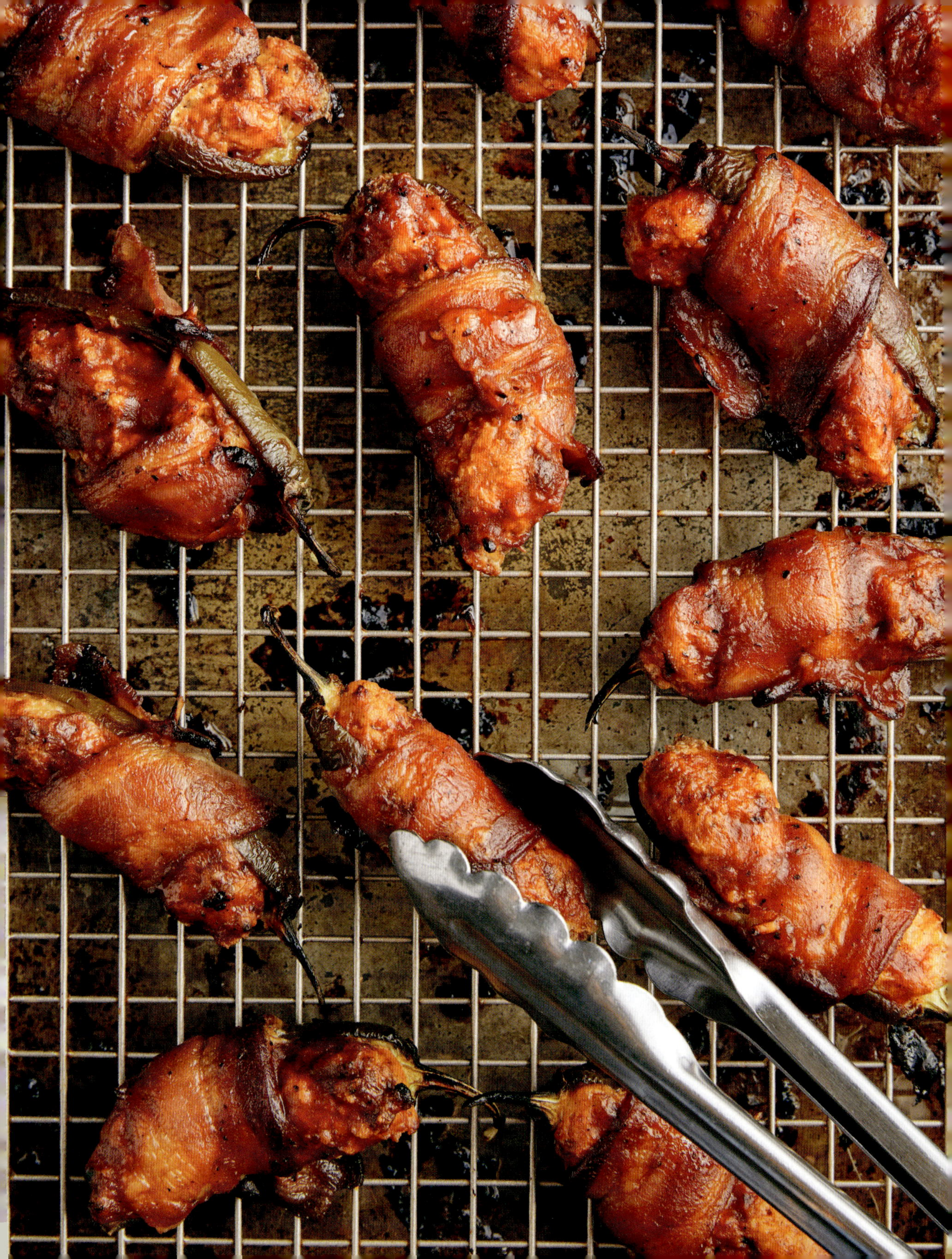

Spicy Pork Canoes with Cilantro Sour Cream

Hawaii holds a special place in my heart. Not only is it my favorite vacation spot, but Tammy and I got married in the backyard of our home on the Big Island of Hawaii. When Noah joined our family, lots of our go-to recipes got a Hawaiian twist. In Texas, these mouthwatering jalapeños stuffed with cream cheese and chorizo, wrapped in bacon, and smoked are referred to as "Texas twinkies." Noah, however, calls them "pork canoes," after Hawaii's iconic outriggers. Whatever you like to call them, dip the flavor explosions in some of our bright, cool cilantro sour cream and you'll have one heck of an appetizer come kickoff. —TERRY

Makes 24 canoes

CILANTRO SOUR CREAM
Makes 1½ cups

1½ cups sour cream

¾ cup finely chopped fresh cilantro

¼ cup fresh lime juice

1 teaspoon ground cumin

½ teaspoon kosher salt

½ teaspoon freshly cracked black pepper

SPICY PORK CANOES

1 cup whipped cream cheese

1 cup shredded Mexican cheese blend

¼ cup panko breadcrumbs

½ cup raw Mexican-style chorizo (see Coach's Corner)

¼ teaspoon kosher salt

¼ teaspoon freshly cracked black pepper

12 large jalapeños, cut in half lengthwise and seeded

12 strips bacon, cut in half lengthwise

1 cup Bradshaw Bourbon Barbecue Sauce (page 141)

To make the cilantro sour cream: Stir together the sour cream, cilantro, lime juice, cumin, salt, and pepper in a small bowl. Set aside until ready to serve.

To make the spicy pork canoes: Combine the cream cheese, Mexican cheese, panko, and chorizo in a medium bowl. Stir until well blended, then season with salt and pepper.

Fill the jalapeño halves with the cheese-chorizo mixture, then wrap each stuffed jalapeño with a half strip of bacon, securing it with a toothpick. (This will prevent the bacon from falling off during the smoking process.)

Preheat an outdoor smoker with hickory, mesquite, or oak to 225°F. (See Grilling and Smoking—a Bradshaw Family Primer, page 27).

When the smoker is at temperature, arrange the stuffed jalapeños on a wire rack and smoke for 30 minutes. If you don't have a smoker that reaches 325°F, smoke at 225°F until the bacon is fully cooked. Remove the smoked jalapeños from the smoker and increase the temperature to 325°F. When the smoker comes to temperature, brush the canoes with the barbecue sauce, return them to the smoker, and smoke until the bacon is fully cooked, about 15 minutes. Brush with additional barbecue sauce before serving with the cilantro sour cream.

COACH'S CORNER

If you prefer this dish to be a little more heart friendly, you can substitute ground turkey or chicken for the chorizo, but we recommend keeping the bacon for flavor.

Spinach Bacon Sports Balls

At first glance, our ingredient list may strike you as a little odd, but trust us, these are tailgate must-haves. Crisp bacon wrapped around spinach, cheese, stuffing, and sausage—how can you go wrong? Tammy and I like to make batches of these and store the raw, bacon-wrapped balls in the freezer. That way, when I invite my friends over for an impromptu cookout—which I do often—we can toss them on the grill or in the oven for a filling, pork-filled snack in minutes. —TERRY

Makes 40 to 45 (1-inch) balls

2 (10-ounce) packages frozen chopped spinach

½ pound bulk breakfast sausage (mild, spicy, or Mexican-style chorizo, depending on your taste)

½ cup hot water

½ cup (1 stick) unsalted butter, melted

1 (6-ounce) box Stove Top Stuffing Mix (about 2 cups)

1 cup grated Parmesan cheese

2 large eggs

1 teaspoon vegetable oil

1 pound bacon (about 14 strips), each strip sliced lengthwise into 3 narrow strips (creating 42 pieces)

Place the frozen spinach in a large skillet over medium-low heat and cover. As the spinach defrosts, use a wooden spoon to break apart the leaves to help it heat faster. Cook until tender, about 5 minutes. Drain well by pressing the spinach in a sieve or colander to extract as much water as possible, and set aside.

Return the skillet to the stove and increase the heat to medium-high. Add the sausage and cook, using a wooden spoon to break up the meat, until browned, 8 or 9 minutes. Drain the fat from the sausage and set aside.

Add the hot water and butter to a large bowl and stir to combine. Add the spinach, sausage, stuffing mix, Parmesan, eggs, and oil. Mix well. Place the mixture in the refrigerator and cool completely, about 1 hour.

Preheat the oven to 375°F. Line a baking sheet with foil and coat with nonstick cooking spray.

Remove the mixture from the refrigerator and form into balls about 1 inch in diameter. Wrap each ball with one strip of bacon and arrange on the baking sheet. Bake until the bacon is crisp, 30 to 35 minutes, turning the balls once about halfway through. Arrange on a platter and serve warm.

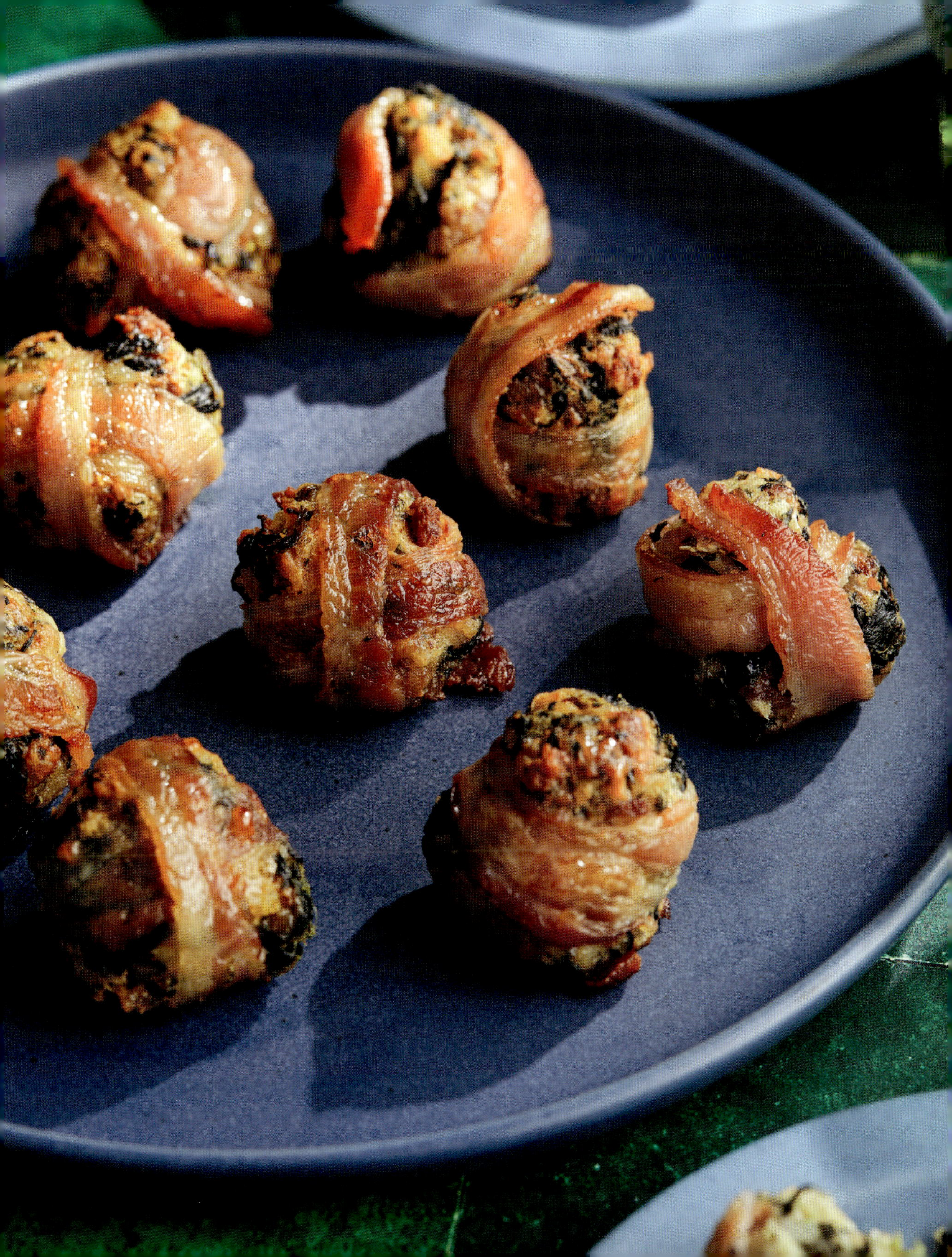

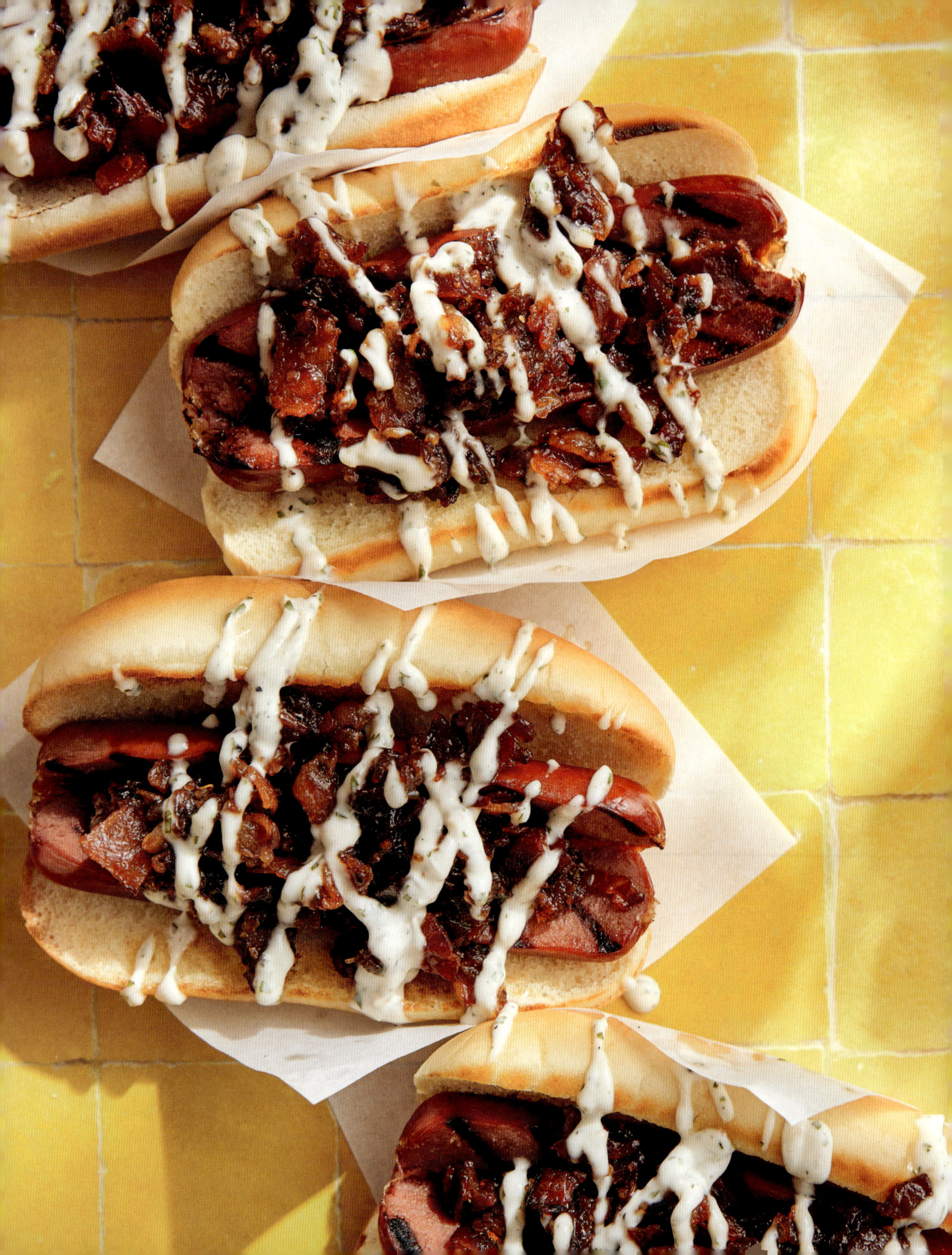

Loaded Wagyu Hot Dogs

I created this hot dog combination for our butcher shop and I'm proud to say it has become a town favorite in McKinney as well as in backyards throughout the region come Sunday. Topped with not one but two savory condiments, this comfort classic takes the humble hot dog to gourmet heights. —NOAH

Makes 4 hot dogs

BACON JAM

1 pound raw bacon, chopped

2 cups finely chopped yellow onions

3 garlic cloves, minced

½ cup packed dark brown sugar

¼ cup maple syrup

¼ cup apple cider vinegar

½ teaspoon freshly cracked black pepper

¼ teaspoon red pepper flakes (optional)

GARLIC AIOLI

1 cup mayonnaise

3 garlic cloves, minced

1 tablespoon fresh lemon juice

1 teaspoon Dijon mustard

Kosher salt and freshly cracked black pepper, to taste

2 tablespoons finely chopped fresh Italian flat-leaf parsley (optional)

4 wagyu hot dogs (see Coach's Corner)

4 hoagie rolls

To make the bacon jam: Add the chopped bacon to a large skillet and cook over medium heat until soft, not crispy, 5 to 7 minutes. Remove the excess bacon fat, leaving 1 to 2 tablespoons of fat in the pan. Add the onions and sauté until softened, 3 to 4 minutes. Add the garlic and cook until fragrant, about 1 minute. Sprinkle the brown sugar over the bacon mixture, then stir in the maple syrup and apple cider vinegar. Season with black pepper and red pepper flakes, if using. Reduce the heat to low and simmer until the mixture reaches a chutneylike consistency, about 30 minutes. Remove from the heat and allow the jam to cool slightly before transferring to an airtight container. Store in the refrigerator for up to 3 weeks.

To make the garlic aioli: Combine the mayonnaise, garlic, lemon juice, and mustard in a bowl and mix thoroughly. Season with salt and pepper. Add the parsley, if using. Cover the bowl and refrigerate for at least 30 minutes before serving.

To cook the hot dogs: Heat an outdoor grill or place a skillet over medium heat. Split the hot dogs down the middle lengthwise, being careful not to cut all the way through. Place them, cut side down, on the grill or in the skillet and cook until golden brown, 4 or 5 minutes. (Note: Use a bacon press or something heavy to keep the hot dogs flat while cooking.) Turn the hot dogs over and repeat on the other side. While the hot dogs are searing, toast the hoagie rolls on the grill or in a second skillet.

To assemble, place a seared hot dog in a toasted roll and spread a generous amount of warm bacon jam on the cut side of the hot dog. Finish with some garlic aioli and serve.

COACH'S CORNER

You're probably asking, "Where in the heck do I find Wagyu hot dogs?" Aside from Noah and Lacey's butcher shop, most grocery chains carry Hempler's or Snake River Farms' version of the gourmet dogs. Wagyu dogs are readily available online too. You can also substitute Kobe hot dogs or the classic all-beef dog.

Bison Burgers with Balsamic Glazed Onions and Hot Honey Mustard

May is National Hamburger Month, so one year Lacey and I created a special burger menu for our shop. She insisted we add this bison burger, to which I reluctantly agreed. The patrons of Hamm's Meat + Market loved the combination of balsamic vinegar–glazed onions, hot honey mustard, and Flamin' Hot Cheetos. Today it remains one of our top sellers. —NOAH

Makes 4 burgers

HOT HONEY MUSTARD

¼ cup Dijon mustard

¼ cup honey

¼ cup sriracha or other hot sauce, plus more to taste

BALSAMIC GLAZED ONIONS

1 large red onion, thickly sliced

2 tablespoons balsamic vinegar

1 tablespoon olive oil

Kosher salt, to taste

1 tablespoon packed dark brown sugar

BISON BURGERS

2 pounds ground bison

Kosher salt and freshly cracked black pepper, to taste

4 ciabatta buns

Dill pickle chips, for serving

2 cups arugula or leaf lettuce and 2 cups crushed Flamin' Hot Cheetos, for serving

To make the hot honey mustard: Sir the mustard, honey, and sriracha together in a small bowl, adjusting the spice to your desired level with additional sriracha to taste. Set aside until ready to use.

To make the balsamic glazed onions: Place the onion in a small bowl and cover with the balsamic vinegar. Let the onion soak for 30 minutes to 1 hour. Heat the oil in a medium skillet over medium heat. Add the onion and season with salt. Cook, stirring occasionally, until softened, about 5 minutes. Add the brown sugar and cook, stirring occasionally, until the onion is caramelized and glazed, 6 to 8 minutes. Remove from the heat and set aside.

To make the burgers: Prepare an outdoor grill to medium-high heat.

Divide the ground bison into four half-pound portions and shape into patties. Season both sides of the patties with salt and pepper. When the grill is at temperature, add the patties and cook to desired doneness, or 4 to 5 minutes per side for medium-rare. Remove the patties to a platter and let them rest for several minutes.

Lightly toast the ciabatta buns on the grill. For each burger, spread a generous amount of hot honey mustard on a bottom bun and add some dill pickles. Place a bison patty on top. Add a handful of arugula and some balsamic glazed onions. Sprinkle with a generous amount of crushed Hot Cheetos. Finish with the top bun and serve.

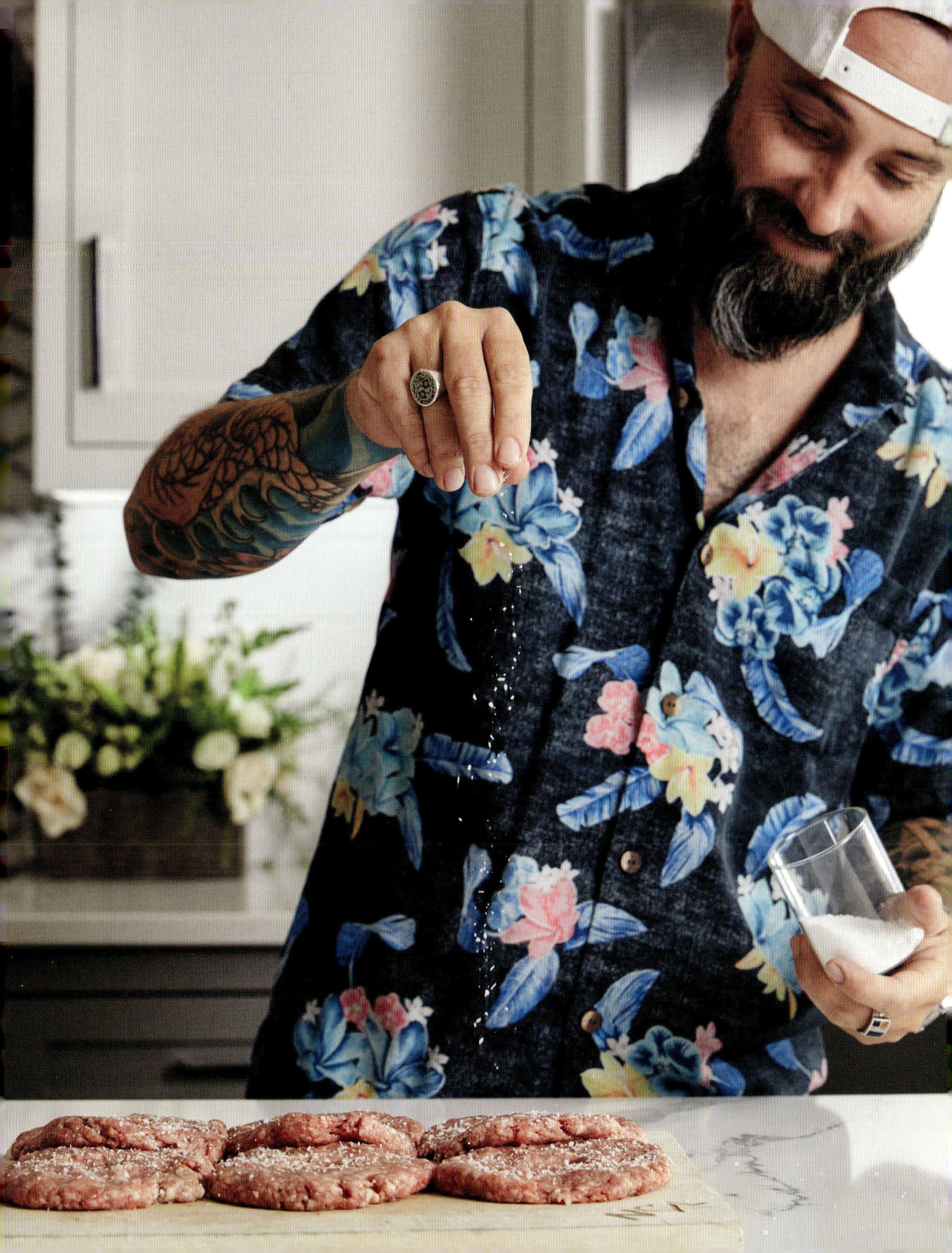

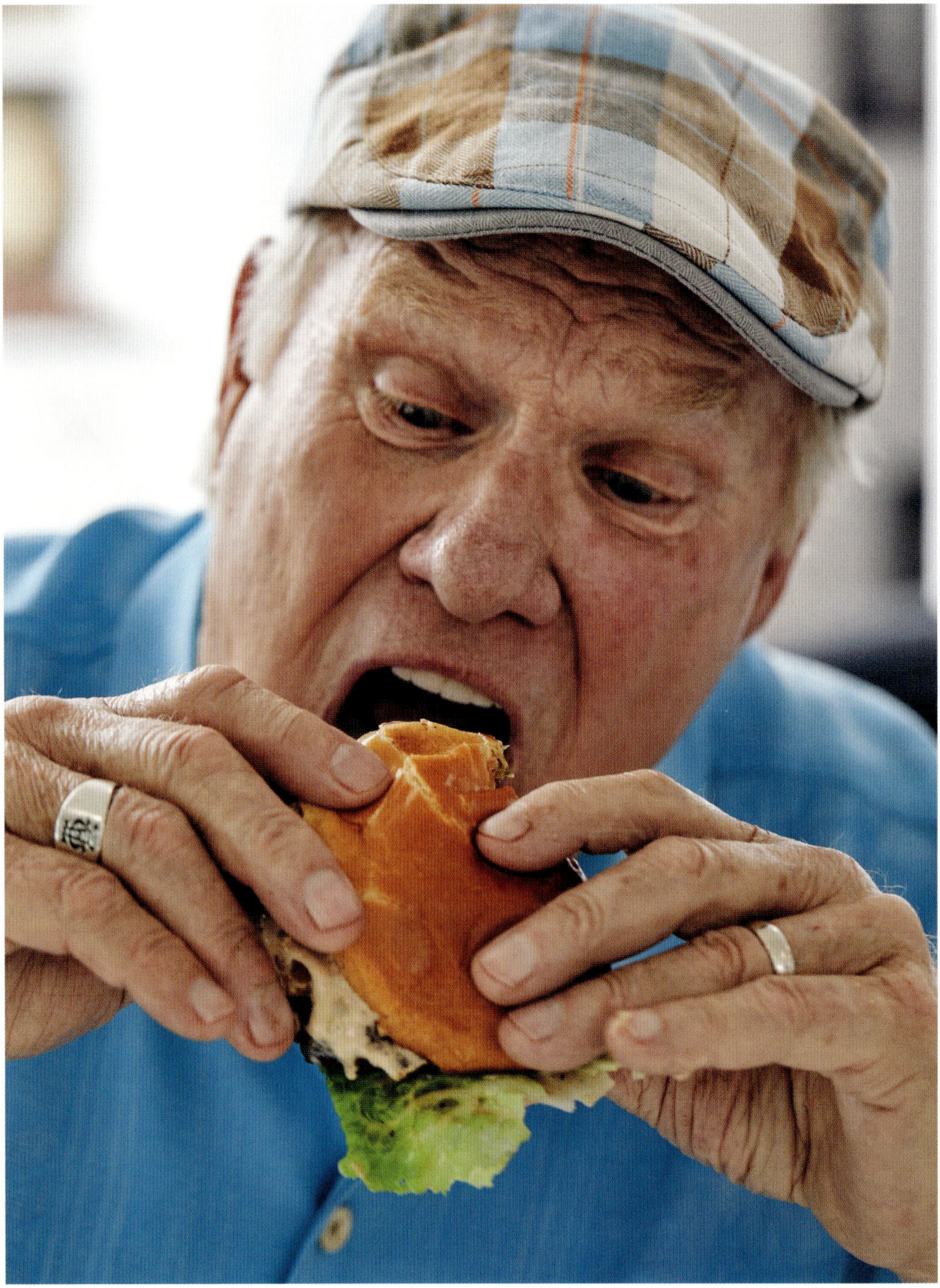

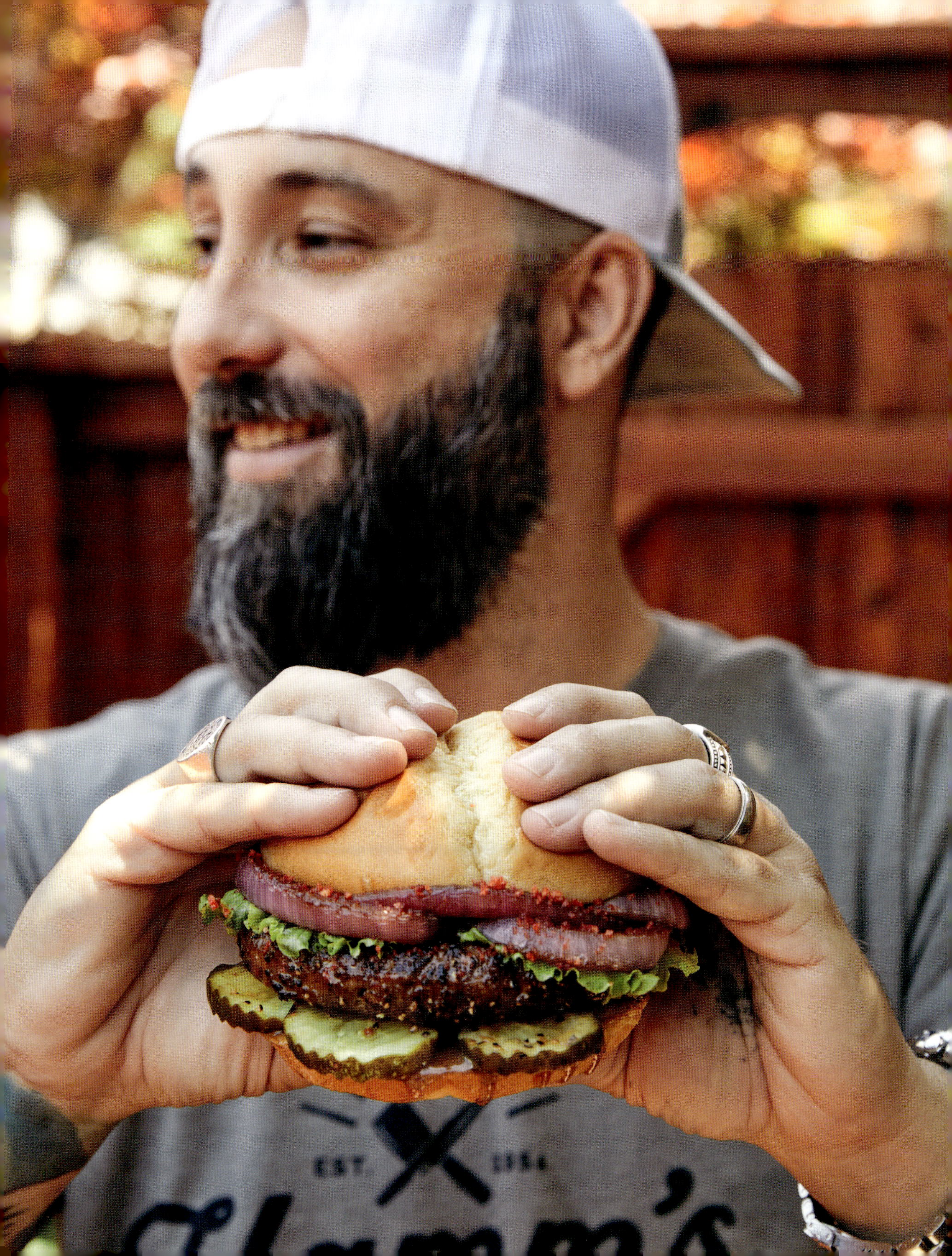
EST.

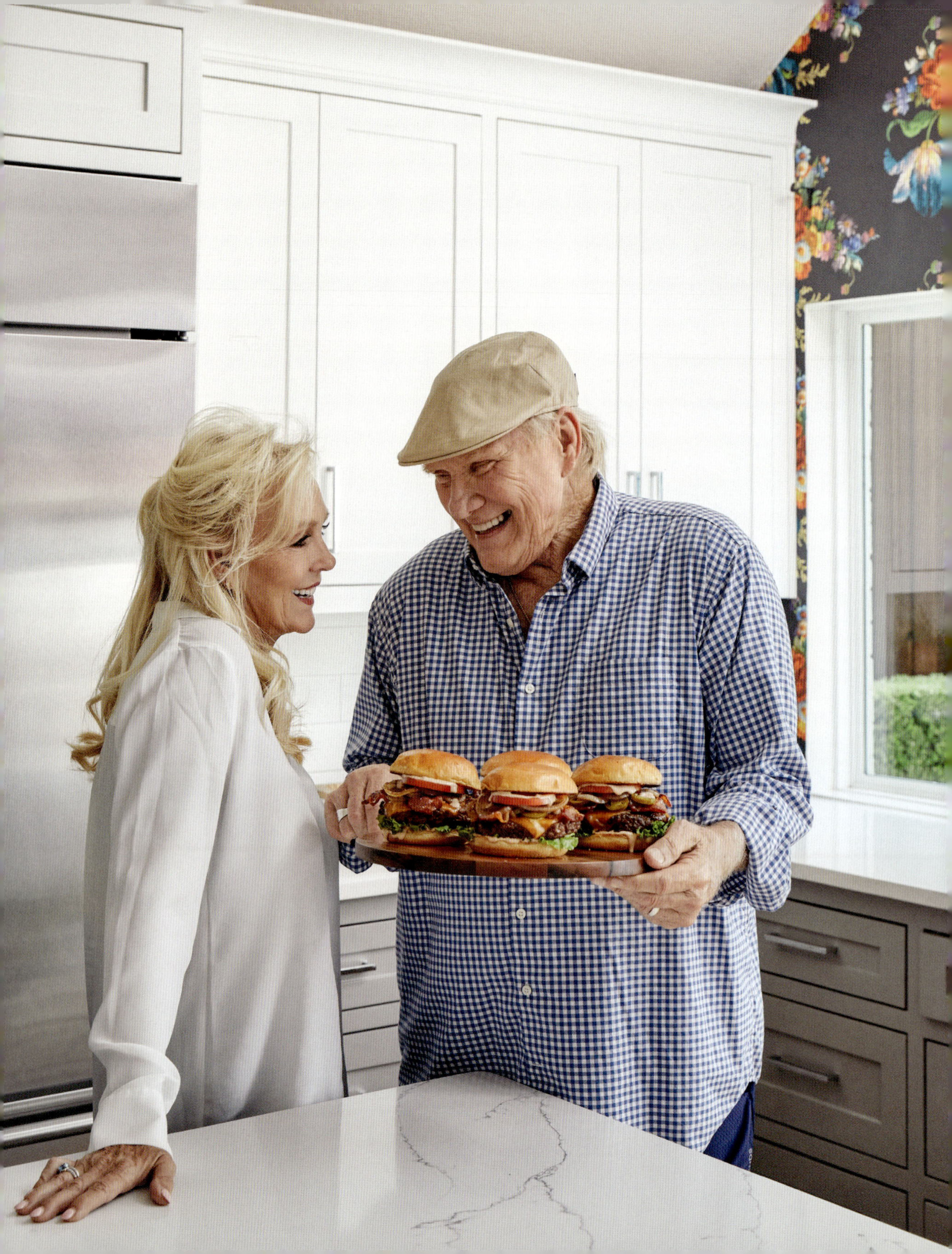

Brisket, Bacon, and Jalapeño Burgers

Noah recently created this mouthwatering hamburger for our butcher shop. When making them at home, ask your butcher to grind some beef brisket. The brisket elevates the burger to the next level as it is very flavorful with the right amount of fat. Top the burger with thick bacon slices, sautéed onion, smoked cheddar, our special burger sauce, and a few pickled jalapeños and you're ready for kickoff. By the way, if you ever have this burger with Terry, make sure to peek under your bun before taking a bite. He likes to spice up the burgers with a smothering of extra jalapeños. Of course, he won't tell you. He'll just wait for your surprised reaction. Take our word for it, your mouth will not fall asleep. —LACEY

Makes 4 burgers

SPECIAL BURGER SAUCE

½ cup mayonnaise

2 tablespoons ketchup

1 tablespoon Dijon mustard

1 tablespoon pickle relish

1 teaspoon Worcestershire sauce

Kosher salt and freshly cracked black pepper, to taste

BRISKET BURGERS

4 thick bacon slices

1 large yellow onion, thinly sliced

Kosher salt, to taste

1 pound ground brisket

Freshly cracked black pepper, to taste

4 burger buns

4 slices smoked cheddar cheese

4 large lettuce leaves, trimmed

Pickled jalapeños, to taste

4 tomato slices

To make the special burger sauce: Stir the mayonnaise, ketchup, mustard, relish, and Worcestershire sauce together in a small bowl. Season with salt and pepper. Refrigerate until ready to use.

To make the brisket burgers: Cook the bacon in a skillet over medium heat until crisp, then use tongs to transfer the bacon to a paper towel–lined plate to drain. Add the onion to the bacon fat in the skillet, season with a little salt, and reduce the heat to low. Sauté the onion, stirring occasionally, until golden brown and caramelized, 10 to 15 minutes. Set aside.

Divide the ground brisket into four equal portions and shape into burger patties. Season with salt and pepper.

Preheat an outdoor grill or stovetop pan over medium-high heat. Cook the seasoned burgers, turning once, to desired doneness, or 4 to 5 minutes per side for medium-rare. (Note: Brisket burgers cook just like regular beef burgers, so cook as you would a typical burger.) While the patties are cooking, lightly toast the buns. During the last minute of cooking, place a slice of smoked cheddar on each patty and cover the grill to melt the cheese. When the buns are toasted and the cheese is melted, remove from the heat.

To assemble each burger, spread a generous amount of the special burger sauce on both halves of a bun. Place a lettuce leaf on the bottom bun and top with a brisket patty. Arrange a bacon slice and a few jalapeño slices on the patty. Spoon sautéed onion on top and cover with a tomato slice. Top with the top bun and serve.

Smoked Brisket Sliders with Homemade Biscuits

When I got the phone call that I would be inducted into the NFL Hall of Fame, I went nuts. But I know you don't get elected by yourself, so I'm sending a big thank-you to all the guys on my team—every one of them deserves the honor. Speaking of team, gather your family and friends together and make a platter of these extra-special sliders, which have earned their own place in the Bradshaw Family Cookout Hall of Fame! —TERRY

Makes 8 to 10 sliders

SMOKED BRISKET

2 tablespoons smoked paprika

1 tablespoon packed brown sugar

1 tablespoon garlic powder

1 tablespoon onion powder

1 teaspoon cumin

1 teaspoon kosher salt

½ teaspoon freshly cracked black pepper

4 pounds beef brisket

1 cup (more or less) yellow mustard

HOMEMADE BISCUITS

2 cups all-purpose flour

1 tablespoon baking powder

½ teaspoon kosher salt

½ cup (1 stick) cold unsalted butter, cubed

¾ cup buttermilk

¼ cup shredded sharp cheddar cheese

¼ cup chopped fresh chives

(continued)

To make the smoked brisket: Preheat an outdoor smoker with hickory, mesquite, or oak to 225°F to 250°F. (See Grilling and Smoking—a Bradshaw Family Primer, page 27.)

While the smoker is preheating, make the rub. In a small bowl, stir together the paprika, brown sugar, garlic powder, onion powder, cumin, salt, and pepper. Coat the brisket on all sides with a layer of yellow mustard, then season the brisket, evenly and generously, with the rub mixture.

Place the seasoned brisket in the smoker, fat side up. For a tender, juicy brisket, smoke until the internal temperature of the brisket reaches 195°F to 205°F, or 1½ hours per pound. Remove the brisket, wrap in foil, and let rest for 30 minutes.

To make the biscuits: Preheat the oven to 450°F. Line a rimmed baking sheet with parchment paper.

Whisk together the flour, baking powder, and salt in a large mixing bowl. Using a pastry cutter or two knives, cut the cold butter cubes into the flour until the mixture resembles coarse crumbs. Add the buttermilk, cheddar, and chives and stir until the dough comes together.

Turn the dough out onto a floured surface and gently knead several times. With a rolling pin, roll the dough to about a ½-inch thickness. Use a 3-inch round biscuit cutter or the rim of a glass to cut out 8 to 10 biscuits and arrange them on the baking sheet with a couple inches of room between each biscuit. Bake until the biscuits are golden brown, 10 to 12 minutes. Set aside.

(continued)

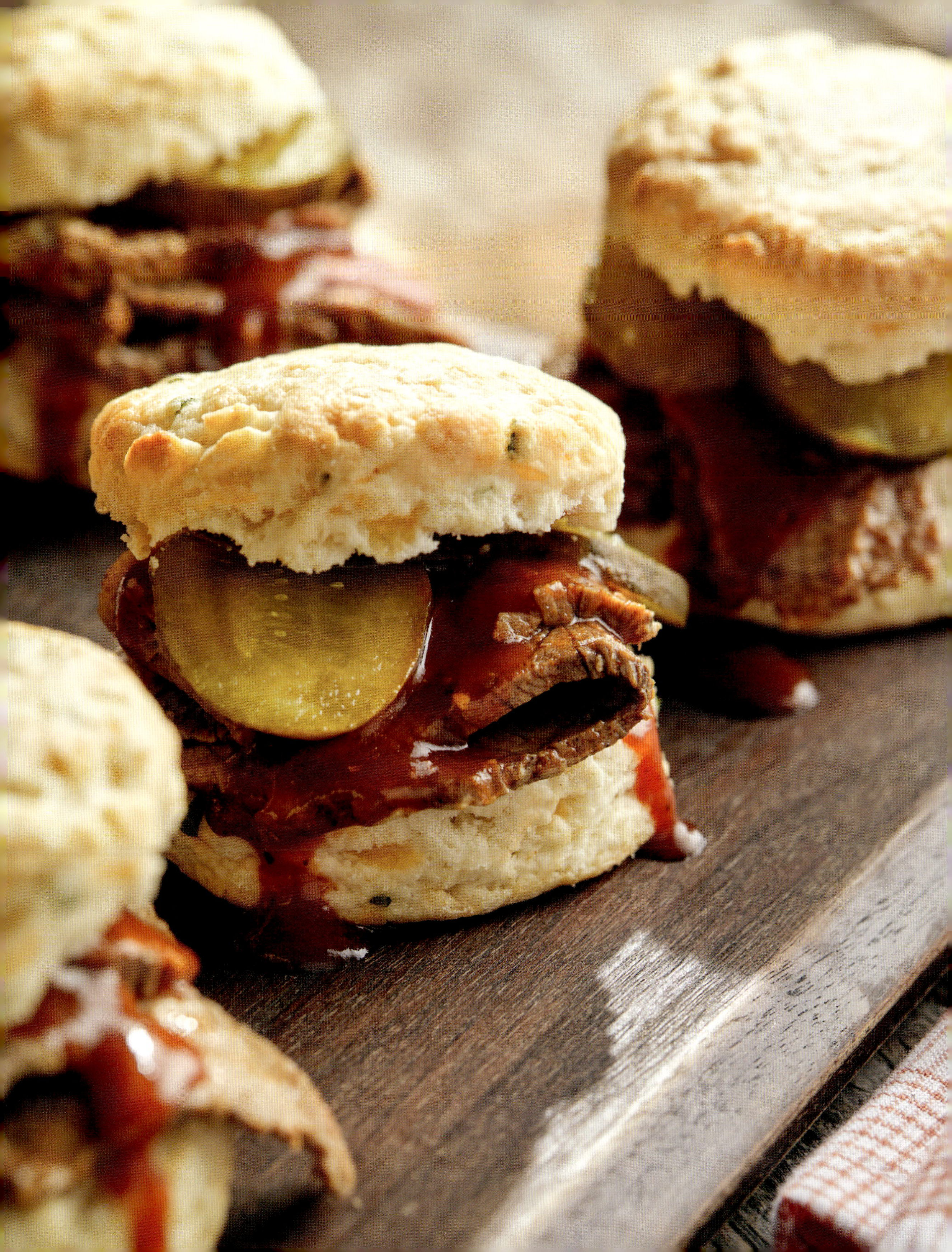

(continued)

Sliced dill pickles, for serving

Dijon mustard, for serving

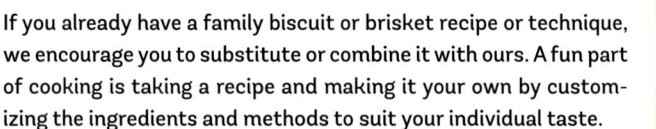

Bradshaw Bourbon Barbecue Sauce (page 141), for serving

When ready to serve, unwrap the brisket from the foil and transfer to a large cutting board. Reserve the jus. Thinly slice the brisket. (Note: there will be plenty of brisket.) Transfer the slices to a bowl or platter and toss with the reserved jus.

Split the biscuits and place slices of smoked brisket on top of the bottom half of each biscuit. Add a slice of dill pickle and drizzle with Dijon mustard and/or barbecue sauce. Top with the other half of the biscuit and serve (see Coach's Corner).

COACH'S CORNER

If you already have a family biscuit or brisket recipe or technique, we encourage you to substitute or combine it with ours. A fun part of cooking is taking a recipe and making it your own by customizing the ingredients and methods to suit your individual taste.

Bradshaw Bourbon Barbecue Sauce

As a chef, I enjoy creating sauces, so naturally when I moved to Texas, I convinced Terry we had to develop a barbecue sauce. Ours pulls the caramel and vanilla notes from the bourbon and combines them with brown sugar and a touch of cinnamon, making this sauce a key ingredient in recipes like our finger-lickin' chicken wings and Terry's legendary beans. —NOAH

Makes 3 to 4 cups

1 tablespoon olive oil

2 cups finely chopped white onions

1 cup straight bourbon whiskey (see Coach's Corner)

½ cup packed dark brown sugar

1½ cups ketchup

½ cup natural rice vinegar

2 tablespoons Worcestershire sauce

1 tablespoon liquid smoke

1 teaspoon garlic powder

1 teaspoon onion powder

½ teaspoon ground cinnamon

Heat the olive oil in a medium saucepan over medium heat. Add the onions and sauté, stirring occasionally, until translucent, about 7 minutes. Carefully stir in the bourbon and brown sugar and continue to cook, stirring frequently, until the sugar is dissolved and the mixture resembles syrup, about 5 minutes. Stir in the ketchup, rice vinegar, Worcestershire sauce, liquid smoke, garlic powder, onion powder, and cinnamon. Bring the mixture to a boil, then reduce the heat to very low. Loosely cover the pan with a screen or lid to prevent splattering. Simmer, stirring occasionally, until the sauce is reduced to your desired consistency, at least 20 minutes. Remove from the heat and set aside. Transfer the barbecue sauce to an airtight container and store in the refrigerator for up to 6 months.

COACH'S CORNER

Save your empty bourbon bottles and tops. They make great vessels to fill with barbecue sauce to gift to your family and friends.

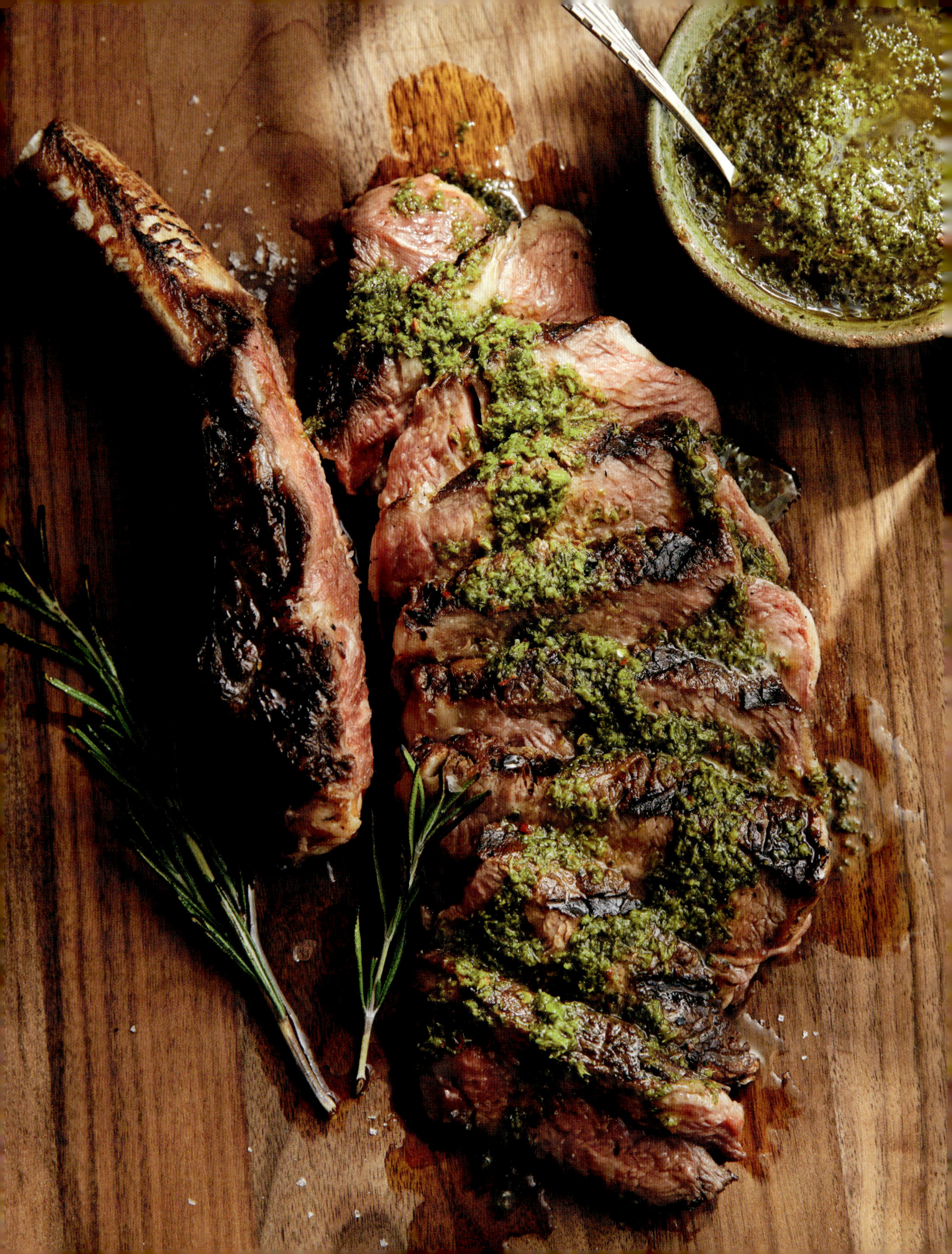

Grilled Tomahawk Steak with Chimichurri

When we want to feature a statement piece at our cookouts, this impressive cut fits the bill. I like to reverse sear this delicious hunk of meat by roasting it in the oven first and then finishing it over an open fire on the grill next to the pool—the same pool I've been pushed into countless times. Of all the steaks, there's nothing that cooks like the tomahawk, delivering succulent, well-marbled meat in a seasoned crust. I'll slice the massive slab off the bone and top it with a zing of chimichurri so everyone can share using their forks or fingers. —TERRY

Serves 2 to 4

CHIMICHURRI
Makes 1 cup

1 cup finely chopped fresh Italian flat-leaf parsley

¼ cup finely chopped fresh cilantro

4 garlic cloves, minced

3 tablespoons red wine vinegar

1 teaspoon dried oregano

½ cup extra virgin olive oil

½ teaspoon red pepper flakes, to taste

Kosher salt and freshly cracked black pepper, to taste

TOMAHAWK STEAK

1 (2-pound) tomahawk steak with exposed bone, 2 to 3 inches thick

2 tablespoons olive oil

2 garlic cloves, minced

Kosher salt and freshly cracked black pepper, to taste

Leaves from 2 sprigs fresh rosemary, divided (optional)

To make the chimichurri: Add the parsley, cilantro, garlic, red wine vinegar, and oregano to a bowl. Mix, then gradually whisk in the olive oil until combined. Season with red pepper flakes, salt, and pepper. You can store the chimichurri in an airtight container in the refrigerator for up to 2 weeks.

Preheat the oven or an outdoor smoker to 250°F. (If using an outdoor smoker, see Grilling and Smoking—a Bradshaw Family Primer (page 27).

To make the tomahawk steak: Rub the steak on all sides with the olive oil, garlic, salt, and pepper. Place the steak on a wire rack set over a rimmed baking sheet. Slowly roast the steak in the smoker or oven until the internal temperature reaches 115°F, 40 to 45 minutes, depending on your oven or smoker.

Preheat a cast-iron skillet or outdoor grill to high heat. Add the steak and sear until a dark crust forms, 2 or 3 minutes per side.

During the last minute of searing, add the leaves from a sprig of rosemary, if using, to the top of the steak for flavor. Remove the steak from the heat and let rest for 10 minutes.

Slice the steak across the bone, then across the grain, top with the chimichurri and garnish with the leaves from a sprig of rosemary, if using, and serve.

COACH'S CORNER

The length of the tomahawk bone can vary, from short to extremely long. It's okay for the bone to extend outside the skillet. Just make sure the meat has good contact with the bottom of the pan.

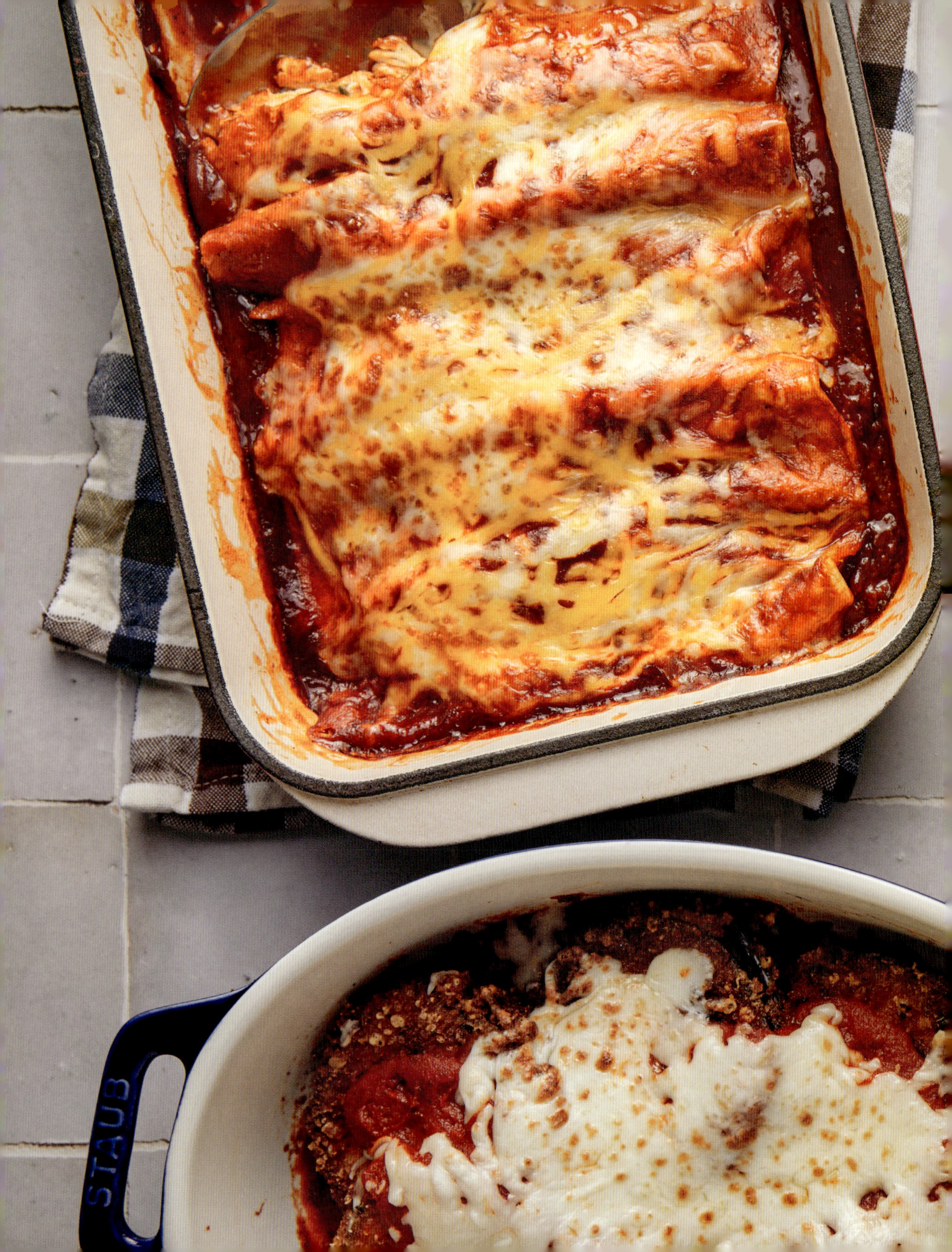
STAUB

4 // Get-Togethers and Potlucks

Aloha Bread

Apple Butter Bread

Cabbage and Potato Kettle

Spicy Italian Sausage,
Vegetable, and Kale Soup

Fire-Roasted Hatch Chile Chicken Stew

Cannellini Chicken Chili

Creamy Sun-Dried Tomato Chicken
with Orzo

Cheesy Chicken Enchiladas

South of the Border Lasagna

Roasted-Chicken Tetrazzini

Sunday Family Casserole

Baked Eggplant Parmesan
with Marinara

Italian Sausage–Stuffed Peppers

Sunday Glazed Meatloaf

WHEN THE BRADSHAWS HOST A POTLUCK, IT'S LIKE A CULINARY competition where everyone's a winner. Each dish tells a story, whether it's Tammy's freshly baked Aloha Bread (page 148) or Terry's Cabbage and Potato Kettle (page 151). The house buzzes with anticipation as the family arrives, each person toting a dish that's been perfected over years of get-togethers. Rachel's Italian Sausage-Stuffed Peppers (page 168) always disappear before you can ask, "May I have another?"

These events inevitably inspire a friendly rivalry over whose dish will be crowned the champion. Once, Terry and Tammy made their classic Sunday Family Casserole (page 165) while Rachel and Chase crafted their Sunday Glazed Meatloaf (page 171). All the grandkids—Jeb, Zurie, Jessie, Cason . . . even some of their friends—were elected the judges. Rachel and Chase's juicy dish with the right amount of Worcestershire sauce and Italian seasoning won hands down. Terry still claims the judging was rigged, but we all know the truth!

As one would expect, the competition doesn't end there. Lacey often impresses with her Baked Eggplant Parmesan with Marinara (page 167), a perfect blend of flavors and textures that warms everyone up. And if you think our cookoff challenge was fun, you should have been there for the infamous Lasagna Face-Off, when Rachel's South of the Border Lasagna (page 162) took center stage alongside Terry's more traditional recipe. It turns out, mixing cuisines is as delightful as mixing family fun!

Aloha Bread

I find breadmaking to be a relaxing process, and the Aloha Bread is one I bake often. This soft and fluffy bread, bursting with sweet pineapple, cherry, coconut, and banana, brings a taste of paradise to any meal. —TAMMY

Makes 2 loaves

1 cup (2 sticks) unsalted butter, at room temperature, plus more for greasing

2 cups granulated sugar

4 large eggs

4 cups all-purpose flour, plus more for flouring the pans

2 teaspoons baking powder

1 teaspoon baking soda

½ teaspoon kosher salt

1 cup mashed ripe banana (2 or 3 bananas)

1 (16-ounce) can crushed pineapple with juice

1 cup flaked sweetened coconut

¼ cup halved maraschino cherries

Preheat the oven to 350°F. Grease and flour two 5 × 9-inch loaf pans.

In the bowl of a standing mixer fitted with a whisk attachment, whip the butter and sugar together until fluffy, about 2 minutes. Add the eggs and continue to whip until incorporated.

Sift the flour, baking powder, baking soda, and salt into a large bowl. Fold in the creamed mixture, then fold in the banana, pineapple, coconut, and cherries, mixing just until combined.

Pour the batter into the prepared pans and bake until a toothpick inserted into the center comes out clean, about 1 hour. Let cool for 10 minutes before removing the loaves from the pans and serving (see Coach's Corner, page 150).

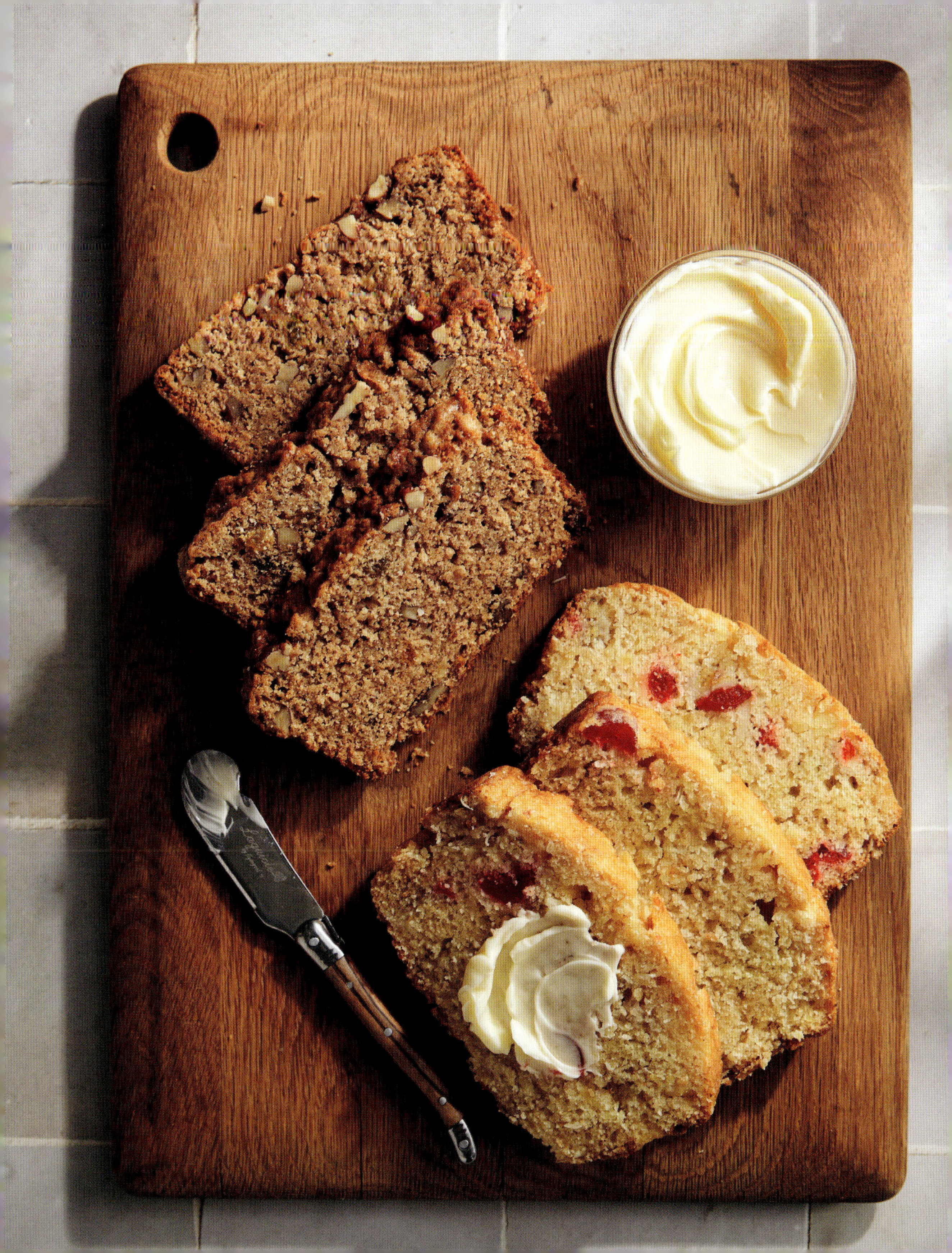

Apple Butter Bread

When Terry and I find ourselves dragging through the doldrums of a cold Texas winter, I'll make Apple Butter Bread to bring a warm smile to our faces. You may not see this bread at a typical get-together or potluck, but you should. It features warm apples and cinnamon while offering a pleasant balance of sweet and crunchy, thanks to the golden raisins and chopped pecans. —TAMMY

Makes 1 loaf

2 cups all-purpose flour, plus more for flouring the pan

1 cup granulated sugar

¼ teaspoon kosher salt

2 teaspoons ground cinnamon

1 teaspoon ground cloves

¼ teaspoon kosher salt

2 large eggs

1 cup (2 sticks) unsalted butter, melted and slightly cooled, plus more for greasing

¾ cup apple butter

2 tablespoons whole milk

½ cup golden raisins

¾ cup finely chopped pecans

Preheat the oven to 350°F. Grease and flour a 5 × 9-inch loaf pan.

In a medium bowl, stir together the flour, sugar, cinnamon, cloves, and salt until combined.

Add the eggs, butter, apple butter, and milk to another bowl and whisk to combine. Stir in the raisins and pecans, then add the wet mixture to the dry ingredients. Mix just until the ingredients are moistened.

Pour the batter into the prepared pan and bake until a toothpick inserted into the center comes out clean, about 70 minutes. Let cool in the pan for 15 minutes before turning the loaf out onto a cutting board. Slice and serve warm (see Coach's Corner).

COACH'S CORNER

The Apple Butter Bread (and the Aloha Bread) will hold up well if you're wanting to bake now and serve later. Just wrap the bread in plastic wrap and store in the refrigerator for up to 3 days, or place the bread in freezer bags and freeze for up to 60 days.

Cabbage and Potato Kettle

If there's one thing I love as much as football, it's cabbage. When the colder months sneak up on us, this hearty and nutritious recipe is the ticket. I wish we had more cold weather here in Texas so I could have this soup more often. It's that good. Tender potatoes and cabbage are simmered in a delicious broth seasoned with onion, celery, and sage. As with many of our recipes, the kettle makes for terrific leftovers—should you find you're left with extra. —**TERRY**

Serves 8 to 10

3 bacon strips, chopped

5¾ cups Homemade Organic Chicken Stock (page 212), divided

½ head green cabbage, chopped

8 cups peeled and rough-chopped Yukon Gold potatoes (about 4 pounds)

1 cup chopped yellow onion

1 cup chopped celery

½ cup (1 stick) unsalted butter

¼ cup all-purpose flour

2 cups whole milk

2 tablespoons chopped fresh Italian flat-leaf parsley

1 tablespoon dried sage

1 teaspoon kosher salt

1 teaspoon freshly cracked black pepper

In a 2-quart saucepan, cook the bacon over medium heat until crisp, 5 to 7 minutes. Add 3 cups of the chicken stock and the cabbage. Stir as the cabbage cooks to make sure any unwilted portion is covered until the cabbage is tender, about 12 minutes. Remove from the heat and set aside.

Add the remaining 2¾ cups chicken stock to a large pot and bring to a boil over medium-high heat. Add the potatoes, onion, and celery and continue to boil until the potatoes are fork tender, 12 to 15 minutes. Remove from the heat and set aside.

Melt the butter in a small saucepan over low heat. Add the flour and whisk until smooth. Add the milk and cook, whisking constantly, until the mixture is smooth and thick, about 3 minutes. Stir in the parsley.

Stir the milk mixture into the pot with the potatoes. Then add the cabbage, bacon, and liquid from the saucepan. Add the sage and stir until all the ingredients are combined. Season with salt and pepper. Return the pot to the stove and warm on medium-low until heated through, about 5 minutes, and serve.

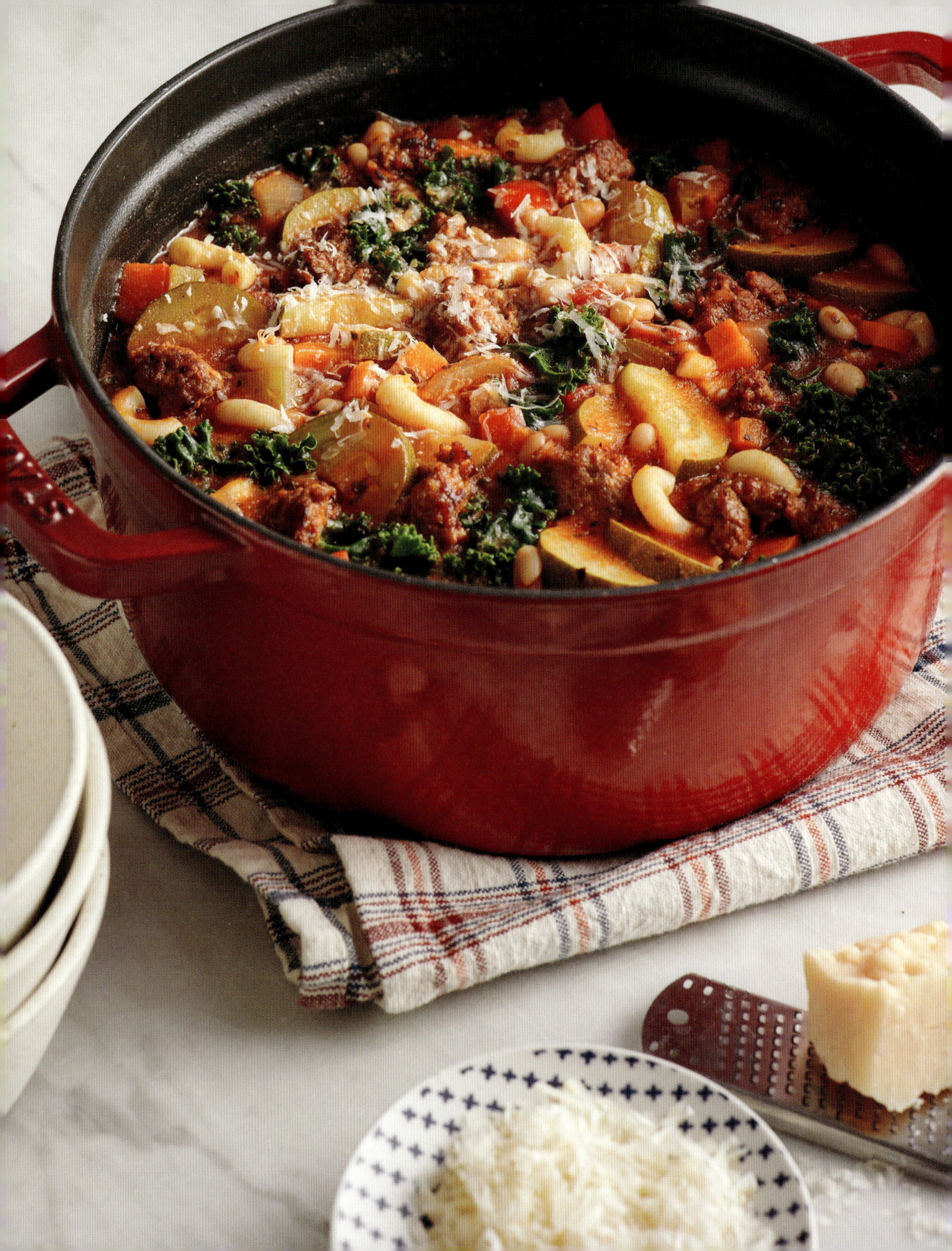

Spicy Italian Sausage, Vegetable, and Kale Soup

When I'm not working, I love to get into the kitchen and start throwing things together in a big pot to simmer all day. This hearty soup is one of them. Spicy Italian sausage adds a kick while the kale provides plenty of texture and nutrition. When it comes to the vegetables, the sky's the limit. I'll add tomatoes, carrots, celery, bell pepper, and zucchini, but you can substitute other vegetables, such as spinach, Swiss chard, cabbage, or whatever else you like. —TERRY

Serves 4

1 cup elbow macaroni

1 pound ground mild or spicy Italian sausage, casings removed

¾ cup diced yellow onion

3 garlic cloves, minced

4 cups Homemade Organic Chicken Stock (page 212), plus more as needed

1 (15-ounce) can cannellini or navy beans, drained and rinsed

1 (14.5-ounce) can diced tomatoes

1 cup chopped red bell pepper

½ cup chopped carrots

¼ cup chopped celery

1 cup tomato sauce

1½ teaspoons dried Italian seasoning

1 cup zucchini, cut in half moons

1 cup chopped stemmed fresh kale

Chopped fresh Italian flat-leaf parsley and Parmesan cheese, for serving

Bring a large pot of well-salted water to a boil. Add the macaroni and cook, stirring occasionally, until al dente, about 8 minutes. Drain and set aside.

Add the sausage to a large pot and cook over medium-high heat, crumbling the sausage with a wooden spoon until no pink remains, 10 to 12 minutes. Add the onion and garlic and cook until the onion begins to soften, about 3 minutes. Stir in the chicken stock, beans, diced tomatoes, bell pepper, carrots, celery, tomato sauce, and Italian seasoning. Bring to a boil, then reduce the heat to a simmer. Cover and cook for 7 minutes. Add the zucchini and cook until the vegetables are tender, 5 to 7 minutes. Additional stock can be added if the mixture begins to get dry. Stir in the kale and macaroni. Cook until heated through and the kale is wilted, 4 to 5 minutes.

Ladle the soup into bowls, garnish with parsley and Parmesan, and serve.

Fire-Roasted Hatch Chile Chicken Stew

The really cool thing about cooking is you get to tell a story about yourself, and my story is all about spice. I love spicy food . . . or *anything* made with hot peppers, for that matter. If you and your guests like heat, this zesty and robust stew will satisfy while celebrating the unique flavors of hatch chiles. We like to serve this hearty and well-seasoned dish with an assortment of toppings. —TERRY

Serves 6

2 tablespoons olive oil

1 small yellow onion, diced

1 cup fresh or frozen corn kernels

4 garlic cloves, minced

1 tablespoon ground coriander

1½ teaspoons ground cumin

¼ teaspoon paprika

¼ teaspoon kosher salt

¼ teaspoon freshly cracked black pepper

3 fresh Hatch chile, roasted, seeded, and diced, or 2 (4-ounce) cans diced green chile

1 (16-ounce) jar salsa verde

4 cups Homemade Organic Chicken Stock (page 212)

1 cup water

Juice of 1 lime

1 rotisserie chicken, meat shredded (3 to 4 cups)

1 tablespoon chopped fresh cilantro

½ cup long-grain white rice, uncooked

Lime wedges, fresh cilantro, tortilla strips, avocado chunks, and sour cream, for serving

Heat the olive oil in a large pot or Dutch oven over medium heat. Add the onion and corn and cook, stirring occasionally, until soft, 6 to 8 minutes. Add the garlic and cook for 1 minute. Stir in the coriander, cumin, paprika, salt, and pepper, then add the chile, salsa verde, chicken stock, water, and lime juice. Stir to combine and bring the mixture to a boil.

Add the chicken and cilantro, reduce the heat to low, and simmer for 20 minutes. Add the rice and cook until the rice is tender, about 15 minutes. Remove from the heat and serve with lime wedges, fresh cilantro, tortilla strips, avocado chunks, and sour cream on the side (see Coach's Corner).

COACH'S CORNER

This soup freezes very well, so you can make a large pot and store the leftovers in an airtight container in the refrigerator for up to 3 days or in the freezer for up to 3 months. When it's time for soup, especially on those cold, cozy Sundays, simply reheat and serve.

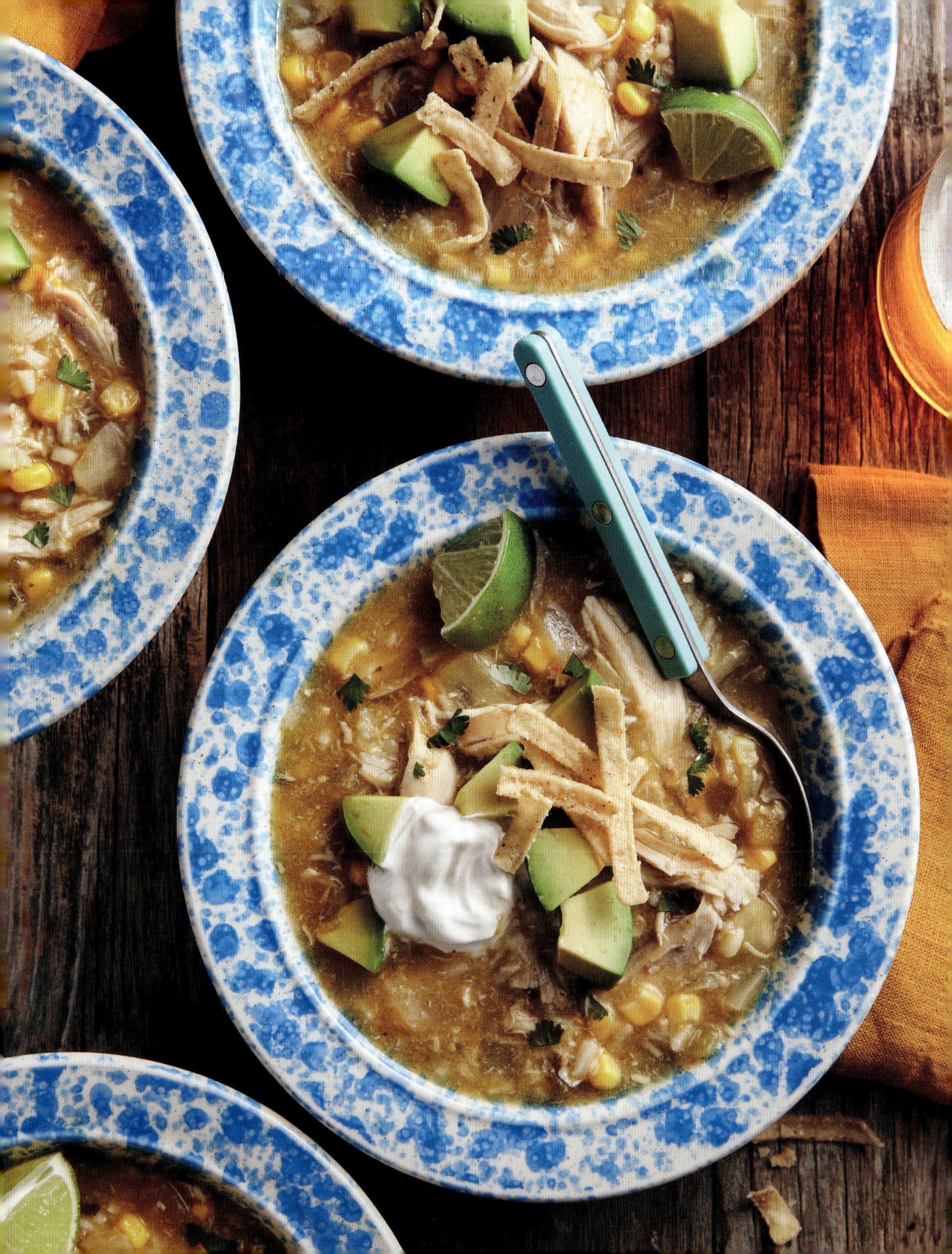

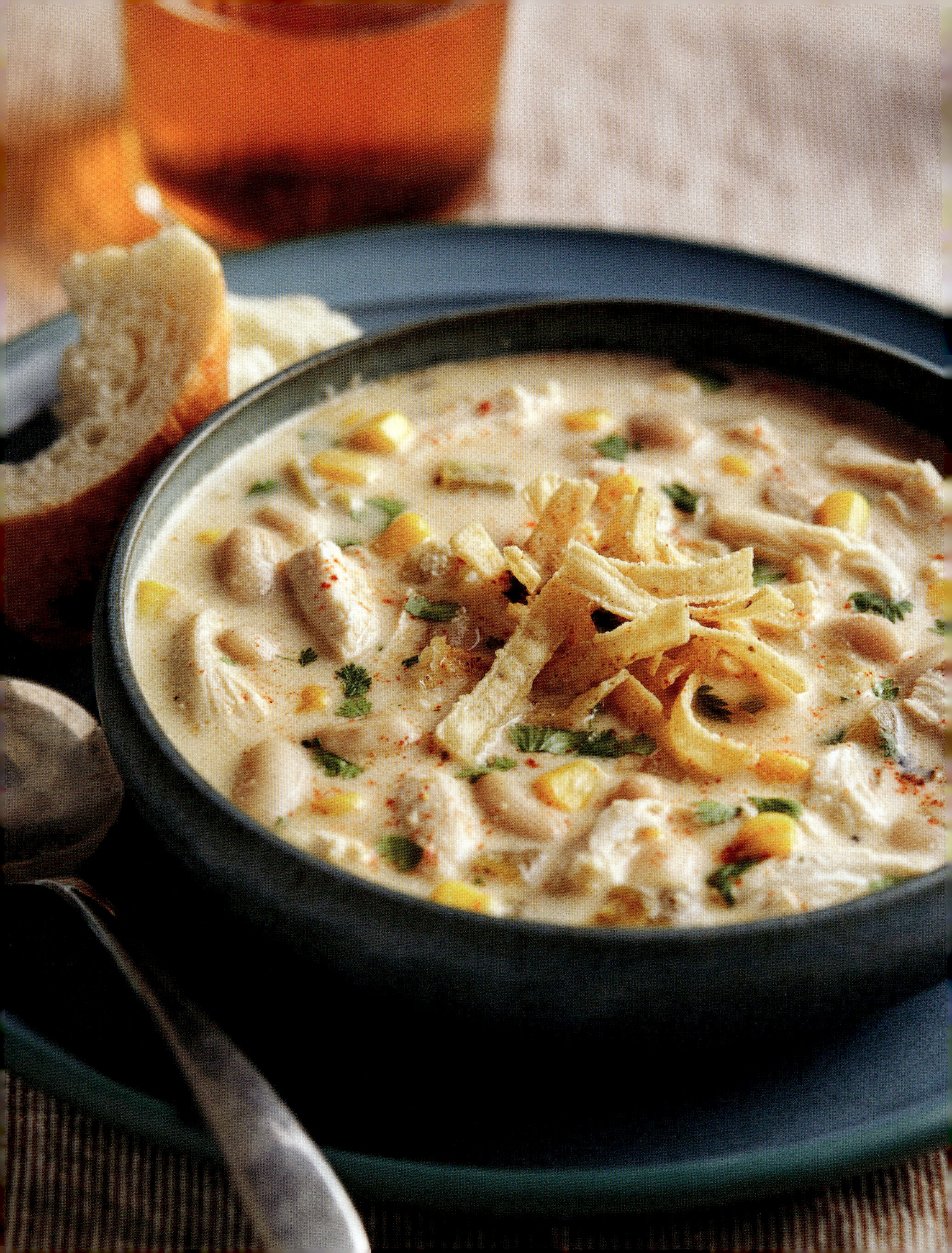

Cannellini Chicken Chili

When your get-together or potluck calls for something to ward off a chill, this cozy white bean chicken chili is the answer. I learned to make this dish in college—it's one of those delicious meals I still enjoy over the course of a week, tasting better and better with each passing day. Today, Chase and I will make this when we're deep into December and there's a good chance there'll be snow on the ground—yes, even in Texas. —**RACHEL**

Serves 6

2 (15-ounce) cans cannellini beans (1 can drained, 1 can with its liquid)

¼ cup olive oil plus 1 tablespoon, divided

1 cup diced yellow onion

4 garlic cloves, finely minced

4 cups Homemade Organic Chicken Stock (page 212) (see Coach's Corner)

2 (7-ounce) cans diced green chilies, drained

1 tablespoon fresh lime juice

1½ teaspoons ground cumin

½ teaspoon paprika

½ teaspoon dried oregano

½ teaspoon ground coriander

¼ teaspoon cayenne pepper, or to taste

¼ teaspoon kosher salt, to taste

¼ teaspoon freshly cracked black pepper

1 (8-ounce) package cream cheese, cut in chunks

2 cups shredded cooked chicken (from about ½ rotisserie chicken)

1 (15-ounce) can whole kernel corn, drained

2 tablespoons chopped fresh cilantro, plus more for serving

Fried tortilla strips, for serving

Add the can of drained cannellini beans to a food processor or blender. With the motor running, slowly add ¼ cup of the olive oil and puree until the mixture is creamy. Set aside.

Add the remaining 1 tablespoon olive oil to a large pot or Dutch oven over medium heat. When the oil is hot, add the onion and sauté, stirring often, until soft, about 4 minutes. Add the garlic and sauté for 1 minute, then stir in the chicken stock, chilies, lime juice, cumin, paprika, oregano, coriander, cayenne, salt, and pepper. Bring to a boil, then add the cream cheese and whisk until melted. Add the blended beans, the remaining can of beans with their liquid, the chicken, and corn. Bring back to a boil, then reduce the heat to low, cover, and simmer for 30 minutes. Serve garnished with chopped cilantro and tortilla strips.

COACH'S CORNER

Home cooks often wonder if there's a big difference between using homemade broth (or stock) and store-bought. The answer is yes. Sure, store-bought broth is more convenient, but if you have the time to simmer chicken bones with vegetables and herbs to extract their flavors and nutrients, you'll find that making homemade stock (page 212) is a fun and rewarding activity that can elevate the taste and nutritional value of your meals. You can also season your broth to taste, whereas store-bought often contains high amounts of sodium, additives, preservatives, and artificial flavors. If you're going to use store-bought, try Better Than Bouillon brand. It's a paste made from premium ingredients, and you just add water.

Creamy Sun-Dried Tomato Chicken with Orzo

Here's another delectable dish for cozy get-togethers. In fact, I gave this recipe to a girlfriend one day and four weeks later, her boyfriend proposed. For all of you out there eager to get engaged, serve this secret dish to your loved one. The chicken is seasoned and seared, then baked in a delicious sauce made with sun-dried tomatoes, garlic, herbs, and spinach. Served over a bed of orzo, it's a delightful and creamy blend of hearty and comforting flavors. —RACHEL

Serves 6

1 tablespoon olive oil

6 medium bone-in, skin-on medium chicken thighs

Kosher salt and freshly cracked black pepper, to taste

3 garlic cloves, minced

1 teaspoon dried oregano

½ teaspoon crushed red pepper flakes, or to taste

¾ cup Homemade Organic Chicken Stock (page 212)

½ cup heavy cream

1 cup chopped sun-dried tomatoes

¼ cup shredded Parmesan cheese

1 cup fresh spinach

1 (16-ounce) box orzo

1 tablespoon chopped fresh Italian flat-leaf parsley (or basil), for serving

Preheat the oven to 350°F.

Add the oil to a large cast-iron skillet over medium-high heat. While the oil is heating, season the chicken thighs with salt and pepper. Add the chicken to the skillet skin-side down and cook until browned, about 4 minutes. Turn the chicken over and cook until browned, about 4 minutes. Remove from the skillet and set aside.

Returning the skillet to the heat, reduce the heat to medium and add the garlic, oregano, and red pepper flakes. Cook until fragrant, about 1 minute. Add the stock, heavy cream, sun-dried tomatoes, and Parmesan. Taste for seasoning and adjust, if necessary, with salt and pepper. Bring to a simmer, then return the chicken to the skillet and coat with the sauce. Turn the thighs skin-side up and stir in the spinach leaves.

Transfer the skillet to the oven and bake until the chicken is cooked through, about 20 minutes.

While the chicken is baking, bring a medium pot of well-salted water to a boil. Add the orzo and stir gently. Return to a boil and cook, uncovered, stirring occasionally, for about 10 minutes or until tender. Remove from the heat and drain.

Divide the orzo among the serving plates. Top with the chicken, sauce, and fresh parsley and serve.

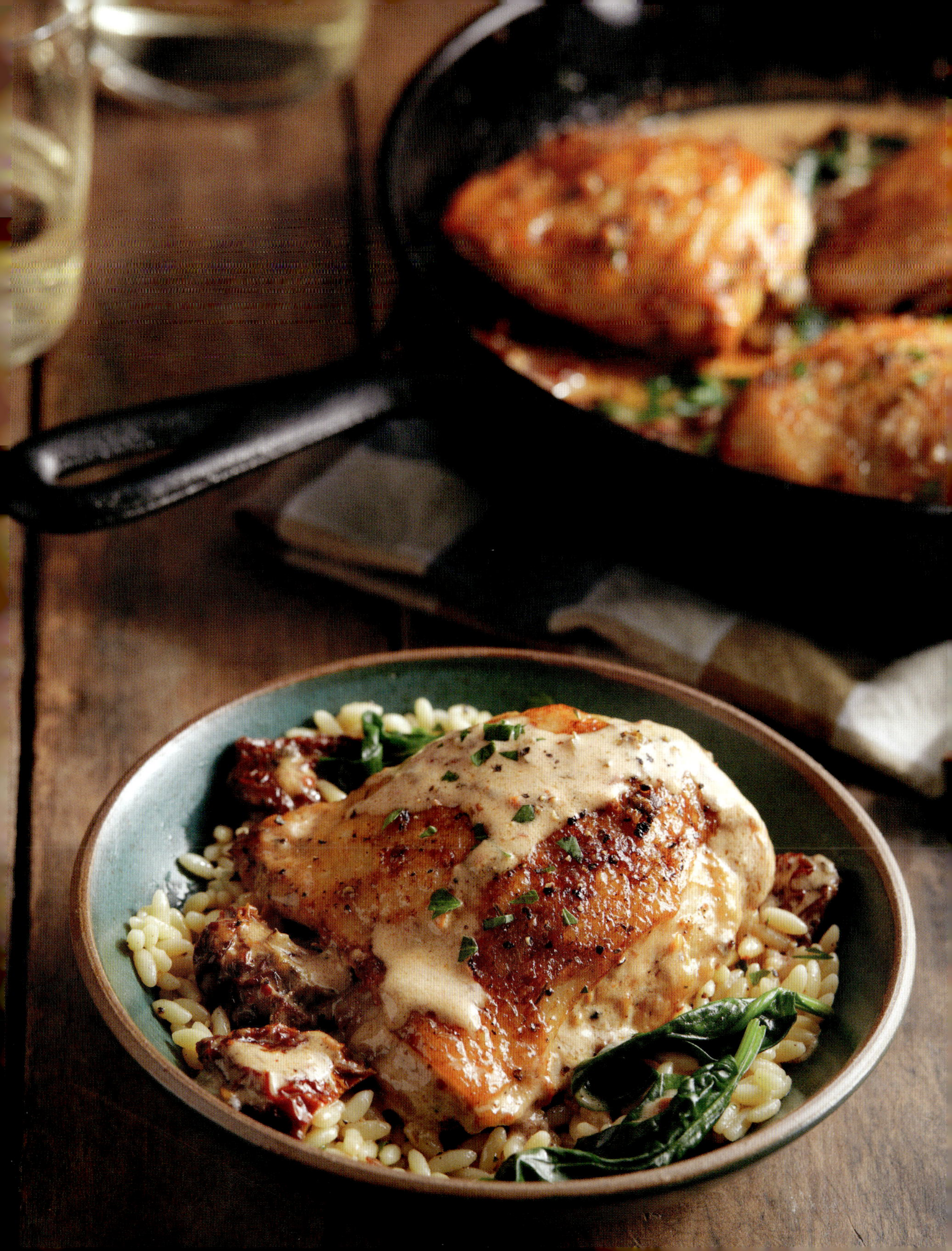

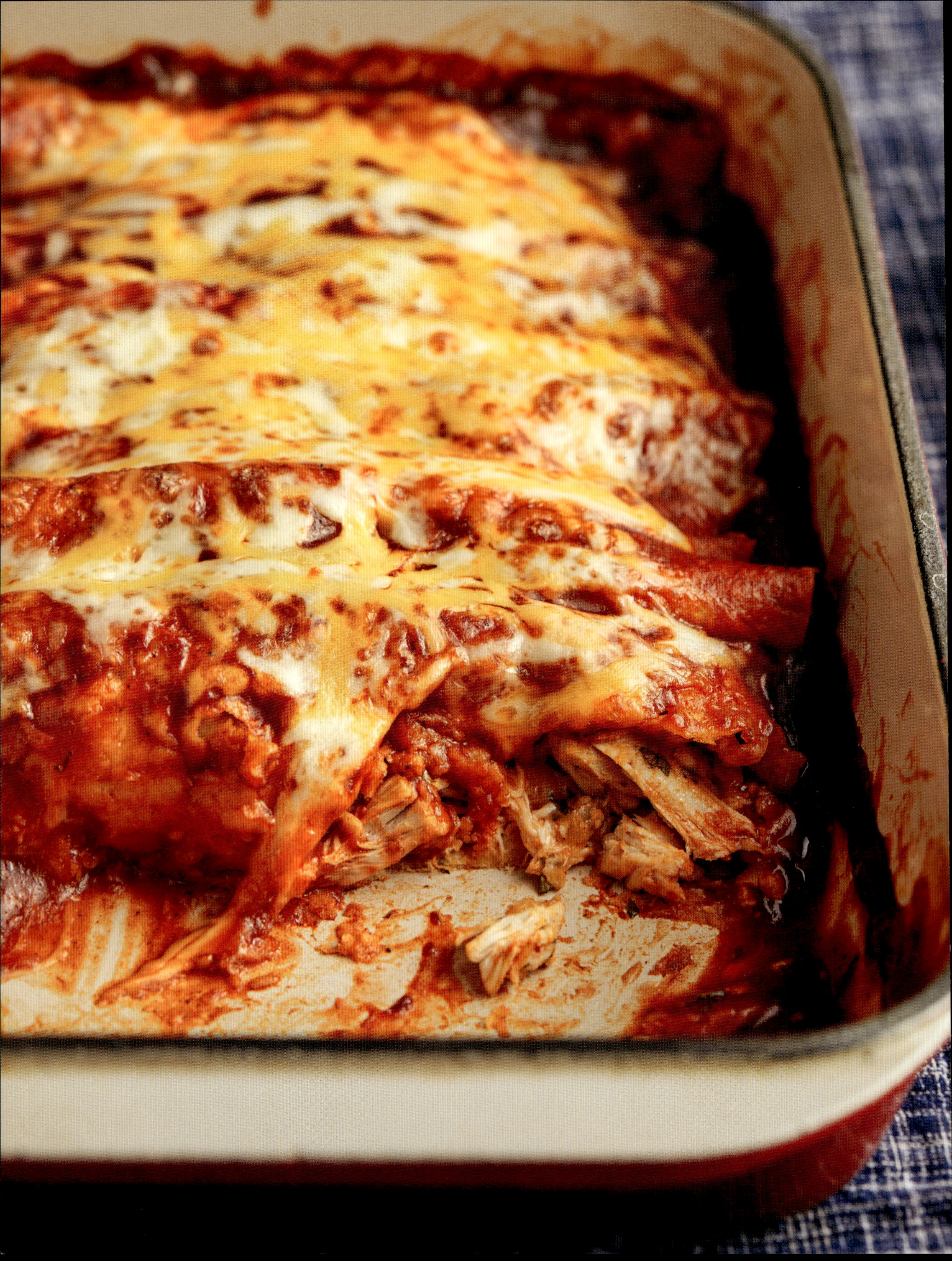

Cheesy Chicken Enchiladas

Being from Texas, we take our Mexican food seriously. These enchiladas feature corn tortillas stuffed with shredded chicken and cheese and topped with what we consider to be the best homemade enchilada sauce. They're then baked until the cheese is melted and bubbly. Sometimes we'll serve the enchiladas with a side of Mexican Street Corn Salad (page 188). —**TERRY AND TAMMY**

Serves 6

RED SAUCE

1 medium yellow onion, diced

1 jalapeño, seeded and chopped

1 tablespoon olive oil

3 medium garlic cloves, finely minced

2 tablespoons chili powder

1 tablespoon packed brown sugar

2 teaspoons ground cumin

½ teaspoon dried oregano

½ teaspoon kosher salt

1 (15-ounce) can tomato sauce

1 cup Homemade Organic Chicken Stock (page 212) or vegetable stock

CHICKEN FILLING

1 to 1½ pounds boneless skinless chicken breasts (2 or 3 large breasts)

Kosher salt, to taste

Nonstick cooking spray

1½ cups shredded sharp cheddar cheese, divided

1½ cups shredded Monterey Jack cheese, divided

½ cup minced fresh cilantro

Juice of 1 lime

12 (6-inch) soft corn tortillas

To make the red sauce. Combine the onion, jalapeño, and oil in a large saucepan and cook over medium heat until the vegetables have softened, 8 to 10 minutes. Stir in the garlic, chili powder, brown sugar, cumin, oregano, and salt. Cook until fragrant, about 1 minute. Add the tomato sauce and stock and stir to combine. (At this point, the sauce can be cooled and stored in the refrigerator for up to 4 days.)

To make the chicken filling: Add the chicken to the pan with the red sauce and bring to a simmer. Reduce the heat to low and continue to simmer, turning the chicken once, until it is fully cooked and registers an internal temperature of 165°F, 15 to 30 minutes. The sauce should have also thickened some. Remove the chicken to a mixing bowl. At this point, if you prefer, you can carefully pour the sauce into a blender and blend until smooth. Season the sauce with salt, if necessary, and set aside.

Preheat the oven to 400°F. Lightly grease a 9 × 13-inch baking dish with nonstick cooking spray.

In the bowl, shred the chicken into bite-sized pieces. Add 1 cup of the cheddar, 1 cup of the Monterey Jack, the cilantro, and lime juice. Mix to combine.

Stack the tortillas on a plate and cover with plastic wrap or damp paper towels. Microwave on high until warm and pliable, 20 to 30 seconds.

Spread a thin layer of the red sauce in the baking dish. Scoop about ⅓ cup of the chicken mixture onto a tortilla and press it evenly down the middle. Tightly roll up the tortilla and lay it seam-side down in the baking dish. Repeat with the remaining tortillas and filling.

Pour the remaining sauce over the enchiladas and top with the remaining ½ cup cheddar and ½ cup Monterey Jack. Cover the baking dish tightly with foil. Bake for 25 minutes, then remove the foil and continue to bake until golden and bubbly, 5 to 10 minutes. Let stand for 10 minutes before serving.

South of the Border Lasagna

This recipe, a south of the border twist on the Italian classic, is from an old notebook of recipes I once made. When I was pregnant, Chase found the book and made the lasagna for me. He says I ate three helpings in one sitting. Of course, I can neither confirm nor deny this. For a potluck, it pairs very well with our Mexican Street Corn Salad (page 188). —RACHEL

Serves 12

Nonstick cooking spray

1 pound (80% lean) ground beef

1 medium white onion, diced

2 garlic cloves, minced

¼ cup taco seasoning

1 (14.5-ounce) can fire-roasted diced tomatoes

1 (4-ounce) can mild green chilies, drained

1 (15-ounce) black beans, drained and rinsed

18 (6-inch) corn tortillas

1½ cups shredded cheddar cheese

1½ cups shredded Monterey Jack cheese

1 medium tomato, diced

1 bunch green onions, green and white parts, sliced, or as needed to taste

Sour cream, for serving (see Coach's Corner)

Preheat the oven to 350°F. Spray a 9 × 13-inch casserole dish with nonstick cooking spray.

Cook the ground beef and white onion in a large skillet over medium heat until the meat is browned and the onion is soft, 10 to 12 minutes. Add the garlic and cook for 1 or 2 minutes. Add the taco seasoning and ¾ cups water and stir until well combined. Add the fire-roasted tomatoes and their juices, the chilies, and black beans. Cook until all the ingredients are heated through, about 5 minutes.

Line the prepared baking dish with 6 tortillas, overlapping slightly to cover the bottom of the dish. Spread one-third of the meat mixture over the tortillas. Sprinkle ½ cup of the cheddar and ½ cup of the Monterey Jack over the meat mixture. Repeat two more times, creating three layers. Cover with aluminum foil and bake until the casserole is bubbly and the cheeses are fully melted, 30 to 40 minutes. Let sit for 10 minutes. Garnish with the diced tomatoes and green onions and serve with a side of sour cream.

COACH'S CORNER

Instead of serving a side of plain sour cream, try the chipotle crema from our Breakfast Tacos (page 64).

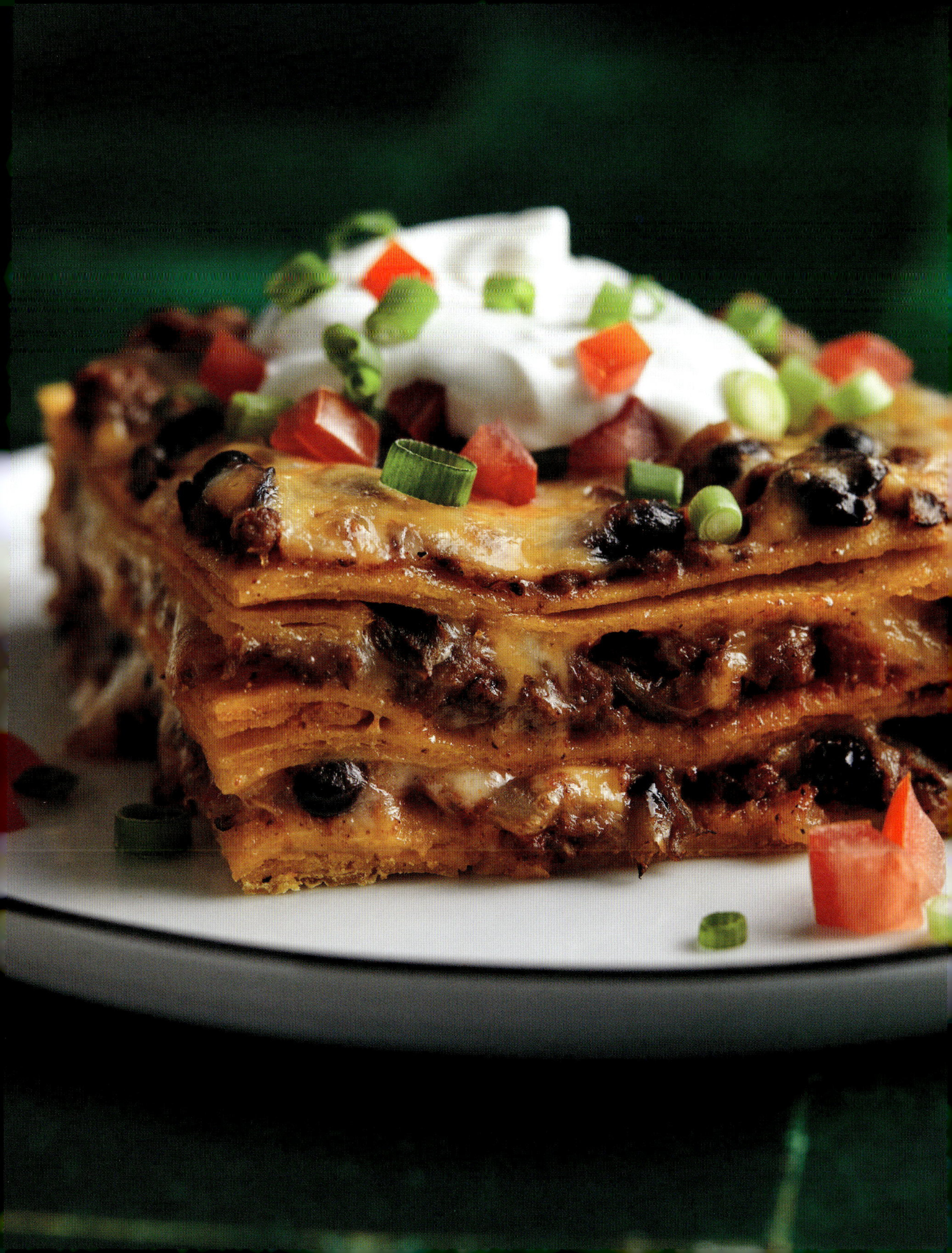

Roasted-Chicken Tetrazzini

I remember coming home from cheerleading during high school and I'd get so excited when I saw chicken tetrazzini on our table. Today, it's one of my go-to recipes, especially on nights when I'm trying to think of what to cook. This is an indulgent bake topped with mozzarella, cheddar, and Parmesan that really transforms a simple rotisserie chicken into something special. —RACHEL

Serves 8

Nonstick cooking spray

1 (16-ounce) box thin spaghetti

1 (10-ounce) can cream of chicken soup

1 (10-ounce) can cream of mushroom soup

1 (16-ounce) container sour cream

½ cup (1 stick) unsalted butter, melted

½ cup Homemade Organic Chicken Stock (page 212)

1 teaspoon kosher salt

½ teaspoon freshly cracked black pepper

¼ teaspoon garlic powder

½ cup frozen peas

1 rotisserie chicken, meat shredded (about 3 cups)

1½ cups shredded mozzarella cheese

½ cup shredded cheddar cheese

2 tablespoons freshly grated Parmesan cheese and chopped fresh Italian flat-leaf parsley, for serving

Preheat the oven to 350°F. Spray a 9 × 13-inch baking dish with nonstick cooking spray.

Bring a large pot of well-salted water to a boil. Add the spaghetti and stir. Return to a boil and cook, uncovered, stirring occasionally, until al dente, about 6 minutes. Drain and set aside.

Add the chicken soup, mushroom soup, sour cream, butter, chicken stock, salt, pepper, and garlic powder to a large bowl and whisk to combine. Stir in the peas, chicken, and cooked spaghetti, and toss until all the ingredients are well combined.

Pour the mixture into the baking dish and top with the mozzarella and cheddar. Cover with foil and bake for 30 minutes. Remove the foil and continue baking until the cheese is melted and the casserole is hot throughout, about 15 minutes. Garnish with Parmesan and parsley. Let stand 5 to 10 minutes before serving.

Sunday Family Casserole

One Sunday afternoon each year, there is a ritual that brings our family together like nothing else: the Super Bowl. If I'm not broadcasting, we will all get together to watch the game and enjoy this Bradshaw classic that represents the simple pleasures of family and food. —TERRY

Serves 6 to 8

Nonstick cooking spray

1 pound (80% lean) ground beef

1½ cups finely chopped yellow onion

1 cup finely chopped green or red bell pepper

2 (14.5-ounce) cans diced tomatoes

1 tablespoon ketchup

1 tablespoon A.1. steak sauce, or your favorite steak sauce

2 tablespoons chopped fresh Italian flat-leaf parsley

1 to 1½ cups elbow macaroni (depending on the meat-to-noodle ratio you prefer)

1 (10.5-ounce) can cream of mushroom soup

Kosher salt and freshly cracked black pepper, to taste

1 cup grated cheddar cheese

Preheat the oven to 350°F. Spray a 3-quart casserole dish with nonstick cooking spray.

Heat a large skillet over medium-high heat and add the ground beef. Cook until browned, about 5 minutes, breaking up the meat with a wooden spoon. Do not drain. Add the onion, bell pepper, tomatoes, ketchup, steak sauce, and parsley. Stir until combined. Reduce the heat to low and simmer, stirring occasionally, for about 30 minutes.

While the beef mixture is simmering, bring a large pot of well-salted water to a boil. Add the macaroni and cook, stirring occasionally, until al dente, about 8 minutes. Drain and transfer to a large mixing bowl.

Add the beef mixture and the cream of mushroom soup to the macaroni and combine. Season to taste with salt and pepper. Transfer the mixture to the prepared casserole dish and top with the grated cheddar. Bake until bubbling and golden brown, about 30 minutes. Let cool slightly before serving.

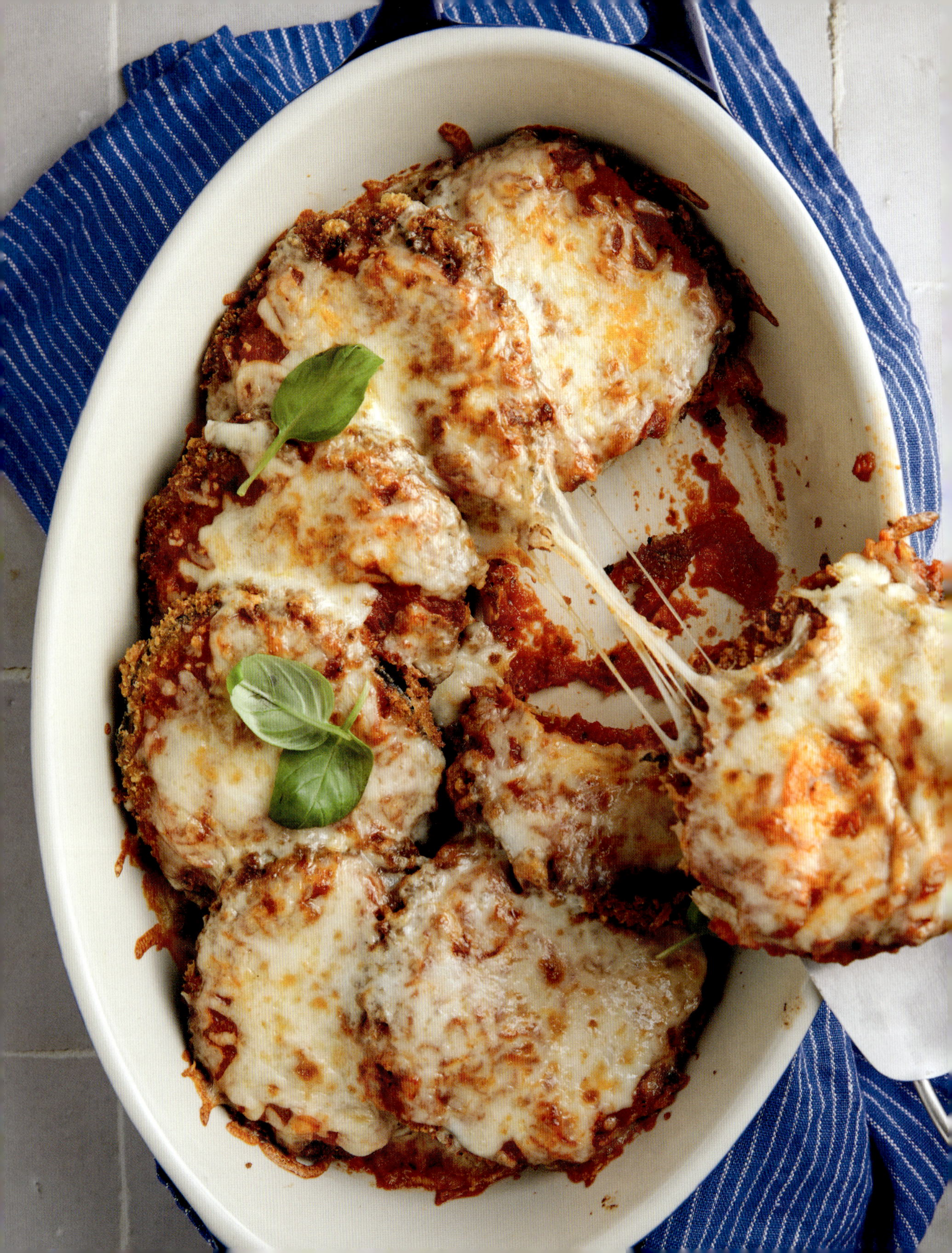

Baked Eggplant Parmesan with Marinara

My late brother Cody loved to cook. When he was a teenager, he took the time to create this wonderful recipe, which he proudly made for me one night. The dish remains one of my all-time favorites. There's nothing like tender slices of seasoned eggplant layered with marinara and melted mozzarella and baked until golden brown. You'll find there's so much depth to this comforting meal. If you're taking this to a potluck, make sure to reheat the dish so it's hot and bubbly when it graces the table. —LACEY

Serves 6

2 medium eggplants, sliced into ½-inch-thick rounds (24 to 28 rounds total)

Kosher salt, to taste

1 cup all-purpose flour

3 large eggs

2 cups panko breadcrumbs

1 cup grated Parmesan cheese

1 teaspoon dried basil

1 teaspoon dried oregano

Freshly cracked black pepper, to taste

Vegetable oil, for frying

4 cups marinara sauce

2½ cups shredded mozzarella cheese

Fresh basil leaves, for serving

Preheat the oven to 375°F.

Place the eggplant rounds on a paper towel–lined rimmed baking sheet. Sprinkle liberally with salt on both sides and let sit for 15 to 20 minutes. Pat them dry with paper towels to remove the moisture.

Set up a breading station with three shallow bowls. Add the flour to the first bowl. Add the eggs to a second bowl and whisk until blended. Add the breadcrumbs, Parmesan, dried basil, oregano, and pepper to a third bowl and mix well.

Add about ¼ inch oil to a large skillet and heat over medium-high until the oil is shimmering.

Working in batches of three or four at a time, dredge the eggplant rounds in the flour, then dip into the beaten eggs, and finally coat evenly in the breadcrumb mixture. Fry the breaded eggplant rounds until golden brown, 2 to 3 minutes on each side. Transfer to a paper towel–lined plate to drain while you fry the remaining slices. (Note: Skim the oil to remove excess breading that could burn, let the pan come back to temp between batches, and add more oil as necessary.)

Spread a thin layer of marinara sauce on the bottom of an 11 × 15-inch baking dish. Arrange a layer of fried eggplant rounds on top of the sauce, using half the slices and slightly overlapping them. Spoon more marinara sauce over the eggplant rounds and spread evenly. Sprinkle half the shredded mozzarella on top of the sauce. Repeat the process to build a second layer, ending with the rest of the mozzarella. Cover the dish with foil and bake for 35 to 40 minutes, or until the mozzarella is melted and bubbly. Remove the foil and bake until the cheese is golden brown, about 10 minutes. Let cool for several minutes, then garnish with the basil leaves and serve.

Italian Sausage-Stuffed Peppers

We often feature these vibrant peppers at our potlucks because they're both easy to make and impressive looking, which is everything you want when feeding a crowd. The real secrets to this dish are the Worcestershire sauce and the Italian sausage. They add that boost of flavor that takes these peppers over the top. If you like spice, substitute hot sausage for the sweet. —RACHEL

Serves 6

Nonstick cooking spray

6 bell peppers (green, red, orange, and/or yellow)

½ pound (80% lean) ground beef

½ pound mild Italian sausage, casings removed

1 small yellow onion, diced

2 garlic cloves, minced

1 (14.5-ounce) can petite diced tomatoes

½ cup raw white rice

1 tablespoon Worcestershire sauce

½ teaspoon Italian seasoning

Kosher salt and freshly cracked black pepper, to taste

2½ cups marinara sauce, divided

½ cup shredded mozzarella or cheddar cheese

Preheat the oven to 350°F. Spray a 9 × 13-inch casserole dish with nonstick cooking spray.

Slice off the tops of the bell peppers and reserve. Remove and discard the stems, seeds, and membranes from the tops and bottoms. Finely chop the tops and set aside.

Bring a large pot of water to a boil and cook the peppers for 5 minutes. (You can also air fry the peppers at 400°F for 5 minutes.) Invert the peppers onto a kitchen towel to drain while you make the filling.

Heat a large skillet over medium-high heat. Add the ground beef, sausage, onion, and garlic. Cook, breaking the meat up with a wooden spoon, until no pink remains, 8 to 10 minutes. Drain off any fat. Add the chopped pepper tops, tomatoes and their juice, rice, 1¼ cups water, Worcestershire sauce, and Italian seasoning. Season with salt and pepper. Bring the mixture to a boil, reduce the heat to low, cover, and simmer until the rice is tender, 15 to 20 minutes. Check after 12 minutes or so, and if the pan looks dry, add ¼ cup water. Remove from the heat and stir in ½ cup of the marinara sauce.

Spread 1½ cups of the marinara in the bottom of the baking dish. Fill the peppers evenly with the sausage mixture and arrange them in the baking dish. Spoon the remaining ½ cup marinara sauce over the tops of the peppers. Cover with foil and bake for 35 minutes. Remove the foil and spoon the sauce from the bottom of the dish over the peppers. Top with the mozzarella and bake, uncovered, until the cheese is melted and the peppers are tender, about 10 minutes. Let cool slightly before serving.

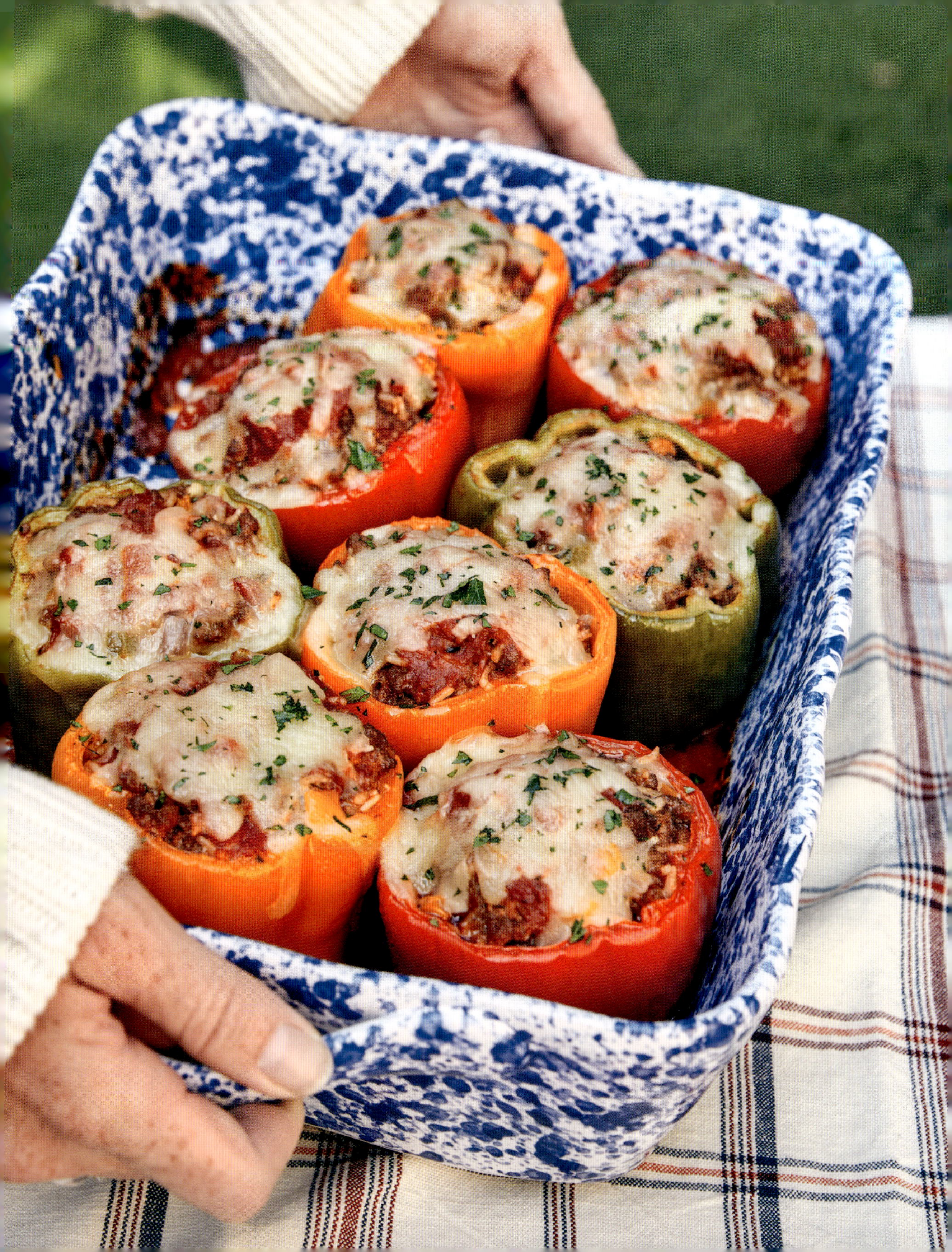

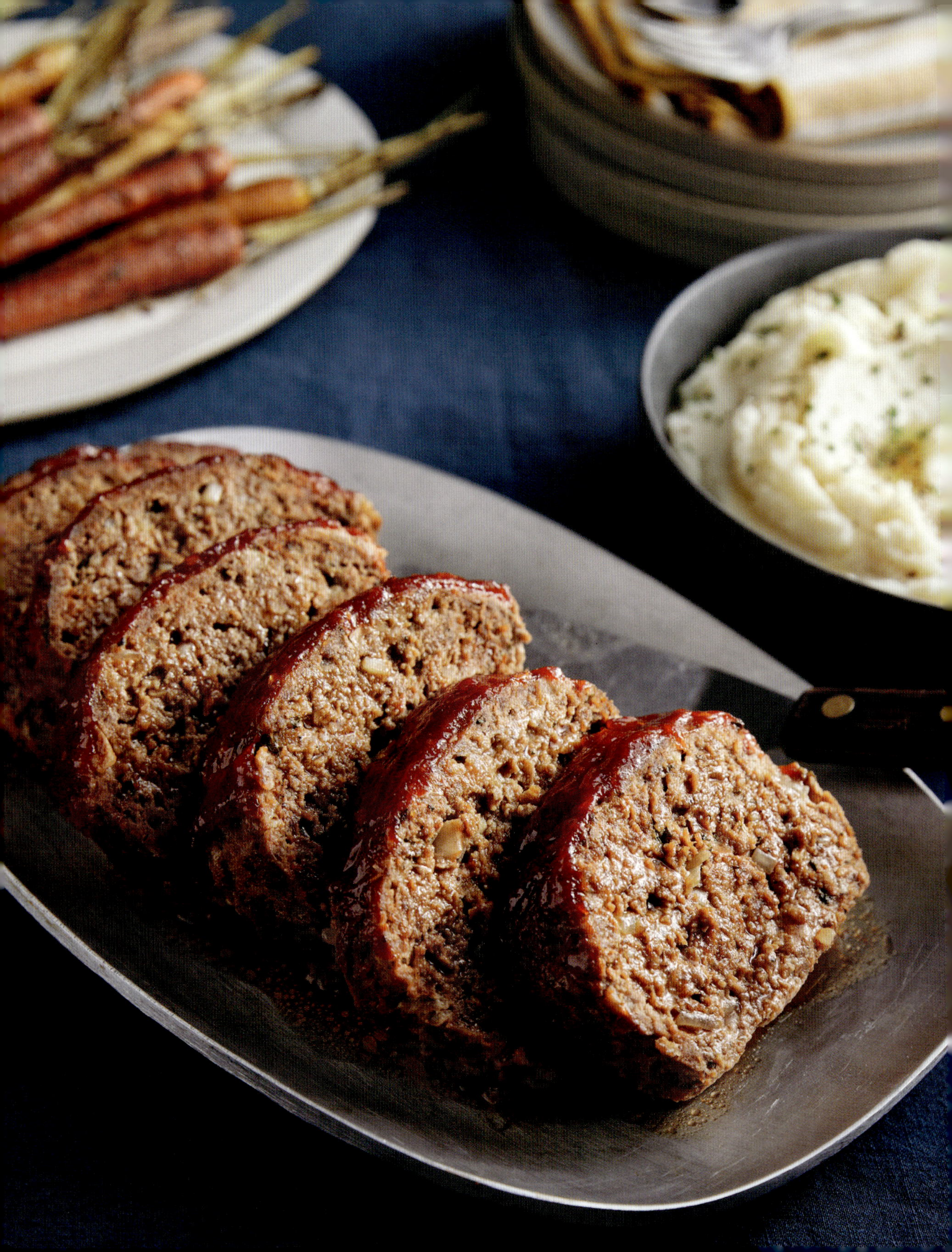

Sunday Glazed Meatloaf

Because Terry and the guys are real meat-and-potato lovers, Sunday dinners wouldn't be complete without a deliciously moist meatloaf on the table. I've tweaked this recipe since college, and it's absolute perfection when we're craving a cozy dish. The glaze adds moisture and a depth of caramelized flavor to the meatloaf. To make the loaf even richer, I'll pour the pan juices over the top just before serving. —RACHEL

Serves 8

MEATLOAF

2 pounds (80% lean) ground beef

1 cup finely chopped yellow onion

¾ cup panko breadcrumbs

2 large eggs

3 garlic cloves, minced

3 tablespoons ketchup

3 tablespoons finely chopped fresh Italian flat-leaf parsley

⅓ cup whole milk

1 teaspoon Worcestershire sauce

1½ teaspoons Italian seasoning

½ teaspoon paprika

1½ teaspoons kosher salt

¼ teaspoon freshly cracked black pepper

GLAZE

¾ cup ketchup

1½ teaspoons white vinegar

2½ tablespoons packed brown sugar

1 teaspoon minced garlic

½ teaspoon onion powder

¼ teaspoon kosher salt

¼ teaspoon freshly cracked black pepper

Preheat the oven to 375°F. Line a 9 × 5-inch loaf pan with parchment paper and set aside.

To make the meatloaf: Add the beef, onion, breadcrumbs, eggs, garlic, ketchup, parsley, milk, Worcestershire, Italian seasoning, paprika, salt, and pepper to a large bowl. With clean hands, gently mix until all the ingredients are combined (see Coach's Corner). Transfer the mixture to the loaf pan and gently press the meat down while shaping evenly in the pan. Bake for 40 minutes.

To make the glaze: Stir together the ketchup, vinegar, brown sugar, garlic, onion powder, salt, and pepper in a bowl. When the meatloaf has baked for 40 minutes, remove it from the oven and spread the glaze over the loaf. Return the loaf to the oven and bake until the internal temperature reaches 160°F, about 30 minutes. Let the meatloaf rest for 10 minutes before slicing and serving with some of the pan juices drizzled on top.

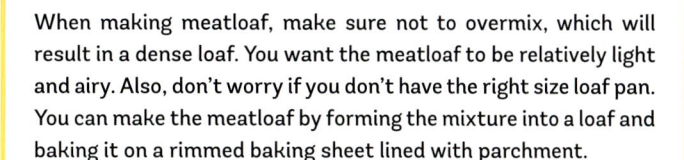

COACH'S CORNER

When making meatloaf, make sure not to overmix, which will result in a dense loaf. You want the meatloaf to be relatively light and airy. Also, don't worry if you don't have the right size loaf pan. You can make the meatloaf by forming the mixture into a loaf and baking it on a rimmed baking sheet lined with parchment.

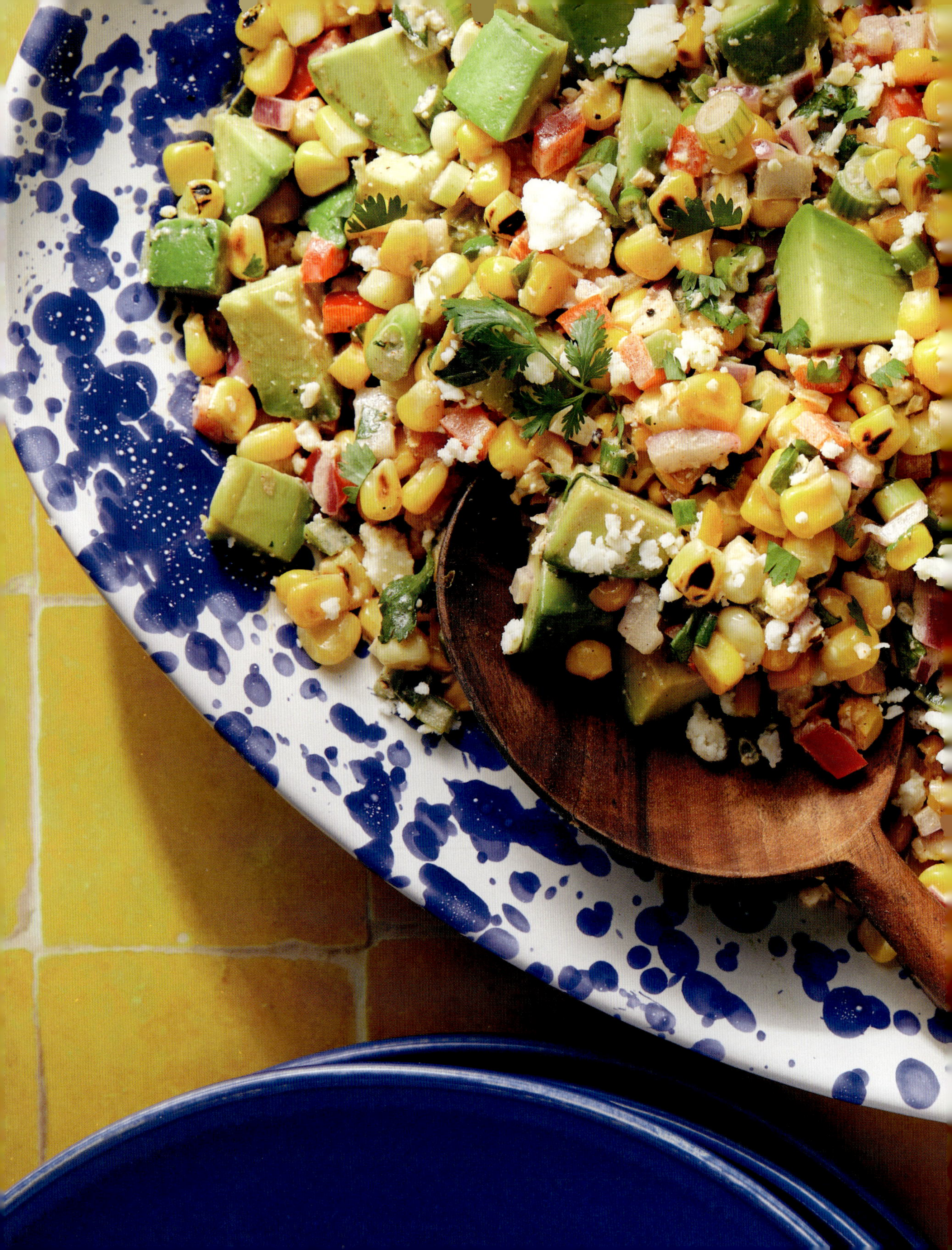

5 // Salads and Sides

Iceberg Salad with Terry's Favorite Dressing

Waldorf Salad with Walnut Pumpkin Seed Brittle

German Country Potato Salad

Red Potato Salad with Pimento and Sweet Pickle

Old-Fashioned Ambrosia Salad

Greek Orzo Salad with Oil, Vinegar, and Honey Dressing

Mexican Street Corn Salad

Missouri Corn Salad with Lime and Paprika

Green Beans with Bacon, Onion, and Garlic

Chicken Stock Scalloped Potatoes

Havarti and Gouda Mac 'n' Cheese

Honey Balsamic Farmers Market Carrots

Terry's Legendary Bradshaw Beans

EVEN AS A FAMILY OF CARNIVORES, THE BRADSHAWS KNOW THE KEY to a perfect meal is all in the sides. Whether it's a summer barbecue or a cozy winter gathering, our table is always loaded with salads and sides that could steal the spotlight from any main dish. Picture Terry re-creating his grandmother Hoodie Baby's Old-Fashioned Ambrosia Salad (page 184) or Noah's Havarti and Gouda Mac 'n' Cheese (page 194), where the gooey cheeses make every bite a comfort-food lover's dream.

Whether Rachel's impressive Waldorf Salad with Walnut Pumpkin Seed Brittle (page 179) and Honey Balsamic Farmers Market Carrots (page 197), inspired by her grandpa, or Lacey's German Country Potato Salad (page 180), or Tammy's Missouri Corn Salad with Lime and Paprika (page 190) that symbolizes her upbringing, these salads and sides are much more than mere supporting players.

But not every dish is what it seems. One year, Terry decided to prank the kids by swapping out his Legendary Bradshaw Beans (page 198) for a "special" batch made with tofu. The looks of betrayal on their faces were priceless! Thankfully, he had the real tray of beef and bacon-loaded beans waiting in the wings.

And let's not forget the classic Iceberg Salad with Terry's Favorite Dressing (page 176), a must-have at every gathering. Nannie's Red Potato Salad with Pimento and Sweet Pickle (page 183) also never fails to bring a smile to everyone's faces. Even more so, our times cooking together set an example for our children, and we make it a priority to share laughter, hugs, and compliments to enrich our family bonds. Every side dish is an opportunity to spread affection and laughter, and maybe a little mischief, too.

Iceberg Salad with Terry's Favorite Dressing

In the summer, a lot of the time we'll just have a big salad for dinner, which includes a lot of great ingredients from our garden, like tomatoes, peppers, and onions. A lighter salad dressing like my favorite, a combo of grapeseed oil and rice vinegar, lets the flavors of our garden vegetables shine through. **—TERRY**

Serves 2

TERRY'S FAVORITE DRESSING
Makes 1½ cups

1 cup grapeseed oil

½ cup natural rice vinegar

Kosher salt and fresh cracked black pepper, to taste

ICEBERG SALAD

¼ large head of iceberg lettuce, torn or shredded

½ cucumber, peeled and thinly sliced

1 ripe tomato, chopped

6 medium radishes, trimmed and thinly sliced

1 green or red bell pepper, stemmed, seeded, and sliced

Kosher salt and freshly cracked black pepper, to taste

To make the dressing: Combine the oil and rice vinegar in a measuring cup or jar. Season with salt and pepper.

To make the iceberg salad: Combine the lettuce, cucumber, tomato, radishes, and and bell pepper in a salad bowl. Add dressing to taste and toss well to coat. Season with salt and pepper, toss again, and serve immediately. Store any leftover dressing in a covered jar and use within a week or so.

COACH'S CORNER

Change up the salad to your liking. Add a little extra crunch with some chopped walnuts, almonds, pecans, or cashews. For a sweeter note, try it with dried cranberries, diced apple, or pear slices. You can serve this salad as a main course, too, by adding some bacon, grilled chicken, diced tofu, sliced steak, beans, or lentils. Or swap some of the veggies for carrots, beets, onions, broccoli, spinach, or mushrooms. Just chop them to a similar size.

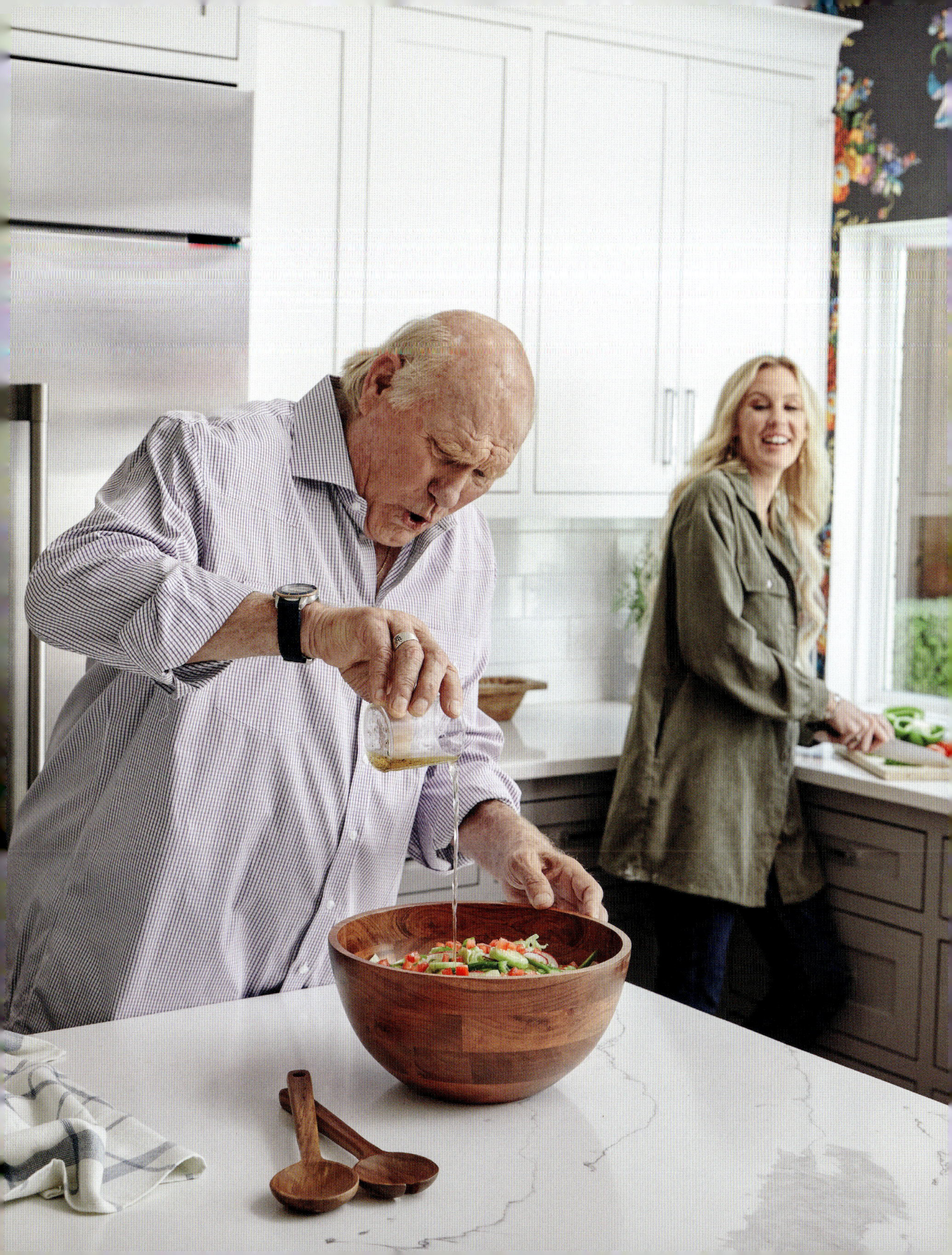

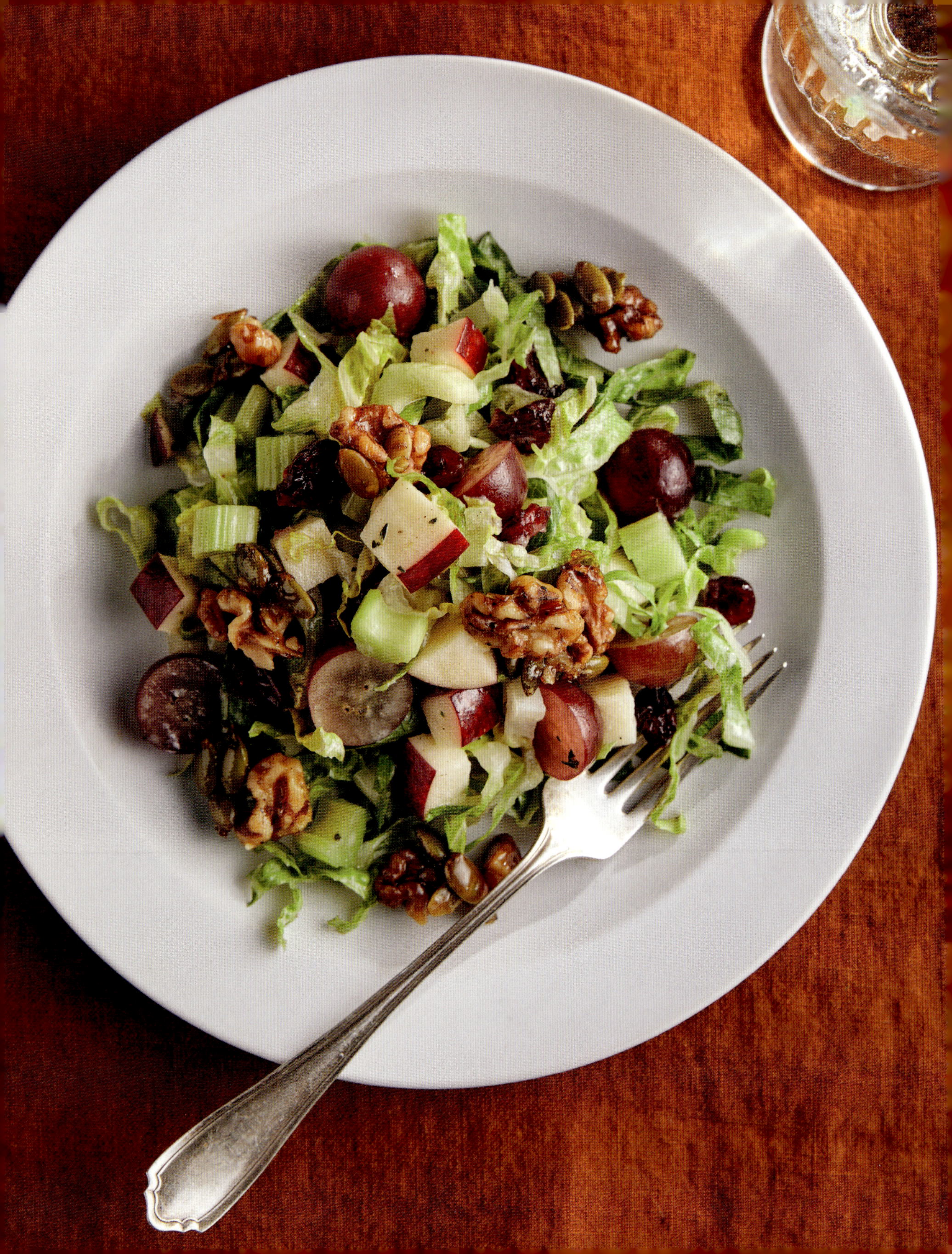

Waldorf Salad with Walnut Pumpkin Seed Brittle

When it's all said and done, this salad will look like it took hours to make when, actually, it takes very little time to prepare. I like it so much I even serve it as a side dish at Christmas. What makes it special are the grapes and dried cranberries for a bit of sweetness and fresh pomegranate seeds for zing. I also like to incorporate walnuts into a crunchy brittle, which I use as a garnish before serving. —RACHEL

Serves 4 to 6

WALNUT PUMPKIN SEED BRITTLE
(see Coach's Corner)

- 1 cup walnut pieces
- ½ cup pumpkin seeds
- ¼ cup maple syrup
- 2 teaspoons olive oil
- ½ teaspoon kosher salt
- ¼ teaspoon freshly cracked black pepper

DRESSING
Makes 1 cup

- ⅓ cup plain or vanilla yogurt
- 2 tablespoons apple cider vinegar
- 1 tablespoon chopped fresh thyme leaves
- 1 tablespoon Dijon mustard
- 1 tablespoon maple syrup
- 1 teaspoon kosher salt
- ½ teaspoon freshly cracked black pepper
- ⅓ cup olive oil

WALDORF SALAD

- 1 large head romaine lettuce, chopped
- 1 cup halved seedless red grapes
- 1 cup sliced celery
- 1 large apple, cored and chopped
- ½ cup dried cranberries
- ¾ cup pomegranate seeds

COACH'S CORNER

Make extra Walnut Pumpkin Seed Brittle and store in an airtight container in a cool, dry place for up to 2 months. It makes for a yummy and crunchy topping on yogurt or ice cream.

To make the brittle: Preheat the oven to 350°F. Combine the walnuts, pumpkin seeds, syrup, olive oil, salt, and pepper in a bowl and mix until the nuts are well coated. Spread out onto a parchment-lined baking sheet. Bake for 10 minutes, then rotate the sheet. Continue to bake until the brittle is golden brown and bubbling, 6 to 8 minutes. Allow to cool completely before breaking the brittle into bite-sized pieces.

To make the dressing: In a medium bowl, whisk together the yogurt, apple cider vinegar, thyme, mustard, syrup, salt, and pepper. Slowly whisk in the olive oil until incorporated.

To make the Waldorf salad: Add the lettuce, grapes, celery, apple, cranberries, and pomegranate seeds to a large bowl. Drizzle about ¼ cup of the dressing, or the amount of your liking, and toss until the leaves are lightly coated. Garnish with some walnut pumpkin seed brittle and serve.

German Country Potato Salad

Growing up, I never liked mustard in my potato salad, so who knew I would come to love this salad, made with whole-grain mustard? This version is tangy and comforting and can be served warm or at room temperature. It features bacon, onion, apple cider vinegar, and a touch of honey for balance. The result is a savory-sweet side dish with a delightful kick. —LACEY

Serves 4 to 6

1½ pounds unpeeled Yukon Gold or red potatoes, cut in ½-inch cubes

6 bacon slices

1 small yellow onion, finely chopped

2 tablespoons apple cider vinegar

2 tablespoons whole-grain mustard

2 tablespoons honey

¼ cup Homemade Organic Chicken Stock (page 212) or vegetable stock

Kosher salt and freshly cracked black pepper, to taste

¼ cup chopped fresh Italian flat-leaf parsley

Chopped fresh chives, for serving

Bring a large pot of well-salted water to a boil. Add the potatoes and cook until fork tender, about 10 minutes. Drain the potatoes and set aside.

Heat a large, high-sided skillet over medium heat. Add the bacon and cook until crisp, 6 to 8 minutes. Remove the bacon to a paper towel–lined plate to drain, then crumble or chop into small pieces. Set aside.

Add the onion to the bacon grease in the skillet and cook over medium heat, stirring occasionally, until translucent, 3 to 4 minutes. Add the apple cider vinegar, mustard, honey, and stock. Stir to combine, scraping up any browned bits from the bottom of the skillet.

Add the cooked potatoes and bacon to the skillet and toss gently until the potatoes are well coated with the dressing. Season with salt and pepper. Reduce the heat to medium-low and cook the potato salad for another 2 minutes. Remove the skillet from the heat and stir in the parsley. Taste and adjust the seasoning, if necessary. Transfer to a serving dish, garnish with chives, and serve warm or at room temperature.

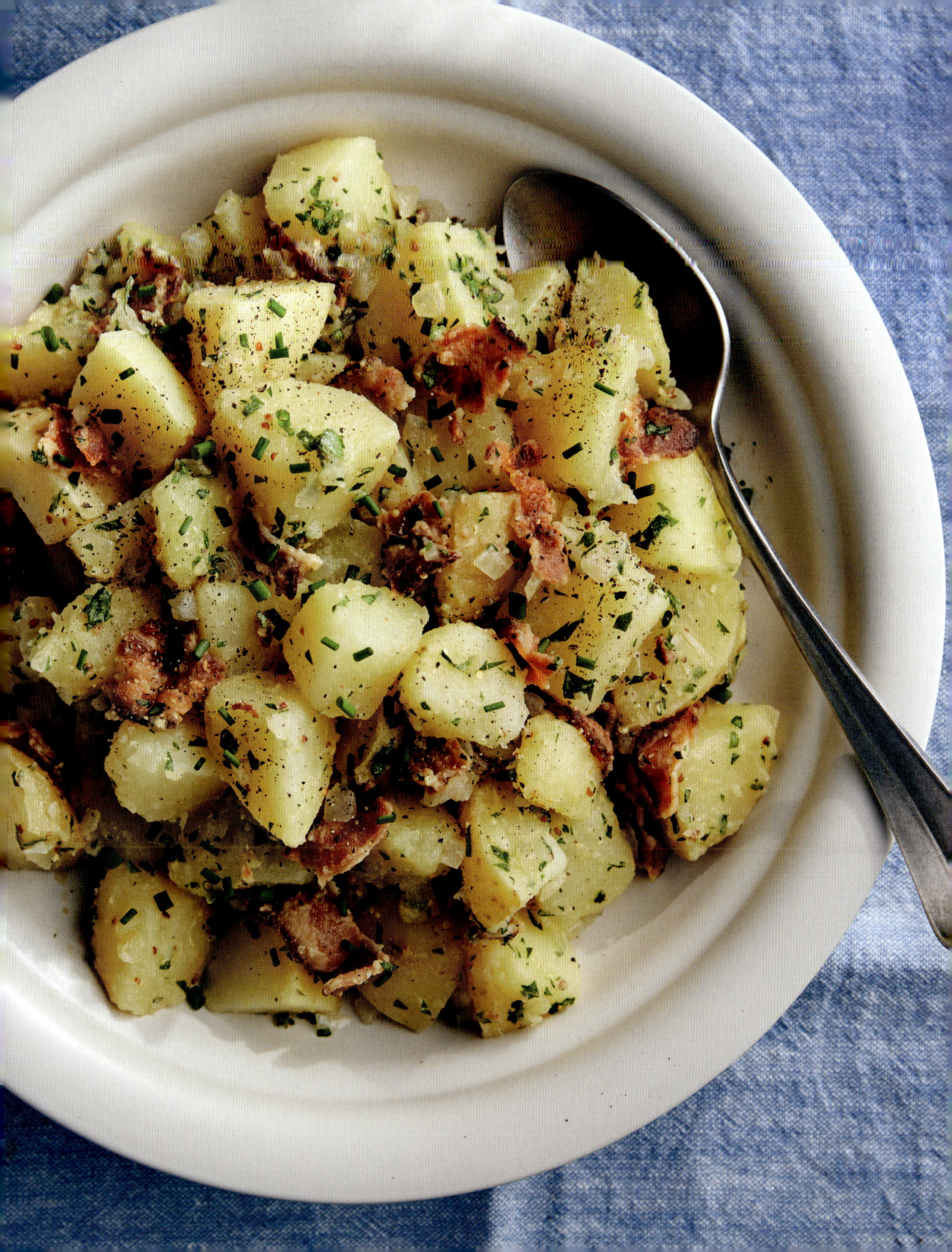

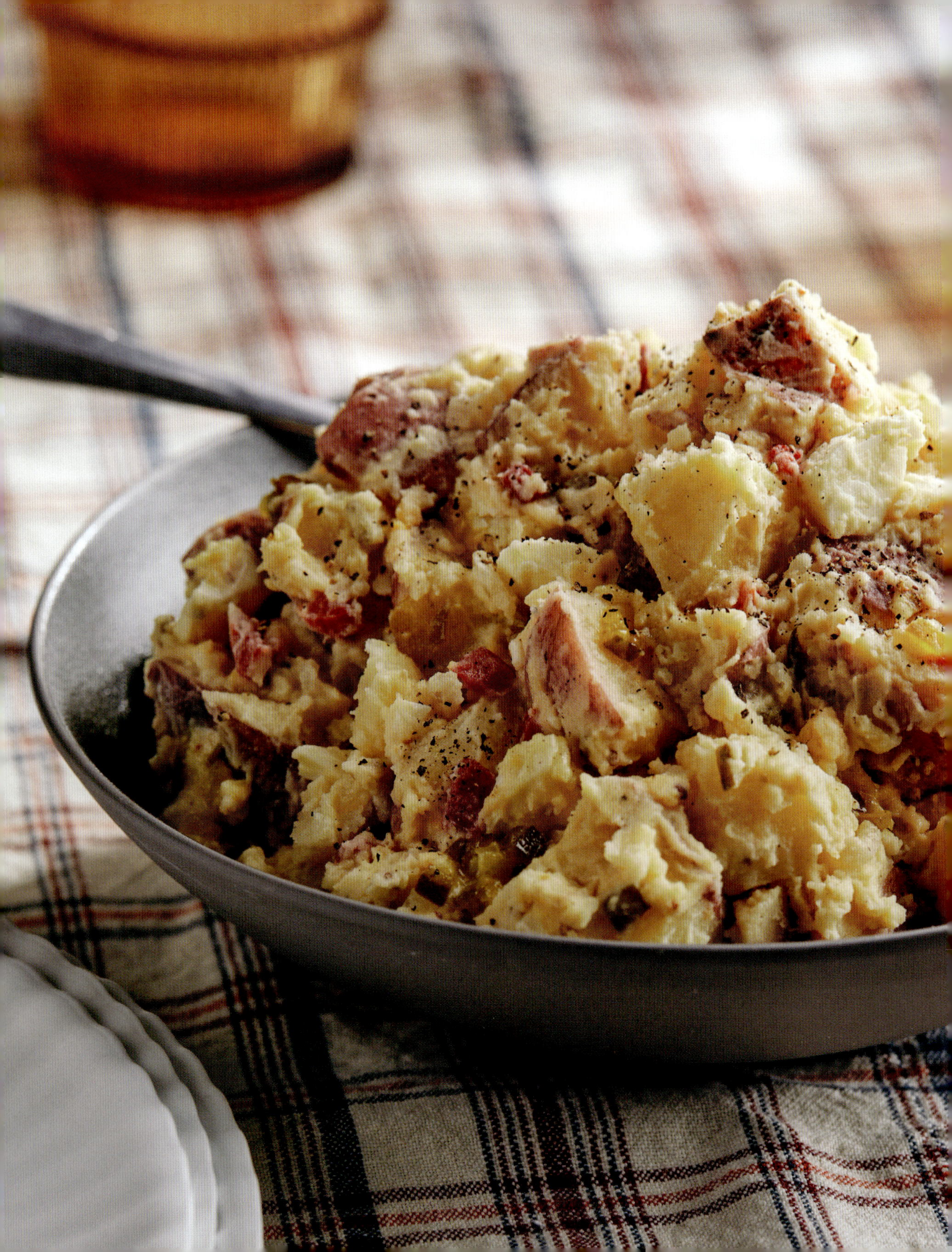

Red Potato Salad with Pimento and Sweet Pickle

My mother began making potato salad decades ago when she was a young bride of sixteen. Over the years, she perfected her recipe, adding a dash of this and a pinch of that until it was just right. As she grew older, she shared her recipe with all of us. Today, at the heart of every Bradshaw family cookout, you'll find a bowl of this potato salad that's spiked with diced pimentos and sweet pickles. —TERRY

Serves 6 to 8

2½ pounds red potatoes, peeled or not

5 hard-boiled large eggs, peeled and mashed

¾ cup diced sweet pickles (or sweet relish)

½ cup Miracle Whip, or more to taste

1 medium yellow onion, diced

1 (2-ounce) jar pimentos, drained

2 teaspoons yellow mustard, or more to taste

Kosher salt and freshly cracked black pepper, to taste

Add the potatoes to a large pot of well-salted water. Bring to a boil over high heat and cook until the potatoes are fork tender, 20 to 25 minutes. Drain the potatoes and place in a large bowl. Partially mash with a potato masher or fork and let cool to room temperature.

Add the eggs, pickles, Miracle Whip, onion, pimentos, and mustard to the potatoes and toss gently. Season with salt and pepper. Adjust the salad by adding more mustard and/or Miracle Whip until you achieve the desired consistency and taste. Cover and refrigerate until ready to serve.

COACH'S CORNER

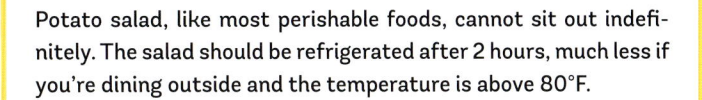

Potato salad, like most perishable foods, cannot sit out indefinitely. The salad should be refrigerated after 2 hours, much less if you're dining outside and the temperature is above 80°F.

Old-Fashioned Ambrosia Salad

This salad holds a special place in my heart. I remember watching my grandmother Hoodie Baby in the kitchen making this salad when I was a little boy. I can still see the bright colors of the fruit and Jell-O. Like many dishes from her era, the ambrosia salad is perfect for potlucks and picnics. **—TERRY**

Serves 12 to 14

1 (20-ounce) can crushed pineapple with juice

1 (6-ounce) package orange Jell-O

1 cup flaked coconut

½ cup chopped pecans

1 (8-ounce) tub Cool Whip

1½ cups cottage cheese

Combine the pineapple (with juice) and Jell-O in a saucepan. Stir over medium heat just until the Jell-O is dissolved. Remove from the heat and stir in the coconut and pecans, then fold in the Cool Whip and cottage cheese. Pour into a 9 × 13-inch glass dish and refrigerate until firm, about 2 hours. Serve chilled.

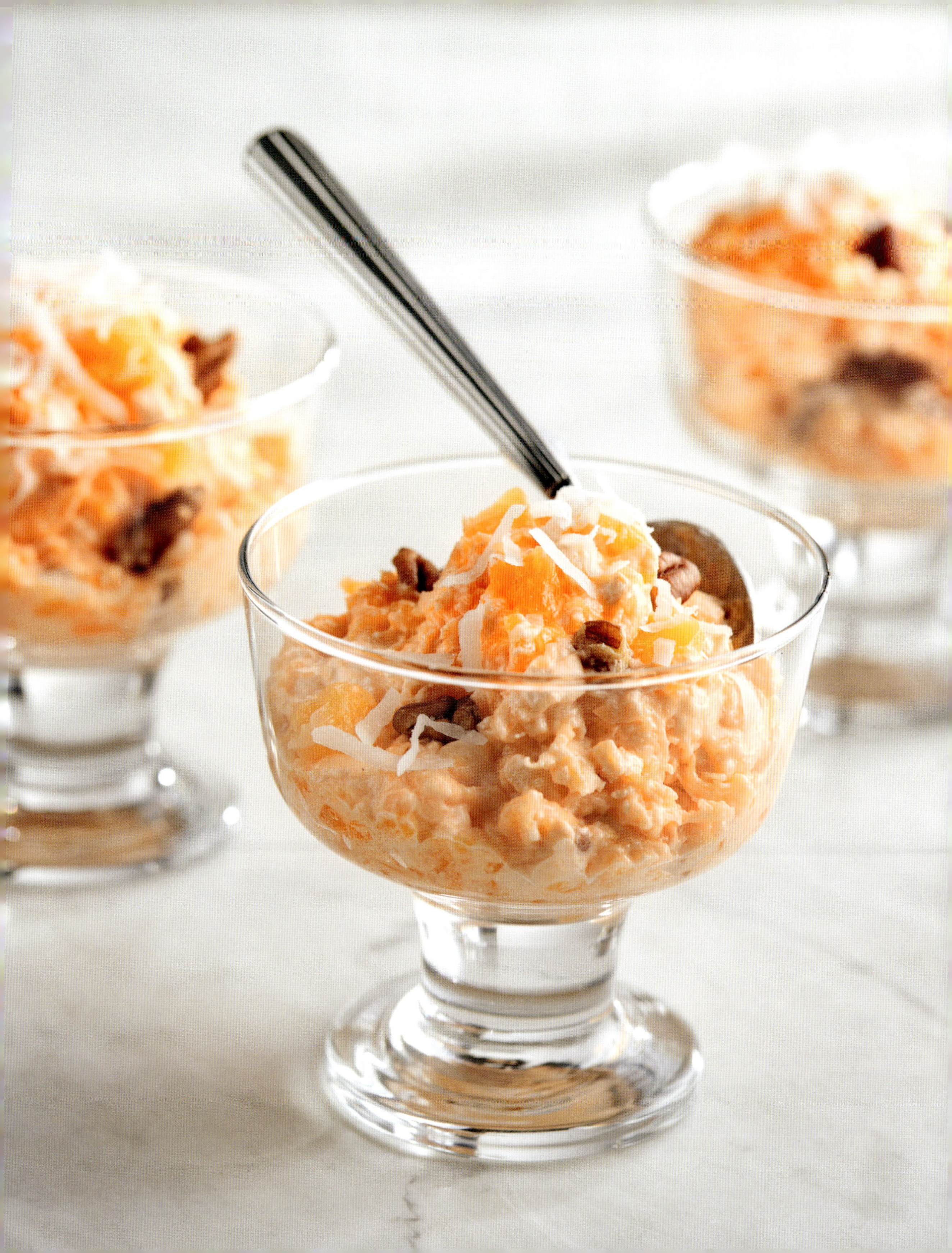

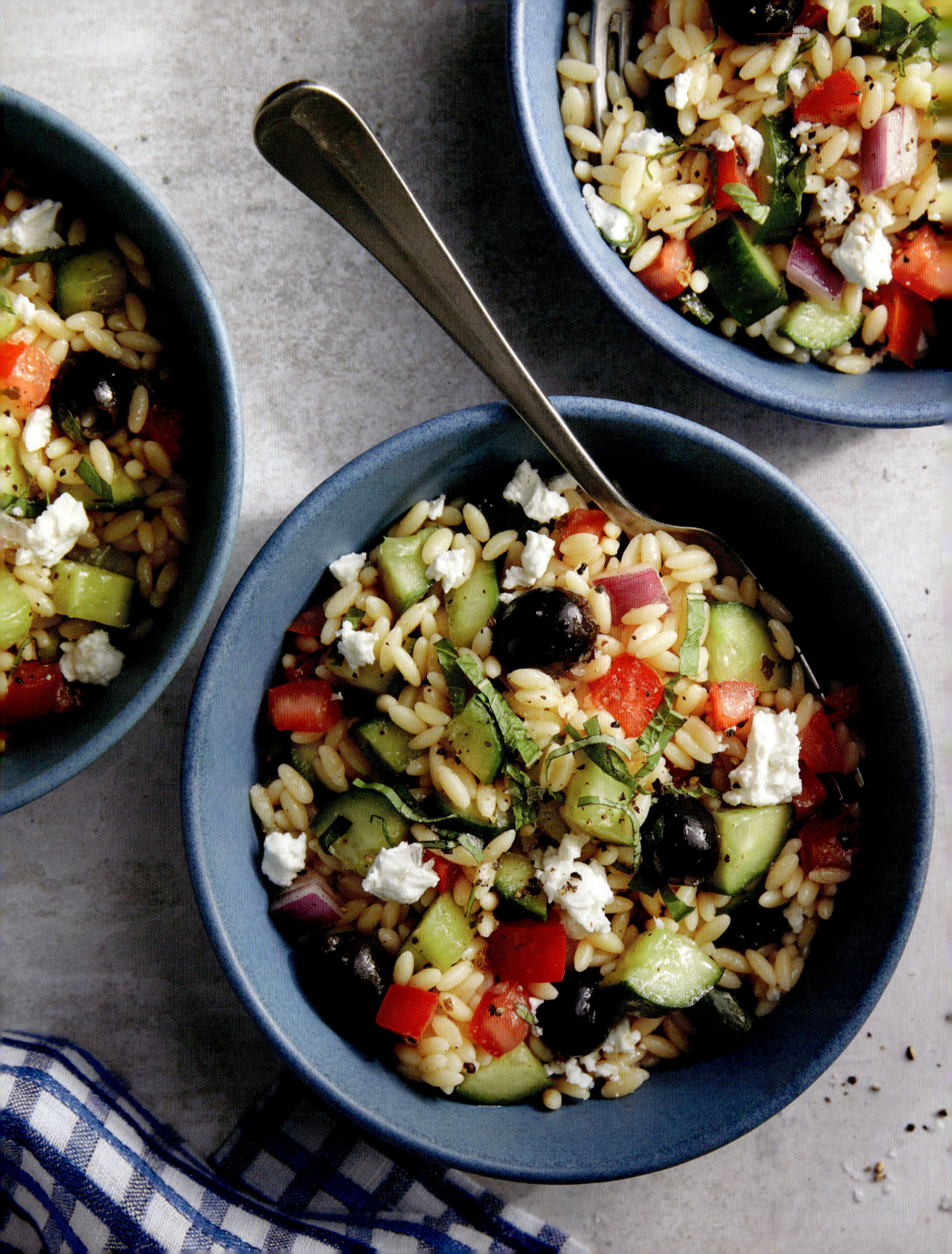

Greek Orzo Salad with Oil, Vinegar, and Honey Dressing

I first made this flavorful salad when I was heading over to my dad's for a crawfish boil and didn't know what to bring. My friend Christina graciously gave me her recipe, which I modified. It's become our "family salad" at virtually every gathering since. It's loaded with orzo, crisp cucumbers, cherry tomatoes, olives, tangy feta cheese, and fresh herbs, with a touch of honey in the dressing for the perfect balance of sweet and savory. —RACHEL

Serves 6 to 8

HONEY DRESSING
Makes about ¼ cup

2 tablespoons olive oil

1 teaspoon white wine vinegar

1 tablespoon red wine vinegar

¼ teaspoon honey

Garlic powder, to taste

Kosher salt and freshly cracked black pepper, to taste

ORZO SALAD

1 cup raw orzo pasta

½ cup crumbled feta cheese

2 tablespoons diced red onion

1¼ cups chopped fresh tomatoes

4 small (pickling) cucumbers, chopped

¼ cup pitted black olives, halved or sliced

¼ teaspoon dried oregano

¼ teaspoon chopped fresh basil

½ teaspoon chopped fresh mint

Kosher salt and freshly cracked black pepper, to taste

To make the dressing: Whisk together the olive oil, white wine vinegar, red wine vinegar, and honey in a small bowl. Season with garlic powder, salt, and pepper. Set aside.

To make the orzo salad: Bring a large pot of well-salted water to a boil. Add the orzo and stir. Return to a boil and cook, uncovered, stirring occasionally, for about 10 minutes. Drain well, then refrigerate until cold.

In a large salad bowl, combine the cold orzo, feta, onion, tomatoes, cucumbers, olives, oregano, basil, and mint. Toss well and season with salt and pepper. Add the dressing and toss to coat. Refrigerate the salad until ready to serve.

Mexican Street Corn Salad

I came up with the name for this fun salad because not only is it a very Mexican-style dish but corn is originally from Mexico—first grown more than ten thousand years ago. In the summer months when the sun is out and the pool is warm and inviting, I'll serve this bright and delicious salad with tortilla chips to scoop up and eat as a dip. —RACHEL

Serves 4

1 tablespoon olive oil

4 cups fresh corn kernels (from about 5 ears), or canned or thawed frozen corn kernels

½ red bell pepper, stemmed, seeded, and chopped

½ small red onion, diced

½ cup chopped fresh cilantro, plus more for serving

6 green onions, green and white parts, sliced

1 jalapeño, stemmed, seeded, and diced

½ ripe Hass avocado, pitted, peeled, and chopped

¼ cup fresh lime juice, plus more to taste

½ teaspoon ground cumin

½ teaspoon smoked paprika

¼ teaspoon kosher salt, plus more to taste

¼ teaspoon freshly cracked black pepper, plus more to taste

2 tablespoons sour cream

2 tablespoons mayonnaise

½ cup crumbled cotija or feta cheese, plus more for serving

Heat the olive oil in a large skillet over high heat. Add the corn and cook, stirring often, until the corn begins to char, 5 to 7 minutes. If you're using thawed corn, you may need a couple minutes extra to get the right charred bits. Transfer the corn to a large bowl and let cool for 5 minutes.

Add the bell pepper, red onion, cilantro, green onions, jalapeño, avocado, lime juice, cumin, paprika, salt, pepper, sour cream, mayonnaise, and cotija to the corn. Stir gently until the ingredients are well combined. Taste and adjust with additional lime juice, salt, and pepper, if necessary. Garnish with additional cotija and cilantro and serve.

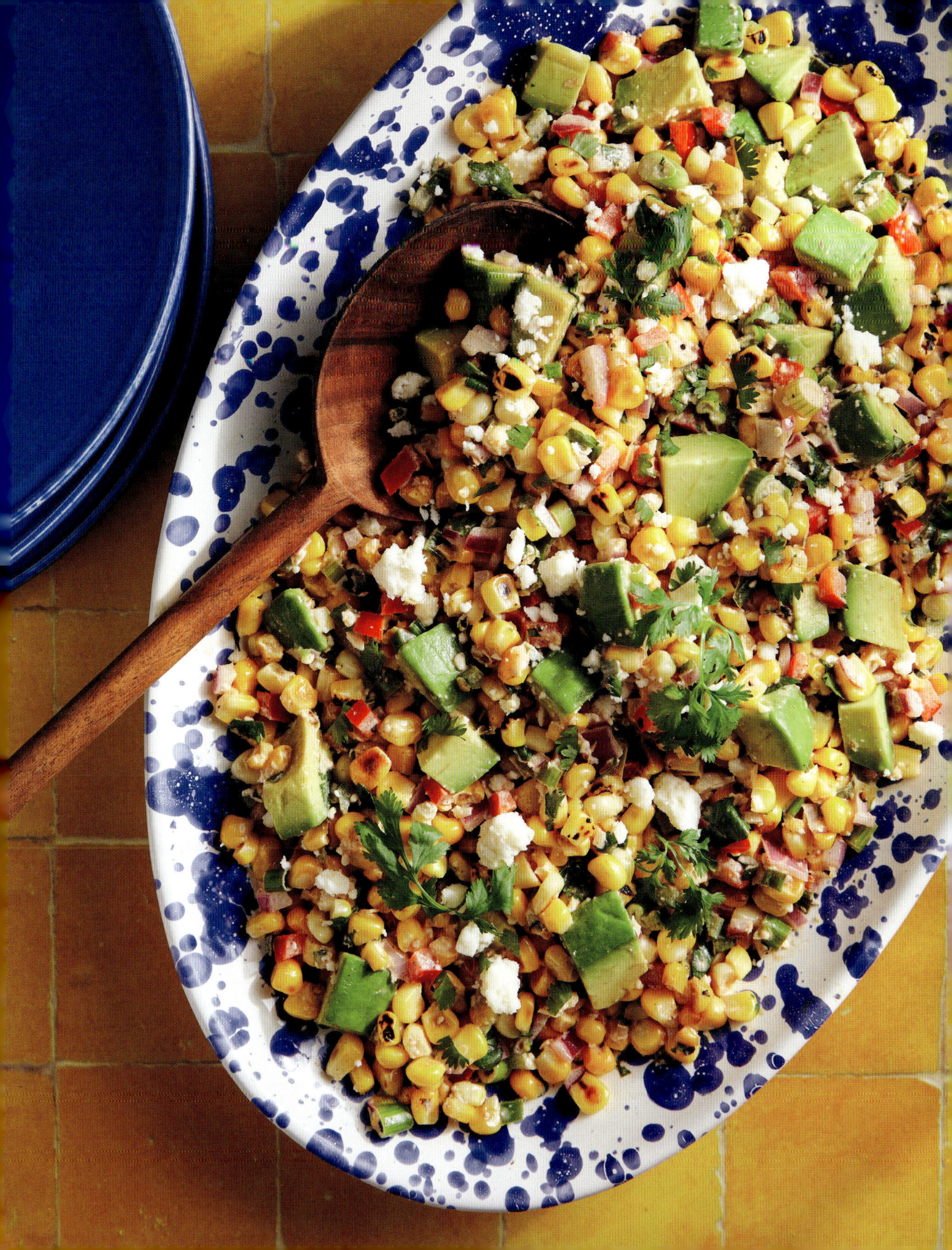

Missouri Corn Salad with Lime and Paprika

Where I grew up in Missouri, this salad, with its coleslawlike texture and south of the border twist, was enjoyed a lot. The combination of sweet corn and the Holy Trinity (celery, bell pepper, and onion) adds the perfect crunch while the creamy mayonnaise and smoked paprika dressing balances the crisp vegetables. I'll often make this salad the night before, then serve it cold the next day along with plenty of corn chips. **—TAMMY**

Serves 8

¼ cup granulated sugar

¼ cup vegetable oil

¼ cup white wine vinegar

2 (15-ounce) cans sweet corn, drained (see Coach's Corner)

½ cup finely chopped celery

1 red bell pepper, stemmed, seeded, and diced

½ cup diced yellow onion

2 tablespoons mayonnaise

⅛ teaspoon smoked paprika, plus more for serving

Kosher salt and freshly cracked black pepper, to taste

Lime wheel, for serving

Combine the sugar, oil, and white wine vinegar in a saucepan. Whisk to combine and simmer over medium heat until the sugar is dissolved, about 3 minutes. Cool to room temperature.

Combine the corn, celery, bell pepper, and onion in a large bowl. Whisk the mayonnaise and paprika into the cooled vinegar mixture and season with salt and pepper. Drizzle ¼ to ½ cup of the dressing over the salad and toss thoroughly. Garnish with a sprinkle of paprika and a lime wheel and serve.

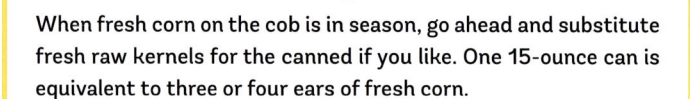

COACH'S CORNER

When fresh corn on the cob is in season, go ahead and substitute fresh raw kernels for the canned if you like. One 15-ounce can is equivalent to three or four ears of fresh corn.

Green Beans with Bacon, Onion, and Garlic

Given Terry's and my crazy schedules, time is a precious commodity, and convenience reigns supreme in the kitchen. Enter the multicooker, a multifunction appliance that can sauté, slow cook, pressure cook, and more. It's a kitchen tool that has revolutionized the way Terry and I cook, even something as humble as garden-fresh green beans. Simply trim the ends of the beans and toss them into the pot after you've sautéed a bit of bacon, onion, and garlic. Add chicken stock and cook until the beans are tender. Season with salt, pepper, and a kick of red pepper flakes, and that's all there is to it. —**TAMMY**

Serves 4

¼ cup diced bacon

1 medium yellow onion, diced

3 garlic cloves, minced

1 pound fresh green beans, cleaned and trimmed

2 cups Homemade Organic Chicken Stock (page 212)

Kosher salt and freshly cracked black pepper, to taste

Crushed red pepper flakes (optional)

Set the multicooker to "sauté" and add the bacon, onion, and garlic. Stir to combine. Cook until the bacon is rendered and the vegetables are soft, 6 to 8 minutes. Add the stock and green beans. Pressure cook on low for 1 minute. Manually release by venting the steam (place a pot holder or kitchen towel over the vent for safety) and then open the lid. Transfer the beans to a platter. Season with salt, pepper, and red pepper flakes, if using, and serve.

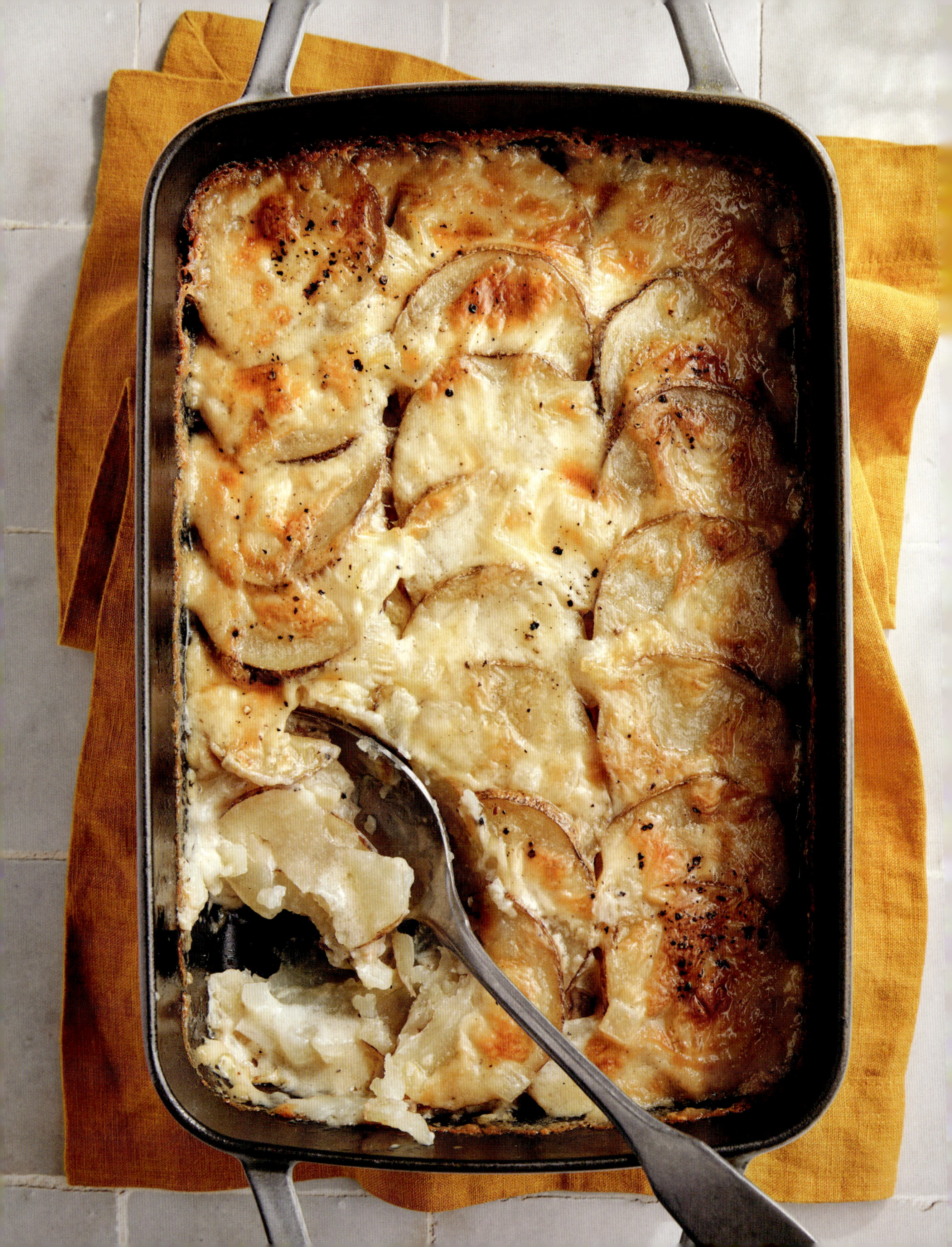

Chicken Stock Scalloped Potatoes

Every year after football season, Tammy and I head over to Hawaii for some rest and relaxation. After about a week, all the kids come over and we'll hang out and cook together. We gravitate toward cozy dishes like this one. The tender potatoes are moist from the flavorful stock, but because it contains no cheese or breadcrumbs, it's on the lighter side, making it the best of both worlds. —**TERRY**

Serves 8 to 10

Nonstick cooking spray

4 tablespoons (½ stick) unsalted butter

1 large yellow onion, diced

2 garlic cloves, minced

¼ cup all-purpose flour

2 cups whole milk

1 cup Homemade Organic Chicken Stock (page 212)

1¼ teaspoons kosher salt, divided

½ teaspoon freshly cracked black pepper, divided

2 pounds russet potatoes, sliced about ⅛-inch thick (see Coach's Corner)

Preheat the oven to 350°F. Spray a 9 × 13-inch baking or casserole dish with nonstick cooking spray.

Melt the butter in a large saucepan over medium-low heat. Add the onion and garlic and cook, stirring occasionally, until the onion begins to soften, 5 to 7 minutes. Add the flour and cook for 1 to 2 minutes. Combine the milk and chicken stock and add to the pan a little at a time, whisking after each addition. When all the liquid has been incorporated, increase the heat to medium and bring to a boil, whisking constantly. Stir in ½ teaspoon salt and ⅛ teaspoon pepper and boil for 1 minute.

Add one-third of the potatoes to the prepared dish and season with ¼ teaspoon salt and ⅛ teaspoon pepper. Pour one-third of the cream sauce over the top. Repeat the layers two more times, ending with cream sauce.

Cover the pan with foil and bake for 45 minutes, then uncover and bake until the potatoes are tender and golden brown, 45 to 60 minutes. If the top isn't brown enough, place the pan under the broiler for 3 to 4 minutes. Let rest for at least 15 minutes before serving.

COACH'S CORNER

If you're making this ahead, you can slice the potatoes and add the slices to a bowl of cold water to prevent browning. Drain just before assembling the dish. To make slicing faster and uniform, use a mandoline.

Havarti and Gouda Mac 'n' Cheese

I made this one day on a whim when Terry and Tammy asked if I could bring a side to one of their fall cookouts. It's been requested by the Bradshaws ever since, especially during the holidays. The creaminess of Havarti and the nuttiness of Gouda create a richer, more indulgent sauce. Tammy says it's her favorite. —NOAH

Serves 6 to 8

Nonstick cooking spray

2 cups elbow macaroni

2 tablespoons unsalted butter

2 tablespoons all-purpose flour

2 cups whole milk

2 cups shredded Havarti cheese

1 cup shredded Gouda or Swiss cheese

¼ teaspoon garlic powder

¼ teaspoon onion powder

Kosher salt and freshly cracked black pepper, to taste

½ cup breadcrumbs (optional)

Chopped fresh Italian flat-leaf parsley, for serving

Preheat the oven to 375°F. Spray a baking dish or casserole dish with nonstick cooking spray.

Bring a large pot of well-salted water to a boil. Add the macaroni and stir to separate the noodles. Return to a boil and cook, uncovered, stirring occasionally, until al dente, about 8 minutes. Drain and set aside.

Melt the butter in a large saucepan over medium heat. Slowly whisk in the flour to create a roux. Cook, stirring constantly, until the roux turns a light golden color, 1 to 2 minutes. Gradually add the milk, whisking continuously to prevent lumps from forming. Cook for 2 to 3 minutes, until the sauce begins to thicken.

Reduce the heat to low and add the shredded Havarti and Gouda. Stir until the cheese is melted and the sauce is smooth and creamy. Season with garlic powder, onion powder, salt, and pepper. Add the macaroni to the sauce, stirring until the macaroni is evenly coated.

Transfer the macaroni and cheese to the prepared baking dish, spreading evenly. Sprinkle with the breadcrumbs, if using, and bake until the top is golden brown and bubbly, about 25 minutes. Let cool for several minutes. Garnish with parsley and serve.

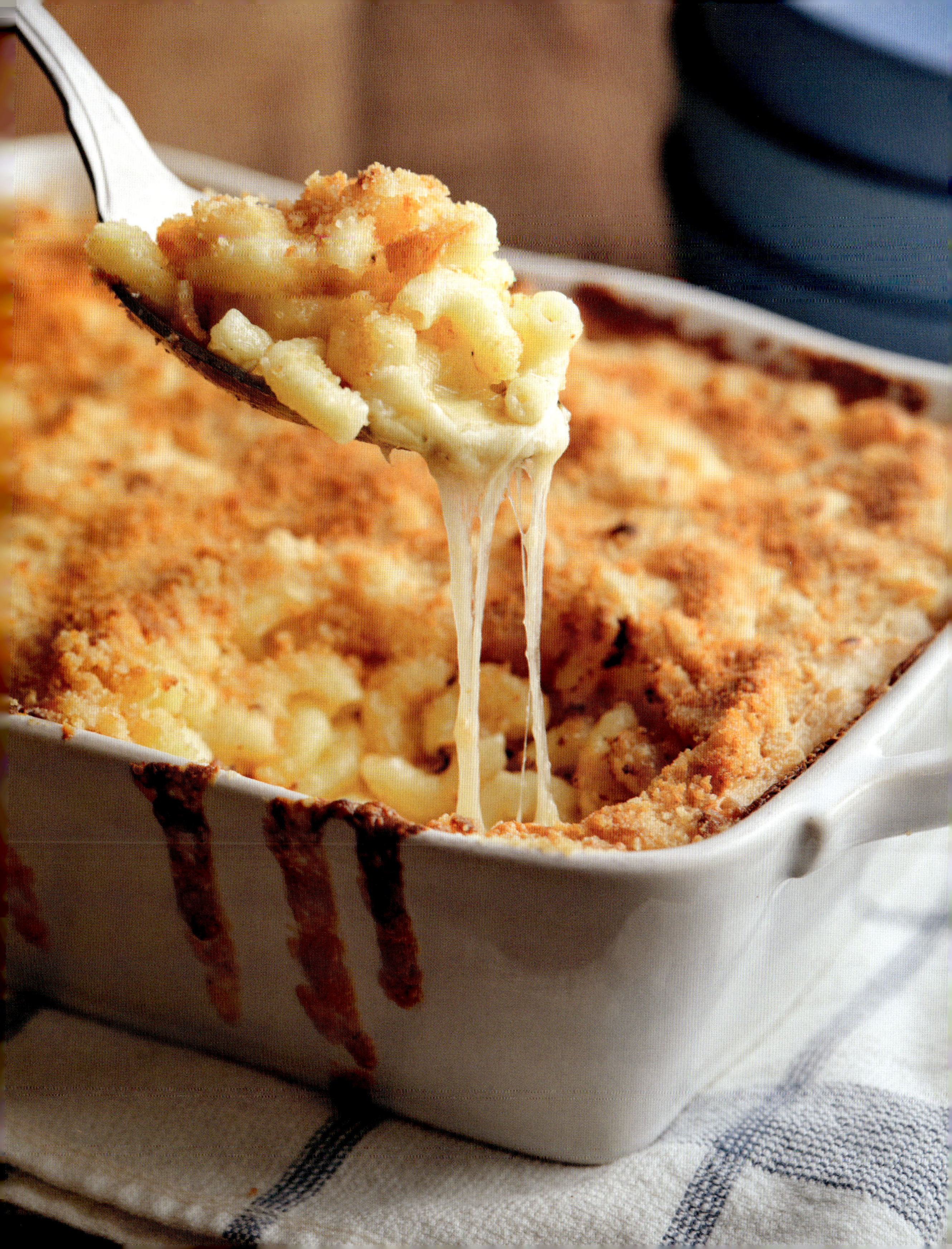

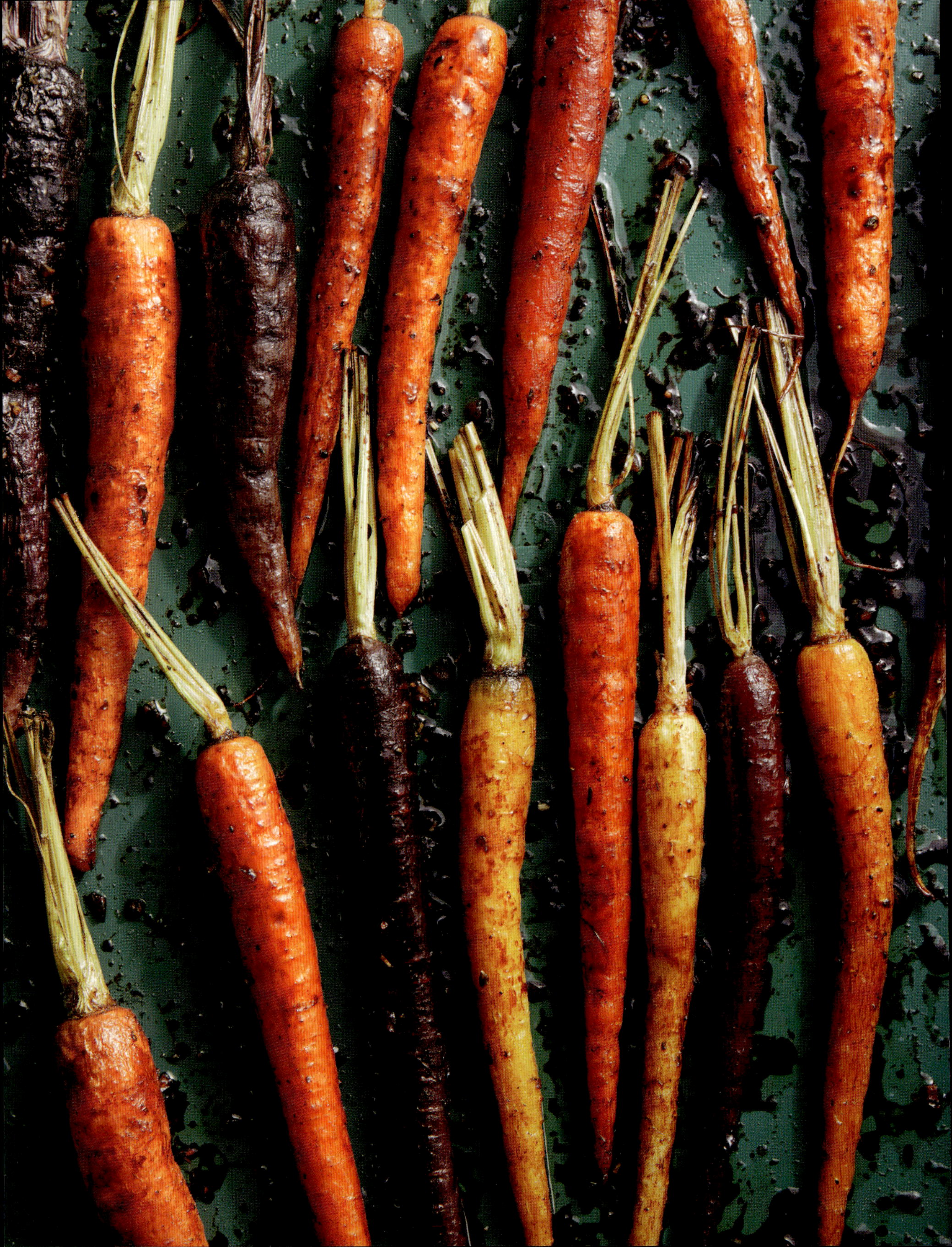

Honey Balsamic Farmers Market Carrots

One year, I found a recipe in my grandpa's old cookbook for roasted carrots. I knew it had to be good, as the page had balsamic stains all over it and still smelled of vinegar. The fact that we have made it a permanent part of our repertoire attests to just how good it is—an assortment of rainbow-colored carrots smothered with a mixture of butter, brown sugar, honey, balsamic vinegar, garlic, and Italian seasoning, then roasted until tender and caramelized. The result is a sweet and tangy side that will make a strong impression at your next gathering. **—RACHEL**

Serves 4 to 6

4 tablespoons (½ stick) unsalted butter

2 tablespoons packed dark brown sugar

2 tablespoons honey

1 tablespoon balsamic vinegar

1 tablespoon minced garlic

1 teaspoon Italian seasoning

2 pounds thin heirloom baby carrots, tops trimmed to about 2 inches (see Coach's Corner)

2 tablespoons olive oil

Kosher salt and freshly cracked black pepper, to taste

Preheat the oven to 400°F.

Combine the butter, brown sugar, honey, balsamic vinegar, garlic, and Italian seasoning in a small saucepan. Cook over medium-high heat, stirring often, until the mixture begins to boil. Remove from the heat.

Toss the carrots with the olive oil and season with salt and pepper. Arrange the carrots in a single layer on a rimmed baking sheet. Pour the butter mixture over the carrots. Bake until the carrots are tender and easily pierced with a fork, 20 to 30 minutes. Transfer to a platter and serve.

COACH'S CORNER

We like to use whole thin carrots, sometimes called baby carrots, but not to be confused with the little carrot nuggets that come in small bags for kids' lunches. The carrots we're referring to are thin, young carrots that are not tough or woody. They are often found at farmers markets or in the organic section of your grocery store. Sometimes they come in multiple colors, which makes for an attractive presentation. Usually, the carrots come with the leafy tops still intact. For a nice presentation, don't cut them off entirely; leave a couple of inches.

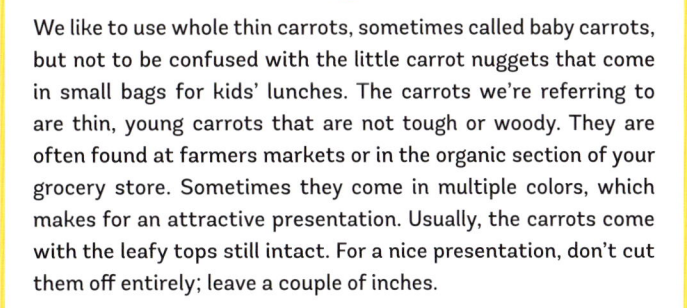

Terry's Legendary Bradshaw Beans

A family meal without Bradshaw Beans just wouldn't be complete. This recipe has been in our family for years. I'm the one who perfected it, although my brother Gary may have something to say about that. I like to spice up the beans with jalapeños and eat on it for a week before freezing what's left for later. Serve the beans as a side or as a main dish. **—TERRY**

Serves 10 to 12

2 pounds (80% lean) ground beef

3 (15-ounce) cans kidney beans, rinsed and drained

3 (15-ounce) cans black beans, rinsed and drained

3 (15-ounce) cans great northern beans, rinsed and drained

1 pound bacon, cut into 1-inch pieces

1 large white onion, diced

2 cups diced green or red bell pepper

1 (or more) jalapeño, stemmed, seeded, and diced (or include the seeds if you like spice)

2 cups Bradshaw Bourbon Barbecue Sauce (page 141), or more to taste

¾ cup packed dark brown sugar

Preheat the oven to 350°F.

Crumble the beef into a large skillet and cook over medium-high heat, using a wooden spoon to break up the meat. When cooked through, about 10 minutes, drain the rendered fat from the pan and transfer the beef to a large heavy-duty all-purpose aluminum pan (approximately 15 × 11 × 2 inches).

Add the kidney beans, black beans, great northern beans, bacon, onion, bell pepper, and jalapeño(s) to the pan with the beef. (Note: The number of jalapeños, and whether you seed them, is entirely up to you and your desired spice level.) With clean hands, mix everything together, adding the barbecue sauce ½ cup at a time until your desired consistency is achieved. (We like using 2 to 2½ cups.) Sprinkle the top with the brown sugar. Cover the pan with foil and bake for 4 hours. Check to make sure there is still enough liquid in the pan after 3 hours (see Coach's Corner). Let cool for 10 to 15 minutes before serving.

COACH'S CORNER

If you'd like to add a touch of smokiness to the dish, transfer the cooked beans from the oven to a preheated outdoor smoker and smoke, uncovered, for about 15 minutes. The natural smoke will really elevate the beans.

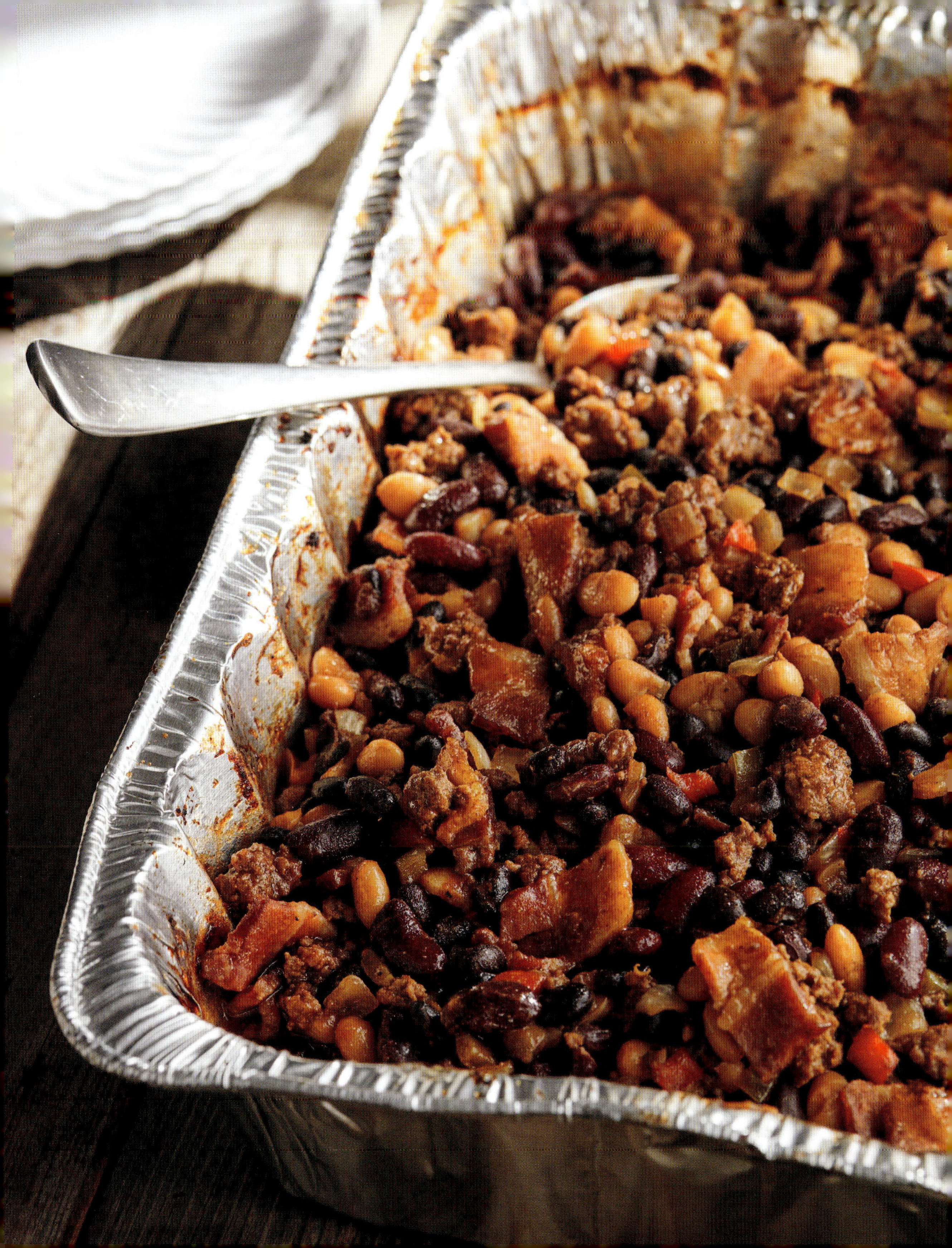

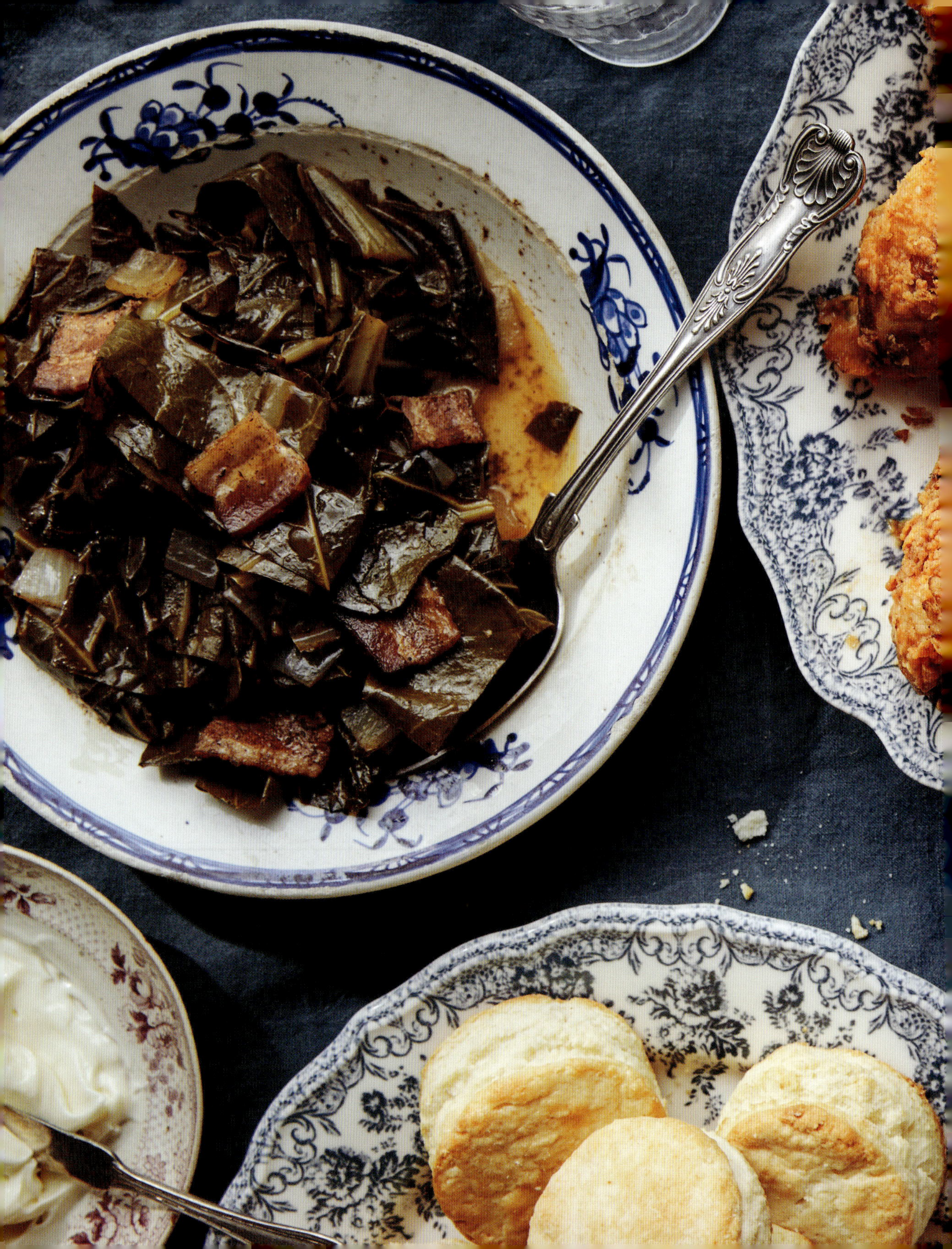

6 // Roots and Relatives

Slow-Cooked Collard Greens with
Bacon, Hot Sauce, and Balsamic

Nannie's Cornbread Dressing

Sweet Potato Casserole
with Chopped Pecans

Fried Green Garden Tomatoes

Homemade Organic Chicken Stock

Buttermilk and Hot Sauce Fried Chicken

Herb-Roasted Chicken and
Biscuit Dumplings

Fried Bologna Sandwich on Texas Toast

Maryland-Style Crab Cakes with
Sweet Pickle Tartar Sauce

Old Bay Shrimp, Andouille,
and Vegetable Boil

Gumbo with Chicken, Andouille,
and Crawfish

Spam (Hawaiian) Musubi
with Homemade Teriyaki Sauce

Terry's Ranch-Style Fish Fry

OUR FAMILY RECIPES ARE MORE THAN JUST FOOD; THEY'RE A WAY TO stay connected to our roots. Each dish is a chapter in our family's story, passed down through generations and flavored with love. Whether it's our spicy Gumbo with Chicken, Andouille, and Crawfish (page 227) and Fried Green Garden Tomatoes (page 209) that transport you straight to Louisiana, or Nannie's Cornbread Dressing (page 206) that makes every holiday meal feel like home, these recipes lay the foundation for our family gatherings.

At these get-togethers, as one could imagine, there's always room for a bit of mischief. One time at the ranch, Noah decided to spice things up for Terry's Ranch-Style Fish Fry (page 233) by sneaking in some ghost pepper hot sauce. Terry loves heat, but when he took a bite, his face turned red as a tomato and he sprinted to the fridge for some milk. The grandkids were in stitches, watching their Pappy fan his mouth with a napkin.

These dishes, with their rich flavors and deep roots, serve as more than just a feast for the senses; they are a testament to the Bradshaw family's culinary journey through generations. Each recipe is a piece of our history, echoing the lessons and affection passed down from our ancestors, who believed in the power of good food to bring people together.

From our Buttermilk and Hot Sauce Fried Chicken (page 213), which pairs well with Lacey's Slow-Cooked Collard Greens with Bacon, Hot Sauce, and Balsamic (page 205), to Noah's Fried Bologna Sandwich on Texas Toast (page 218), a nostalgic treat that transports us back to simpler times spent with those we love, these dishes remind us the simplest meals carry the most heart.

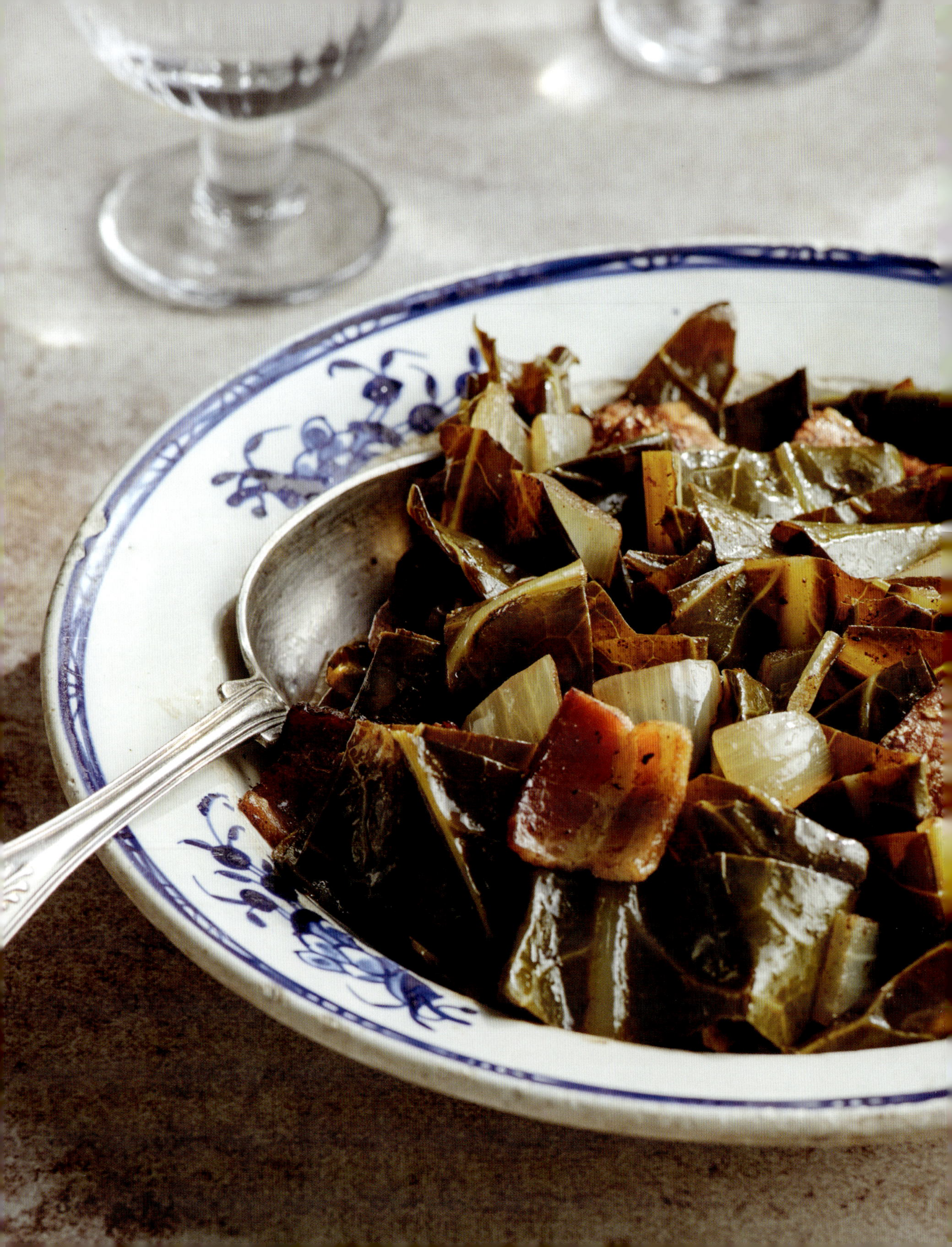

Slow-Cooked Collard Greens with Bacon, Hot Sauce, and Balsamic

Collards are a must at every Bradshaw fish fry. When Noah and I lived in Hawaii, we found it difficult to find fresh collards, so we planted some in our backyard. If you have a sunny spot at home with well-drained soil, we encourage you to plant collard greens, too. When making these flavorful, nutritious greens, layer all the ingredients and do not stir; just let them do their thing. Collards start out bitter, but their flavor will soften and become more mellow the longer you cook them (but don't overcook or they'll turn mushy). If collards are out of season, you can substitute mustard greens. Like good barbecue, the secret is to not rush the cooking process—do it low and slow. —LACEY

Serves 6 to 8

4 bunches fresh collard greens (about 2 dozen leaves)

2 cups chopped thick-cut bacon

2 cups finely chopped white onions

½ cup (1 stick) unsalted butter, cut into tablespoon-sized pieces

½ cup Louisiana's Pure Crystal Hot Sauce (or your favorite brand)

½ cup Chef Noah's Hawaiian Chili Water (optional)

¾ cup balsamic vinegar

Kosher salt and freshly cracked black pepper, to taste

Rinse the collard greens and chop coarsely. For more crunch, leave the stems; for a softer collard, remove the stems; or do half and half.

Place the chopped greens in a large (6.5-quart) pot or Dutch oven. You may need to press them down to make room for the other ingredients. Sprinkle the bacon on top of the greens, followed by a layer of all the onions. Top with the butter, then add the hot sauce, chili water, if using, and balsamic vinegar. Sprinkle generously with salt and pepper, then fill the pot with just enough water to cover the greens (about 10 cups).

Place the pot over medium heat and partially cover so steam can escape. Cook without stirring until the collards are tender and the bacon is cooked through, about 1 hour. Strain the collards into a large colander, then return them to the pot. Stir until all the ingredients are combined, then transfer to a platter and serve.

Nannie's Cornbread Dressing

Cornbread dressing has adorned our holiday tables for generations. For me, this dressing is a taste of home. Before my mother passed, she shared her recipe, which had brought so much joy to her in the kitchen. Year after year, we continue to honor her memory and spirit by making her savory cornbread dressing for Thanksgiving and Christmas. —TERRY

Serves 6 to 8

Nonstick cooking spray

½ cup (1 stick) butter

2 cups finely chopped yellow onions

1 cup chopped celery

10 cups crumbled premade cornbread

1½ tablespoons dried sage

1 tablespoon freshly cracked black pepper

4 large eggs

1 quart Homemade Organic Chicken Stock (page 212)

Preheat the oven to 450°F. Spray a 3-quart glass baking dish with nonstick cooking spray.

Melt the butter in a large skillet over medium heat. Add the onions and celery and cook, stirring occasionally, until softened, 6 to 7 minutes. Transfer the vegetables to a large mixing bowl. Add the cornbread, sage, pepper, eggs, and chicken stock. Mix well to combine. The dressing should have a batterlike consistency so it can be poured into the prepared baking dish.

Add the dressing to the baking dish and bake until it is bubbling and golden brown on top, about 30 minutes. If the top is browning too quickly, cover with aluminum foil. Let cool for 5 minutes before serving.

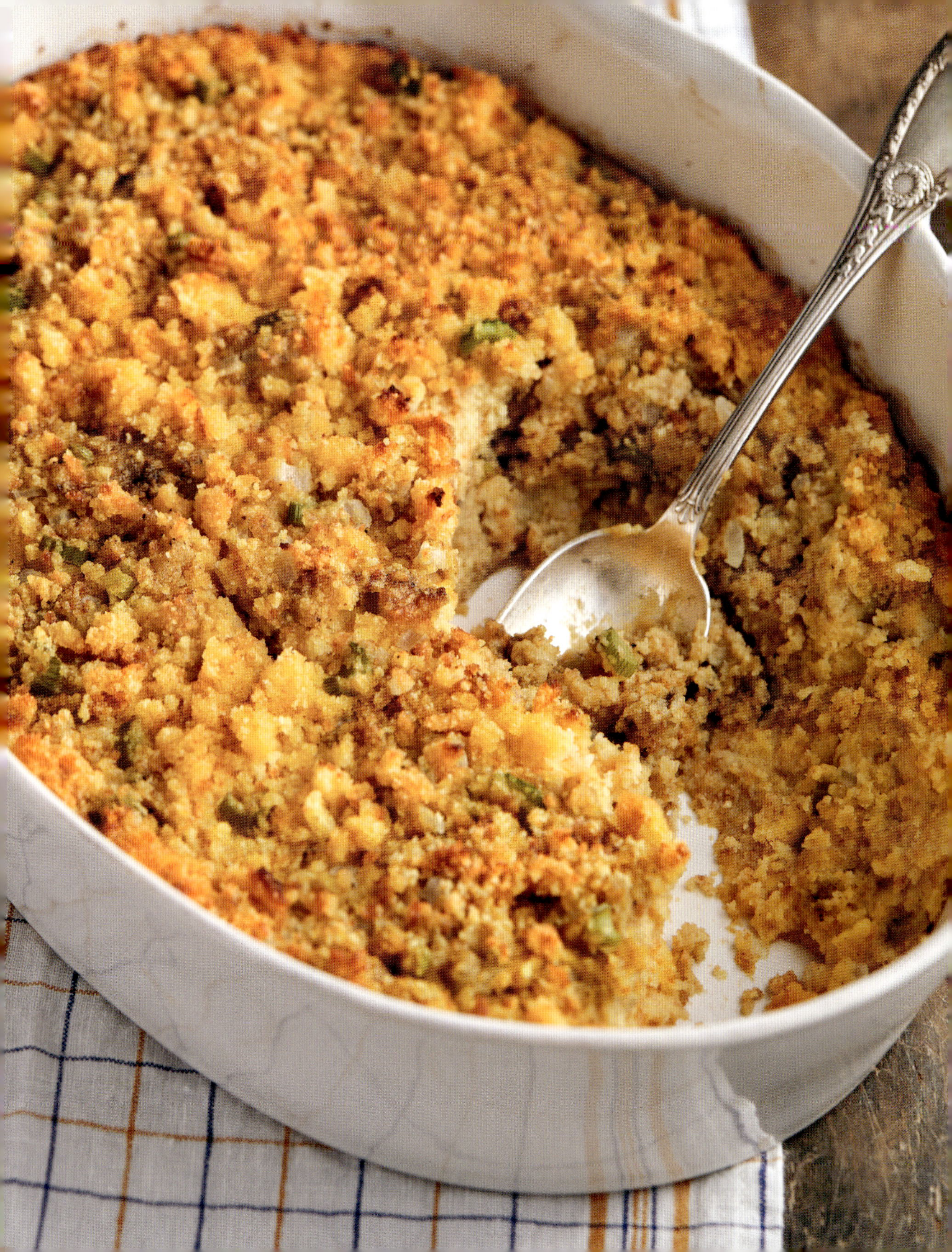

Sweet Potato Casserole with Chopped Pecans

We love hosting Christmas at our home. And when the entire Bradshaw clan is over, our kitchen bustles with activity. Because our feast tends to be very Southern influenced, sweet potato casserole always makes an appearance. The crunchy, nutty topping enhanced with brown sugar and a hint of vanilla never fails to put smiles on our faces. —TAMMY

Serves 12

Nonstick cooking spray

4 or 5 large sweet potatoes, peeled and cut in 1-inch cubes

1/3 cup granulated sugar

1 3/4 sticks unsalted butter, melted

2 large eggs

1 tablespoon pure vanilla extract

3 3/4 cups packed dark brown sugar

1/3 cup whole milk

1/3 cup all-purpose flour

1 cup coarsely chopped pecans

Preheat the oven to 350°F. Spray a 9 × 12-inch baking dish with nonstick cooking spray.

Fill a large pot with water and bring to a boil over high heat. Add the sweet potatoes and boil until fork tender, 8 to 10 minutes. Drain the potatoes in a colander, then transfer to a large bowl.

Using a potato masher, mash the sweet potatoes until smooth. Add the granulated sugar, melted butter, eggs, and vanilla and combine thoroughly. Spread the potato mixture in the prepared baking dish.

Add the brown sugar, milk, flour, and pecans to the same large bowl. Mix well, then slowly pour over the sweet potato mixture, spreading evenly.

Bake until the topping is set, 60 to 70 minutes. Let cool slightly before serving.

Fried Green Garden Tomatoes

Come summer, our garden is filled with so many plump, ripe tomatoes that we pick some of the firmest tomatoes before they have a chance to turn red for this Southern classic. Whether served as an appetizer, side dish, or in a sandwich, these iconic treats never fail to impress. —**TERRY AND TAMMY**

Serves 4

4 large green tomatoes
1 cup whole milk
1 cup all-purpose flour
½ cup cornmeal
Vegetable oil, for frying (about 1 quart)
2 teaspoons kosher salt
¼ teaspoon freshly cracked black pepper

Slice each tomato into approximately ¼-inch-thick rounds. Transfer the slices to a bowl and add the milk, making sure the slices are completely submerged. Set aside.

In a shallow bowl, whisk together the flour and cornmeal.

Heat the oil in a large high-sided skillet over medium-high heat to 350°F. Use a candy or digital thermometer to check the temperature.

One at a time, remove the tomato slices from the milk and dredge in the flour-cornmeal mixture, gently shaking off the excess. When the oil is at temperature, working in batches, add the tomatoes to the hot oil in a single layer, making sure the slices don't touch. Season with salt and pepper as the tomatoes fry. Cook, turning often, until both sides are golden brown, 4 to 5 minutes per side. Drain the tomatoes on a paper towel–lined plate. Serve warm.

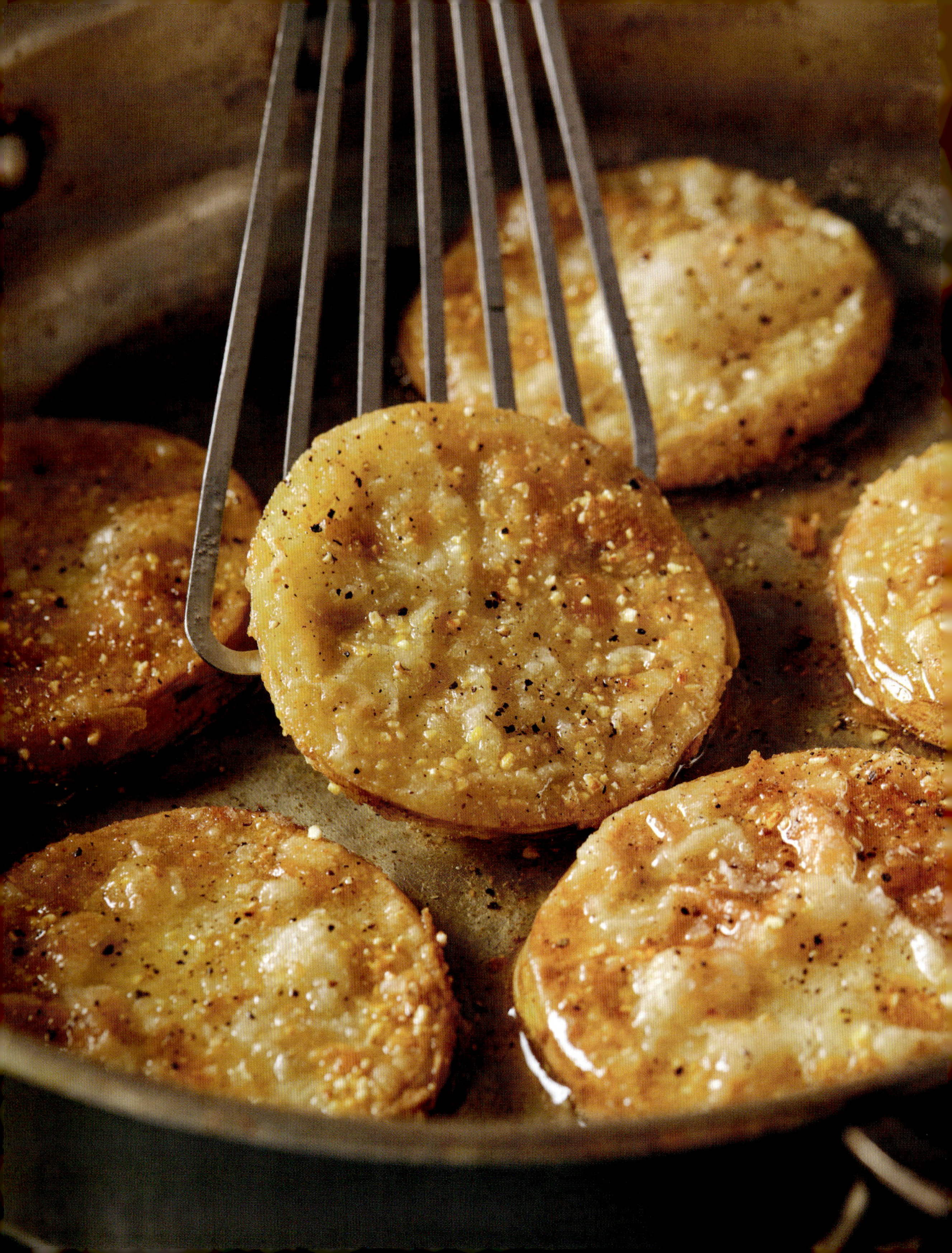

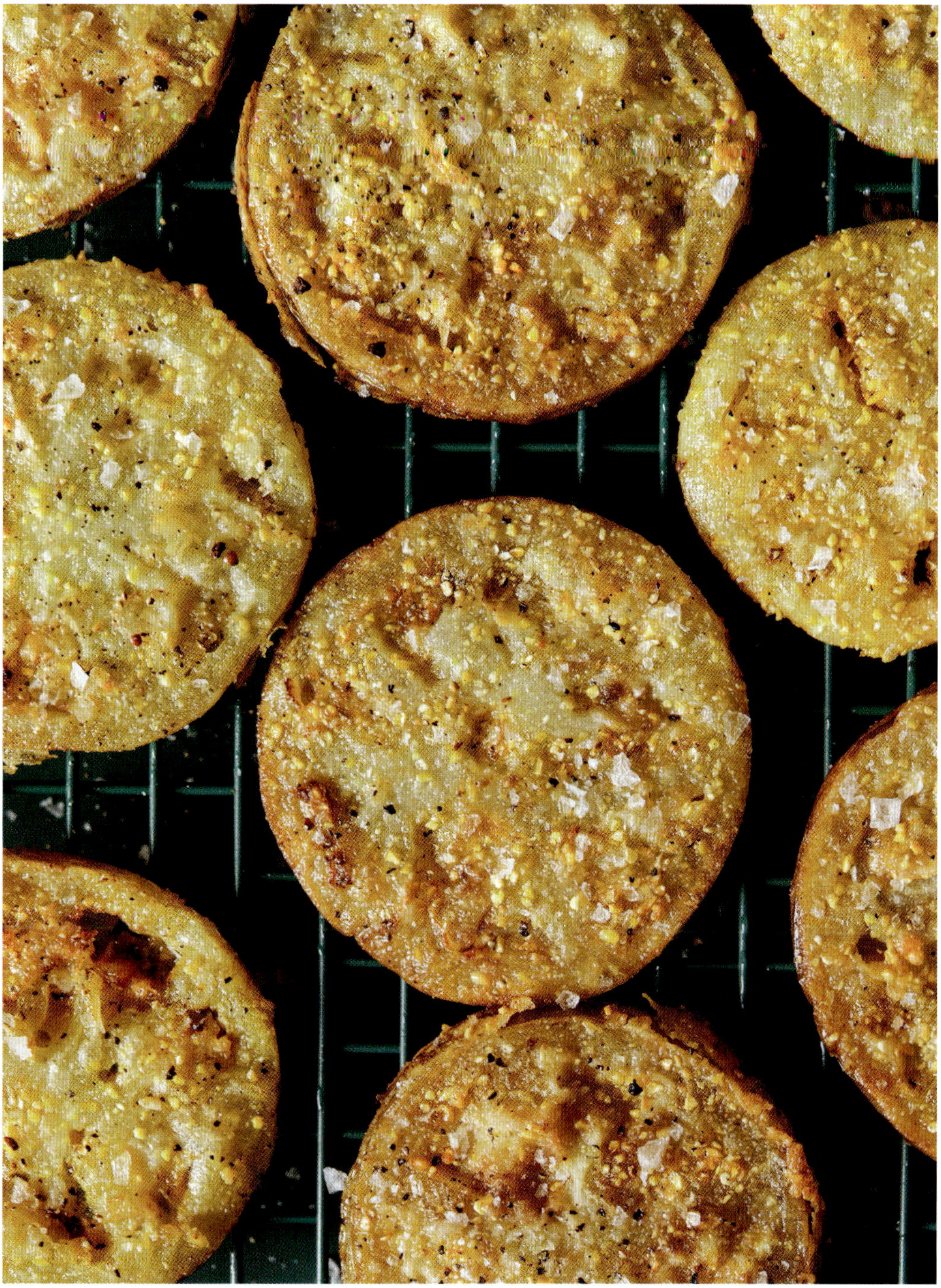

Homemade Organic Chicken Stock

This homemade stock has a nutritious, flavorful base made by simmering an organic chicken (and its bones) with fresh vegetables and herbs. The simple stock, filled with essential nutrients, offers a rich taste without all those preservatives, additives, and excess salt like the stocks you find in the grocery store. Use this stock in any of our recipes that call for chicken stock to enhance the depth of flavor of the dishes. —NOAH

Makes 8 cups

1 (4-to-5-pound) organic chicken (see Coach's Corner)

1 bunch fresh Italian flat-leaf parsley

2 or 3 bay leaves

4 or 5 sprigs fresh thyme

2 or 3 garlic cloves

1 teaspoon kosher salt

1 teaspoon freshly cracked black pepper

Place the chicken in a large pot and add 8 cups water, or enough to cover the chicken. Add the parsley, bay leaves, thyme, garlic, salt, and pepper. Bring to a boil over medium-high heat, then reduce the heat to a gentle boil. Continue boiling until the chicken is cooked and the meat falls off the bone, 3 to 4 hours. Remove from the heat and strain the stock. Let the carcass cool, discard the skin and bones, and use the cooked chicken for our chicken and dumplings (page 217) or other recipes that call for rotisserie chicken.

COACH'S CORNER

We always prefer to make our stock from a bird we've roasted ourselves. The key difference between a home-roasted or home rotisserie chicken (if you use your rotisserie feature on your outdoor grill) and store-bought is that you can control the salt. We eat a lot of chicken, and that's why we like to roast our chickens ourselves. Same with chicken stock.

Buttermilk and Hot Sauce Fried Chicken

There are certain dishes Noah believes made me fall in love with him. Well, I made this dish for Noah to fall in love with me. I served this chicken alongside creamy mashed potatoes, our slow-cooked collard greens (page 205), and homemade biscuits (page 138). Let's just say marriage discussions started the following day. Marinating the chicken is vital to this recipe, as the buttermilk and hot sauce help to tenderize and infuse the chicken with savory and spicy flavor. The longer you marinate, the better the bite. —LACEY

Serves 4 to 6

2 cups buttermilk

½ cup Frank's RedHot sauce, to taste (see Coach's Corner)

8 chicken pieces (preferably a mix of thighs and drumsticks)

Vegetable oil, for frying

2 cups all-purpose flour

1 teaspoon kosher salt

1 teaspoon freshly cracked black pepper

1 teaspoon paprika

1 teaspoon garlic powder

Combine the buttermilk and hot sauce in a large bowl and mix well. Add the chicken, making sure the pieces are fully submerged. Cover the bowl with plastic wrap and refrigerate for at least 2 hours, preferably overnight.

Heat at least 3 or 4 inches of oil in a deep fryer or large pot over medium-high heat, until the oil reaches 350°F, using a digital or candy thermometer to check the temperature. You may need to adjust the heat to get the oil temperature just right.

In a large bowl, whisk together the flour, salt, pepper, paprika, and garlic powder. Remove the chicken from the buttermilk marinade, allowing the excess to drip off. Dredge each chicken piece in the seasoned flour mixture, ensuring they are evenly coated, shaking off any excess flour. In batches, carefully add the chicken to the hot oil, being careful not to crowd the pieces. Fry the chicken, turning occasionally, until the coating is golden brown and the chicken is cooked to an internal temperature of 165°F, 7 to 8 minutes. Make sure the oil returns to 350°F before you add the next batch. (If the chicken starts to get too dark before it's cooked through, transfer the pieces to a baking sheet and finish in the oven at 350°F until the internal temperature of 165°F is reached.) Drain the chicken on a paper towel–lined plate. Once all the chicken is fried, transfer to a platter and serve.

COACH'S CORNER

Select your favorite hot sauce, but we use a combination of Frank's RedHot with Chef Noah's Hawaiian Chili Water, at a 4:1 ratio of hot sauce to chili water.

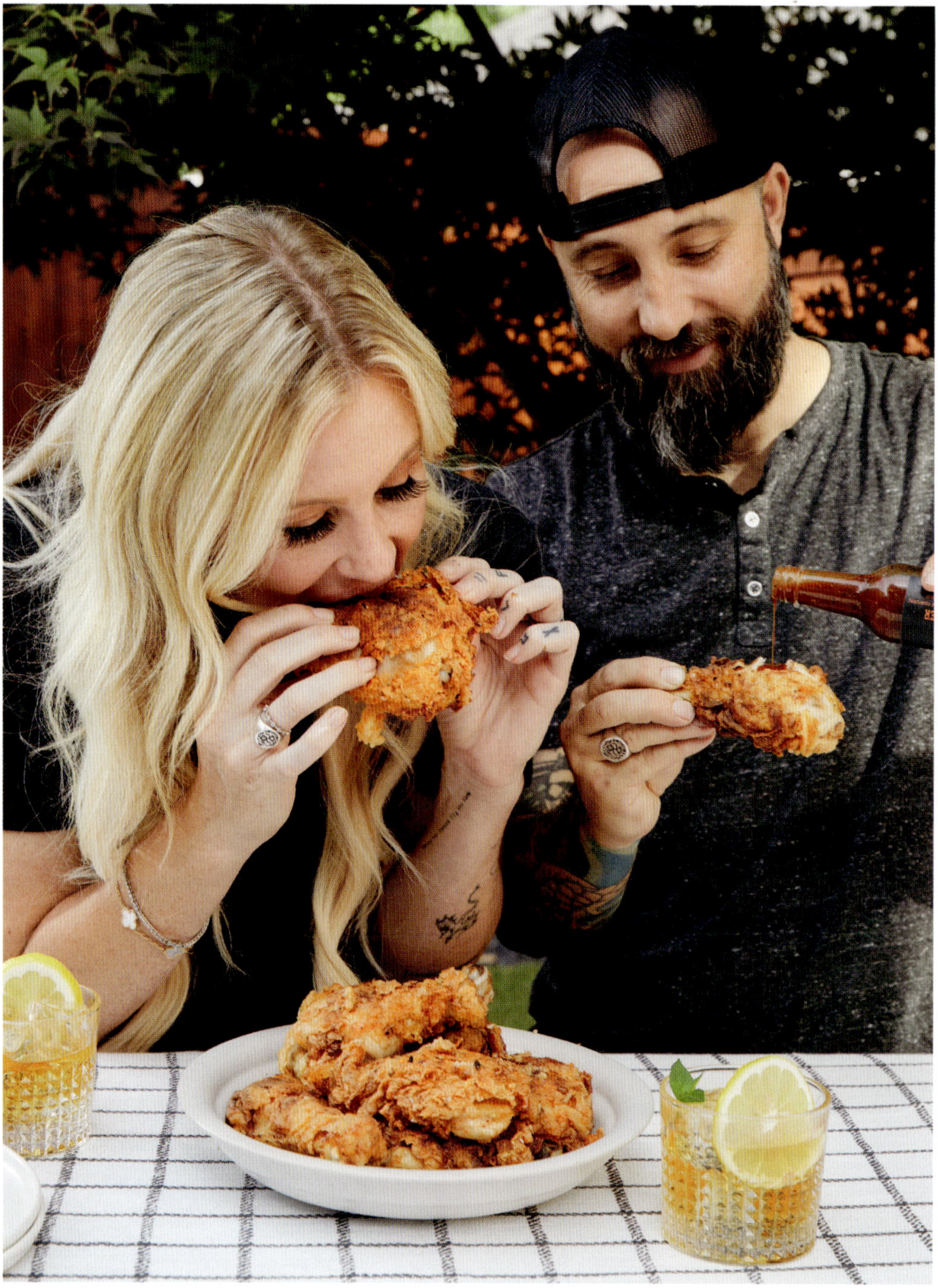

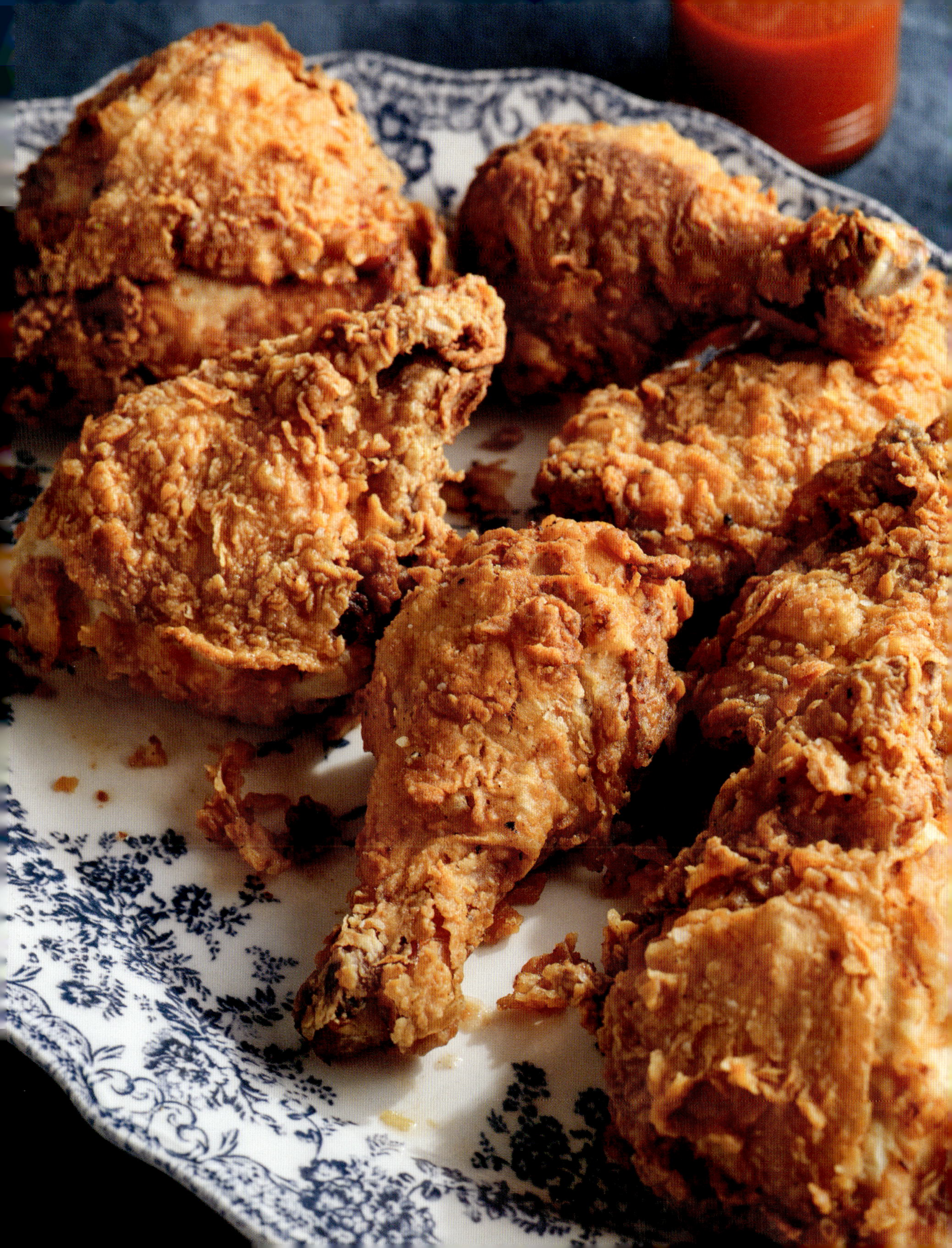

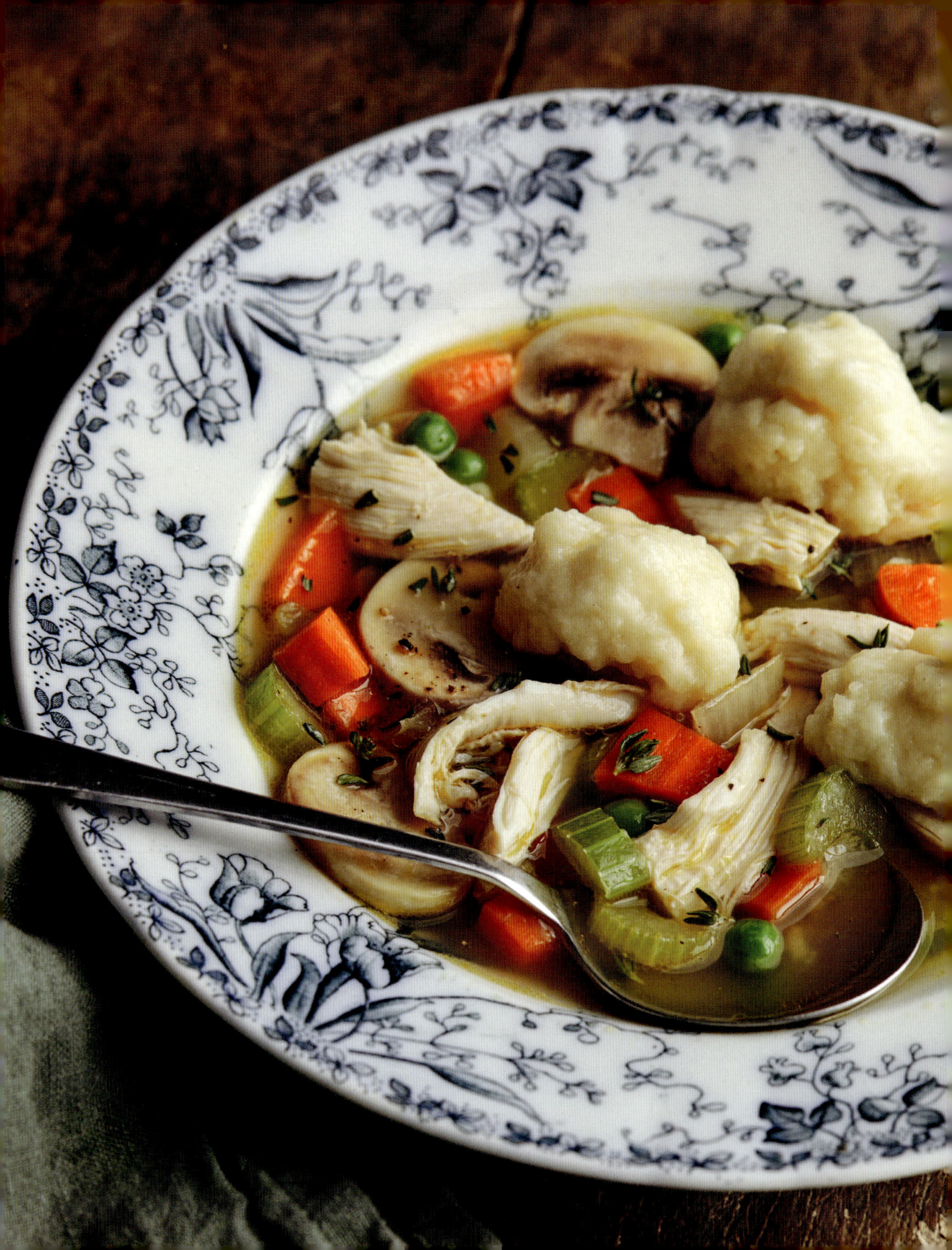

Herb-Roasted Chicken and Biscuit Dumplings

This soul-warming dish, loaded with tender chunks of chicken, fresh garden vegetables, and fluffy dumplings, reminds us of a cross between chicken noodle soup and a thick, hearty stew. It's also one of the easiest ways to get our kids to eat their vegetables. We like to add heaps of different veggies, and pretty much any vegetable works. Just be wary of canned peas. They can have a strong flavor when added to the mix. —**LACEY**

Serves 6 to 8

1 tablespoon olive oil

2 cups diced carrots

4½ cups diced celery

1 large white onion, diced

2 or 3 garlic cloves, chopped

Broccoli, corn, mushrooms, fresh or frozen peas, chopped zucchini (optional)

½ teaspoon kosher salt

¼ teaspoon freshly cracked black pepper

1 rotisserie chicken, meat shredded (about 3 cups)

8 cups Homemade Organic Chicken Stock (page 212)

1 tablespoon minced fresh thyme, fresh Italian flat-leaf parsley, or dried Italian seasoning (optional)

3 cups Bisquick

1 cup whole milk

Heat the olive oil in a large pot over medium-low heat. Add the carrots, celery, onion, and garlic, plus any additional vegetables you'd like to include. Season with salt and pepper. Sauté, stirring occasionally, until the carrots are slightly soft, 10 to 12 minutes. Add the chicken and chicken stock, and season to taste with thyme. Bring to a rolling boil.

Measure the Bisquick into a bowl. Slowly whisk in the milk, mixing until the consistency is between biscuit batter and pancake batter. Carefully add spoonfuls of the batter to the boiling liquid. Cover and continue to boil until the dumplings are soft and fluffy on the inside and wet and dense on the outside, 12 to 15 minutes (remove one and check it). Remove the stew from the heat once the dumplings are cooked through and let cool slightly before dividing among individual bowls and serving.

Fried Bologna Sandwich on Texas Toast

My grandmother often made this for my mom and me, and we both love it. I shared the recipe with Noah while convincing him we should add a taste of home to the menu at our butcher shop. He was reluctant because he didn't grow up eating such a thing, but when we added the sandwich, it instantly became a bestseller. Customers often tell us, "My grandparents used to make me Fried Bologna Sandwiches. I'm so grateful you have it on your menu, because we can't find it anywhere." If you haven't tried this classic before, you're in for a real treat. —LACEY

Makes 2 sandwiches

1 tablespoon butter or oil, or more for sautéing

4 (¼-inch-thick) slices deli bologna

4 tablespoons mayonnaise, to taste

4 slices thick-cut bread (Texas toast style)

4 slices American cheese

2 thick slices large ripe tomato

Heat the butter or oil in a large skillet over medium heat. Add the bologna and fry until the slices are lightly browned and slightly crisp, 1 or 2 minutes on each side. Remove the skillet from the heat and set the slices aside.

To assemble the sandwich, spread about 1 tablespoon mayonnaise evenly on each of two slices of bread. Add a slice of cheese to one of the slices, followed by two slices of fried bologna, a thick slice of tomato, then another slice of cheese. Top with the other slice of bread. Repeat the process to make the second sandwich.

Once the sandwiches are assembled, place them back in the skillet and place over medium heat. Add a little more butter or oil if necessary. Cook until the bread is golden brown and the cheese is melted, 2 to 3 minutes on each side. Pressing down gently on the sandwiches with a spatula while cooking will help flatten them and ensure even browning. Once the sandwiches are cooked to your liking, remove from the skillet and let cool for 1 or 2 minutes. Slice each sandwich diagonally and serve.

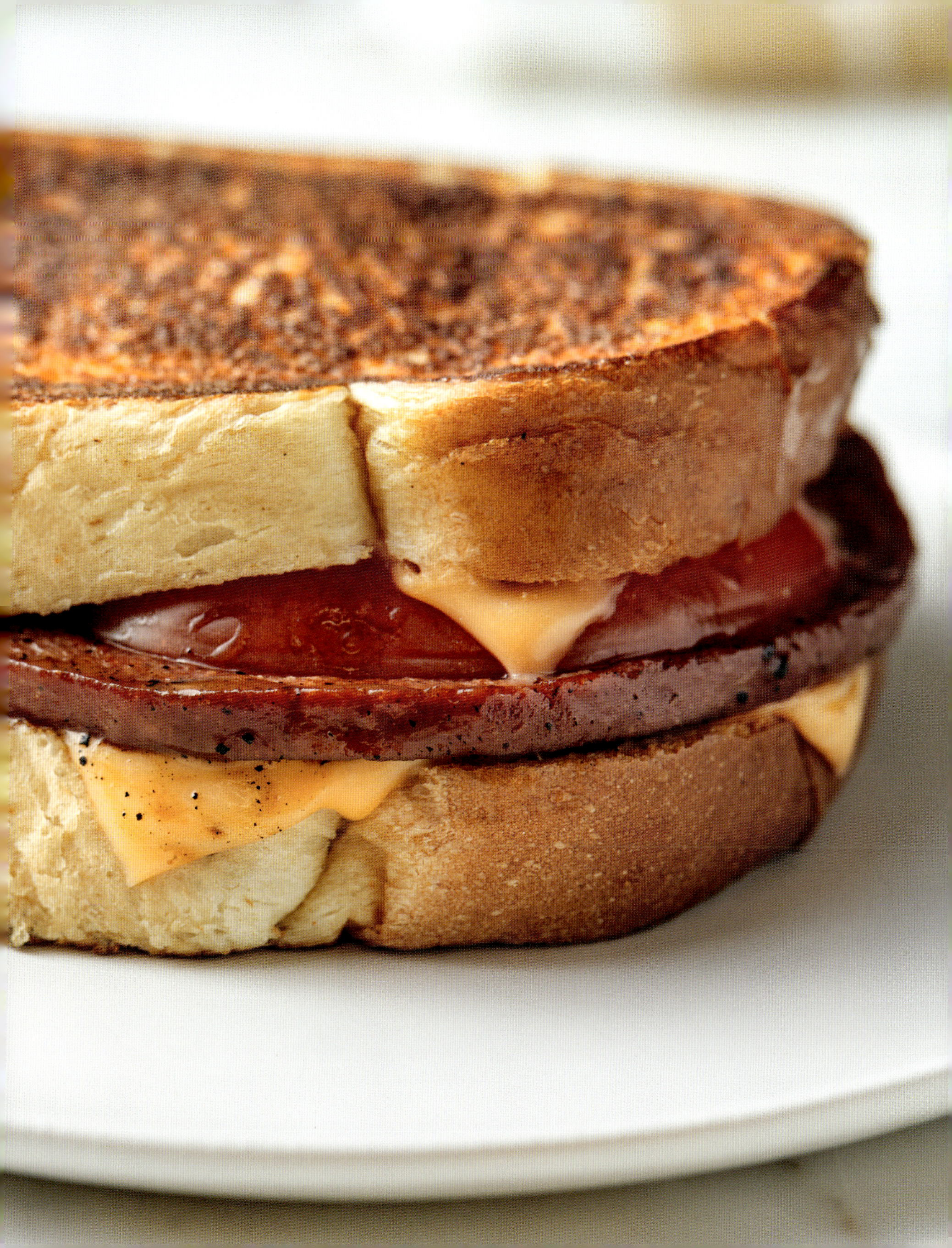

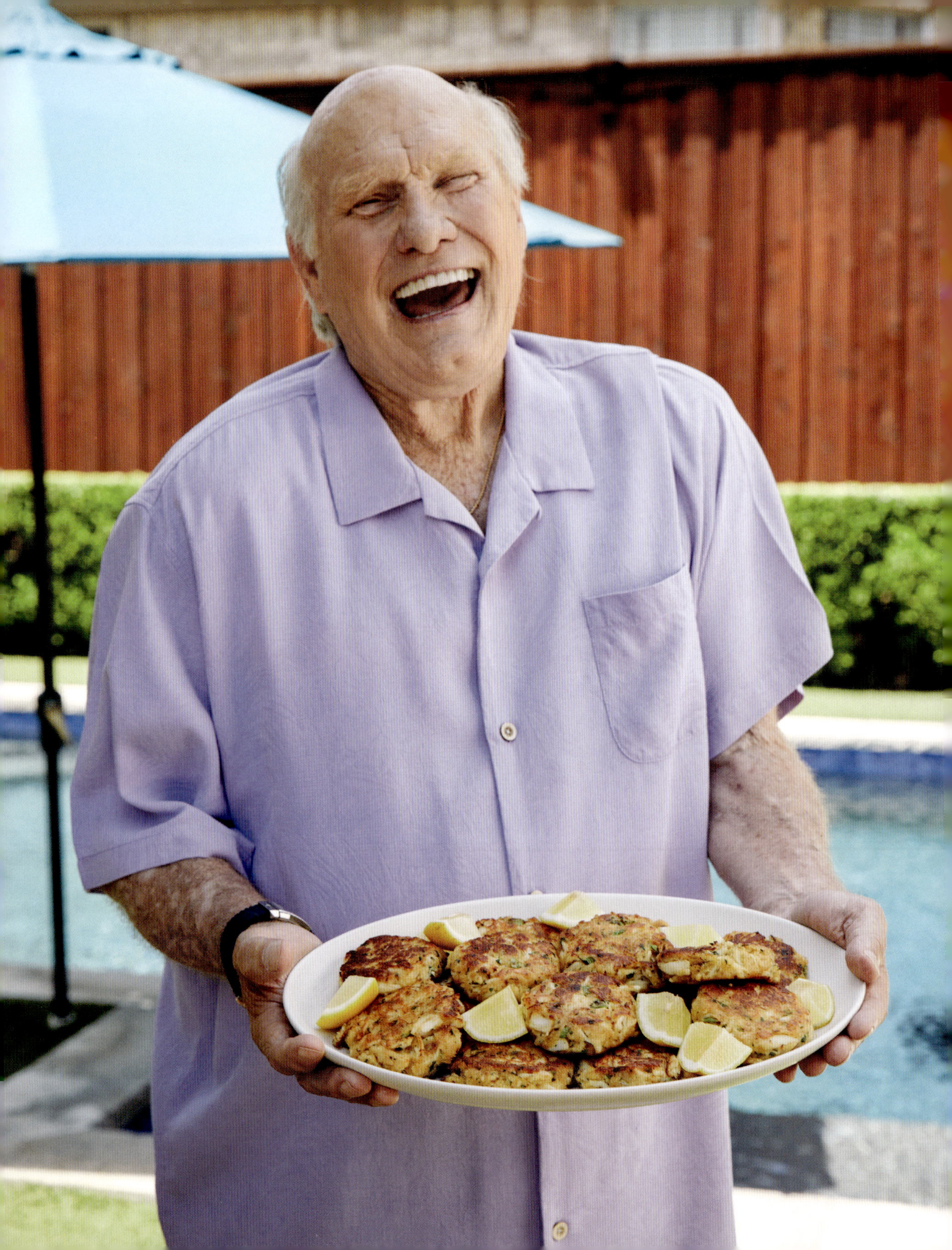

Maryland-Style Crab Cakes with Sweet Pickle Tartar Sauce

Growing up, we did a lot of traveling once dad was finished playing football. One year, we visited the East Coast, where we stopped at a tiny little seaside restaurant that served the most delicious crab cakes we'd ever had. This recipe always comes out when we're craving something with crab. The moist cakes are filled with so much crabmeat—seasoned with a touch of mayo, Dijon, Worcestershire, and Old Bay, and very few breadcrumbs. The sweet pickle tartar sauce is the perfect accompaniment to these zesty bites. —RACHEL

Makes 6 crab cakes

SWEET PICKLE TARTAR SAUCE
Makes 1 cup

1 cup mayonnaise

1½ tablespoons sweet pickle relish

1 teaspoon Dijon mustard

1 tablespoon minced red onion

1 to 2 tablespoons fresh lemon juice, to taste

⅛ teaspoon kosher salt

⅛ teaspoon freshly cracked black pepper

CRAB CAKES

2 large eggs

2½ tablespoons mayonnaise

1½ teaspoons Dijon mustard

1 teaspoon Worcestershire sauce

1 teaspoon Old Bay Seasoning

¼ teaspoon kosher salt

¼ cup finely diced celery

2 tablespoons finely chopped fresh Italian flat-leaf parsley

1 pound fresh-picked crab meat

¾ to 1 cup panko breadcrumbs

Vegetable or canola oil, for frying

Lemon wedges, for serving

To make the tartar sauce: Add the mayonnaise, relish, mustard, onion, and lemon juice to a bowl and whisk until combined. Season with salt and pepper. Cover and refrigerate until ready to serve.

To make the crab cakes: Add the eggs, mayonnaise, Dijon mustard, Worcestershire sauce, Old Bay, and salt to a large bowl and whisk until combined. Stir in the celery and parsley, then gently fold in the crabmeat and ¾ cup of the panko until just combined; if the mixture looks too wet, add the remaining ¼ cup. With damp hands, shape the mixture into six evenly sized cakes about 3 inches in diameter and place on a parchment-lined rimmed baking sheet. Cover and refrigerate for at least 2 hours to set the cakes.

Heat about ¼ inch of oil in a large nonstick pan over medium heat. Add the crab cakes to the hot oil, cooking in batches if the pan is crowded, and cook until golden brown, about 3 minutes per side. Cover the pan with a screen while frying, as the oil may splatter. Drain the crab cakes on paper towels. (Note: If cooking in batches, place the cakes in a warm 250°F oven until all the cakes are cooked.) Serve warm with the tartar sauce.

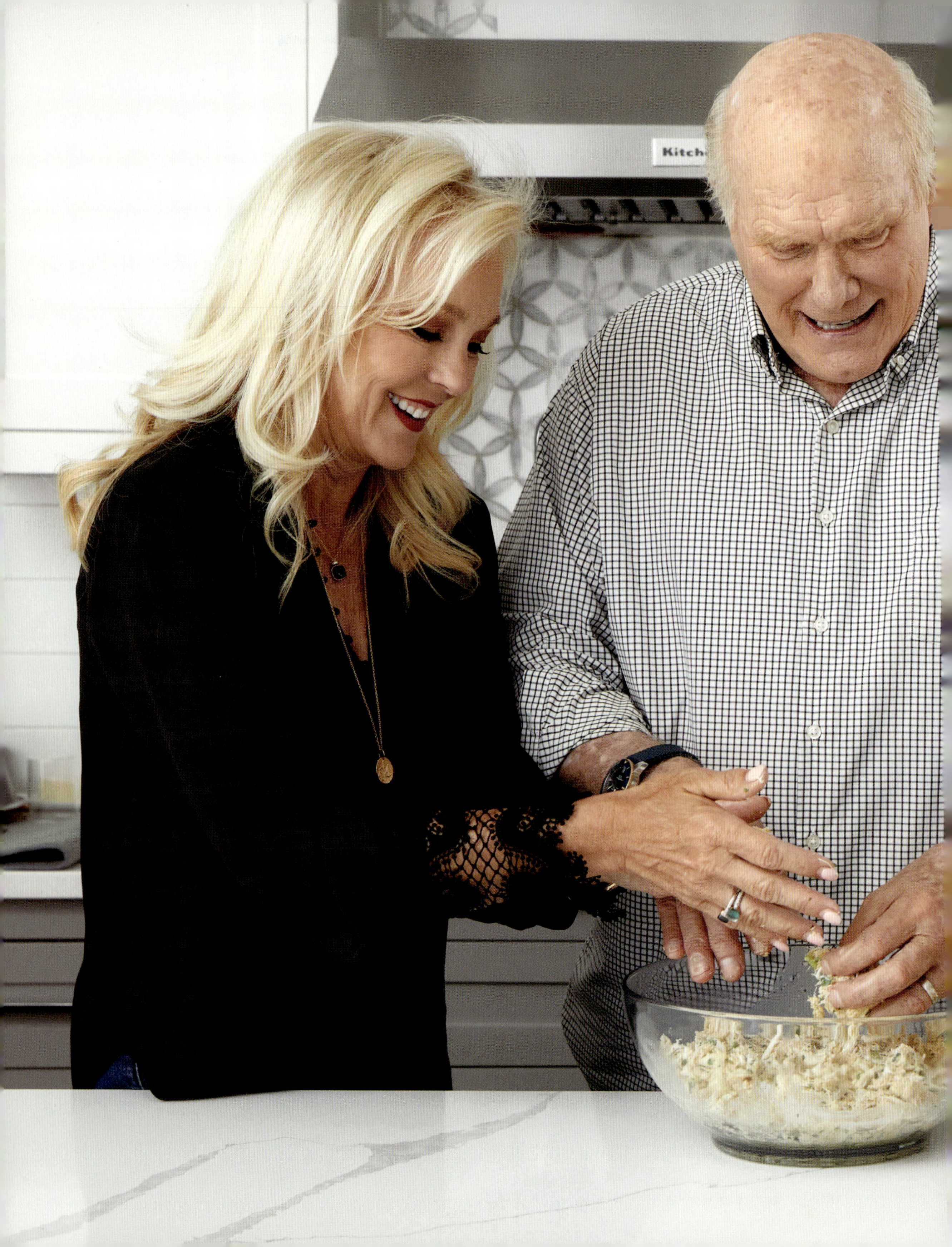

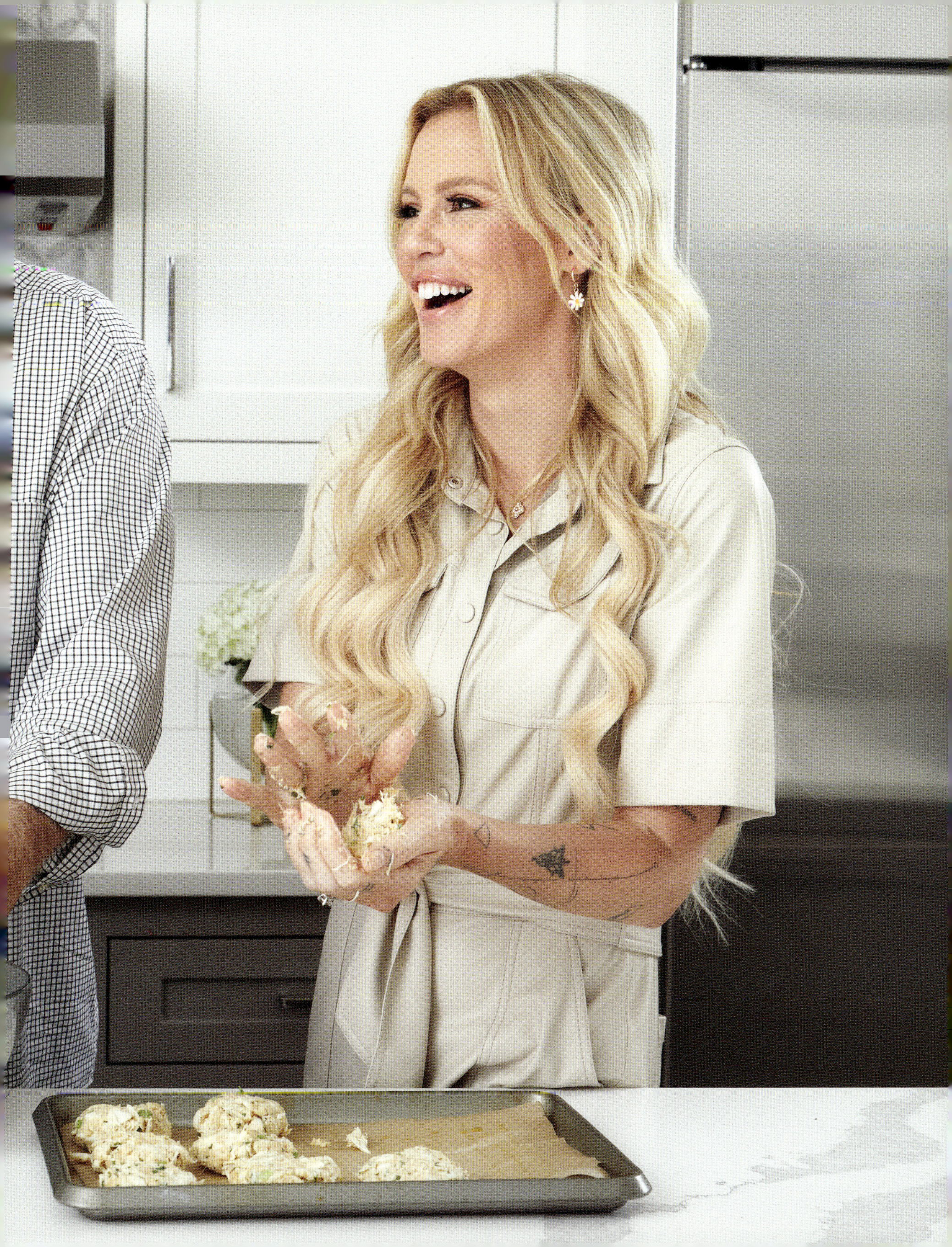

Old Bay Shrimp, Andouille, and Vegetable Boil

It wasn't long ago that I visited the very house I grew up in, in Shreveport, Louisiana. When I walked into the kitchen, I could instantly see my mom cooking up a big boil while I sat at the dining table watching *The Howdy Doody Show* on the brand-new black-and-white television my parents had just bought. As a Louisiana native, I take gumbos and boils seriously, and this recipe from Rachel is a winner. If you're ready to be transported to the bayou, boil some plump shrimp along with red potatoes, corn on the cob, okra, and smoked sausage in a large pot of well-seasoned water and you'll be on your way. Serve with a garnish of Old Bay and some buttered French bread rolls on the side. —TERRY

Serves 6 to 8

3 lemons

1 heaping cup Old Bay Seasoning

6 garlic cloves, smashed

1 medium yellow onion, peeled and cut into 6 pieces

1 pound small red potatoes (about 10), halved

4 ears of corn, shucked and cut into 3-to-4-inch pieces

3 cups sliced fresh okra pods, or 1 (16-ounce) package sliced okra, thawed from frozen

1 pound smoked andouille sausage or kielbasa, cut into 1-inch pieces

2 pounds raw (31/40) shrimp, peeled and deveined, tails on (see Coach's Corner)

3 tablespoons unsalted butter, melted

2 tablespoons chopped fresh Italian flat-leaf parsley, for serving

Fill a large pot with 3½ quarts of cold water. Cut two of the lemons in half, squeeze the juice into the water, and add the rinds. Add the Old Bay, garlic, and onion. Bring to a boil. Add the potatoes and cook until just tender, 10 to 12 minutes. Add the corn, okra, and sausage and cook for another 3 to 4 minutes. Add the shrimp and cook until pink and opaque, 2 to 3 minutes.

Reserve 1 cup of the cooking liquid, then drain the shrimp and vegetables and transfer to a large serving bowl. Whisk the melted butter into the reserved broth, then pour the broth over the shrimp, sausage, and vegetables. Garnish with chopped parsley. Cut the remaining lemon into wedges and serve on the side.

COACH'S CORNER

Feel free to swap out the shrimp for crawfish, a seasonal Southern seafood delicacy that cooks just like shrimp. These freshwater crustaceans are tender and sweet and make for an excellent change of pace if you're looking to liven up your boils. If unavailable at your local market or grocery store, live or frozen crawfish can be ordered online.

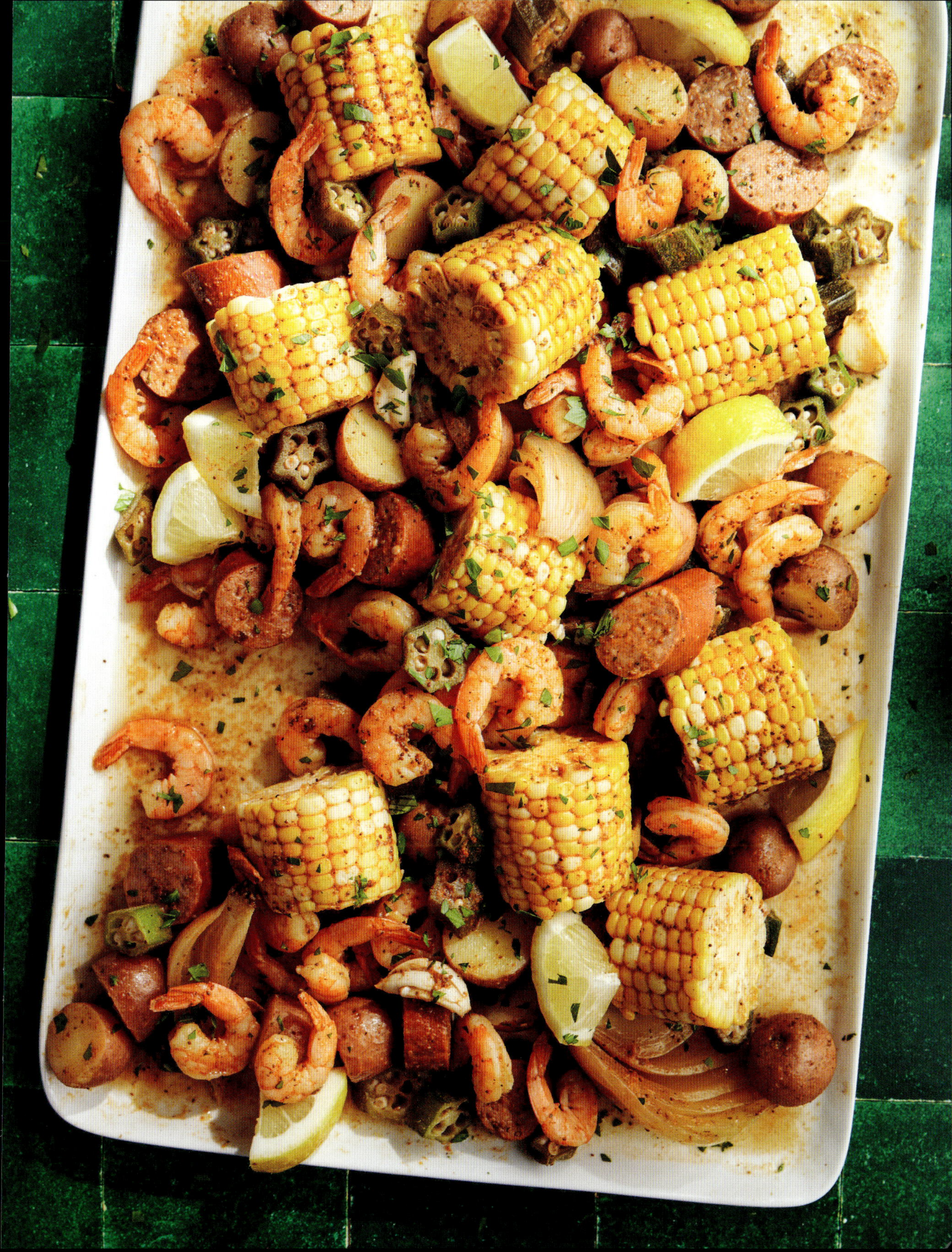

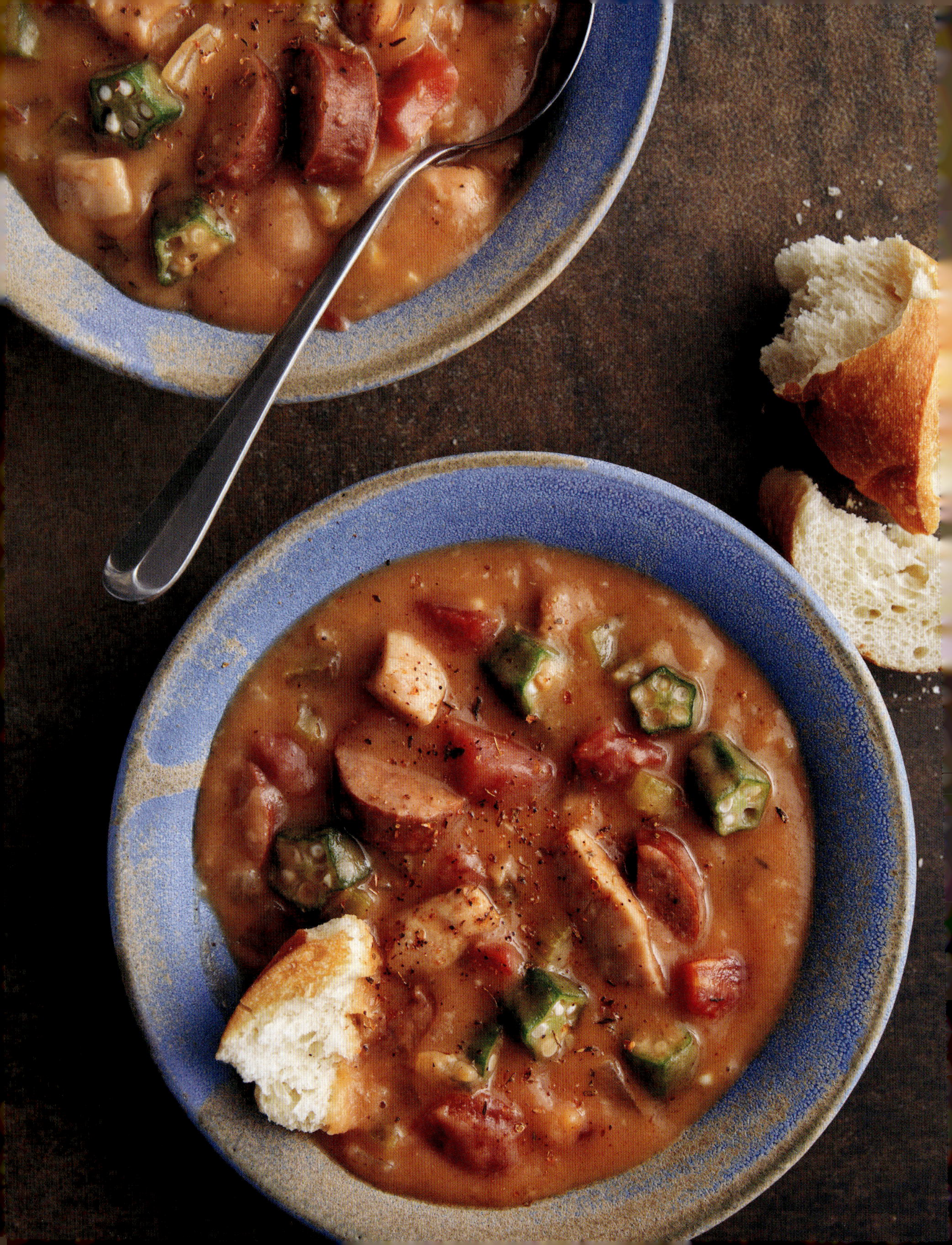

Gumbo with Chicken, Andouille, and Crawfish

We love Southern stews, and this rich and comforting gumbo, filled with tender chicken, spicy andouille sausage, and a medley of vegetables, is one we serve often. Making homemade gumbo does take some time, but it's worth it, in my opinion. I usually start several hours before everyone comes over to hang out and enjoy some down-home Southern cooking. We're not fans of seafood in our gumbo, but feel free to add shrimp. We also won't make the gumbo too spicy. When we serve it, we'll include the spice on the side, so guests can season the gumbo to their liking. —TAMMY

Serves 10 to 12

5 boneless, skinless chicken thighs (about 2 pounds), cut into ½-inch pieces

2 tablespoons Slap Ya Mama Cajun Seasoning (original blend), plus more to coat chicken and for serving

Kosher salt and freshly cracked black pepper, to taste

1 tablespoon vegetable oil, plus more if needed

1 (13.5-ounce) package andouille sausage link, sliced in half lengthwise then into ½-inch pieces

¾ cup (1½ sticks) unsalted butter

1 cup all-purpose flour

2½ cups diced yellow onions

2 bell peppers, stemmed, seeded, and diced

4 garlic cloves, chopped

5 celery stalks, diced

2 quarts Homemade Organic Chicken Stock (page 212)

1 (15-ounce) can diced tomatoes

1 tablespoon Worcestershire sauce

1 teaspoon Tabasco hot sauce, plus more for serving

15 fresh okra pods, cut into rounds, or 1 (16-ounce) package sliced okra, thawed from frozen

1 pound raw peeled crawfish or raw peeled shrimp (optional)

Your choice of condiments, including additional Cajun seasoning, chopped green onions, filé powder, and hot sauce, for serving

French bread and rice

(continued)

(continued)

Add the chicken thighs to a bowl and season with ½ tablespoon of the Cajun seasoning, salt, and pepper. Toss to coat evenly. Set aside.

Heat the oil in a large Dutch oven or other heavy-bottomed pot over medium-high heat. Add the chicken and sauté, stirring occasionally, until golden brown and cooked through, 8 to 10 minutes. Add the sausage to the pot. If the pot is too dry, add a little more olive oil. Cook, stirring occasionally, for 5 minutes. Remove the chicken and sausage from the pot and set aside.

Remove the pot from the heat and let cool for 1 minute. Add the butter and return the pot to the stove over medium-low heat. When the butter is melted, stir in the flour. Cook, stirring constantly, until the color and consistency of the roux is like dark brown peanut butter. This can take anywhere from 15 to 30 minutes (see Coach's Corner).

When the roux is ready, add the onions and bell peppers. Cook for 3 minutes, stirring often, then add the garlic and celery. Season again with salt and pepper. Cook for 5 minutes, stirring often, then add the chicken stock along with the tomatoes, Worcestershire sauce, hot sauce, and the remaining 1½ tablespoons of Cajun seasoning. Stir well. Increase the heat to high and bring to a boil. Stir in the chicken and sausage, the okra, and crawfish or shrimp, if using. When the gumbo returns to a boil, reduce the heat to medium-low, partially cover the pot, and simmer for 30 minutes. Serve with bread, rice, and your choice of condiments.

COACH'S CORNER

Getting the roux right is the most important part of making gumbo, and it's the step many home cooks struggle with. For those of you who don't know what a roux is, it's essentially the thickening agent for the gumbo. The flour-and-butter mixture should be cooked until it turns dark brown. The key is to stir continually. Don't walk away when making roux, as the mixture will quickly burn.

Spam (Hawaiian) Musubi with Homemade Teriyaki Sauce

Because Hawaii is Terry's favorite place to visit, and we and our children used to live in the Aloha State, we had to throw an island dish into this chapter. Spam musubi is a staple in our household and a popular Hawaiian snack that features a slice of grilled Spam atop a block of sushi rice that is wrapped with a strip of nori seaweed. It's Zurie and Jeb's favorite snack—they'd eat it every day if they could. These Hawaiian bites are easy to make and they're perfect for a beach or park snack. For this recipe, you'll need a musubi mold, which is available online. —NOAH AND LACEY

Makes about 8 assorted musubi

SUSHI RICE
Makes 2 cups cooked rice

2 cups sushi rice (see Coach's Corner)

4 cups water

1 tablespoon natural rice vinegar

1 tablespoon granulated sugar

1 teaspoon sea salt

TERIYAKI SAUCE
Makes 1 cup

1 tablespoon cornstarch

¼ cup water

½ cup soy sauce

¼ cup packed dark brown sugar

2 tablespoons honey

2 garlic cloves, minced

1 teaspoon grated fresh ginger

1 tablespoon sesame oil

SPAM MUSUBI

1 tablespoon vegetable oil

1 (12-ounce) can Spam, sliced ⅜-inch thick (about 8 slices)

4 sheets nori (seaweed), cut into strips

Furikake seasoning (optional)

(continued)

(continued)

To make the sushi rice: Rinse the sushi rice under cold water until the water runs clear. In a rice cooker or a medium-sized pot, combine the rinsed rice and water. Cook on high until boiling. Cover, reduce the heat to low, and cook until the rice is tender and the water has been absorbed, 18 to 20 minutes. In a small bowl, mix the rice vinegar, sugar, and salt until dissolved. Gently fold into the cooked rice and let the rice cool slightly before using.

To make the teriyaki sauce: In a small bowl, stir together the cornstarch and water until well combined. In a small saucepan, add the soy sauce, brown sugar, honey, garlic, and grated ginger and whisk to combine. Bring to a simmer over medium heat, then whisk in the cornstarch mixture. Continue to cook and whisk until the sauce thickens, 5 to 7 minutes. Remove from the heat, stir in the sesame oil, and set aside to cool.

To make the musubi: Heat the vegetable oil in a large skillet over medium-high heat. Add the Spam slices and cook until golden brown and slightly crisp on both sides, about 4 minutes per side. Remove from the heat.

To assemble, lay a sheet of plastic wrap on a clean work surface. Place the musubi mold on top of the plastic wrap. Fill the mold with a thin layer of the sushi rice, pressing it down with the top portion of the mold to compress firmly. Place a slice of Spam on top of the rice. Carefully remove the mold, leaving a compact block of rice and Spam. Wrap a strip of nori around the musubi, sealing the ends with a bit of water. Transfer to a plate. Repeat with the remaining rice and Spam slices, or make other versions. For example, follow the same procedure as above, but this time spoon a small amount of teriyaki sauce over the Spam. Or add another layer of rice on top of the Spam, pressing it down firmly again.

Season with furikake seasoning, if you like, and serve.

COACH'S CORNER

Buying prepared sushi rice is very convenient when making Spam Musubi. You can find prepared rice at your favorite Asian restaurant or sushi bar and in Asian stores and grocery stores that make and sell prepared foods. For this recipe, buy 2 pounds of prepared rice.

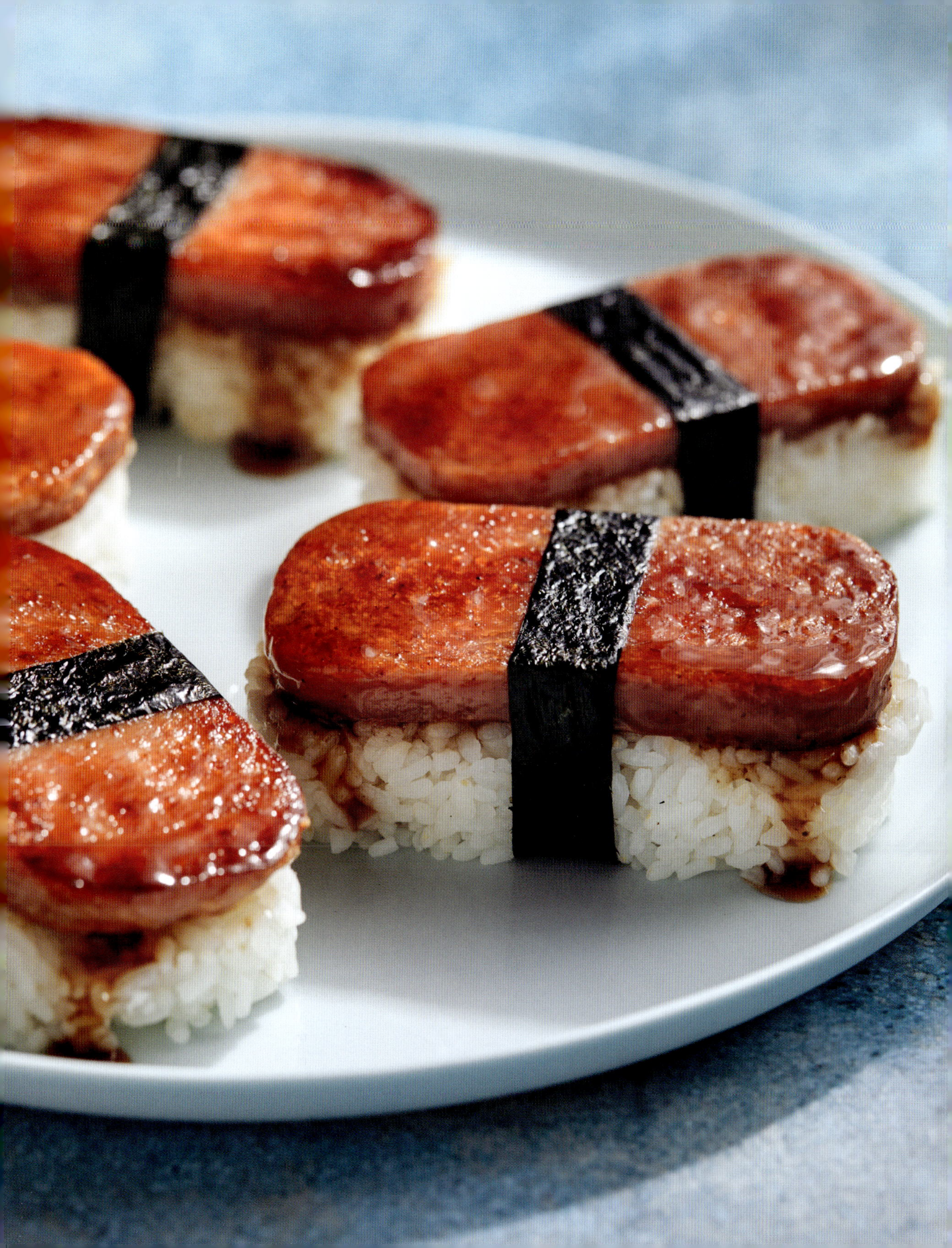

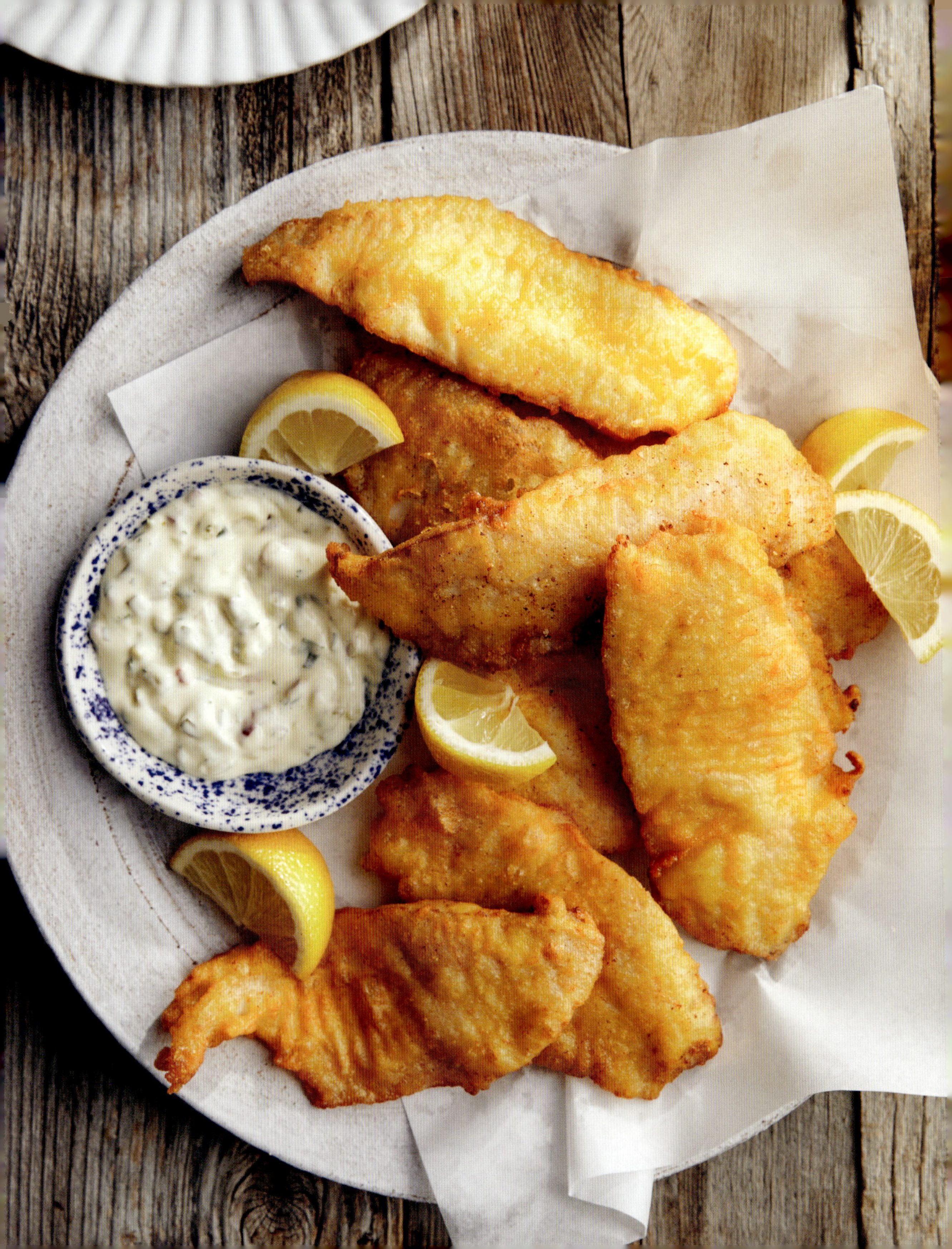

Terry's Ranch-Style Fish Fry

I host a fish fry so often that I had a large deep fryer built into my outdoor kitchen. My family tells me I'm notorious for buying too much fish, and that a fish fry turns into an all-day affair, but to my mind there's nothing worse than not having enough food. I don't want to run out. For me, the aroma of sizzling fish mingled with laughter and fun equals a perfect summer day. You can double this recipe if you're cooking for more people. —**TERRY**

Serves 4

4 fresh catfish fillets (about 1½ pounds total)

1 cup buttermilk

1 tablespoon hot sauce

Vegetable oil, for frying

1 cup cornmeal

½ cup all-purpose flour

1 teaspoon salt

1 teaspoon garlic powder

1 teaspoon paprika

½ teaspoon freshly cracked black pepper

½ teaspoon cayenne pepper (optional)

Fresh Italian flat-leaf parsley (optional) and lemon wedges, for serving

Rinse the catfish fillets under cold water, and pat dry with paper towels.

Add the buttermilk and hot sauce to a shallow dish and whisk to combine. Submerge the catfish into the mixture, making sure the fillets are fully coated. Cover and refrigerate for at least 30 minutes (or up to 2 hours) to marinate.

When ready to fry, heat at least 4 inches of vegetable oil in a medium stockpot or deep fryer over medium-high heat until the oil reaches 350°F.

While the oil is heating, add the cornmeal, flour, salt, garlic powder, paprika, black pepper, and cayenne (if using) to a shallow dish. Mix well.

Remove the catfish from the marinade, allowing any excess to drip off. Dredge each fillet in the cornmeal mixture, pressing the fillets into the mixture to evenly coat on all sides. In batches to avoid overcrowding the pan, carefully place the coated fillets into the hot oil, and fry until golden brown and crispy, 3 to 4 minutes per side. The internal temperature of the fish should reach at least 145°F. Use a slotted spoon or tongs to transfer the fried catfish to a paper towel–lined plate to drain any excess oil.

Arrange the catfish on a platter while hot and garnish with parsley, if using. Serve with lemon wedges, for squeezing over the top.

COACH'S CORNER

To ensure the fish are crispy and not soggy, follow these easy steps: (1) Proper coating: Make sure the fillets are well coated with the cornmeal mixture. This creates a crispy outer layer. (2) Oil temperature: The oil needs to be hot (350°F). If the oil is not hot enough, the fish will absorb more oil, making it greasy and soggy. Use a thermometer to check the oil temperature before frying. (3) Avoid overcrowding: Fry the fillets in batches to prevent the oil temperature from dropping. If the temperature drops, the fish will absorb more oil and the coating may not crisp up properly. (4) Drain excess oil: After frying, place the catfish on a wire rack or paper towel–lined plate to drain any excess oil. This helps maintain crispiness.

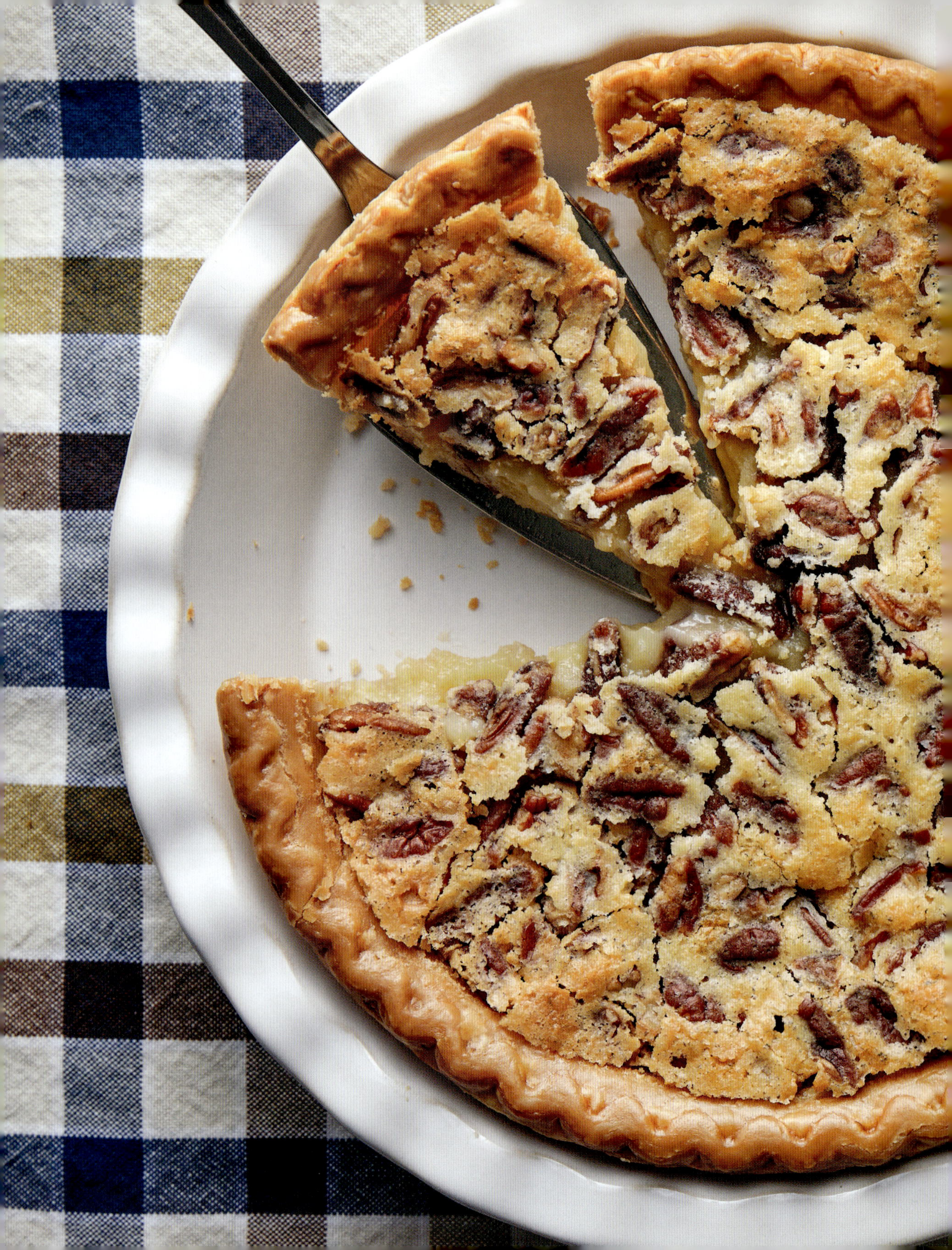

Crispy Egg Rolls with Shrimp, Sprouts, and Peanut Butter, 73, *92*, *93*
Famous Gridiron Nine-Layer Dip, 73, 102, *103*
Fourth and One Bourbon Smash, 73, *76*, *77*
Gainesville Grande Margarita, 82, 113
Garlic Pull-Apart Pigs in a Blanket, 22, *71*, 73, 90, *91*
Hawaiian Summer Tuna Fish Dip, 22, 106, *107*
Homemade Focaccia with Herb Dipping Oil, 86, *87*
The Immaculate Refreshment, 78, *79*
Missouri Crab Grass Dip, 73, *104*, 105
Nannie's Ranch Crackers, 70, 73, 83
Poppa Hester's Savory Herb Pimento Cheese, 22, *70-71*, 98, *99*
Ranch-Style Pretzel Snacks, *71*, 73, *84*, 85
Sriracha Curry Dip, 73, *108*, 109
Toasted Ham and Swiss Cheese Sliders, *96*, 97
Steak "Fries," Chicken-Fried, with Zesty Dip, 94, *95*
Steak, Grilled Tomahawk, with Chimichurri, 113, *142*, 143
Stock, Homemade Organic Chicken, 212
stock, store-bought, 157

Sunday Family Casserole, 147, 165
Sunday Glazed Meatloaf, 147, *170*, 171
Super Bowl, 13, 90, 165
sushi rice, prepared, 230
Sweet Orchard Peach Cobbler, 14, 237, 252, *253*
Sweet Potato Casserole with Chopped Pecans, 208
Swiss Cheese and Toasted Ham Sliders, *96*, 97

T

Tacos, Breakfast, with Chipotle Crema, 64, *65*, 162
Tartar Sauce, Sweet Pickle, *220*, 221, *222-23*
Teriyaki Sauce, Homemade, 24, 229-30, *231*
Terry's Favorite Dressing, 24, 175, 176, *177*
Terry's Favorite Omelet, 68
Terry's Legendary Bradshaw Beans, 14, 21, 23, 141, 175, 198, *199*
Terry's Ranch-Style Fish Fry, 14, 203, *232*, 233
Texas Toast, 67
   Fried Bologna Sandwich with, 203, 218, *219*
thermometers, cooking with, 28, 233
Toad in the Hole, 66, 67
Toasted Ham and Swiss Cheese Sliders, *96*, 97
Tomatoes, Green, Fried, *201*, 203, 209, *210-11*

Tomato, Sun-Dried, with Chicken and Orzo, 158, *159*
Tuna Fish Dip, Hawaiian Summer, 22, 106, *107*

V

Veggie, Shrimp, and Andouille Boil, Old Bay, 224, *225*
vertical water smokers, 28-29
Villa Grande Mexican Restaurant, Gainesville, Texas, 82

W

Waffles, Cinnamon Apple, 24, 35, *48*, 49
Wagyu Hot Dogs, Loaded, 22, *130*, 131
Waldorf Salad with Walnut Pumpkin Seed Brittle, 175, *178*, 179
Walnut Pumpkin Seed Brittle, 175, *178*, 179
Warm Chocolate Chip Cookies with Sea Salt, 256, *257*, 262
Weiss, Jessie, 15, 147
Weiss, Scott, 15
Wild Blackberry Muffins with Powdered Sugar, *238*, 239

Z

Zesty Dip, 94, *95*

Scalloped Potatoes, Chicken Stock, 24, *192*, 193
Shrimp, Andouille, and Veggie Boil, Old Bay, *224*, *225*
Shrimp, Garlic, in Phyllo Cups with Cheddar and Bacon, *111*, *116*, 117
Shrimp, Sprouts, and Peanut Butter Egg Rolls, Crispy, 73, *92*, 93
sides and salads
   Chicken Stock Scalloped Potatoes, 24, *192*, 193
   Creamy Vanilla Fruit Salad, *40*, 41
   German Country Potato Salad, 175, 180, *181*
   Greek Orzo Salad with Oil, Vinegar, and Honey Dressing, *186*, 187
   Green Beans with Bacon, Onion, and Garlic, 24, 191
   Havarti and Gouda Mac 'n' Cheese, 175, 194, *195*
   Honey Balsamic Farmers Market Carrots, 175, *196*, 197
   Iceberg Salad with Terry's Favorite Dressing, 24, 175, 176, *177*
   Mexican Street Corn Salad, 161, 162, *172-73*, 188, *189*
   Missouri Corn Salad with Lime and Paprika, 175, 190
   Old-Fashioned Ambrosia Salad, 14, 175, 184, *185*
   Red Potato Salad with Pimento and Sweet Pickle, 175, *182*, 183
   Terry's Legendary Bradshaw Beans, 14, 21, 23, 141, 175, 198, 199
   Waldorf Salad with Walnut Pumpkin Seed Brittle, 175, *178*, 179
Simple Syrup, 77
Slap Ya Mama Original Blend Cajun Seasoning, 22
Sliders, Smoked Brisket, with Homemade Biscuits, *110-11*, 138-40, *139-40*
Sliders, Toasted Ham and Swiss Cheese, *96*, 97
Slow-Cooked Collard Greens with Bacon, Hot Sauce, and Balsamic, *200*, 203, *204*, 205, 213
smoked dishes. *See* grilled and smoked dishes
smokers and smoking tips, 24, 27-29, *28*
snacks. *See* starters and snacks
soups and chili. *See also* sides and salads
   Cabbage and Potato Kettle, 147, 151
   Cannellini Chicken Chili, 24, *156*, 157
   Fire-Roasted Hatch Chile Chicken Stew, 154, *155*
   Gumbo with Chicken, Andouille, and Crawfish, 22, 24, 203, *226*, 227-28
   Spicy Italian Sausage, Vegetable, and Kale Soup, *152*, 153
   Stock, Homemade Organic Chicken, 212
   stock, store-bought, 157
Southern Living, 49
South of the Border Lasagna, 147, 162, *163*
Spam (Hawaiian) Musubi with Homemade Teriyaki Sauce, 24, 229-30, *231*
Spicy Breakfast Casserole with Onion and Bell Peppers, 60
Spicy Italian Sausage, Vegetable, and Kale Soup, *152*, 153
Spicy Pork Canoes with Cilantro Sour Cream, 21, 113, *126*, 127
Spinach Bacon Sports Balls, 113, 128, *129*
Sprouts, Shrimp, and Peanut Butter Egg Rolls, Crispy, 73, *92*, 93
Sriracha Curry Dip, 73, *108*, 109
starters and snacks. *See also* sides and salads
   Beet Deviled Eggs, *88*, 89
   Blond Bomber, 73, 74, *75*
   Cheesy Smoked Buffalo Chicken Dip, 22, 73, *100*, 101
   Chicken-Fried Steak "Fries" with Zesty Dip, 94, *95*

Pickle, Sweet, Tartar Sauce, 220, 221, *222–23*
piecrusts, premade, 22
Pigs in a Blanket, Garlic Pull-Apart, 22, *71*, 73, 90, *91*
Pillsbury Grands! Original Flaky Layers Biscuits, 22
pimentos, *20*
    in Poppa Hester's Savory Herb Pimento Cheese, 22, *70–71*, 98, *99*
    in Red Potato Salad with Pimento and Sweet Pickle, 175, *182*, 183
Pineapple, Crushed, and Pecans with Cherry Crisp, 237, *254*, 255
Pittsburgh Steelers, 13, 78, 101
Poppa Hester's Savory Herb Pimento Cheese, 22, *70–71*, 98, *99*
Pork Belly Bites, Smoked Maple-Bourbon, 124, *125*
Pork Canoes, Spicy, with Cilantro Sour Cream, 21, 113, *126*, 127
Potato and Cabbage Kettle, 147, 151
Potatoes, Scalloped, with Chicken Stock, 24, *192*, 193
Potato Salad, German Country, 175, 180, *181*
Potato Salad, Red, with Pimento and Sweet Pickle, 175, *182*, 183
potluck dishes. *See* get-together and potluck dishes

Pretzel Snacks, Ranch-Style, 71, 73, *84*, 85
Pudding, Banana, with Nilla Wafers, 237, 240, *241*, 260
Pumpkin Seed Walnut Brittle, 175, *178*, 179

Q

Quiche, Bacon, Onion, and Mushroom, 35, *62*, 63

R

Ranch Crackers, Nannie's, *70*, 73, 83
Ranch-Style Pretzel Snacks, 71, 73, *84*, 85
Red Potato Salad with Pimento and Sweet Pickle, 175, *182*, 183
ribs. *See* grilled and smoked dishes
Roasted-Chicken Tetrazzini, 164
roots and relatives dishes. *See also* get-together and potluck dishes
    Buttermilk and Hot Sauce Fried Chicken, *200–201*, 203, 213, *214–15*
    Fried Bologna Sandwich on Texas Toast, 203, 218, *219*
    Fried Green Garden Tomatoes, *201*, 203, 209, *210–11*
    Gumbo with Chicken, Andouille, and Crawfish, 22, 24, 203, *226*, 227–28

    Herb-Roasted Chicken and Biscuit Dumplings, 21, *216*, 217
    Homemade Organic Chicken Stock, 212
    Maryland-Style Crab Cakes with Sweet Pickle Tartar Sauce, *220*, 221, *222–23*
    Nannie's Cornbread Dressing, 203, 206, *207*
    Old Bay Shrimp, Andouille, and Veggie Boil, 224, *225*
    Slow-Cooked Collard Greens with Bacon, Hot Sauce, and Balsamic, *200*, 203, *204*, 205, 213
    Spam (Hawaiian) Musubi with Homemade Teriyaki Sauce, 24, 229–30, *231*
    Sweet Potato Casserole with Chopped Pecans, 208
    Terry's Ranch-Style Fish Fry, 14, 203, *232*, 233

S

Sausage and Cheddar Cheese Biscuits, *56*, 57, 58, *59*
Sausage Gravy, Nannie Bradshaw's, 35, 57, 58, *58–59*
Sausage, Italian, Stuffed Peppers, 147, 168, *169*
Sausage, Spicy Italian, Vegetable, and Kale Soup, *152*, 153

Lemon–Olive Oil Cake, Italian, *250*, 251
Lime and Paprika with Missouri Corn Salad, 175, 190
Lit'l Smokies, 20, 22
Loaded Wagyu Hot Dogs, 22, *130*, 131
Louisiana Coconut Cream Pie, 248, *249*

M

Mac 'n' Cheese, Havarti and Gouda, 175, 194, *195*
Maple-Bourbon Pork Belly Bites, Smoked, 124, *125*
Maryland-Style Crab Cakes with Sweet Pickle Tartar Sauce, 220, 221, *222-23*
Meatloaf, Sunday Glazed, 147, *170*, 171
Mexican Street Corn Salad, 161, 162, *172-73*, 188, *189*
Missouri Corn Salad with Lime and Paprika, 175, 190
Missouri Crab Grass Dip, 73, *104*, 105
Mushroom, Bacon, and Onion Quiche, 35, *62*, 63
Musubi, Spam (Hawaiian), with Homemade Teriyaki Sauce, 24, *229-30*, 231

N

Nannie Bradshaw's Sausage Gravy, 35, 57, 58, *58-59*
Nannie's Cornbread Dressing, 203, 206, *207*
Nannie's Ranch Crackers, *70*, 73, 83
NFL Hall of Fame, 138
Nilla Wafers with Banana Pudding, 237, 240, *241*, 260

O

offset smokers, 28-29
Old Bay Shrimp, Andouille, and Veggie Boil, 224, *225*
Old English Cheese Spread, 20, 22
Old-Fashioned Ambrosia Salad, 14, 175, 184, *185*
Old-Fashioned Blackberry Pie, 22, 237, 244, *245*
Olive Oil–Lemon Cake, Italian, *250*, 251
Omelet, Terry's Favorite, 68
One-Skillet Breakfast Frittata, 61
Onion and Bell Peppers with Spicy Breakfast Casserole, 60
Onion, Bacon, and Garlic with Green Beans, 24, 191
Onion, Bacon, and Mushroom Quiche, 35, *62*, 63
Onions, Glazed, with Bison Burgers and Hot Honey Mustard, 113, 132, *133*

Ooey Gooey Apple Monkey Bread, 22, 35, *44*, 45
Orzo Salad, Greek, with Oil, Vinegar, and Honey Dressing, *186*, 187
Orzo with Chicken and Creamy Sun-Dried Tomato, 158, *159*
Overnight Stuffed Brioche French Toast Casserole, 52, *53*

P

Pancakes, Funfetti Chocolate Chip Banana, 21, 35, 46, *47*
pantry items, suggestions for, 20, 21-22
Pappy's Midnight Spoon, 259
Paprika and Lime with Missouri Corn Salad, 175, 190
Peach Cobbler, Sweet Orchard, 14, 237, 252, *253*
Peanut Butter, Shrimp, and Sprouts Egg Rolls, Crispy, 73, *92*, 93
Pecan Buttermilk Pie, *234-35*, 237, *246*, 247
Pecans and Crushed Pineapple with Cherry Crisp, 237, *254*, 255
Pecans, Chopped, with Sweet Potato Casserole, 208
Peppers, Italian Sausage-Stuffed, 147, 168, *169*
Pickle, Sweet, in Red Potato Salad with Pimento, 175, *182*, 183

268 INDEX

Finger-Lickin' Barbecue Bourbon Chicken Wings, 21, 22, 113, 114, *115*, 141
Garlic Shrimp, Cheddar, and Bacon Phyllo Cups, *111*, *116*, 117
Grilled Tomahawk Steak with Chimichurri, 113, *142*, 143
Juicy Braised Korean Short Ribs, 24, 118, *122*, 123
Loaded Wagyu Hot Dogs, 22, *130*, 131
Smoked Brisket Sliders with Homemade Biscuits, *110-11*, 138-40, *139-40*
Smoked Maple-Bourbon Pork Belly Bites, 124, *125*
Spicy Pork Canoes with Cilantro Sour Cream, 21, 113, *126*, 127
Spinach Bacon Sports Balls, 113, 128, *129*
Grilled Tomahawk Steak with Chimichurri, 113, *142*, 143
grills and grilling tips, 24, 27-29
Gumbo with Chicken, Andouille, and Crawfish, 22, 24, 203, *226*, 227-28

H

Ham and Old English Cheese Casserole, 22, 51, *54-55*
Ham and Swiss Cheese Sliders, Toasted, *96*, 97
Hamm's Meat + Market, McKinney, Texas, 14, 63, 132
Harris, Franco, 78
Havarti and Gouda Mac 'n' Cheese, 175, 194, *195*
Hawaiian Summer Tuna Fish Dip, 22, 106, *107*
Herb Dipping Oil, 86, *87*
Herb Pimento Cheese, Poppa Hester's Savory, 22, *70-71*, 98, *99*
Herb-Roasted Chicken and Biscuit Dumplings, 21, *216*, 217
Hester, Jebediah, 15, 67, 94, 147, 229, 237
Hester, Lacey, *12*, 14-15, *16-18*, *36*, *38-39*, 108, *177*, *214*, *223*
Hester, Noah, *12*, 14-15, *16*, *18*, 21, *28*, *39*, *81*, *104*, *108*, *133*, *135*, *214*
Hester, Zurie, 15, 46, 85, 94, 147, *229*
Homemade Biscuits, 213
  Smoked Brisket Sliders with, *110-11*, 138-40, *139-40*
Homemade Focaccia with Herb Dipping Oil, 86, *87*
Homemade Organic Chicken Stock, 212
Honey Balsamic Farmers Market Carrots, 175, *196*, 197
Honey Mustard, Hot, with Bison Burgers and Glazed Onions, 113, 132, *133*
"Hoodie Baby" (Terry's grandmother), 13-14, 19, 184, 252
Hot Dogs, Loaded Wagyu, 22, *130*, 131
Houston Life, 78

I

Iceberg Salad with Terry's Favorite Dressing, 24, 175, 176, *177*
The Immaculate Refreshment, 78, *79*
Italian Olive Oil-Lemon Cake, *250*, 251
Italian Sausage-Stuffed Peppers, 147, 168, *169*

J

Jalapeño, Brisket, and Bacon Burgers, *136*, 137
Juicy Braised Korean Short Ribs, 24, 118, *122*, 123

K

Kale and Vegetable Italian Sausage Soup, Spicy, *152*, 153
Kamado Joe Big Joe grill, 27
Keller's Granny Smith Apple Turnovers, 237, *242*, 243
kitchen tools, must-have, 23-24, *25*, 28

L

Lasagna, South of the Border, 147, 162, *163*

egg dishes *(continued)*
  Toad in the Hole, *66*, 67
Eggplant Parmesan with Marinara, Baked, 147, *166*, 167
Egg Rolls, Crispy, with Shrimp, Sprouts, and Peanut Butter, 73, *92*, 93
electric smokers, 28–29
Enchiladas, Cheesy Chicken, *160*, 161

F

Famous Gridiron Nine-Layer Dip, 73, 102, *103*
Finger-Lickin' Barbecue Bourbon Chicken Wings, 21, 22, 113, 114, *115*, 141
fire extinguishers, 28
Fire-Roasted Hatch Chile Chicken Stew, 154, *155*
Fish Fry, Terry's Ranch-Style, 14, 203, *232*, 233
Focaccia, Homemade, with Herb Dipping Oil, 86, *87*
Fourth and One Bourbon Smash, 73, *76*, 77
Frank's RedHot Sauce, *20*, 21–22, 114, 213
French Toast Casserole, 19, 50, 52
  Overnight, with Stuffed Brioche, 52, *53*
Fried Bologna Sandwich on Texas Toast, 203, 218, *219*
Fried Chicken, Buttermilk and Hot Sauce, *200–201*, 203, 213, *214–15*

Fried Green Garden Tomatoes, *201*, 203, 209, *210–11*
Frittata, One-Skillet Breakfast, 61
Fruit Salad, Creamy Vanilla, *40*, 41
Funfetti Chocolate Chip Banana Pancakes, 21, 35, 46, *47*

G

Gainesville Grande Margarita, 82, 113
Garlic, Bacon, and Onion with Green Beans, 24, 191
Garlic Pull-Apart Pigs in a Blanket, 22, *71*, 73, 90, *91*
Garlic Shrimp, Cheddar, and Bacon Phyllo Cups, *111*, *116*, 117
German Country Potato Salad, 175, 180, *181*
get-together and potluck dishes. *See also* roots and relatives dishes
  Aloha Bread, 147, 148, *149*
  Apple Butter Bread, 150
  Baked Eggplant Parmesan with Marinara, 147, *166*, 167
  Cabbage and Potato Kettle, 147, 151
  Cannellini Chicken Chili, 24, *156*, 157
  Cheesy Chicken Enchiladas, *160*, 161
  Creamy Sun-Dried Tomato Chicken with Orzo, 158, *159*

  Fire-Roasted Hatch Chile Chicken Stew, 154, *155*
  Italian Sausage-Stuffed Peppers, 147, *168*, *169*
  Roasted-Chicken Tetrazzini, 164
  South of the Border Lasagna, 147, 162, *163*
  Spicy Italian Sausage, Vegetable, and Kale Soup, *152*, 153
  Sunday Family Casserole, 147, 165
  Sunday Glazed Meatloaf, 147, *170*, 171
Gouda and Havarti Mac 'n' Cheese, 175, 194, *195*
Gravy, Nannie Bradshaw's Sausage, 35, 57, 58, *58–59*
Greek Orzo Salad with Oil, Vinegar, and Honey Dressing, *186*, 187
Green Beans with Bacon, Onion, and Garlic, 24, 191
grilled and smoked dishes
  Asian-Inspired Sticky-Finger Ribs, 113, 118, *119–20*
  Bison Burgers with Balsamic Glazed Onions and Hot Honey Mustard, 113, 132, *133*
  Bradshaw Bourbon Barbecue Sauce for, 21, 141
  Brisket, Bacon, and Jalapeño Burgers, *136*, 137

Chicken Stock, Homemade Organic, 212
Chicken Stock Scalloped Potatoes, 24, *192*, 193
Chicken Tetrazzini, Roasted, 164
Chicken Wings, Finger-Lickin' Barbecue Bourbon, 21, 22, 113, 114, *115*, 141
Chicken with Creamy Sun-Dried Tomato and Orzo, 158, *159*
Chile, Hatch, Fire-Roasted with Chicken Stew, 154, 155
Chimichurri with Grilled Tomahawk Steak, 113, *142*, 143
Chipotle Crema with Breakfast Tacos, 64, *65*, 162
Chocolate Chip Banana Funfetti Pancakes, 21, 35, 46, *47*
Chocolate Chip Cookies with Sea Salt, Warm, 256, *257*, 262
Cilantro Sour Cream with Spicy Pork Canoes, 21, 113, *126*, 127
Cinnamon Apple Waffles, 24, 35, *48*, 49
Cinnamon Doughnuts, Baked, 23, *32-33*, 42, 43
Cobbler, Sweet Orchard Peach, 14, 237, *252*, 253
Coconut Cream Pie, Louisiana, 248, *249*
Cody (Tammy's son), 14, 167

Collard Greens, Slow-Cooked, with Bacon, Hot Sauce, and Balsamic, *200*, 203, *204*, 205, 213
Cookies, Warm Chocolate Chip with Sea Salt, 256, *257*, 262
Cornbread Dressing, Nannie's, 203, 206, *207*
Corn Salad, Mexican Street, 161, 162, *172-73*, 188, 189
Corn Salad, Missouri, with Lime and Paprika, 175, 190
Crab Cakes, Maryland-Style, with Sweet Pickle Tartar Sauce, *220*, 221, *222-23*
Crackers, Nannie's Ranch, *70*, 73, 83
Crawfish, Chicken, and Andouille Gumbo, 22, 24, 203, *226*, 227-28
Creamy Sun-Dried Tomato Chicken with Orzo, 158, *159*
Creamy Vanilla Fruit Salad, *40*, 41
Crispy Egg Rolls with Shrimp, Sprouts, and Peanut Butter, 73, *92*, 93
Curry Sriracha Dip, 73, *108*, 109

D

desserts and sweets
Banana Pudding with Nilla Wafers, 237, 240, *241*, 260

Buttermilk Pecan Pie, *234-35*, 237, *246*, 247
Cherry Crisp with Crushed Pineapple and Pecans, 237, *254*, 255
Italian Olive Oil–Lemon Cake, *250*, 251
Keller's Granny Smith Apple Turnovers, 237, *242*, 243
Louisiana Coconut Cream Pie, 248, *249*
Old-Fashioned Blackberry Pie, 22, 237, 244, *245*
piecrusts, premade, for, 22
Sweet Orchard Peach Cobbler, 14, 237, *252*, 253
Warm Chocolate Chip Cookies with Sea Salt, 256, *257*, 262
Wild Blackberry Muffins with Powdered Sugar, *238*, 239
Doughnuts, Baked Cinnamon, 23, *32-33*, 42, *43*
Dressing, Nannie's Cornbread, 203, 206, *207*
Dumplings, Herb-Roasted Chicken and Biscuit, 21, *216*, 217

E

egg dishes
Beet Deviled Eggs, *88*, 89
and peeling eggs, tips for, 89
Terry's Favorite Omelet, 68

Bradshaw Bourbon Barbecue Sauce, 21, 141
The Bradshaw Bunch (TV show), 14
Bradshaw, Erin, 14–15
Bradshaw, Gary, 198
Bradshaw, Nannie (Terry's mother), 49, 58, 83, 183, 206
Bradshaw, Rachel, 14–15, *17, 36, 39, 43*
Bradshaw, Tammy, *12*, 14–19, *26, 104, 108, 136, 222*
Bradshaw, Terry, *12*, 13–19, *26, 80, 104, 108, 134, 136, 177, 220, 222, 258*
breakfast and brunches
    Bacon, Onion, and Mushroom Quiche, 35, *62*, 63
    Baked Cinnamon Doughnuts, 23, *32–33*, 42, *43*
    Breakfast Tacos with Chipotle Crema, 64, *65*, 162
    Brunch Punch, 24, 35, *36, 37, 38–39*
    Cinnamon Apple Waffles, 24, 35, *48*, 49
    Creamy Vanilla Fruit Salad, *40*, 41
    French Toast Casserole, 19, 50, 52
    Funfetti Chocolate Chip Banana Pancakes, 21, 35, 46, *47*
    Ham and Old English Cheese Casserole, 22, 51, *54–55*

Nannie Bradshaw's Sausage Gravy, 35, 57, 58, *58–59*
One-Skillet Breakfast Frittata, 61
Ooey Gooey Apple Monkey Bread, 22, 35, *44*, 45
Overnight Stuffed Brioche French Toast Casserole, 52, *53*
Sausage and Cheddar Cheese Biscuits, *56*, 57, 58, *59*
Spicy Breakfast Casserole with Onion and Bell Peppers, 60
Terry's Favorite Omelet, 68
Toad in the Hole, *66*, 67
Breakfast Tacos with Chipotle Crema, 64, *65*, 162
Brisket Burgers with Bacon and Jalapeño, *136*, 137
Brisket Sliders, Smoked, with Homemade Biscuits, *110–11*, 138–40, *139–40*
Brunch Punch, 24, 35, *36*, 37, *38–39*
Buttermilk and Hot Sauce Fried Chicken, *200–201*, 203, 213, *214–15*
Buttermilk Pecan Pie, *234–35*, 237, *246*, 247

C

Cabbage and Potato Kettle, 147, 151
Cannellini Chicken Chili, 24, *156*, 157

Carrots, Farmers Market, with Honey and Balsamic, 175, *196*, 197
Cason (Rachel's son), 15, 86, 147
Chase (Rachel's husband), 15, 60, 90, 157, 239, 251
Cheddar, Garlic Shrimp, and Bacon Phyllo Cups, *111*, *116*, 117
Cheesy Chicken Enchiladas, *160*, 161
Cheesy Smoked Buffalo Chicken Dip, 22, 73, *100*, 101
Chef Noah's Hawaiian Chili Water, *20*, 21, 114, 213
Cherry Crisp with Crushed Pineapple and Pecans, 237, *254*, 255
Chicago Bears, 13
Chicken and Biscuit Dumplings, Herb-Roasted, 21, *216*, 217
Chicken, Andouille, and Crawfish Gumbo, 22, 24, 203, *226*, 227–28
Chicken Cannellini Chili, 24, *156*, 157
Chicken Dip, Cheesy Smoked Buffalo, 22, 73, *100*, 101
Chicken Enchiladas, Cheesy, *160*, 161
Chicken-Fried Steak "Fries" with Zesty Dip, 94, *95*
Chicken, Fried, with Buttermilk and Hot Sauce, *200–201*, 203, 213, *214–15*
Chicken Stew with Fire-Roasted Hatch Chile, 154, *155*

Index

A

Aloha Bread, 147, 148, *149*
Ambrosia Salad, Old-Fashioned, 14, 175, 184, *185*
Andouille, Chicken, and Crawfish Gumbo, 22, 24, 203, *226*, 227–28
Andouille, Shrimp, and Veggie Boil, Old Bay, 224, *225*
Apple Butter Bread, 150
Apple Cinnamon Waffles, 24, 35, *48*, 49
Apple Monkey Bread, Ooey Gooey, 22, 35, *44*, 45
Apple Turnovers, Keller's Granny Smith, 237, *242*, 243
Asian-Inspired Sticky-Finger Ribs, 113, 118, *119–20*

B

Bacon, Brisket, and Jalapeño Burgers, *136*, 137
Bacon, Garlic Shrimp, and Cheddar Phyllo Cups, *111*, *116*, 117
Bacon, Onion, and Garlic with Green Beans, 24, 191
Bacon, Onion, and Mushroom Quiche, 35, *62*, 63
Bacon Spinach Sports Balls, 113, 128, *129*

Bacon with Slow-Cooked Collard Greens, Hot Sauce, and Balsamic, 200, 203, *204*, 205, 213
Baked Cinnamon Doughnuts, 23, *32–33*, 42, *43*
Baked Eggplant Parmesan with Marinara, 147, *166*, 167
Balsamic and Honey Farmers Market Carrots, 175, *196*, 197
Balsamic with Slow-Cooked Collard Greens, Bacon and Hot Sauce, 200, 203, *204*, 205, 213
Banana Chocolate Chip Funfetti Pancakes, 21, 35, 46, *47*
Banana Pudding with Nilla Wafers, 237, 240, *241*, 260
bar tools, basic, 23–24
Beans, Terry's Legendary Bradshaw, 14, 21, 23, 141, 175, 198, *199*
Beet Deviled Eggs, *88*, 89
Bell Peppers and Onion with Spicy Breakfast Casserole, 60
biscuit dishes
    Herb-Roasted Chicken and Biscuit Dumplings, 21, *216*, 217
    premade biscuit dough for, 22

    Sausage and Cheddar Cheese Biscuits, *56*, 57, 58, *59*
    Smoked Brisket Sliders with Homemade Biscuits, *110–11*, 138–40, *139–40*
Bison Burgers with Balsamic Glazed Onions and Hot Honey Mustard, 113, 132, *133*
Bisquick Original Pancake and Baking Mix, 21
Blackberry Pie, Old-Fashioned, 22, 237, 244, *245*
Blackberry, Wild, Muffins with Powdered Sugar, *238*, 239
Blond Bomber, 73, 74, *75*
Bologna Sandwich, Fried, on Texas Toast, 203, 218, *219*
bourbon
    in Bradshaw Bourbon Barbecue Sauce, 21, 141
    in Finger-Lickin' Barbecue Bourbon Chicken Wings, 21, 22, 113, 114, *115*, 141
    in Fourth and One Bourbon Smash, 73, *76*, 77
    in Smoked Maple-Bourbon Pork Belly Bites, 124, *125*

263

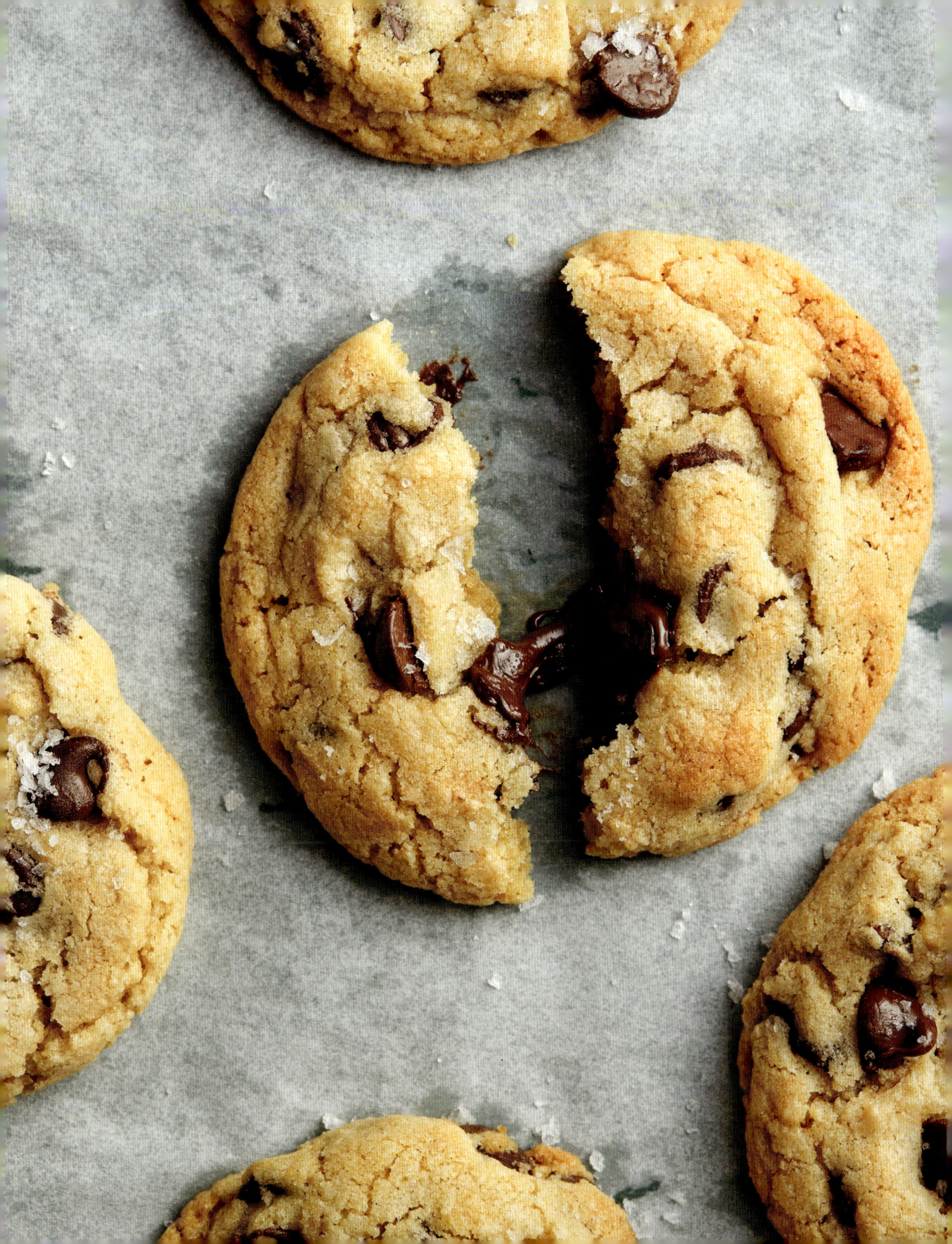

Acknowledgments

The Bradshaw Family would like to personally thank the following for their assistance and support with this cookbook:

James Beard Award-winning author James O. Fraioli and Culinary Book Creations; Stephanie Wilson and Wicked Creative; Ray Graj and Graj + Gustavsen; Janis Donnaud and Janis A. Donnaud and Associates; Charity Burggraaf and Charity Burggraaf Photography; Texas food stylists Stephanie Jo Greenwood and Amanda Mobley; Seattle food stylists Theresa Gilliam and Tyler Hill; editor Pam Krauss and the Artichoke Group; and the entire team at Flatiron Books, including Megan Lynch, Julie Will, Sydney Jeon, and Frances Sayers.

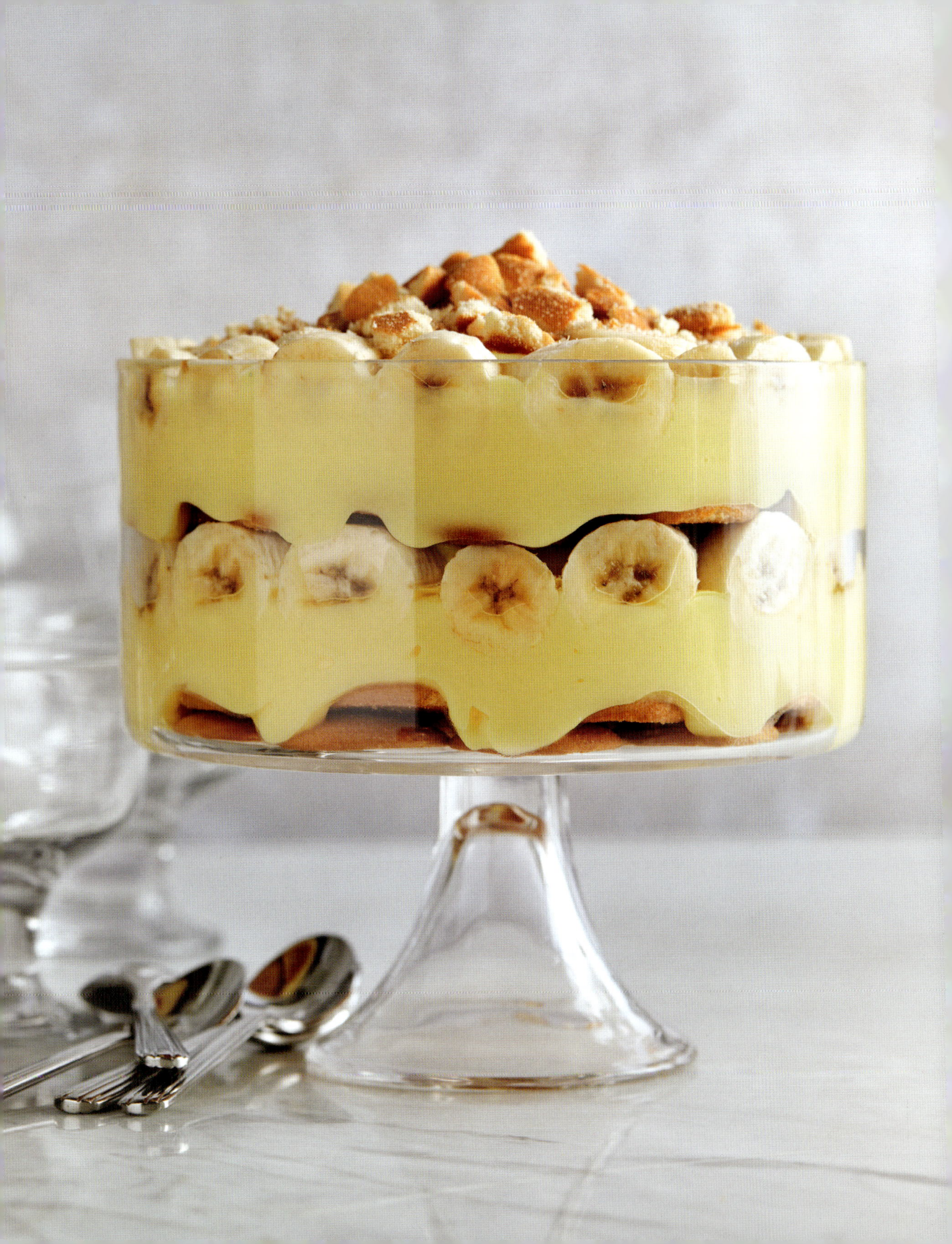

Pappy's Midnight Spoon

This recipe is not a true dessert, but a family joke we have to include. Picture a large spoon topped with either peanut butter or ice cream. When all our families are over at Terry and Tammy's, we always know when Pappy has a midnight snack, because there'll be a large spoon on the kitchen counter the following morning. We don't say anything, but we still can't figure out why Terry can't get his spoon into the sink. Of course, he'll deny it, saying, "It wasn't me. I don't get up during the night." —**NOAH**

Serves 1

1 heaping tablespoon peanut butter or whatever flavor ice cream is in your freezer

Grab a spoon from the drawer between 11 p.m. and 3 a.m. Take the spoon to the pantry or freezer and scoop up a heaping portion of peanut butter or ice cream. Devour immediately, then leave the used spoon on the counter for your family to find the next morning. Return to bed.

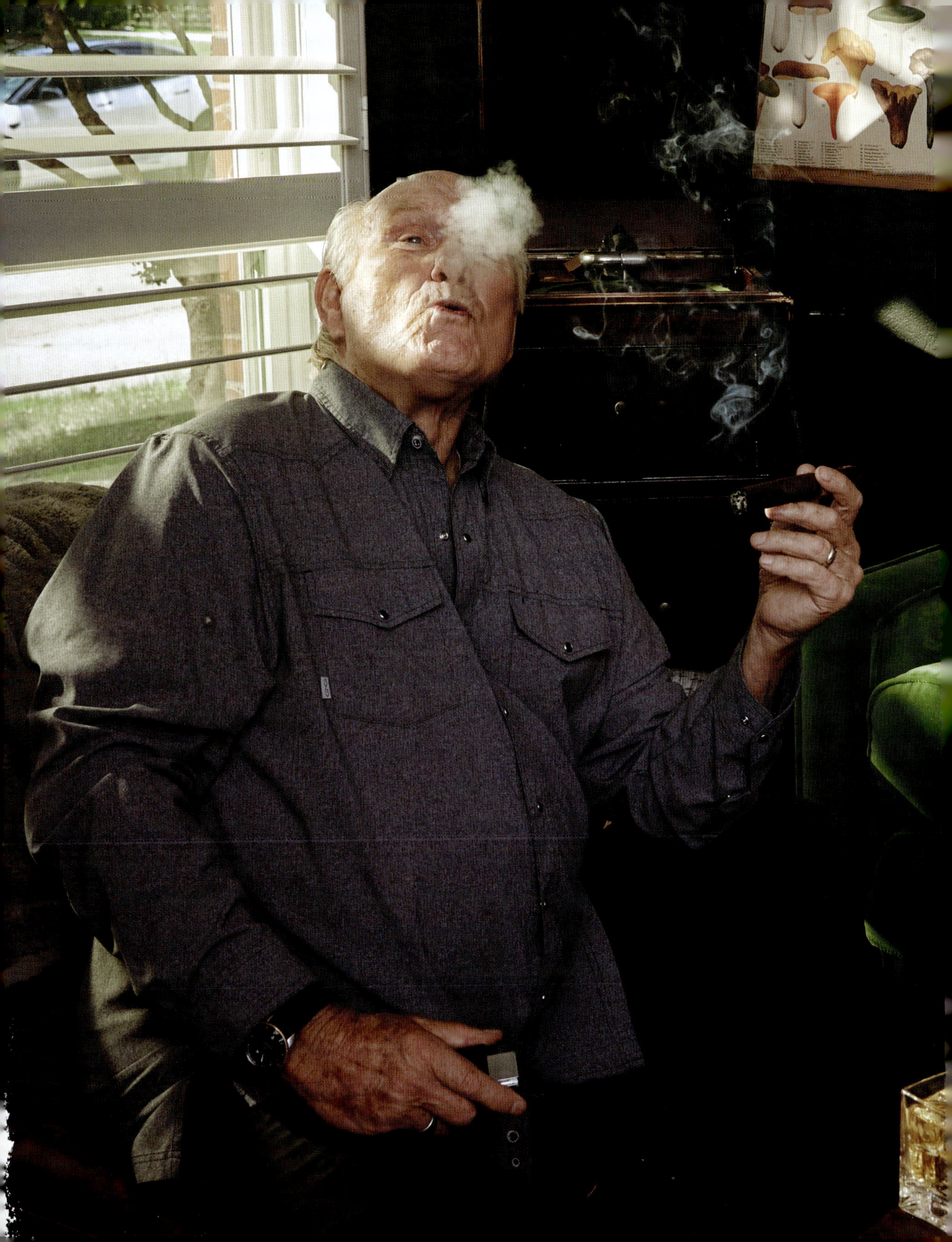

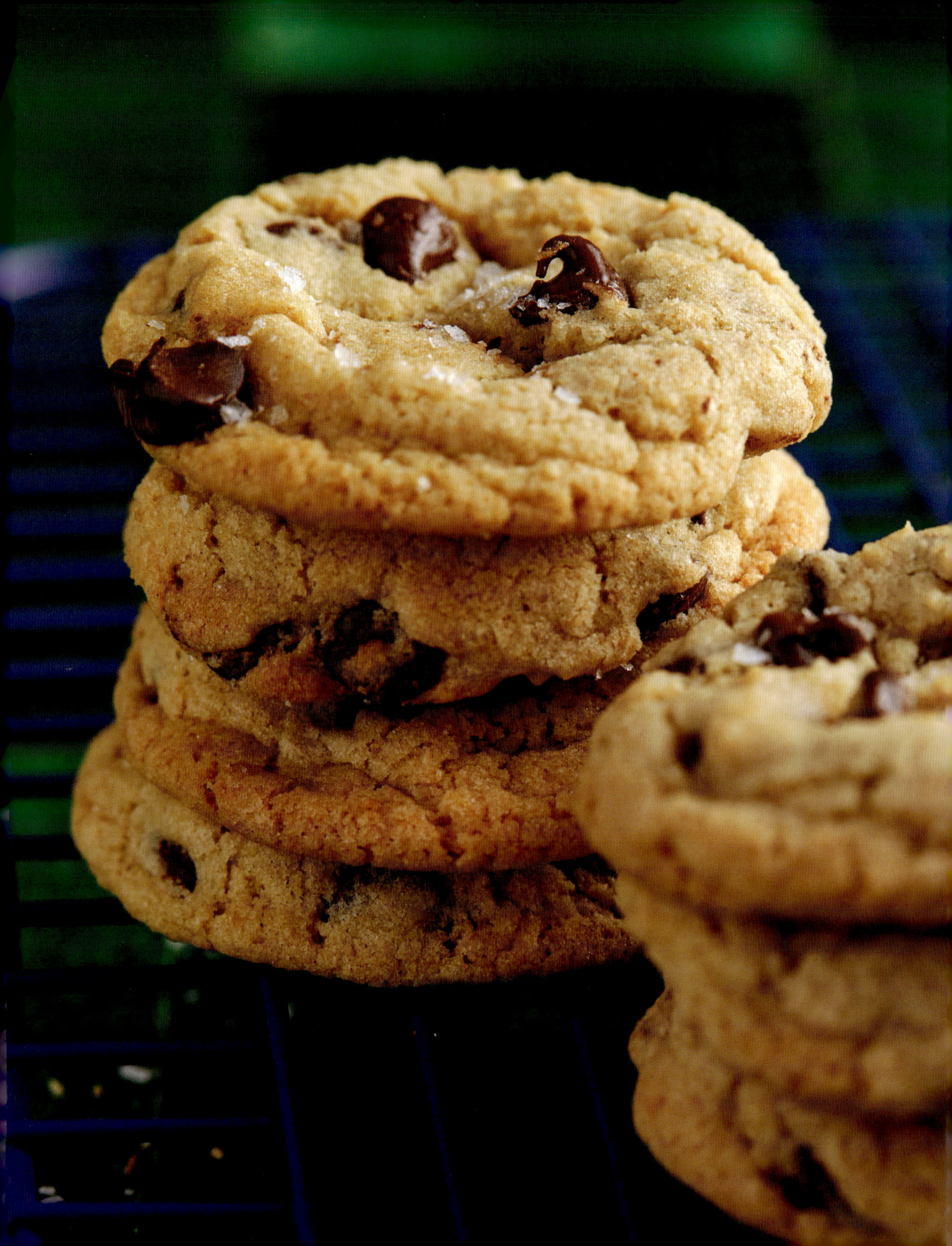

Warm Chocolate Chip Cookies with Sea Salt

My "baking era" started when I was pregnant, and, naturally, I was obsessed with cookies. I now make these warm chocolate chip cookies with sea salt time and time again, and they've become my go-to anytime our family or friends invite Chase and me over. Note I said warm, because these are especially enticing when they are still a bit gooey in the center. —RACHEL

Makes about 3 dozen cookies

3 cups all-purpose flour

1 teaspoon baking soda

½ teaspoon baking powder

2 teaspoons flake sea salt, plus more for serving

1 cup (2 sticks) butter, softened

1 cup granulated sugar

1 cup packed dark brown sugar

2 large eggs

2 teaspoons pure vanilla extract

2 cups (14 ounces) chocolate chips

Preheat the oven to 375°F. Line two rimmed baking sheets with parchment paper and set aside.

Whisk together the flour, baking soda, baking powder, and salt in a large bowl.

Combine the butter, granulated sugar, and brown sugar in another large bowl and mix. Add the eggs and vanilla and whisk until well combined, about 1 minute. Add the wet ingredients to the dry ingredients and mix just until blended. Fold in the chocolate chips.

Roll 2 to 3 tablespoons (depending on how large you like your cookies) of dough into a ball and place on one prepared baking sheet, about 2 inches apart. Repeat with the remaining dough. Bake until the cookies are just barely starting to turn brown, 8 to 10 minutes. Let them sit on the baking sheet for 2 minutes before removing to a cooling rack. Sprinkle with some flake sea salt and serve.

Cherry Crisp with Crushed Pineapple and Pecans

I love whipping up this dessert for Terry and the kids. Not only has the recipe been in our family for many years but it's also a simple dish made with ingredients that we always have in our pantry. We like to describe it as soft, a bit gooey, and delicious. Try it with a scoop of vanilla ice cream. —TAMMY

Serves 6 to 8

- 1 (21-ounce) can cherry pie filling
- 1 (8-ounce) can crushed pineapple, drained
- 1 (15.25-ounce) box yellow cake mix
- ⅓ cup vegetable oil
- 3 large eggs
- 1 cup water
- 1 cup chopped pecans
- 4 tablespoons (½ stick) butter, melted, plus more for greasing

Preheat the oven to 350°F. Grease a 9 × 9-inch baking dish.

Add the cherry pie filling to the prepared baking dish, spreading it in an even layer. Layer the drained pineapple on top of the cherry filling.

In a large bowl, combine the cake mix, oil, eggs, and water and blend with an electric mixer at low speed until moistened, about 30 seconds. Increase the speed to medium and beat for 2 minutes. Fold in the chopped pecans.

Carefully pour the batter over the pineapple and cherry filling without disturbing the fruit. Drizzle with the melted butter. Bake until bubbly and a toothpick inserted in the center comes out clean, 40 to 45 minutes. Let cool slightly before serving.

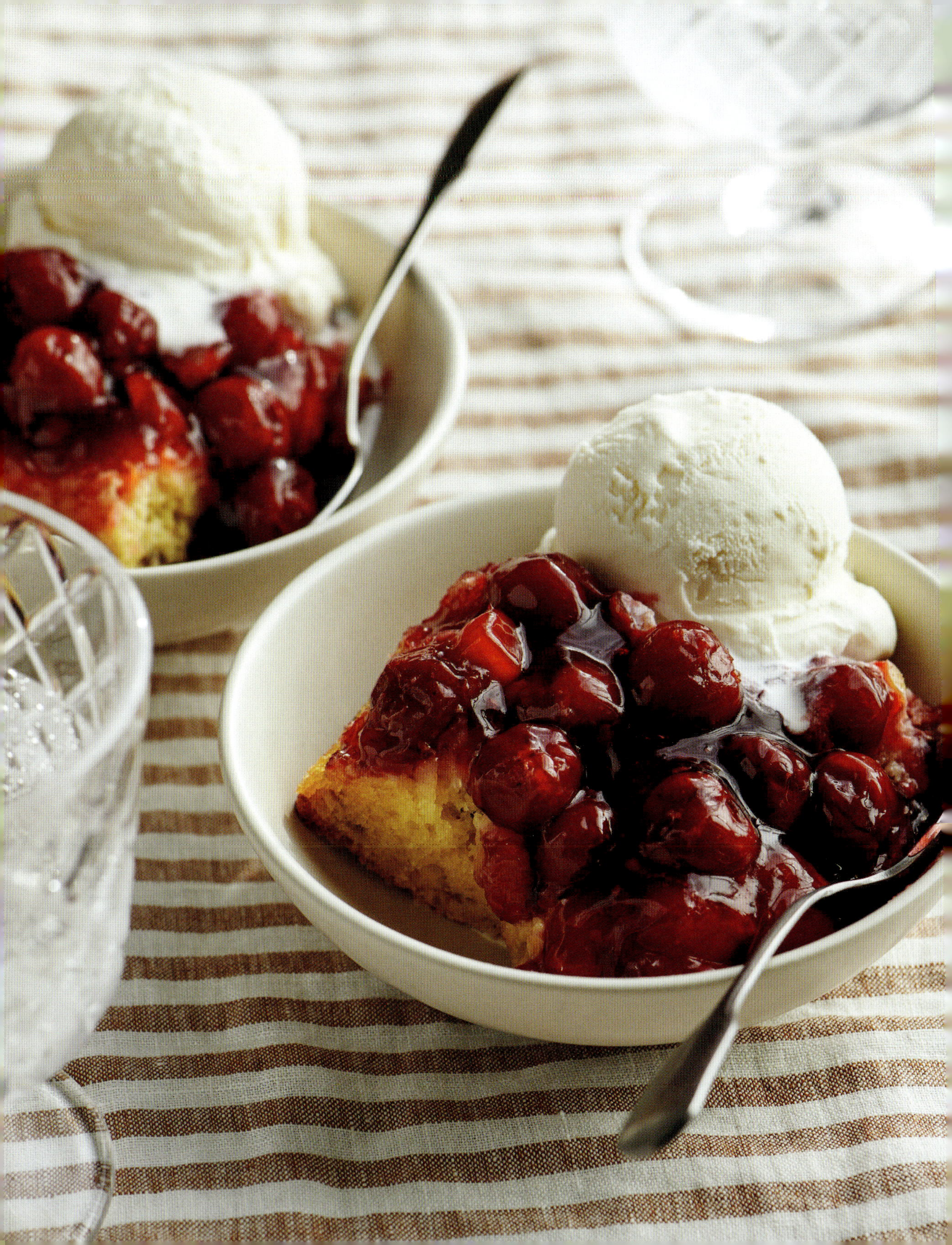

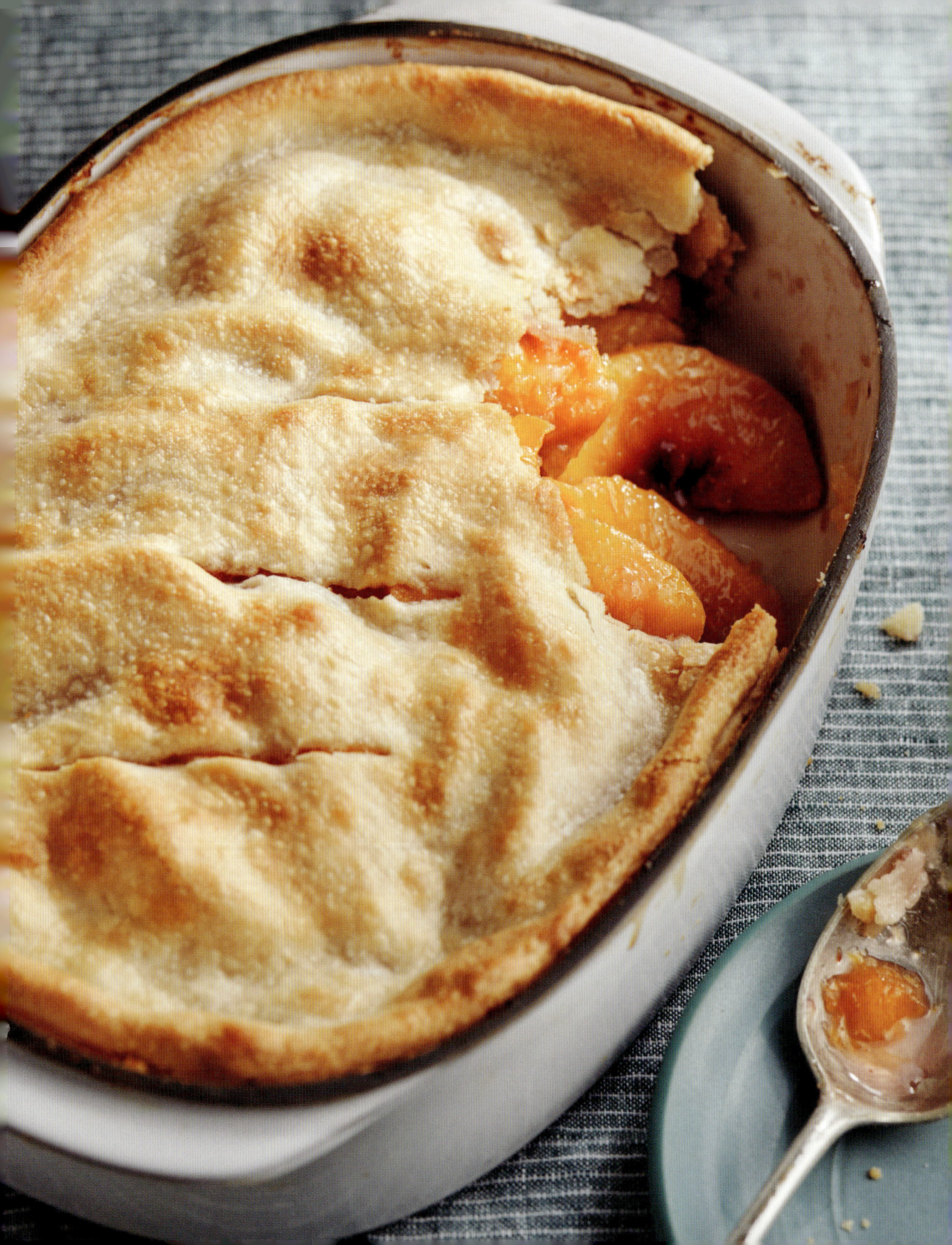

Sweet Orchard Peach Cobbler

There's something about the warm Southern sun that seems to create the perfect peach. Growing up in Louisiana, I would pick peaches with my mother and grandmother Hoodie Baby at an orchard near our house. The ripe, juicy peaches often ended up in a cobbler like this one. For the cobbler crust, we prefer a biscuitlike dough to a cakelike batter. We think it offers a better textural contrast to the tender fruit. —TERRY

Serves 8 to 10

FILLING

1 cup granulated sugar

2 cups all-purpose flour

6 cups peeled, pitted, and sliced fresh ripe peaches (see Coach's Corner)

CRUST

¾ cup all-purpose flour

¼ cup granulated sugar

1 teaspoon kosher salt

¾ cup vegetable shortening

½ cup cold water

4 tablespoons (½ stick) cold unsalted butter, cut into small cubes, plus more for greasing

Vanilla ice cream, for serving (optional)

Preheat the oven to 350°F. Grease a 9 × 9-inch baking dish.

To make the filling: Add the sugar and flour to a large mixing bowl and mix with a fork until combined. Fold in the peaches, mix gently, and set aside while you assemble the crust.

To make the crust: Add the flour, sugar, salt, and shortening to a large mixing bowl. Mix with a fork until crumbly. Add ¼ cup of the cold water and mix until a shaggy dough forms, adding more cold water, 1 tablespoon at a time, as needed. Knead the dough on a well-floured surface until a smooth ball forms. Divide the dough ball into two parts with slightly more dough for the bottom crust. Using a rolling pin, roll out each portion to ¼-inch thickness.

Line the prepared baking dish with the larger bottom dough. Spoon the peach filling on top and dot with the butter. Place the remaining dough on top of the filling, tucking in the edges and pressing them against the sides of the dish to seal. Cut a pattern of slits into the top dough so steam can escape as the cobbler bakes.

Bake until bubbly and the top crust is golden brown, about 60 minutes. Serve warm with vanilla ice cream, if using.

COACH'S CORNER

If fresh ripe peaches aren't available, you can use canned peaches. Just make sure to drain the syrup. Because canned peaches are typically very sweet, cut back on the amount of sugar.

Italian Olive Oil–Lemon Cake

Chase and I went to Italy on our honeymoon, and that's where we discovered this to-die-for olive oil cake. When we're after a light, summery treat or a sophisticated dinner party dessert, we'll reach for this recipe. The moist, tender cake combines the richness of olive oil with the bright, tangy flavor of fresh lemons. We then enhance the texture with a bit of yogurt. One bite and you'll agree this cake is a refreshing alternative to traditional butter-based cakes. **—RACHEL**

Serves 8

Nonstick cooking spray
1¼ cups all-purpose flour
⅔ cup granulated sugar
½ teaspoon baking powder
¼ teaspoon baking soda
¼ teaspoon kosher salt
⅔ cup olive oil
½ cup plain traditional-style Greek yogurt
2 large eggs
Zest of 1 lemon, plus more for serving (optional)
3 tablespoons fresh lemon juice
Powdered sugar, for serving (optional)

Preheat the oven to 350°F. Spray a 9-inch round cake pan with nonstick cooking spray.

Whisk together the flour, granulated sugar, baking powder, baking soda, and salt in a large bowl. Create a well in the center of the flour mixture and add the olive oil, yogurt, and eggs. Whisk the wet ingredients into the flour mixture. Add the lemon zest and juice and use a wooden spoon or spatula to stir until there aren't any lumps.

Pour the batter into the prepared pan and bake until a toothpick inserted in the center comes out clean, 30 to 35 minutes. Allow to cool in the pan for at least 10 minutes. Garnish with powdered sugar and lemon zest, if using, and serve.

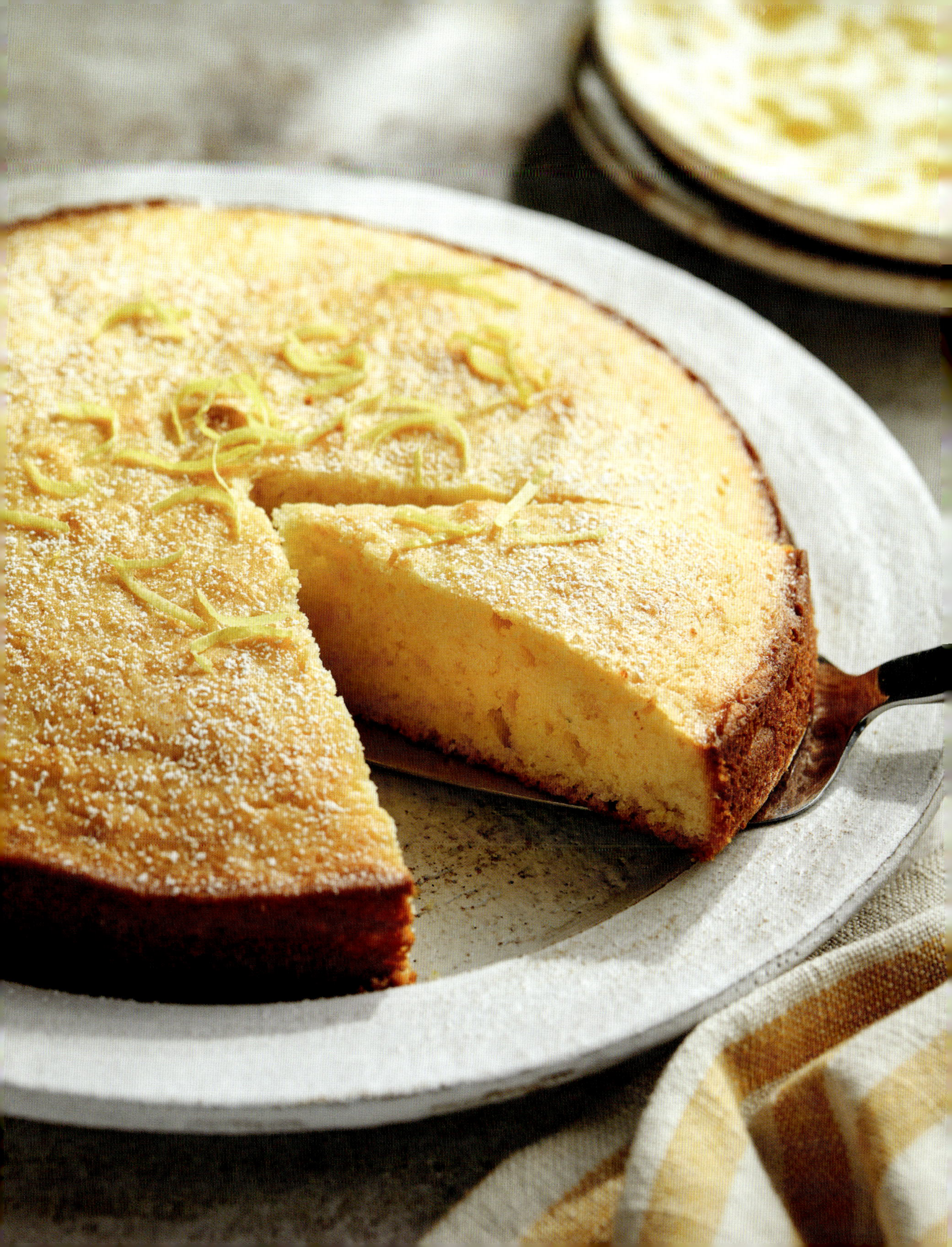

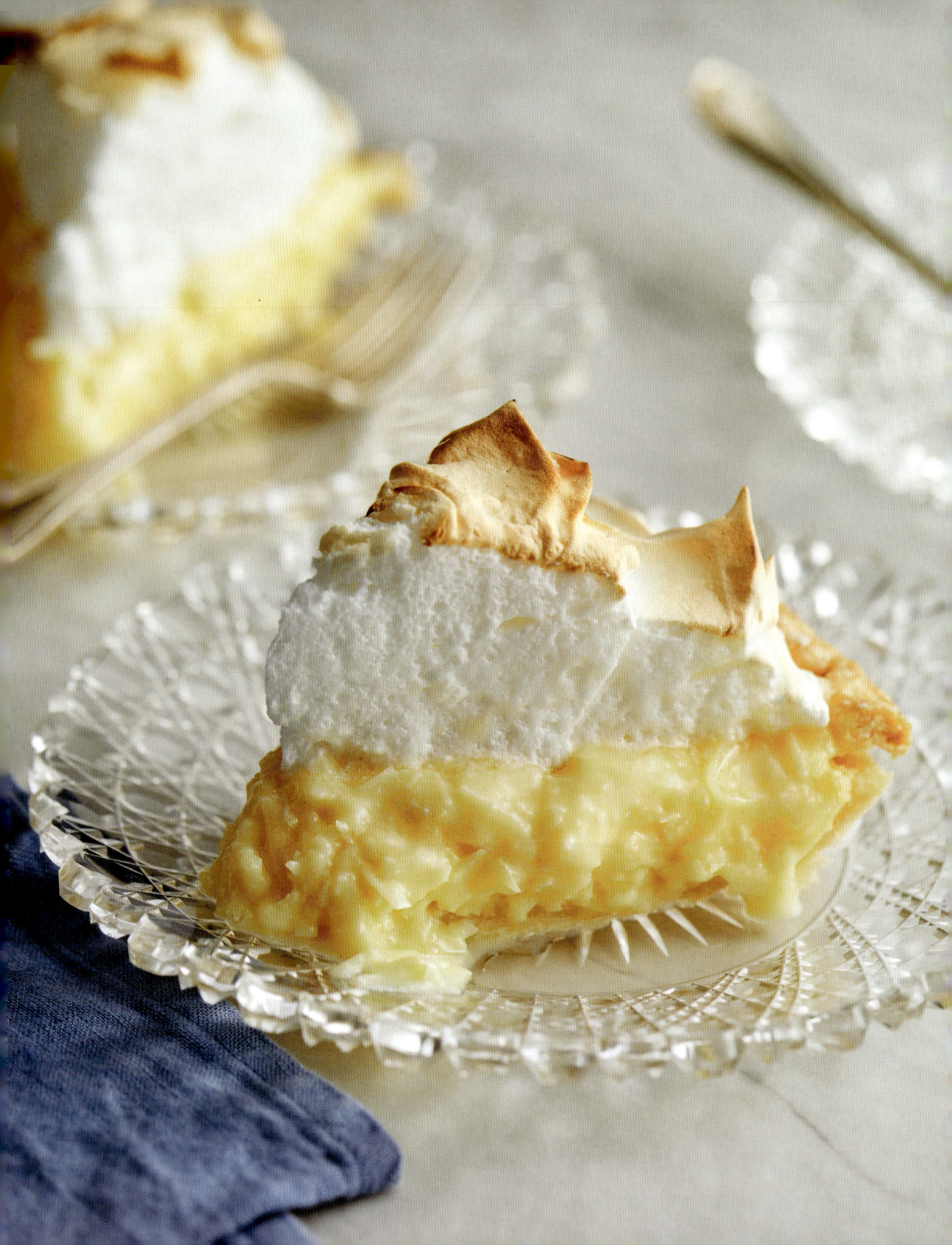

Louisiana Coconut Cream Pie

Here's another dessert that immediately transports me back to my childhood in Louisiana and a much simpler time. We top the thick and creamy coconut custard with a fluffy meringue and bake it to a golden brown. The result is a classic pie with perfect texture and flavor that's not overly sweet. **—TERRY**

Serves 6

1 (9-inch) premade pie shell

2 heaping tablespoons all-purpose flour

1¾ cups granulated sugar, divided

2 cups whole milk, divided

4 large eggs, separated

2 tablespoons (¼ stick) butter

1 (14-ounce) package flaked coconut

1 teaspoon pure vanilla extract

Preheat the oven to 350°F.

With a fork, poke holes in the bottom of the pie shell and fill with pie weights or dried beans. Bake until golden brown, 25 to 30 minutes. Set aside to cool.

Combine the flour, 1¼ cups of the sugar, 3 tablespoons of the milk, and the egg yolks in a deep saucepan. Whisk over medium heat while adding the butter, coconut, vanilla, and remaining milk. Continue to cook, stirring constantly, until thickened, 8 to 10 minutes. Pour into the baked pie shell and set aside.

To make the meringue, add the egg whites and remaining ½ cup sugar to a bowl. Use an electric mixer or whisk to beat until stiff peaks form.

Spoon the meringue onto the pie using the back of the spoon to make swirls and peaks and spreading all the way out to the crust all the way around. Bake until golden brown, 10 to 15 minutes. Let the pie cool completely before cutting and serving. The filling will thicken as it cools.

Buttermilk Pecan Pie

This sweet and nutty pie is similar to a traditional pecan pie, but creamier, thanks to a custard-like filling. The subtle tang from the buttermilk elevates this pie even more. At home, we like to pair the pie with a cup of hot apple cider or a rich coffee for a decadent ending to a special meal. **—TERRY AND TAMMY**

Serves 6

- 1 (9-inch) premade pie shell
- 2 cups granulated sugar
- 3 tablespoons all-purpose flour
- ¼ teaspoon kosher salt
- 3 large eggs
- 1 cup buttermilk
- ½ cup (1 stick) butter, melted
- 2 teaspoons pure vanilla extract
- ½ cup chopped pecans

Preheat the oven to 300°F.

With a fork, prick holes in the bottom of the pie shell and fill with pie weights or dried beans. Par-bake the shell until golden brown, 15 to 18 minutes. Set aside.

Whisk together the sugar, flour, salt, eggs, buttermilk, and vanilla in a large bowl until combined and free of lumps. Fold in the chopped pecans, then pour the filling into the prepared pie shell in an even layer.

Bake the pie on the center rack until a toothpick inserted in the center comes out clean, about 90 minutes. Serve warm or at room temperature. Cover and refrigerate any leftovers for up to 3 days.

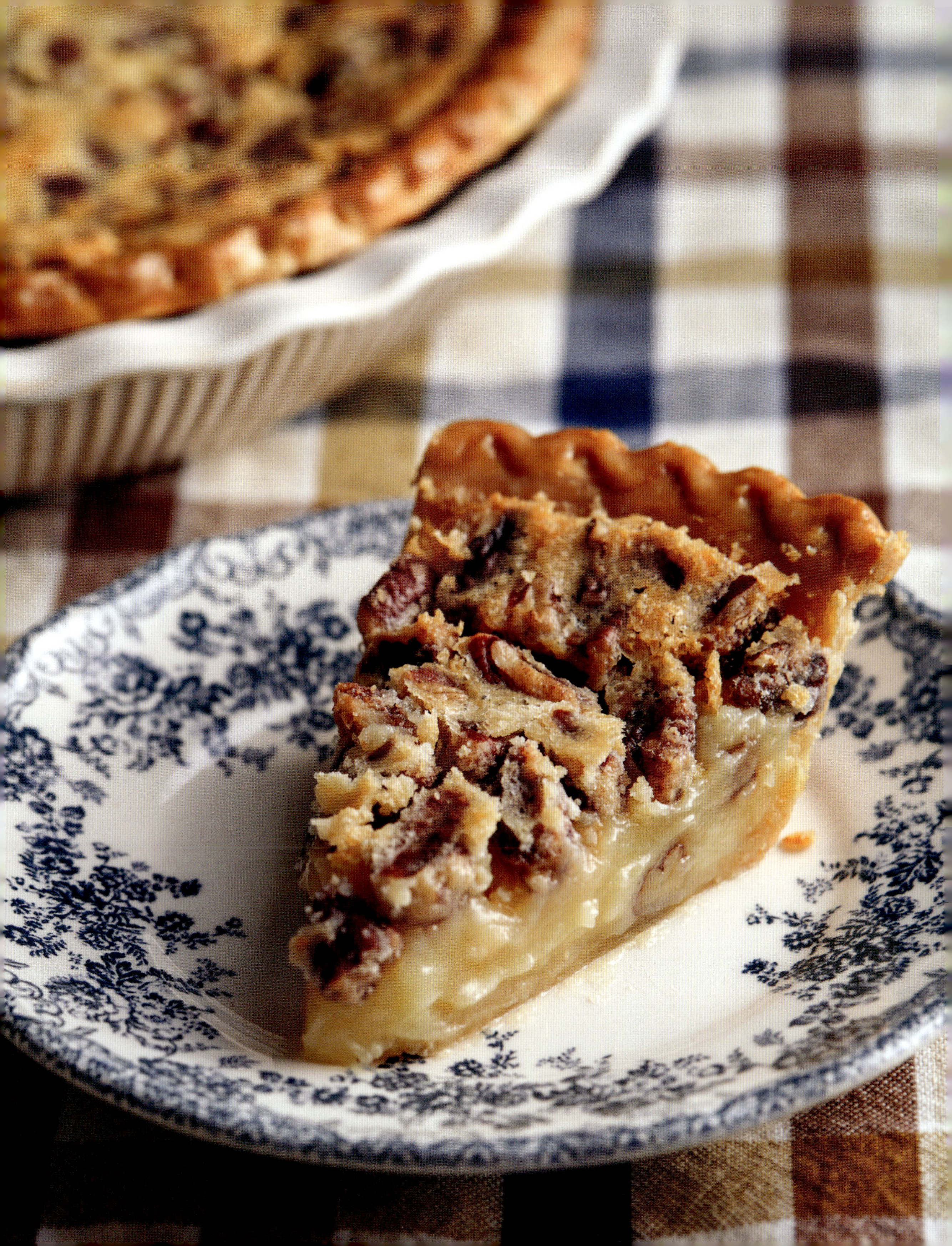

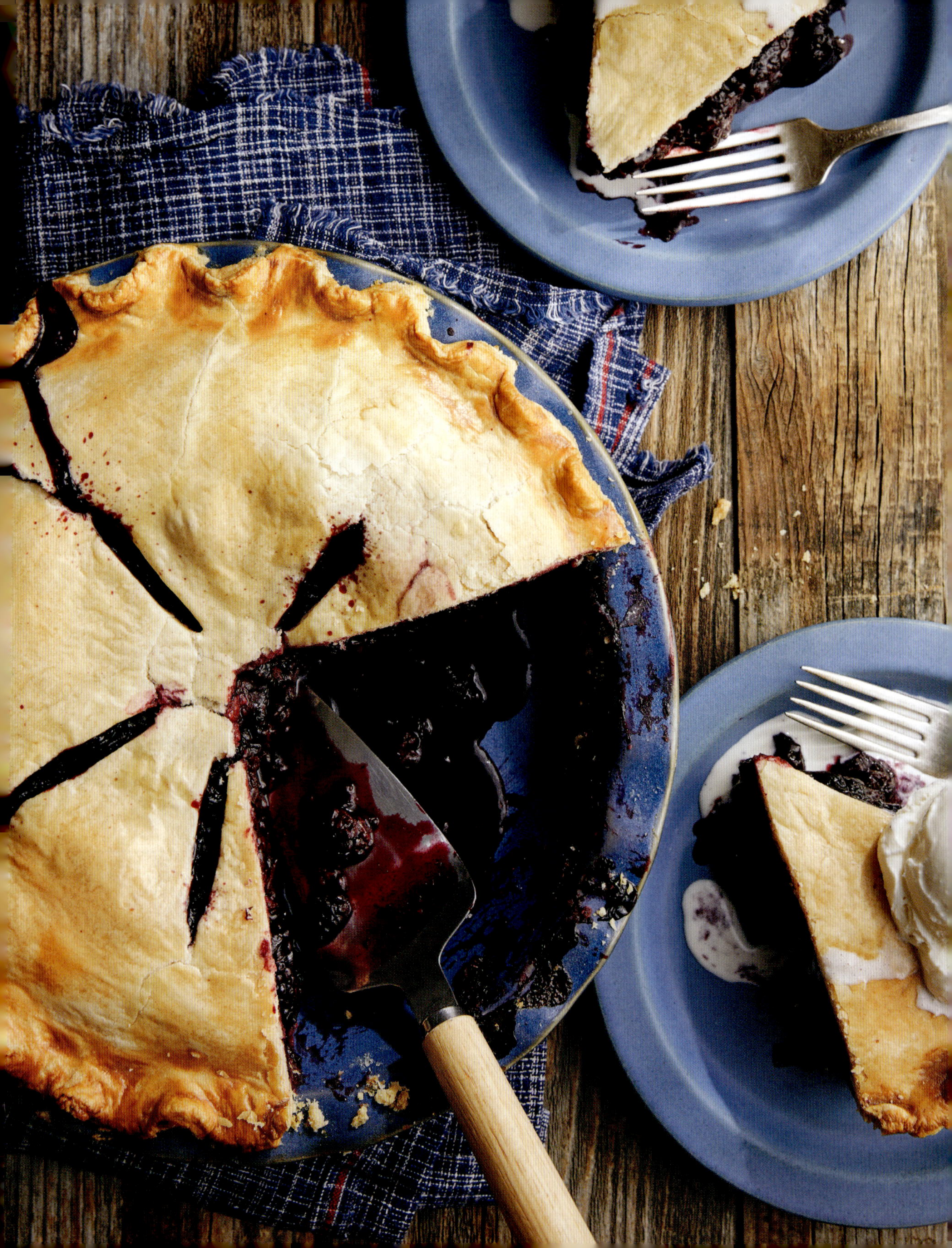

Old-Fashioned Blackberry Pie

If you like blackberries, you'll want to try this delicious summer dessert. We gently toss the berries with sugar, a touch of lemon, and a hint of spice, then bake until bubbly and fragrant within a flaky, golden crust. Chase and I like to serve the pie slightly warm with a scoop of vanilla ice cream or a dollop of whipped cream. —**RACHEL**

Serves 6

5 to 6 cups fresh blackberries, rinsed and dried

½ to ¾ cup granulated sugar (depending on the sweetness of the berries)

6 tablespoons cornstarch, all-purpose flour, or instant tapioca

1 teaspoon lemon zest

1 teaspoon fresh lemon juice

½ teaspoon ground cinnamon

¼ teaspoon almond extract

2 premade piecrusts

Preheat the oven to 400°F.

Add the blackberries, sugar, cornstarch, lemon zest, lemon juice, cinnamon, and almond extract to a large bowl. Gently fold the berries until they are well coated with the mixture. Let the berries stand for 30 minutes to release their juices.

Roll out one of the premade piecrusts and fit it into a 9-inch pie dish. Press it gently into the pan and trim any excess dough hanging over the edges. Fill the piecrust with the berry mixture.

Roll out the second piecrust and place it over the top of the filling. Or cut it into strips and arrange in a lattice pattern. If leaving whole, make a couple slits in the top crust to allow steam to vent. Trim the edges and crimp to seal the top and bottom crusts together. Place the pie dish on a baking sheet to catch any juices that bubble over and bake on the middle rack in the oven for 30 minutes.

Reduce the heat to 350°F and place a sheet of aluminum foil or a pie protector over the top crust to protect the edges and tops from getting too dark. Bake until the crust has browned and the filling is bubbly, about 30 minutes. Place on a wire rack to cool completely before serving. Reheat the pie in the microwave or oven if you like to enjoy your pie warm, as the Bradshaws do.

Keller's Granny Smith Apple Turnovers

In Keller, Texas, a quaint suburb of Dallas where my great-grandfather lived, there was a little doughnut shop that made the best strudels and turnovers. He used to stop there and bring us back doughnuts and pastries. The shop closed, but our version of their apple turnovers keeps the tradition alive. Serve these pockets of homemade goodness with ice cream after a fabulous dinner, or in the morning with a cup of fresh-brewed coffee. —RACHEL

Makes 8 turnovers

1 (17.3-ounce) package Pepperidge Farm Puff Pastry Sheets, thawed

1 tablespoon butter

3 Granny Smith apples, peeled, cored, and diced into 1/3-inch pieces (about 6 cups)

1/4 cup packed dark brown sugar

1 teaspoon pure vanilla extract

1/2 teaspoon ground cinnamon

1/8 teaspoon kosher salt

1 egg, beaten with 1 tablespoon water

Coarse sugar such as Sugar in the Raw, for serving

Remove both sheets of puff pastry from the box and remove the outer wrapping. Thaw the sheets until the pastry unfolds easily, but no more than 40 minutes.

While the dough is defrosting, melt the butter in a medium saucepan over medium heat. Add the diced apples and cook, stirring occasionally, until softened, 5 to 7 minutes. Reduce the heat to low and stir in the brown sugar, vanilla, cinnamon, and salt. Continue to simmer until the apples are soft and caramelized, 3 to 5 minutes. Remove from the heat and set aside.

Preheat the oven to 400°F. Line a rimmed baking sheet with parchment paper.

Using a rolling pin, roll the first sheet of thawed puff pastry to an 11-inch square. With a pizza cutter or kitchen knife, cut the dough into four equal-sized squares. Spoon 2 to 3 tablespoons of the reserved apple filling onto half of each square, leaving at least a 1/2-inch border. Brush the edges lightly with egg wash (just enough to seal), fold over the opposite corner of the filling, bring the edges together, and crimp firmly with a fork. Arrange the filled turnovers on the prepared baking sheet, leaving at least 1 inch between them. Repeat with the second sheet of puff pastry to make eight turnovers in total.

With a paring knife, cut two or three small slits in the top of each turnover. Brush the tops with the remaining egg wash, top with a sprinkling of coarse sugar, and bake until golden brown and puffed, about 20 minutes. Serve warm.

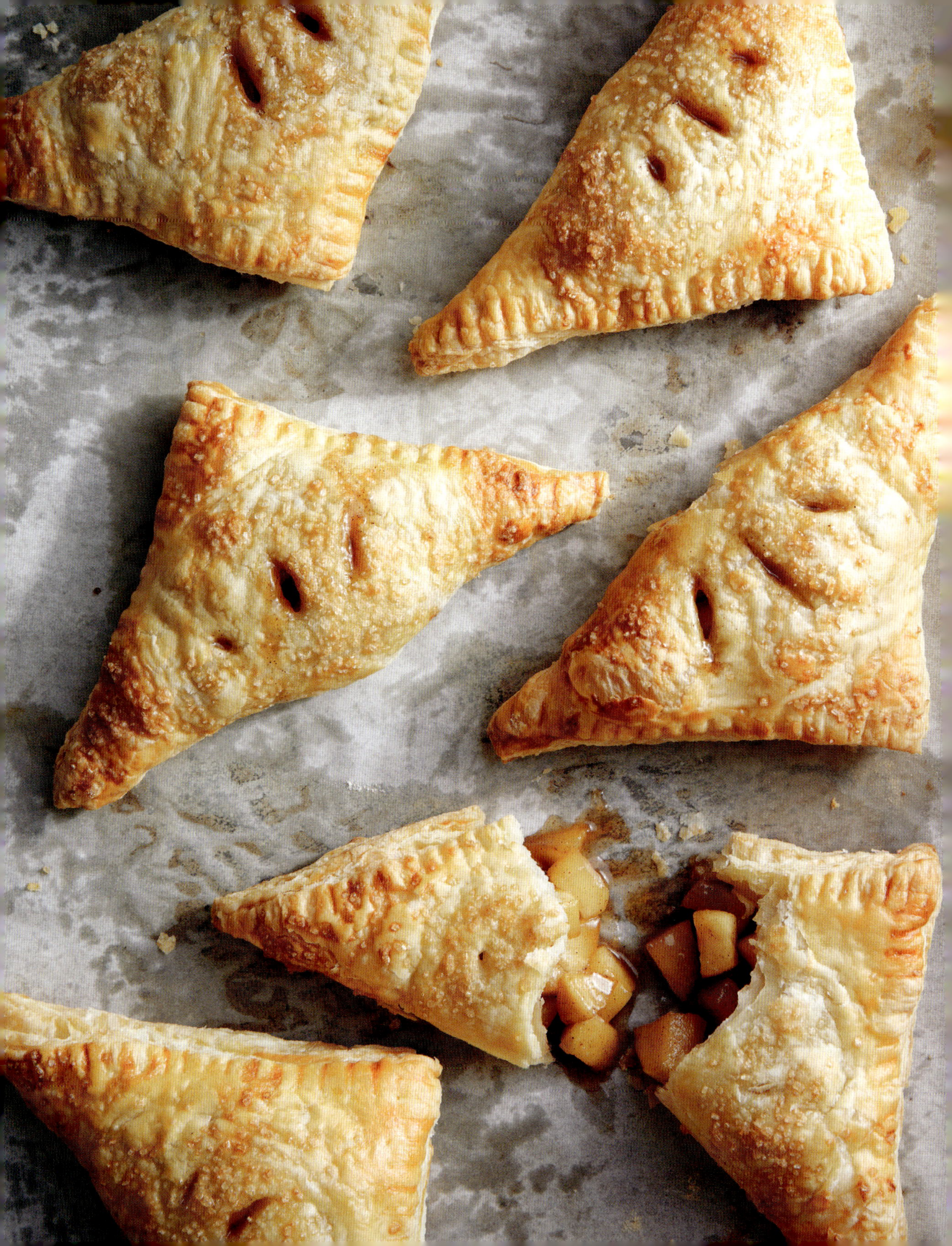

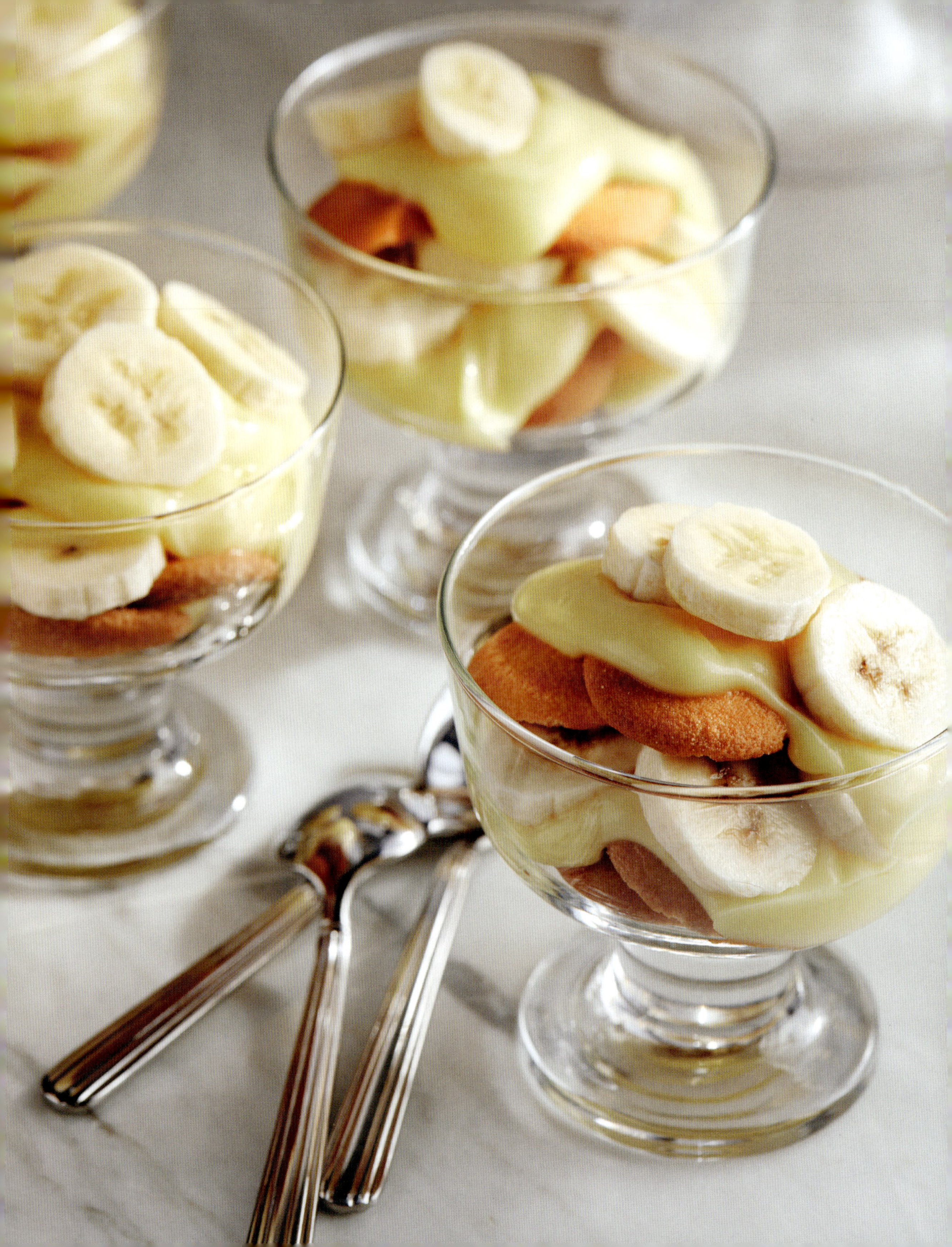

Banana Pudding with Nilla Wafers

My mother loved her Southern dishes, and this pudding was one of my favorites growing up. When we make it, I like to double up on the wafers because it really adds to the flavor. We also crush some extra wafers as a topping and serve the pudding warm, but it's also excellent chilled. You can make this in individual serving bowls or in one large serving dish, whichever you prefer. —TERRY

Serves 6

- ¾ cup granulated sugar
- 3 tablespoons cornstarch
- ¼ teaspoon kosher salt
- 2 cups whole milk
- 2 large egg yolks
- 1½ teaspoons pure vanilla extract
- 1 (15-ounce) box Nilla wafers, or to taste
- 2 to 3 ripe bananas, sliced

Add the sugar, cornstarch, and salt to a medium saucepan and whisk to combine over medium heat. Gradually add the milk and whisk until smooth, then whisk in the egg yolks. Slowly bring to a boil, 5 to 8 minutes, whisking frequently, then boil until thickened, about 2 minutes. Whisk in the vanilla, remove from the heat, and let cool to room temperature.

Line a 2-quart round glass baking dish or 6 to 8 individual dessert glasses with a single layer of cookie wafers. Top with some of the pudding and a layer of sliced bananas. Keep layering until the dish is filled. Sprinkle the top with crushed wafers, if desired. Serve warm or refrigerate until chilled.

Wild Blackberry Muffins with Powdered Sugar

My husband, Chase, has a quaint little river house in Arkansas that we visit year-round. When family and friends come over, we'll have everyone create a dish to serve. Chase's Aunt Mary once made blueberry muffins, and they were the most delicious little treats. One day, I re-created the recipe using wild blackberries and they turned out well. A light dusting of powdered sugar adds to the sweetness, perfectly complementing the tartness of the berries. —RACHEL

Makes 16 to 18 muffins

2½ cups all-purpose flour

1 tablespoon baking powder

½ teaspoon baking soda

½ teaspoon kosher salt

½ teaspoon ground cinnamon

1 cup granulated sugar

2 large eggs

1 cup sour cream

½ cup (1 stick) unsalted butter, melted and slightly cooled, plus more for greasing

1 teaspoon whole milk

1 teaspoon pure vanilla extract

2 cups fresh wild blackberries, halved (see Coach's Corner)

Powdered sugar, for serving

Preheat the oven to 400°F. Grease the cups of two 12-cup muffin pans or insert 18 paper muffin cups.

Whisk together the flour, baking powder, baking soda, salt, and cinnamon in a large bowl. To another large bowl, add the granulated sugar, eggs, sour cream, butter, milk, and vanilla and whisk until combined. Add the wet mixture to the dry mixture and stir with a wooden spoon or silicone spatula just until the dry ingredients are moistened. The batter should be very thick, like a moist dough rather than a batter. Fold in the berries.

Divide the dough evenly among the muffin cups, filling each no more than three-quarters full. (You may not fill all 18.) Bake until a toothpick inserted into the middle of one or two muffins comes out clean, 18 to 22 minutes. Allow to cool in the pan for a few minutes before dusting the tops with powdered sugar and serving warm.

COACH'S CORNER

If blackberries are out of season, you can use frozen berries. We recommend that you don't thaw the berries beforehand. This will ensure they don't sink to the bottom of the mixture while baking. They also won't burst or have their color bleed, making your muffins purple.

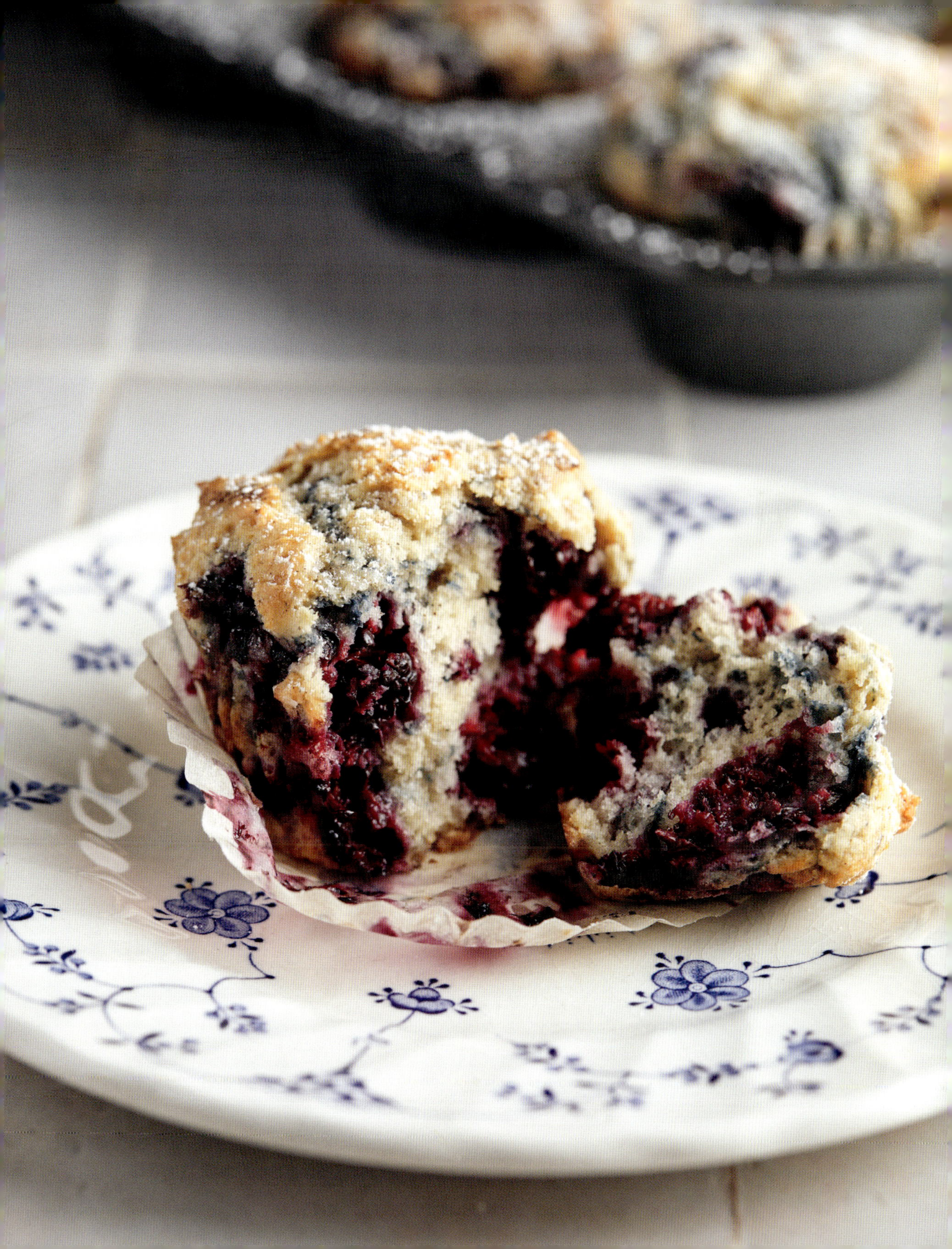

IN OUR FAMILY, DESSERT IS SERIOUS BUSINESS. THE SWEET TREATS we serve are as big and bold as Texas itself, and we don't skimp on the sugar. From Keller's Granny Smith Apple Turnovers (page 243), a recipe we can trace back to Terry's grandfather, to Hoodie Baby's Sweet Orchard Peach Cobbler (page 252), which tastes like a summer day in a bowl, our desserts are the perfect ending to any meal.

Dessert time is about indulging in flavors that evoke happiness and togetherness. During one family reunion, we celebrated Jeb's birthday. Noah filled the piñata not just with candy but also a few random ranch items—like tiny packets of horse treats, plastic farm animals, and miniature cowboy hats. When the piñata broke open, the kids' confused looks turned into giggles as they tried to figure out what to do with all the extra "goodies." As the children entertained themselves with their newfound toys, we enjoyed generous portions of sweet and nutty Buttermilk Pecan Pie (page 247) and luscious, juicy Old-Fashioned Blackberry Pie (page 244)—both served with scoops of vanilla ice cream.

Our time-honored Bradshaw desserts, from Terry's Banana Pudding with Nilla Wafers (page 240) to Tammy's delicious Cherry Crisp with Crushed Pineapple and Pecans (page 255), make any meal one to remember. Carefully crafted and lovingly served, these desserts embody the joy we find in coming together to enjoy the sweeter side of life.

**Wild Blackberry Muffins
with Powdered Sugar**

Banana Pudding with Nilla Wafers

Keller's Granny Smith Apple Turnovers

Old-Fashioned Blackberry Pie

Buttermilk Pecan Pie

Louisiana Coconut Cream Pie

Italian Olive Oil–Lemon Cake

Sweet Orchard Peach Cobbler

**Cherry Crisp with Crushed
Pineapple and Pecans**

**Warm Chocolate Chip Cookies
with Sea Salt**

Pappy's Midnight Spoon

7 // Desserts and Sweets